Portuguese Africa

Portuguese Africa

JAMES DUFFY

HARVARD UNIVERSITY PRESS

Cambridge, Massachusetts

1961

Second Printing

Distributed in Great Britain by
Oxford University Press, London

Publication of this book has been aided by a grant
from the Ford Foundation

Maps by Samuel H. Bryant

Library of Congress Catalog Card Number: 59-7650

Printed in the United States of America

PREFACE

Of the modern European powers Portugal has the longest colonial record in Africa. Since about 1500 the major areas of Portuguese interest in Africa have been below the equator, in Angola and Moçambique, where Portugal has been engaged, with varying intensity, in commercial, military, and colonizing campaigns. In the course of this work I have attempted to trace the historical contact of Portugal with the lands and peoples of Angola and Moçambique and to interpret the significance of her activities there. I have not sought to write a comprehensive account of African and Portuguese life in the two areas. I have chosen to emphasize those aspects of the Portuguese occupation which seem properly to characterize recurrent colonial problems and attitudes. To the best of my knowledge, a co-ordinated single-volume study of Angola and Moçambique does not exist, and I hope that this book will contribute, if only superficially, to an understanding of Portuguese policies and traditions in Africa.

I am aware that the title *Portuguese Africa* is somewhat of a misnomer, since I touch but lightly on Portugal's possessions in West Africa north of the equator — São Tomé, the Cape Verdes, and Portuguese Guinea. These regions have had, I realize, occasional importance in Portugal's colonial schemes in Africa, but the greater part of that country's policy and enterprise has been directed toward Angola and Moçambique, and it is to these two overseas provinces that one usually refers when speaking of Portuguese Africa. I should also point out that for convenience I have taken the liberty of using the words "colony" and "province" interchangeably to designate Angola and Moçambique, frequently for periods when these terms were either not in common acceptance or when one word or the other was given specific reality by colonial legislation.

In the course of developing the subject I shall be compelled in a number of chapters to dwell primarily on one or another aspect of a complex problem. So as to bring before the reader the total picture in these chapters I make reference to associated problems. In some instances this has led to a repetition which I have unfortunately been unable to avoid. I also realize that the manner of presentation has led me to omit material which might fruitfully have been included, and I deeply regret these inadequacies.

In general I have used the Portuguese version of African proper names in Angola and Moçambique, although these may occasionally be at variance with English usage. I believe that most of the time these names will be easily recognizable. Portuguese orthography and accentuation, which have undergone many major revisions in the last hundred years, are another problem, and, as Professor Charles Boxer remarks in his preface to *Salvador de Sá*, one can only plead guilty to being inconsistent. All translations in the work are my own.

The study resulting in this publication was made under a fellowship granted by The Ford Foundation. However, the conclusions, opinions, and other statements in this publication are those of the author and are not necessarily those of The Ford Foundation. The American Council of Learned Societies has made a grant-in-aid to help in the preparation of the manuscript. I wish to acknowledge the assistance given by Brandeis University. And I thank all those persons at home and abroad who so generously helped me in so many different ways.

June 1958   James Duffy

Contents

MAPS

ILLUSTRATIONS

(Photographs courtesy of the Agência Geral do Ultramar)

Portuguese Africa

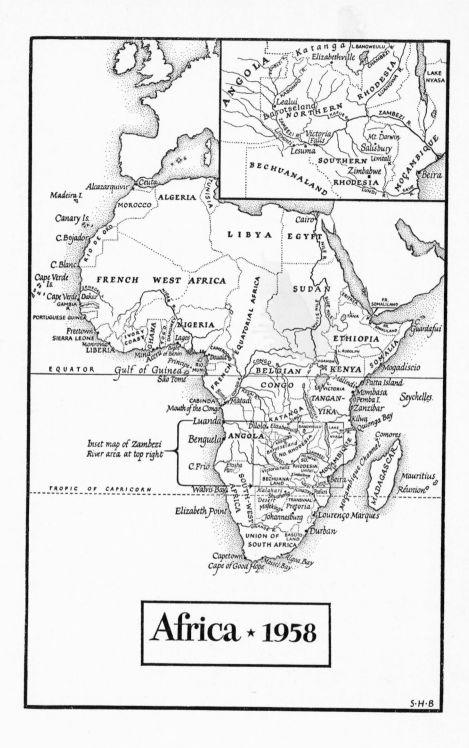

INTRODUCTION

Today Angola and Moçambique are more than place-names on the map of Africa. After four and a half centuries frequently marked by isolation, neglect (save for the ruthless exploitations of the slave trade), and frustration, the two colonies seem to have achieved at last some of their great expectations. Although still among the most under-developed areas of the continent, the Portuguese possessions have in the last two decades undergone almost startling material transforma-tions. They no longer stand on the edge of Africa's development and crises. Politically and economically Angola and Moçambique have been drawn into the realities of modern colonialism, and it is now impossible to discuss the fate of Africa below the equator without giving thoughtful consideration to the present and future roles of the Portuguese African provinces.

The dreams of a Portuguese colony stretching in a bold swath across southern Africa from the Atlantic to the Indian Ocean died in 1890, but the territories of Portuguese West and East Africa are still considerable, making Portugal, as her statesmen sometimes like to boast, the world's third largest colonial power. Comprising some 780,000 square miles (Angola, 481,000 square miles, and Moçambique, almost 298,000), their total area is roughly equal to that of Western Europe. The population of the two provinces is not so impressive. Moçambique has perhaps five and a half million inhabitants, while Angola has slightly over four million. Almost 99 per cent of the popu-lation is African.

Angola, now the Cinderella colony of the Portuguese empire, is a solid block of territory extending from the mouth of the river Congo to the desert of South-West Africa; it is bounded on the north by the Belgian Congo, in the east by the Belgian Congo and Northern Rho-desia, and in the south by Bechuanaland and South-West Africa. From an arid coastal strip the land rises eastward in a series of terraces to the central and southern plateaus of Bié and Huíla. Here in the deep central area of the province lies the watershed for the Kasai-Congo and Zambezi rivers and for the lesser streams, the Cuanza and Cunene. In the plateau country, with its healthful air and adequate rainfall, stretches the expanding frontier of Portuguese settlement in Angola. In the north the semitropical districts of Malange and Cuanza Norte also offer rich possibilities for plantation commerce.

Moçambique, shaped roughly like a Y, lies at the southern extension of the Great Rift Valley. Her western frontier touches, in succession, the Union of South Africa, the Rhodesias, and Nyasaland, and the northern boundary is with Tanganyika. Not so favored geographically as Angola, Moçambique is dominated by a long low coast which is for the most part moist and malarial. Only in the upper reaches of the Zambezi, which bisects the province, and in the highlands of Portuguese Niassa, are conditions equivalent to those of the Angolan plateau. Though situated some degrees farther south than Angola, Moçambique is a more tropical land; its pace of existence is more leisurely and its promise of exploitation less.

Angola and Moçambique are lands of extremes. In perhaps no other region of Africa has the presence of a colonial power been so clearly impressed as on the cities and towns of Portuguese Africa. In a sense they are Portugal. In the most ancient coastal cities or in the newest towns of the interior, the architecture, the streets, the city squares, the gardens and parks, the color, the spirit, the whole way of life is fundamentally Portuguese. But beyond the towns, in the bush, in the African fields and villages, one has the feeling that little has changed in four hundred years, and in many of these areas the influence of the Portuguese occupation may hardly be said to exist. Only a stretch of rail track, a well-kept road, or an isolated Portuguese house betrays the advance of Europe.

In comparison with their more prosperous neighbors, Angola and Moçambique are today far from being rich, but viewed against the disappointments of previous centuries the colonies' prosperity is little short of miraculous. Much of the present expansion in the economies of Angola and Moçambique is based on selective agricultural crops and the transit trade through several excellent ports. The verified mineral deposits of the two colonies offer no great encouragement for the future; the diamond mines of Angola's Lunda district and the oil field near Luanda are the only proved mineral deposits of great value in either province.[1] Industry is still rudimentary and, apart from the various fish products from southern Angola, serves mostly to satisfy local needs.[2] The export economy of Portuguese Africa — with the exception of Angolan diamonds — rests squarely on agricultural prod-

ucts, on the African crops of cotton and cereals [3] and on the plantation
crops of sugar, sisal, copra, coffee, and tea.[4]

The large deep-water ports of Lobito, Luanda, Lourenço,
Marques, and Beira, and the lesser ports of Moçâmedes in southern
Angola and Nacala in northern Moçambique — which figure prominently in the development plans for these two areas — are Portuguese Africa's greatest natural assets; [5] no other African territory is so
gifted with a profusion of truly excellent natural harbors. The ships
of many flags that call at the ports of Angola and Moçambique are
the most visible examples of the colonies' recent economic progress,
for although the majority of the cargo passing through the ports is
transit trade, a growing percentage of it is local exports and imports.
Tools, industrial and railway machinery, and vehicles from the United
States, England, and West Germany, wine and cotton goods from
Portugal, and countless lesser items from a dozen other countries
satisfy the increasing demands of Angola and Moçambique. Portuguese African crops and a handful of manufactured products flow
steadily to Europe, America, and other parts of Africa.[6] The diverse
nature of this trade has brought the provinces into ever closer contact with the other countries of the world.

A complex of rail lines links Lobito, Beira, and Lourenço Marques
with the rail systems of central and southern Africa,[7] and local lines
penetrate the interior of both colonies.[8] The construction of all-
weather roads and bridges is a major project in the development
schemes for Angola and Moçambique (about fifteen million dollars
have been budgeted for road and bridge construction in Angola and
about eight million for similar works in Moçambique). Government-
operated air lines offer efficient and expanding service between the
cities and larger towns.

Angola and Moçambique are changing fast. Colonization schemes,
hydro-electric projects, agricultural stations, and mineral survey missions all give evidence of the even greater expectations Portugal holds
for Angola and Moçambique. In the old coastal towns, in new towns
in the interior, and in white agricultural colonies a growing Portuguese
immigration swells the European population — and creates problems
for the future. There is a sentiment abroad in Portugal and in Africa
that the age of material promise has finally arrived. If the Portuguese
are more expansive than fearful about the shape of events to come in
Angola and Moçambique, their optimism in part derives from the
feeling that they have survived the vicissitudes of the past and that at
no time in their history have the colonies been better prepared to face
the future. But the weight of tradition rests heavily in Portuguese

Africa. In spite of genuine material progress, the Portuguese presence in Africa today is still characterized by ignorance, repression, and a careless exploitation of the African people, and in purely human terms the lessons of the past offer little hope for the future.

I

THE CONGO EXPERIMENT

O N the southern bank of one of the world's great rivers the Portuguese crown in the sixteenth century attempted a modest program of co-operation and development with a primitive people, which, compared with the policies of many European powers in the nineteenth and twentieth centuries, remains, in some of its ideals, a model of diplomatic understanding and restraint. Although the substance of events in the Congo kingdom fell far short of the royal vision (from the beginning of Portuguese colonization in Africa, one is confronted by the gap between the administrative dream, contained in elegant legislation, and the reality), nevertheless the story of Portugal's conduct in the first half of the sixteenth century has captured the imagination of panegyrist and critic alike.

Official Portuguese design in the Congo was not military conquest, administrative domination, or even primarily commercial exploitation, goals which at one time or another determined Lusitanian policy in the Indian Ocean in the sixteenth century. Instead, the crown sought to establish with the African potentate a relationship founded on alliance, plans for the spread of a Christian European cultural pattern, and simple economic agreements. In practical terms Portugal hoped to use the conversion of a supreme African chief in order to evangelize his people, to guarantee her own favored economic position in the area, and to make contact with the Ethiopian kingdom of the supposedly Christian Prester John.

That the Portuguese accepted the paramount chiefs of the Congo as equals and that their penetration into the area was generally marked by pacific relations with the African has come to have special and, possibly, distorted significance in the twentieth century when the whole endeavor is viewed against the subsequent background of European exploitation of Africa. The significance is further colored by the fact that their activities in the Congo represented the first substantial contact of a European nation with black Africa. One is faced, on one hand, by fanciful interpretations of what was, and on the other, by bitter conjectures of what might have been. For the defenders of Portuguese imperialism, the Congo experiment represents the founding of colonial traditions which continue to the present day. Here they find abundant historical example for avowed sentiments of racial equality, for sincere attempts to educate and Christianize the African — with the African's consent — and for relatively disinterested economic and military assistance. The critics of the Portuguese see a cause that was lost. When the Congo adventure failed, as it was doomed to do because of Portuguese commitments in the East which drained the mother country of men and resources, and the slave trade became the dominant interest in the Congo and Angola, the failure is viewed as a singular betrayal of the African. "Seldom," writes Basil Davidson, "was there a more obvious example of people asking for bread and being given a stone." [1] Ultimately, however, what the Portuguese did or did not accomplish in the Congo is neither a triumph nor a betrayal. It is a segment of European history in Africa which at an early date offers insight into the problems of African colonization.

In the middle months of the year 1483, Captain Diogo Cão — whose abilities as navigator and explorer have led some to consider him the leading Portuguese mariner of his century — arrived at the mouth of a majestic brown river whose current swept fresh water twenty leagues into the Atlantic. He had reached the Congo or, in Portuguese nomenclature, the Zaire, a derivation of a native word meaning "the river that swallows all others." On the left bank of the massive stream Cão and his men put into shore; on a spit of land they erected a stone *padrão* bearing the arms of Portugal and the bare facts of their visit. Having briefly established friendly relations with the leaders of a Negro community situated there, Cão left four Portuguese companions to be conducted with gifts and messages to the paramount chief dwelling in the interior and pursued his explorations southward.

The first contact between European and African in the regions of the Congo is almost casual. Doubtless the inhabitants of the area were

sufficiently astonished at the appearance of white visitors from the
sea, but for the Portuguese the Congo encounter was only another in
a progression of landfalls along the humid coast. From this first visit
there is little to indicate the extraordinary shape of events soon to
take place, and certainly there is no realization in contemporary accounts that the Congo kingdom and the lands adjacent to the south
would some day form the bulk of a modern colonial empire. Such
indifference should not come as a surprise. By 1480 Portuguese preoccupations were not for this section of the African coast. They were
for the southern promontory of the continent and the open searoads
beyond to the wealth of the Indies. The discovery of the Congo
was merely another in a series of discoveries that had been continuing
with regularity since late in the first third of the century.

By a set of curious and probably exaggerated circumstances, the
year 1415 has emerged as one of the decisive dates in Portuguese
imperial destiny. In 1415 João I, the first king in the new dynasty of
Avis, carried the battle against the Moors across the sea to the North
African fortress-port of Ceuta. The expedition was the initial move
in a Moroccan campaign indirectly associated with subsequent West
African exploration. It is one of the first in a chain of events linking
Europe with the East by ship, for it was here that João's third son,
Henry, was reinforced by evidence and rumor in his determination
to reach the far side of the African continent by sea.

The figure of the man responsible for directing the first half-
century of African exploration was cast in the particular heroic mold
so respected by the Portuguese. Prince Henry, the Navigator, was, if
we are to believe the historians of his time, devout, humorless, austere;
he possessed an extraordinary capacity for patient hopeful planning,
confident in the eventual success of his schemes. His dedication to
discovery — and not the accident of his English blood, as many have
claimed — has made him the most internationally famous member of
Portuguese royalty. His practical and idealistic motives, trade and
evangelization, are still voiced in the twentieth century to justify
Portuguese colonialism in Africa.

Expeditions along the coast were initially slow and painstaking;
only the settlement of the Canary Islands in 1424 represents a clear-
cut indication of Henry's progress. During this period coasting was
an uncertain adventure, reflecting the lack of geographical knowledge
and the fears of the mariners. In 1434 Gil Eanes succeeded where he
had failed the year before in rounding the menacing Cape Bojador,

and for the next thirty years successful voyages continued pushing beyond that point. In 1436 Eanes and Gonçalves Balaia reached the Río de Oro, and the 1441 expedition of Nuno Tristão and Antão Gonçalves made its way to Cape Blanc. From the latter voyage dates the beginning of Portugal's West African slave trade. As a reward for the first visible profits after long years of sacrifice, Henry received from his brother the king a commercial monopoly in the new-found lands; his mariners were granted a plenary indulgence from the Pope in the unhappy event that they should die while spreading Christian civilization in Africa. In the next fifteen years, the probing caravels passed Cape Verde and beyond, to the Gambia, now not only carrying on the work of exploration, but serving as well the scattered fortresses and factories Henry had ordered built in their wake.

From the trading posts came human and material wealth sufficient to silence the intermittent complaints from critics of Henry's work. Some of the first products to reach Portugal and Europe were exotica (birds, monkeys, feathers), but the bulk of commerce coming from West Africa was gold, most of it black. A great part of the history of Portuguese Africa is written in terms of slavery; much of the controversy associated with that area for the following four centuries has its origin in the 1440's when men like the chivalresquely named Lançarote de Lagos — one of Henry's financial aides — began in earnest to exploit a trade that was shortly to introduce into Portugal, if one is to give credence to the extravagant figures of the humanist Damião de Gois, some ten to twelve thousand African slaves a year, a part of whom by the turn of the century, if one is to believe another, unlikely figure, made up one-tenth of Lisbon's population. Economically, the practice proved a temporary boon to the hard-pressed labor market in Portugal. From the Church's point of view, the practice was held defensible in terms of spiritual salvation. Finally, the Portuguese claim that their buying and selling of Africans (facilitated by the mortal enemies of Christian Portugal, Mohammedan slave dealers) was an accepted custom of the day, soon to be shared by other European nations, and they add, with considerable justification, that the slave in Portugal was treated liberally and humanely.

Occasional ambushes by militant Africans did not discourage the Portuguese explorers. Nor did the death of Prince Henry in 1460. In the two years after his death, Pero de Sintra surveyed much of the Sierra Leone coast, and in the early 1470's Portuguese ships sailed below the equator. In 1474 Afonso V invested his son and heir João with the responsibility for affairs in Guinea and the investigation of the seas beyond. João possessed an Henriquean vision and pertinacity:

during his reign (1481–1495) Diogo Cão came upon the Congo and Dias rounded the Cape of Good Hope. Before the end of the century da Gama made his way to India.

The hundred years after Ceuta are the grandiose century of Portuguese exploration and expansion. They encompass an age which, beginning with Henry and ending with Afonso de Albuquerque, includes captains and warriors like Cão, Bartolomeu Dias, Cabral, Vasco da Gama, Francisco d'Almeida. They furnish a seemingly endless source of inspiration to chroniclers, poets, scientists, in Portugal and abroad, who so define, elaborate, and redefine past glories that these years have become an age of supermen whose inspiration is still a living presence in Portuguese colonial thought. While the study of Portuguese Africa is only in passing concerned with their heroics, many of the current attitudes in every part of the Lusitanian world have their nationalistic foundation in the *século maravilhoso*.

On his return from a brief survey of the arid shore south of the Congo, Diogo Cão put in at the village where he had left the four-man embassy to the paramount chief of the area. Discovering that his companions had been retained at the Manicongo's court, the captain seized four Africans from among those who had come to visit the ships. Though the men were clearly taken as hostages for the safety of the Portuguese ambassadors — if indeed they were still alive — Cão attempted to make it clear to the local prince, a relative of the supreme chief, that his subjects would be returned in fifteen months. It is by no means certain that Diogo Cão's motives were as benevolent as subsequent interpretation has held them to be, but what is certain is that his action was turned into a masterstroke of diplomacy by the Portuguese king and his advisers.

Hopes of establishing contact with the kingdom of Prester John undoubtedly influenced the decision of João II to treat the Congo captives in a lordly manner. An alliance with the Manicongo seemed to offer an excellent opportunity to penetrate the interior of the continent in an attempt to reach this goal. Accordingly, every effort was made to impress the hostages with the wealth and spiritual values of the Portuguese. They were regarded as guests of the crown, were handsomely clad and housed, and were introduced into the mysteries of the national language and faith. The treatment was not wasted on the unsophisticated visitors. From victims of a kidnapping, which had sorely distressed the Congo king, the four Africans were transformed into messengers of good will who were able to explain to their chief far better than any Portuguese the benefits to be gained from friendship with the Europeans.

The return of Diogo Cão to the Congo in 1484 or 1485 was more a triumphal embassy than another voyage of exploration. He carried rich presents for King Nzinga-a-Cuum (or Nzinga Nkuwu) and the traditional messages of hope that he would put aside his idols and embrace the Christian faith. When the expedition reached the Congo, the exchange of hostages was easily arranged, the Portuguese rejoining their compatriots and the Africans going to the capital to astound their fellows by their bizarre dress and miraculous stories of distant Portugal. Cão sent promises to follow them after exploring still further the southern coast.

On this trip the captain sailed beyond the present-day frontier between Angola and South-West Africa. Returning to the river, he went upstream its navigable limits, to the falls above Matadi, where on a face of rock he had inscribed, "Here came the ships of the illustrious D. João of Portugal . . ." Diogo Cão and a company of men then went inland to the capital Mbanza. Delighted with the visit of the white men, Nzinga-a-Cuum proved receptive to the Christian religion and to the promise of further visits from the Portuguese. He prepared a small group of his people to be sent to Portugal to be trained in European ways, and asked that João II send missionaries, builders, and farmers to instruct his people.

Portuguese intelligence of the Congo kingdom, based on the reports of Diogo Cão's two voyages, was necessarily scant, as in fact was all of their knowledge of West Africa in back of the coast, and the notions of João and his advisers about the chief with whom they were treating were equally vague.[2] It is apparent from the outset that the crown believed — or wished to believe — that it was dealing with a king of more sophistication and greater political power than was actually the case. (The same misconception prevailed with regard to the Monomotapa, apparent supreme ruler of the interior of Moçambique in the middle of the sixteenth century.) That this mistaken attitude has become one of the legends of Portuguese colonial history is partly in recognition of the dignities conferred upon the Manicongo by João II and Manuel, for there is no evidence that the Manicongo's people enjoyed a civilization more advanced than they do today.

The king of the Congo in the late fifteenth and early sixteenth centuries was paramount chief of a loose confederation of tribal organizations over which he could usually claim authority, but his suzerainty was not always stable. The geographical limitations of his realm were roughly the Congo River in the north (although at times he held the obedience of tribes on the other side of the river), the Dande in the south, the Cuango River in the east, and the Atlantic Ocean to the west. The kingdom was split into six provinces, governed by lesser chiefs. These offices were more or less hereditary, but it was not unknown for a chief to take over by force. Over these so-called provinces the Manicongo's authority was supreme in the sixteenth century, after which it diminished. The Manicongo also claimed the allegiance of the kingdom of Ndongo (Angola), but his influence there waned perceptibly as the sixteenth century progressed, thanks in part to the intervention of Portuguese slave dealers.[3]

The response of João II to the Manicongo's request for assistance makes it clear that the Portuguese king considered the mission of more than passing importance. A fleet of three ships under the command of the *fidalgo* Gonçalo de Sousa — who died of the plague during the voyage and was replaced by his nephew Rui de Sousa — was dispatched to the Congo late in 1490. The embassy consisted of priests, skilled workers, and Africans who had been tutored in a Portuguese monastery. The cargo included tools, presents for the king and his family, and numerous religious objects. The purpose of the expedition was eminently peaceful; the company was to evangelize and in a sense nationalize, to seek alliance not conquest. Arriving at Pinda (the Portuguese anchorage not far from the present port of Santo António do Zaire) in March 1491, the company undertook the march to the kraals of Nzinga-a-Cuum, about one hundred and twenty-five miles from the river's mouth. When the chief was advised of their approach he sent two captains to accompany them. In Mbanza a throng of Africans, "playing different kind of instruments . . . barbarously out of tune . . . and the king on a high platform, on an ivory seat . . . awaited the ambassador and the vicar and received them with honors and extraordinary attentions." [4]

The history of the Portuguese expansion records few contacts with any African or Asian people which began so auspiciously. Within a month the Manicongo was baptized, taking the Christian name of João. Other notables of the court and one son followed the lead of the chief. Nor was Portuguese assistance entirely spiritual. Before their return to Portugal, Rui de Sousa and his men joined the convert chief to put down a rebellion of the Anzicos, a tribe inhabiting the northern coast and some islands at the mouth of the Congo. Rui de Sousa then sailed for Portugal, leaving behind, in a climate which had already begun to take a fearful toll of European lives, four priests, a number of lay brothers, and several Portuguese soldiers who had instructions to discover a route leading to Prester John and India.

From the departure of Rui de Sousa for Portugal in 1495 until 1505 or 1506, when Afonso succeeded to his father's ivory seat, little is known of the progress of events in the lands of the Manicongo. Portugal herself in the last decade of the fifteenth century was preoccupied with other problems, and relations with a primitive African kingdom were largely forgotten. In 1495 Manuel, *O Venturoso*, came to the Portuguese throne, and with the voyage of da Gama at the end of the century, the attentions of the new monarch were attracted by the more brilliant promises of Indian commerce. The absence of an official Portuguese population in the Congo, save for the few priests and explorers left behind in 1492, was a misfortune in Portuguese policy which was partly responsible for the ultimate failure of the Congo experiment. Certainly it contributed to the creation of conditions there which were to bedevil the black and white inhabitants of the region for a long time. In the absence of fortress, factory, or royal representative in the Congo, the Portuguese residents of the newly populated São Tomé island (a strange mixture of religious exiles, criminals, and adventurers) began about 1500 to exercise their trading prerogatives along the southern coast. Since São Tomé had no native labor force to work the incipient sugar plantations, this trade was mostly in slaves. Not much later São Tomé became the slave center for the whole lower Guinea coast and the Congo. To protect the supply of workers and expand the traffic in slaves, the Portuguese on São Tomé quite naturally sought to fill the vacuum of Portuguese influence in the Congo, to the detriment of relations between Portugal and the African kingdom.

A second result of Portugal's temporary abandonment was a period of internal strife within the region. After his impulsive acceptance of Christianity, the African chief João, encouraged by a second son and royal advisers, lapsed into his tribal habits. The monarch seems principally to have been exasperated by the restraints of monogamy. In his disaffection with European ways, João turned against his son and heir apparent, Afonso, and expelled him to the province of Sundi. Into exile with the young prince went two of the Portuguese priests. The priests, harried by royal antagonism, had been able to make little progress with the Congo people and concentrated their attentions on Afonso, his chosen friends, and his mother Leonor. Success rewarded their efforts when Afonso, despite his younger brother's militant opposition, succeeded to his father's throne.

The long reign of Afonso I, Christian king of a pagan land, represents the golden age, from a European point of view, of the Congo. "Never again will an African kingdom," observes R. E. G. Armattoe, "exhibit so much refinement and so much grace. The lessons of its fall," he adds, "must be a warning to all Africans to eschew the outward manifestations of an alien civilization. A civilization to endure must be founded on the sound foundation of native institutions and must fulfill the legitimate aspirations of its people." [5] Whatever the causes for the failure of a Christian Congo, few may be attributed to the aspirations of Mbemba-a-Nzinga, Afonso I. Ten years of Portuguese clerical instruction had produced more than a superficial imitator of European ways; they had created a man whose counterpart may be found in some of the Oxford-educated African princes of the twentieth century. Afonso's contact with his own traditions was broken, but his opportunity to change the customs and destiny of his own people was destroyed by one of the side effects — the slave trade — of the civilization he had accepted. Afonso was also more than an ignorant princeling in the hire of the Portuguese. One of the earliest examples of Portuguese success at assimilation, the young king was a Christian, versed in the foreigner's language, and familiar with Portuguese history and traditions. His reign was marked by a steadfast, though frustrated, dedication to bring the benefits of a European civilization to the Congo. His greatest flaw was a naïve refusal to believe that some Portuguese were able to betray the virtuous principles he had been taught to hold. A memorial to the unhappy monarch is the statement of the famous nineteenth-century missionary to the Congo, Father António Barroso: "A native of the Congo knows the name of three kings: that of the present one, that of his predecessor, and that of Afonso." [6]

Events in the Congo from the beginning of Afonso's reign until 1512 were characterized by the intrigues of the *donatário* (proprietary landlord, or lord proprietor) of São Tomé, Fernão de Melo, and by the immorality of the second group of missionary priests sent out in 1508 at the request of Afonso. Commercially, the Congo had become a dependency of São Tomé, and it was with Fernão de Melo that Afonso was obliged to treat, unaware, perhaps, that Melo represented his own interests, not King Manuel's. There was little else Afonso could do in his isolation; his letters to Lisbon were frequently destroyed at São Tomé, his messengers were delayed or turned back or even taken into slavery. Nor was the example offered by the missionaries of 1508 such as to impress either the Portuguese or the Africans.[7] Afonso received the thirteen or fifteen priests with jubilant plans for educating and evangelizing his people, but a number of the fathers, succumbing to the moral and physical climate of the capital, found the buying and selling of slaves, in some cases with funds given them by

Afonso, more lucrative. Instead of living together in the large residence prepared for them, each set himself up in private quarters, one with an African mistress by whom he had a child. Others complained about the conditions surrounding them and demanded to be sent home, and only a few remained in the Congo, where the last member of the group died in 1532.

Against this background and in response to the complaints of Afonso, King Manuel moved to salvage the situation. He had composed an unusual document which has been widely interpreted as one of the theoretical cornerstones of Portuguese colonial policy. This *regimento*, or set of instructions, consisted of thirty-four points, in none of which is there a suggestion of authoritarian restraint on the people of the Congo. The man bearing the *regimento*, Simão da Silva, was to be roughly the equivalent of adviser to or resident officer in the African court and supervisor of Portuguese action there.

The *regimento* covered four areas of instruction. The first considered the help and advice Simão da Silva was to give to Afonso in the organization of his kingdom, and it is this section that the Portuguese hail as a case in point for their sixteenth-century efforts at cultural assimilation. Simão da Silva was to teach the Portuguese manner of conduct in war and justice, and for this purpose he was accompanied by a scholar with the code of Portuguese law. On points of conflict between African custom and Portuguese law, Simão da Silva was to try to explain and then yield if necessary. He was to describe the organization and procedures of the Portuguese court down to the matter of table service. In local wars he was at liberty to assist the king when there appeared to be no danger of heavy Portuguese casualties. Churches and residences were to be built under his supervision. In all matters he was to move with tact and discretion, to offend no one, but to create where possible an African parallel to Portuguese society.

The second group of instructions was meant to assure the mission's success and to counteract the harm that had been done in the previous decade. Manuel placed control of the Congo's Portuguese community in Simão da Silva's hands. He commanded the people accompanying da Silva to live in peace with the Africans and avoid incidents; those who disobeyed were to be punished, although in all matters of misconduct, the Portuguese reserved extraterritorial privileges. Priests were to live together and to refrain from accepting money from Afonso. Those who abused the native population were to be sent immediately to Lisbon. Simão da Silva was also to survey the religious situation in the Congo and force all priests who had not con-

ducted themselves decorously to return home. Any slaves they possessed were to be sent to Portugal on another ship at the owner's expense!

The last two sections of the *regimento* demonstrated Manuel's
practical nature, for herein he was concerned with commerce and
geography. The resident officer must explain to Afonso "as honestly
as he could" that it would be a pity for Portuguese ships carrying expensive cargo and personnel to depart from the Congo with empty
holds. What assistance Manuel had rendered, to be sure, "was the result of the love of one king for another and for the honor and service
of Afonso," but Manuel would not be disappointed to see his ships
come home loaded with slaves, copper, and ivory to defray the expenses he had voluntarily shouldered. So that there should be no mistake, da Silva's responsibility to obtain some form of payment was
repeated three times in the *regimento* and a royal factor was sent to
the Congo. Finally, the resident was to obtain all the geographical
and political knowledge possible of the area: the Congo and its source,
the size and spread of the population, the military strength and loyalty
of the petty chiefs, the centers of trade and communication. Manuel
and his advisers were not yet willing to put aside the possibility of a
trans-African route to the lands of Prester John and the East.

Having disposed of the order of business, the Portuguese monarch
invited Afonso to send an embassy of a dozen noblemen and their at-
tendants to Portugal, whence they would be dispatched with all honor
at Portuguese expense to Rome for an audience with the Pope. The
embassy would include Afonso's son Henrique, already in Portugal.
Thus, suggested Manuel, would the Christian faith be propagated
more readily in pagan lands. He did not suggest that Portuguese prestige in Rome would be further enhanced by the appearance of the
mission.[8]

Viewed superficially the document seems to offer no more than
the trappings of a European court in exchange for slaves, and it is at
once apparent that Manuel hoped to perpetuate an alliance which, although it promised little, at the same time would cost him little. But
in considering the course of events in the Congo from the hopeful
beginnings in 1482 and realizing that the abuses associated with the
São Tomé slave trade could still in 1512 have been checked, one is
forced to speculate on what might have been. It is difficult to envision,
given the assuredly primitive nature of Congo society, the complete
projection there of European civilization, but it is entirely consistent
with the terms of the *regimento* and with the character of Afonso to
see the establishment of a Portuguese protectorate which, with

thoughtful assistance and guidance, could have fulfilled the aspirations of both monarchs for the gradual transformation of Congo society. Such assistance implied, however, a disinterested investment of men and authority far greater than Portugal was prepared to give, concerned as she was with the exploitation of the East. And so what might have been — the creation of a Europeanized community within the framework of an African national state — became instead the frustrated strivings of an African chief, against the opposition of Portuguese freebooters and against a strongly dissident element in his own people, for the attainments of a European culture.

The failure of the *regimento*, which is the high point of official policy in the Congo, to achieve its purpose and the dissipation of subsequent opportunities were mostly caused by Portuguese indiscipline. Even if Simão da Silva had not died of fever shortly after his arrival at Pinda, his instructions vis-à-vis the Portuguese there were probably doomed to failure in the absence of means to implement them. By the time he had reached the Congo, intrigues having their origin in São Tomé, which was determined to protect its slaving monopoly, had created such an atmosphere of hostility toward him that he feared to leave his ship and sent a physician as his representative to Afonso. The chief, apprised of the scope and nature of the embassy, attempted at once to throw off the burdensome influence of Captain General Melo, asking da Silva to proceed with all haste to Mbanza to punish his arrogant countrymen. Simão da Silva perished on his trip through the interior.

Alvaro Lopes, the factor appointed by Manuel to represent royal commerce in the Congo, carried the title of succession, but a delay between the time of da Silva's death and the arrival of Lopes' ship gave the Portuguese at Mbanza a chance to solidify their position. Lopes, short-tempered and direct in his dealings, was within a year compromised and forced to leave the realm, and the *regimento* was of course ignored. Priests traded in slaves; others, in spite of Afonso's protests, kept African mistresses. A revolt among some slaves being taken to Pinda for export caused smoldering resentments to flare up. In desperation, Afonso directed a long letter to Manuel wherein he reviewed the plots and disturbances caused in his kingdom during the last eight years by unruly Portuguese profiteers and slave trade agents from São Tomé. Naïvely he suggested that he be given jurisdiction over the island. Again he pled for more priests and teachers. In his final lines he wrote, "And we beg Your Highness not to leave us unprotected or allow the Christian work done in our kingdom to be lost, for we alone can do no more." [9]

Disappointed with the results of his correspondence with the Portuguese court, the black king began to emerge as a more independent — and isolated — ruler. The privilege of appointing the Portuguese resident adviser remained his, which gave him control over at least one segment of the white population in the Congo, the partisans of the resident. There was no inclination in Portugal to discourage this tendency toward independence from Portugal's guidance. Where Manuel had made distracted attempts to maintain friendly relations with Afonso, João III — who ruled after 1519 — paid him little heed. West African policy now centered on the island of São Tomé, whose administration had been taken over by the crown in 1522. Its prosperous sugar plantations, its safe haven for Indies ships, and its growing importance as the leading slave entrepôt on the African coast gave the island economic advantages the Congo kingdom did not have. In 1534 the town of São Tomé was made a city and the seat of a bishopric.

In the early 1520's the resident officer Manuel Pacheco was Afonso's strong right arm. He restrained the more extreme behavior of the Portuguese, and he fostered the chief's spirit of self-reliance. Afonso's letters to the Lisbon court became less pleading and humble, more formal and forceful. Apparently it was with the advice of Pacheco and another resident adviser, Gonçalo Pires, that Afonso took a small step to control the slave trade, convinced now that João would not intervene. Twenty-five years of slaving, during most of which Afonso had innocently inflamed Portuguese desires by his lavish gifts of slaves to Manuel and his subsidy to the missionaries (the slaves being a form of currency),[10] had left their mark on the Congo. The traffic was causing revolts and fears of depopulation. Traders and their agents in the interior paid no heed to Afonso's authority and cared little whether their purchases were captives of war or the chief's subjects. To protect his own people Afonso in 1526 set up a slavery commission of three chiefs to ascertain whether Negroes shipped from the country were in effect captives and not free men.

In the same year, 1526, Afonso directed another letter to Lisbon asking for fifty missionaries.[11] Six of the fathers, he hoped, would be from the same order which had educated his son Henrique, now Bishop of Utica and Vicar Apostolic of the Congo. Henrique had returned to his father's land in 1521 after thirteen years in Europe. Through Manuel's perseverance, Pope Leo X reluctantly elevated the young African to the office of Bishop of Utica *in partibus infidelium*, setting aside the canonical age limit. The appointment was a political stratagem, but with his consecration in Lisbon in 1520, Henrique became the first — and the last — Negro bishop in the Congo. He remained an auxiliary, however, to the Bishop of Madeira, receiving his instructions through São Tomé. His role in the evangelization of his people was insignificant. Constrained by his father from leaving the capital, he was a witness to the laxity and selfishness of the white clergy, whose scorn he suffered. In the middle 1530's Henrique died, a useless product of Afonso's vanity and two nations' aborted hopes.

The creation of a bishopric in São Tomé was viewed as an insult by Afonso, although there was no justification for a bishopric in the Congo, and spiritual subordination to the hated island was cruelly felt. The years since the death of Manuel had brought many disaffections, of which this was but one more. One remnant of former amity remained, however, as Portugal continued to educate the young sons of Congo chiefs. For their instruction the historian João de Barros composed a Portuguese grammar. The scholars' passage to Lisbon was not always without interference at São Tomé, whose desire, even now as a crown colony, was to keep the Congo as nothing more than a warehouse for slaves: some students disappeared, others were put ashore along the coast, and others were delayed. A number of the Africans educated in Portugal remained there, one as a distinguished teacher of Latin and rhetoric; most returned to their country to take their places in the oppressive artificial environment of Mbanza.

The last decade of Afonso's reign drew to a close amid complaints and corruption. Afonso, now old, forgotten by Europe and isolated from his people, became tired and discouraged, more interested in the affairs of his vanity than in his country. The Portuguese, with their celebrated adaptability to any culture or climate, lingered in that backwater of imperial design, quarrelsome, meddling, scheming for the king's favors and attention. How many Portuguese resided in the Congo in the 1530's, for example, can only be estimated. Probably there were never more than two hundred white men there, enjoying an influence out of all proportion to their number. Their mulatto children became functionaries, agents of the slave trade, lesser members of the clergy. Children of two worlds, they paid allegiance to neither and were as responsible as their fathers for the constant turmoil that beset the Congo. After a five-year absence Manuel Pacheco had returned in 1531, but he was unable to cope with the resurgence of factionalism. In the stale abandoned world of the Congo which gave little opportunity for valor or ambition, the Portuguese plotted for or against Afonso, keeping his kingdom in a state of artificial frenzy.[12]

Manuel Pacheco, Alvaro Peçanha, Gonçalo Nunes Coelho all appealed in vain to João III in Portugal. They swore that troubles with

the African population rested in the egotism and greed of the Portuguese, and they advised their king to replace every civil and religious
officer in the Congo kingdom. For all of their flaws the European
clique around Afonso made his last years less fretful. In them he found
support to turn aside Lisbon's half-hearted efforts to explore the
Congo and look for metals, development projects which did not
coincide with the Manicongo's own plans. Also the Europeans helped
the great chief extend the limits of his kingdom in the name of Christianity — and for themselves, in the name of slavery. The tensions
built up in these chaotic years, however, were to explode in the years
to come when the patient restraint of Afonso had disappeared.

In the early 1540's Afonso died. The facts of the succession are
clouded, although it was attended by a violent struggle between
Afonso's son Pedro and Diogo, one of the chief's nephews. Pedro became king, enjoying the support of the Europeans who had held
Afonso's favor, but he could not command the loyalty given his
father. In a short time around the figure of Diogo there emerged an
embittered opposition of jealous Portuguese and Africans hostile to
the old order. The accumulation of ill-assorted resentments burst
forth in a bloody revolt which resulted in the flight of Pedro and the
usurpation of his throne by Diogo. Pedro, from the asylum of the
church where he stayed until his death in 1566, made representations,
through his partisans who had taken refuge in São Tomé, to the Pope
and João III, both of whom, if they were at all aware of events in the
Congo, observed a discreet neutrality. From 1545 Diogo was the effective ruler of the Congo. The years of his reign were to begin the
final decline of the Portuguese policy of maintaining, in theory at
least, the independent integrity of the Congo and were to see the
emergence of Angola as the area of principal Lusitanian interest.

The situation by 1545 defied solution and Diogo, although impulsive and arbitrary in many of his actions, was usually a puppet in
the hands of his advisers. The issue of slavery daily grew more troublesome. In the early years of the century the *donatário* of São Tomé had
enjoyed exclusive slaving rights in the Congo, but gradually his agents
were replaced by permanent Portuguese residents of the Congo, who
penetrated all parts of the interior inciting wars and purchasing subjects from the Manicongo's petty chiefs. The chaos resulting from the
competition was such that once the Portuguese king's authority was
established on São Tomé and the traffic became a royal monopoly to
be let to slaving companies, Afonso and Pacheco attempted to control
the export of slaves for economic and demographic reasons.[13] Because
of these measur⸻ ⸻ ⸻rs taken in the next fifteen years, the local

traders and their half-caste sons resented Afonso and his advisers. When the opportunity came, they strongly supported Diogo, hoping once more to establish free trade in the interior. To a large extent they attained their goal.

In March 1548, the first Jesuit mission, three priests and the lay teacher Diogo de Soveral, set foot on the bank of the river, bearing a letter of recommendation to the African chief. With their usual energy they set about the task of housecleaning: 2,100 baptisms were recorded in the first four months; three churches were erected, one of which, dedicated to the Savior, gave the capital city of Mbanza its new and permanent name of São Salvador; Master Soveral was busily educating six hundred children in different schools. But the Jesuits were less successful in bringing a moral order to the Portuguese community; on the contrary, it was not long before some were contaminated by the prevailing morality and frictions. Father Jorge Vaz in his first years of residence collected sixty slaves for embarkation and sale. The Jesuits also made the mistake of siding with the camp of the deposed Pedro and wrote João that evangelization was impossible until Diogo was replaced. In an atmosphere of antagonism their work was of little profit, and by 1552 the first Jesuit mission had departed in failure.

The 1550's in the Congo kingdom were enlivened by bickerings and violent reprisals. The governor of São Tomé in a long letter to João III upbraided Diogo and his court for abusing the Jesuits and robbing slave dealers, and he urged the Portuguese king to declare an economic boycott of the river. Diogo replied that the Jesuits were guilty of loose conduct and of outraging his royal dignity by calling him an ignorant dog.[14] A second Jesuit mission in 1553 fared as badly as the first. The priests found that Diogo, following the example of many Europeans, had surrounded himself with concubines and showed other signs of reverting to pagan ways. Without royal support — Diogo forbade his subjects to attend Jesuit schools or churches — the missionaries could do little and withdrew in 1555.

In the last years of Diogo's life the Congo moved still further from the orbit of Portuguese influence. The ingrown clique of black, brown, and white inhabitants, having thwarted all efforts to curb them, brought the Congo to its period of greatest isolation since the voyages of Diogo Cão. João III, who in later life seems to have suffered mild compunctions over his previous neglect of the region, suggested to the aged stalwart Manuel Pacheco that he might be able to bring harmony to the Congo. Pacheco hesitantly accepted the commission, but when he reached São Tomé and was told of the vindictive regard in which he was held by Diogo and his own countrymen, he realized that there was nothing he could do and went no further.

The death of Diogo in 1561 produced a bloodbath greater than the one which brought him to power, as the Congo community turned on itself again in the battle for succession. The reign of the heir apparent, Afonso II, an illegitimate son of Diogo, was brief. He was murdered by his brother Bernardo while attending Mass. From the subsequent confusion, in which black and white citizens perished with surprising lack of discrimination, the same Bernardo emerged as supreme chief. During the civil war, the Congo was closed to ships from São Tomé, and the slave trade passed openly to Angola.

Its violence spent, the kingdom of the Congo entered into a peaceful period in the 1560's which was no more than a lull before the final storm. Bernardo, with the white population now diminished and apathetic, ruled reasonably and tranquilly, having only occasional difficulties with the Europeans. He exchanged friendly notes with the Portuguese crown and showed himself amenable to permitting exploration for copper in his territories. Bernardo probably died in battle against the rebellious Anzicos in 1567. The following year the cannibalistic Jagas,[15] in company with the equally ferocious Anzicos, descended upon the Congo. The new king, Alvaro, the chiefs of the land, and the Portuguese community fled before the host to the safety of Hippopotamus Island (sometimes referred to as Elephant Island) in the middle of the river. From there Alvaro sent a courier to young Sebastião of Portugal for assistance. Sebastião responded with unusual speed, sending in 1570 Captain Francisco de Gouveia and six hundred men. He joined forces with the exiles and during the next two years the combined army drove the Jagas from the land. Afterwards Gouveia built a strong wall around the city of São Salvador. In gratitude for the restoration of his kingdom, Alvaro formally acknowledged vassalage to the king of Portugal. He agreed to send tribute each year of one fifth of the yearly collection of cowrie shells, the currency of the realm which could always be exchanged for slaves. Even though Sebastião answered graciously, advising Alvaro only to be a good Christian, by this symbolic act the first and most significant period of Portuguese Congo history came to a close. The Congo kingdom retained its theoretic independence and was not formally annexed to Angola until 1883.

Except for furnishing slaves and a field for missionary activities, the Congo was gradually eclipsed by the rise of Angola in the last quarter of the sixteenth century. Alvaro directed a continuing flow of ambassadors to the Cardinal Henrique and Philip II of Spain and

Portugal, among them the redoubtable Duarte Lopes, first celebrated explorer of equatorial Africa,[16] asking for missionaries in return for mining concessions. In 1584 three Discalced Carmelites arriving in São Salvador found there four priests and an inadequate clerical staff, all ignorant and corrupt. In spite of their warm reception by Alvaro the Carmelites were convinced by the spiritual poverty of the city, the destruction wrought by constant slaving, the tenacity with which the majority of the Africans clung to their own beliefs, and the climate that the task was a hopeless one. They withdrew in 1589.

In 1596 São Salvador was hopefully raised to the rank of city and made the seat of the bishopric of the new diocese of the Congo and Angola, but even this recognition did not halt the decline. By 1615 most traces of Christian life had disappeared; the white population had died, fled, or been absorbed. The Congo chiefs became more and more despotic and the unity of the kingdom crumpled. São Salvador was a deserted city in 1690, its twelve churches in ruins, its walls and fortress in ruins. Stanley, who explored the area in 1874–1879, professed that he could find no trace of Portuguese civilization, no mark of their sovereignty.

In such a manner one of the unique European experiments in Africa petered out. Although in the sixteenth century a policy of colonization meant not much more than the evangelization of a heathen people, the story of the Congo, even in its failure, stands for more. It stands for the pacific good intentions, seldom realized, of the Portuguese crown, and it stands for the faith of an African chief in his alliance with a European power. For eighty years the paramount chief was political ruler of his kingdom with authority which frequently extended over the Portuguese residing there. Portuguese intervention was officially limited to commerce and religion; if these activities more often than not merged with political matters, the fault lay more with the African king and his chosen Portuguese advisers than with crown policy. There is no suggestion of official Portuguese tyranny or occupation during these years. The original desire of Portugal to create a civilized African state contiguous geographically with the illusory Ethiopia of Prester John went by the boards, but the Portuguese profess that more lasting values were created in the Congo. As a result of the entry of white traders and settlers there emerged in the sixteenth century a bi-racial community. The practice of easy assimilation with the African, which was to continue in other parts of the continent for four hundred years, is one example of why, the Portuguese maintain, even today they enjoy a comparative lack of racial tensions in their African colonies.

In conflict with the practice of assimilation and with the willingness of the Portuguese king to accept his African counterpart as a brother was the Congo slave trade. "At the side of the missionary who carried salvation," Father Barroso lamented, "was the buyer of men who destroyed the ties linking father to son and mother to daughter." [17] The degradations and frictions arising from the slave trade and the demands of the empire in the East, which distracted Lisbon's interest from the Congo in the crucial years of the Portuguese-African alliance, were responsible for the failure of the experiment. Without encouragement and moral authority, it succumbed to the purely material exploitations which have so often characterized the presence of Europe in Africa.

II

MOÇAMBIQUE AND THE TRADITION

I N sharp contrast with the shape of events in the Congo kingdom was Portuguese activity on Africa's east coast. Frequently historical currents in Portugal's African provinces east and west have
failed to run parallel, although Portuguese presence in both Angola
and Moçambique has been generally characterized by a decline from
early promise into a protracted state of neglect and confusion. The
reasons for the divergence of interests in the two colonies are necessarily complex, but the principal factors have been, as one might expect, geographic and economic. Angola, forty to sixty days across the
Atlantic from Brazil, early in its development became the Black
Mother, supplier of slaves for three centuries to the American plantations. Its political orientation was toward Brazil. Slavery in Moçambique, although the *bête noire* of David Livingstone, never achieved
Angolan proportions. The Portuguese in East Africa were originally
concerned with the promotion and protection of trade in the Indian
Ocean and with the pursuit of gold and silver in the mines of Manica.
Their political orientation was toward India — even after the final
collapse of the eastern empire. The relation of the Portuguese forts,
most of them north of the present Moçambique-Tanganyika frontier,
and settlements to Indian commerce points up the political implication absent in Angola, that the Portuguese in East Africa were for almost two hundred years in military and commercial conflict with the
Arab city-states. To a lesser extent, the nature of the native populations and the emergence of the Zambezi *prazos* also gave Moçambique
a different character. The first century of occupation saw in East

Africa the formation of the traditional mold of Portuguese expansion in the East: the establishing and fortifying of points along the coast for the protection and dissemination of trade. Where satisfactory alliances could be made with local leaders, the Portuguese eschewed the use of arms; defiance, on the other hand, was met, where feasible, by a show of strength and a puppet king was set up to protect the invader's interests.[1]

The continuity of expansion along the African west coast which had led Diogo Cão to the Congo and beyond was unbroken. Shortly after Cão's return in 1486 from his second expedition, João II pressed the search for the continent's end with greater haste. A year later a fleet of three vessels under the command of Bartolomeu Dias sailed from Lisbon. By early December of 1487 Dias had reached Walvis Bay and had by the end of the month sailed beyond Elisabeth Point. In the following days, out of sight of land and possibly driven by storms, he rounded the Cape of Good Hope. When, by sailing northward, the ships made land again, they were in the vicinity of Mossel Bay. Here the company rested and replenished the water supply. At Algoa Bay the protests of the crew, exhausted by hunger, grew so vehement that Dias agreed to proceed only several days more, after which he reluctantly turned the prows of his caravels southwest. On the return voyage they passed within sight of the redoubtable promontory so long the object of Portugal's aspirations, to which Dias gave the name Cape of Good Hope.

Nine years passed before another expedition set forth from the Tagus. The strange lapse of time must be explained by a number of reasons, chief among which is probably the long delay in Lisbon's receiving information on the fate of an overland mission to India by Pero da Covilhã and Afonso de Paiva, who had left Portugal at the same time as Dias' expedition. Covilhã reached Calicut, possibly returning to Cairo by way of the east coast of Africa. From Cairo Covilhã sent his king a report which made abundantly clear the wealth of the East, the extent of trade in the Indian Ocean, and the ease of navigation from the southeast coast of Africa to India.[2] With this intelligence João's successor Manuel ordered a fleet of four ships to be made ready. In the selection of commander, Bartolomeu Dias was passed over in favor of Vasco da Gama.[3] In July 1497 the small fleet sailed.

The captain reached Moçambique harbor early in March 1498. For several days the sheik of the island — which was under the suzerainty of the sultanate of Kilwa — apparently thought the Portuguese were some sort of Moslem traders, while da Gama believed that the island population was a neo-Christian community. But both illusions were soon dispelled, and by March 27, when favorable winds permitted the European ships to depart, the town had been raked by Portuguese cannon.[4] Further up the coast, at Mombasa, negotiations again began auspiciously, if hesitantly, although there is reason to believe that the ruler of Mombasa, apprised of the flare-up at Moçambique, intended harm to the Portuguese fleet. In any case, after an initial exchange of presents and representatives (the Portuguese sent two convicts with some beads) the situation deteriorated. An Arab attempt to sabotage da Gama's ships failed, and the captain sailed north to Malindi, capturing a loaded dhow along the way. In spite of da Gama's continuing high-handed manner — he held an official messenger hostage in order to obtain a pilot to guide him across the Indian Ocean — Malindi was favorably disposed to European presence, either because of her animosities against Mombasa and Kilwa or her fear of superior Portuguese arms. The town proved Portugal's only consistently loyal ally on the whole coast during the sixteenth century. Da Gama visited the harbor again on his homeward voyage and was able to carry to King Manuel protestations of friendship from at least one East African principality. As for other Arab cities, da Gama's belligerent behavior, which ran counter to sixty years of Portuguese policy on the west coast of Africa, partly counterbalanced the remarkable nature of his achievement and stirred up needless antagonisms.

Only in that area of the interior of Moçambique lying behind the coastline from Sofala to Quelimane did the Portuguese make substantial contact with the black African population during the sixteenth and seventeenth centuries. For the rest they were dealing with a coastal people, Arab or Swahili. The Moslem sphere of influence extended as far south as Sofala, although scattered trading settlements existed in the hinterland. Some of the main towns on the eastern fringe were Mogadishu, Pate (Patta Island), Malindi, Mombasa, Pemba, Zanzibar, Kilwa, Moçambique; such travelers as Ibn Batuta have recorded their prosperity and beauty. Da Gama spoke of the fine stone houses and the air of elegance in the local courts and markets. By all accounts it was a world comparable, if not superior, in material culture to Portugal in 1500. Political unity among these city-states was a transitory burden. Each fiercely defended its own political and commercial independence and at no time did there exist an East African nation or empire, although the stronger towns dominated or influenced their neighbors at certain times in their history. Mombasa, Mogadishu, or Pate held sway over their neighbors, and at the moment of Portuguese entry into the Indian Ocean, Kilwa was mistress of the lands and commerce to the south, including the vital Sofala gold trade. Portugal was able in part to exploit the differences between the Arab communities, but she was also to discover that in their latent hostility to the European interlopers there was strong unity.

In 1500 the origins of Arab dominance reached more than a thousand years into the past, and Arab captains probably traded the East African coast centuries before that. Evidence is constantly appearing to show that the trading civilization of East Africa was a very old one and penetrated much deeper into the interior than has been supposed. From the eighth century on, the area was progressively peopled by Arabs and to a lesser extent by Persians; later an Indian immigration added to the cosmopolitan complexion of the coast. The Swahili community probably formed the bulk of each city's population, although political administration remained in the hands of an Arab aristocracy which imposed its religion and a variation of its language. The management of much of the commerce in the cities seems gradually to have passed into the hands of the Indian residents; in the interior, Swahili merchants — traditionally referred to as Arab traders — carried on most of the trade. East Africa itself was commercially a part of the mercantile complex of the Indian Ocean, and the Arabs thrived in their role as middlemen who brought the products of India and the Middle East to Africa. These manufactured goods (cloth, metal, adornments) were traded primarily for ivory, gold, and slaves. Local manufacture or large-scale agriculture held little interest for the Arabs, who found it more profitable to send their dhows to the trading emporia of the Indian Ocean. Their caravans penetrated the continent regularly in search of slaves — some of whom were shipped to points as distant as China — but their influence on the African tribes of the interior usually decreased in ratio to the distance from the coast.

The northern frontier of modern Moçambique is Cape Delgado, which has roughly demarked the extent of Portuguese authority in that direction since about 1700. But even earlier Cape Delgado represented a symbolic point on the East African coast: to the south the Portuguese, having made Moçambique island their source of power, brought under their domination the Arab population all the way to Sofala; to the north the Portuguese were never able, either through their steadfast alliance with Malindi or through the construction of the massive Fort Jesus at Mombasa, to impose a lasting control; and by 1700 a resurgence of Arab power had effectively eliminated Portuguese traders and soldiers from the score of coastal towns in which they had tenaciously, if intermittently, held sway.

One of the facts of the Portuguese empire in the East is that East

Africa played at all times a secondary role in it, and this may be one reason why the Portuguese still retain the province of Moçambique and very little else of their former eastern possessions. North of the Rovuma River along the coasts of Tanganyika, Kenya, and southern Somalia, present-day traces of Portuguese influence are slight: Fort Jesus, the remains of smaller forts, and the memories of crooked little Portuguese Street in Zanzibar. Portuguese contact with the pattern of life here was superficial, maintained only by passing carracks and coasters and by small detachments of traders and garrisons of soldiers. No real attempts at settlement were made, and the Portuguese population north of Cape Delgado was always smaller than south of it. Portugal derived little profit from her tenure, but what she did accomplish was to destroy once and for all most of the prosperous and lively Arab city-states which she found there.

With the dispatching of the 1505 fleet to India, twenty-three ships under Francisco d'Almeida, Portuguese policy was directed toward the establishing of commercial monopoly in the Indian Ocean. D'Almeida's orders called for a factory to be built at Sofala to manage the flow of gold — which had already reached fantastic proportions in the Portuguese imagination — from the "mines of Ophir." Kilwa and Mombasa were to be subjugated and all Arab shipping, save that from Malindi, driven from the seas. D'Almeida attacked Kilwa on a pretext, and the fortress of Santiago was built there and garrisoned. Mombasa was bombarded, burnt, and pillaged. As a result of d'Almeida's voyage along the East African coast, the two pillars of Arab authority were split, but hostilities were created which were to plague the Portuguese for the next two hundred years.

By 1510 hardly a town along the coast failed to acknowledge European supremacy. The quick success of Portuguese arms, however, had created a surprising spirit of resistance. The fortress at Kilwa had to be abandoned after seven years of Arab hostility and boycott. By 1528 Mombasa had regained so much of her former arrogance that the Portuguese once more saw fit to demolish the town. Nor were the Portuguese able to guarantee their commercial monopoly. The Arabs preserved of their former trade a measure sufficient for their survival, and a contraband commerce sprang up between East Africa and India which the Portuguese captain at Malindi was unable to suppress. A recognition of this failure was found in the Portuguese policy to release certain areas and products of trade to Arab merchants willing to purchase the rights.

But through most of the sixteenth century the Arab world in Africa was never sufficiently strong or united to confront the Portuguese. Nor did the Europeans have the personnel or the inclination to expand their control over the area. The king's representative at Malindi collected tribute from the various cities and regulated commerce as best he could through his factors. In the 1580's a Turkish adventurer, Mir Ali Bey, stirred his co-religionists at Mogadishu, Pate, and Mombasa to rebellion. Only through a large punitive armada from India and a temporary alliance with the Zimba, a Bantu people who had stormed their way northward to the gates of Mombasa, were the insurrectionists put down and Mombasa once more devastated.

The episodes of the 1580's convinced Portugal that Moçambique island was too distant and Malindi too weak to exert effective domination over the coast, so in 1593 Fort Jesus was constructed at Mombasa, which now became the administrative center of the north in place of Malindi. The building of Fort Jesus brought a temporary rash of activity in adjacent ports. Zanzibar boasted a larger European population than ever before. Pemba and smaller towns developed a flourishing exchange of products, and African staples like slaves and ivory found their way to India with regularity. The first thirty years of the seventeenth century were probably the period of greatest Portuguese solidarity in the area.

In the meantime the strength of the empire in the East was being sapped by the English and Dutch, one of the factors making the Portuguese position north of Cape Delgado untenable. The city-states found an ally in the Oman Arabs who had recovered enough of their former power to listen sympathetically to appeals from their East African brethren. The half-century from 1650 to 1700 records the vicissitudes of Moslem and Christian alike. The struggle was nearly equal, and had it taken place a hundred years earlier Portugal would have prevailed. Now she had neither the ships nor her ancient vigor to cope with the constant pressure from the north and the scores of revolts bursting like firecrackers at her skirts. At the end of the century the thirty-three-month siege by an expedition from Oman rendered Fort Jesus. Help from Goa was not sufficient to save the fort, in which about 2,500 Portuguese, Arabs, Swahili, and Indians perished from disease and hunger,[5] and with the fall of Mombasa one of the two bastions in East Africa was reduced (a Portuguese force briefly held the fort from 1728 to 1730). Within a few years the remnants of Portuguese authority were concentrated on the island of Moçambique. From then on, as if by tacit agreement, Arab rule north of Cape Delgado was accepted as supreme, and the Portuguese mandate to the south was not seriously challenged.

Although factories were established at both Sofala and Moçambique within seven years of da Gama's first voyage, Sofala, the gate-
way to gold, retained a more powerful hold on official imagination
during the first several decades of the century. Part of Francisco
d'Almeida's fleet of 1505 had paused there to construct a fortress. The
Portuguese convinced the sheik of the Arab trading village of the advantages to be gained from their friendship and protection; accordingly, he granted them permission to put up a mud and wattle fort
and several houses for the king's officers and men. In the first months
of the occupation trade flourished, since the Portuguese cut off communication with the Arab markets. Finally, the exasperated Moslem
traders prevailed upon the sheik to dislodge the intruders, but the
sheik fell leading an attack by a native army. A more reasonable man
was put in his place by the Portuguese.

The outpost consolidated its position in the next several years.
Under a series of energetic captains, the bulwarks were reinforced
with stone. A fairly steady movement of gold from the Manica mines
fed the aspirations of the slowly increasing European population, although neither then nor later did the supply from the interior measure
up to the expectations of the crown, which was misled by such exaggerated accounts as those of Diogo de Alcovaça, a short-term visitor
to Sofala in 1506, and Afonso de Albuquerque. Even during the years
1506–1510 the receipts from Sofala scarcely sufficed to maintain the
fortress with its unnecessarily large administrative personnel and constant demand for outside provisions. When the interior was peaceful,
Arab and Swahili traders from Manica and Mashonaland made their
way to the coast; but frequently tribal wars prevented their passage.
Other Arab merchants, their trade withering under the close control
exercised by the Portuguese at Sofala, sought to bypass their once
prosperous port. An enterprising sheik of the Angoche Islands set up
a new line of communication with the interior. He sent his boats
down the coast and up one of the mouths of the Zambezi; some leagues
up the river, the goods were transhipped to canoes, and from still
another point further upriver were carried by caravans into the lands
of the Monomotapa, paramount chief of the central area of Moçambique province, for barter at a fair in one of the principal villages. The
king's factor at Sofala in 1511 urged Manuel to stifle Angoche by a
strict blockade of that section of the coast; in this manner both the
Arabs and Africans would be forced to come to terms with Sofala.
Two years later another factor, elaborating on the situation, tried to
impress upon the king that the supply of gold was not as great as had
been imagined, its sources scattered over a wide area, and that it was

certainly not sufficient for both Arab and Portuguese markets.[6] Such negative reports, however, were not especially welcomed in Lisbon and were seldom heeded.

The situation at Sofala became worse in the years from 1510 to 1530. Sporadic attempts to suppress the smuggling from Angoche failed. In back of Sofala the principal African chief imposed his own blockade on the fortress, cutting off its communication in every direction except the sea. Furthermore, Portuguese coastal vessels often indulged in trade for their own purpose, not the crown's, a circumstance which further cut into the royal factor's business. In desperation the Sofala factor in 1530 advocated the establishment of a supply route from Malindi to Sofala using Arab ships. By controlling the price of Cambay cotton and beads in Malindi and ivory and gold in Sofala, Portugal could, he argued, circumvent her subjects' dishonesty and assure a fixed steady profit at little cost to herself. Such dealings with heretics did not receive royal approval, but it is significant that at an early date the Portuguese in the East realized their country's commercial limitations. Later in the century, when the Portuguese penetrated the interior, the trade in gold and ivory showed a relative increase, and many of the spices sent from the East were paid for in African gold. But even then the amount was disappointingly uncertain.

In these years much of the knowledge of the hinterlands of Sofala came as a result of the extraordinary journeys of António Fernandes, probably a convict left on the coast in 1505 by d'Almeida. Fernandes made his way into the interior seeking information on the gold country. On two trips he explored the area roughly comprising the modern district of Manica and Sofala and the eastern half of Southern Rhodesia. Fernandes recommended that the Portuguese go up the Save and Lundi rivers and establish a factory which would be in a position to tap directly the gold fields of the Monomotapa. But Portuguese penetration, when it came, was to be up the Zambezi, and for fifty years the Save valley route remained untried. Like much of Portugal's African exploration in the interior of the continent, Fernandes' effort was an isolated incident, unrelated to any consistent program of discovery or development. The only useful purpose these journeys and others like them served was centuries later to bolster Portuguese claims of priority in their abortive attempts to effect a territorial transcontinental union of Angola and Moçambique.

That part of Moçambique visited by António Fernandes was inhabited by the Makalanga, with whom the Portuguese had more contact in early centuries than they did with any other Bantu people. The

Makalanga in 1500 had come to the lands between the Save and the Zambezi comparatively recently, probably from northwest Rhodesia, and had incorporated their predecessors in the area or pushed them to the south, as the Makalanga themselves were to be assimilated or displaced by the Barotse in the eighteenth century. The various tribes forming the Makalanga community were in a frequent state of unrest in one part of the country or another. The Portuguese entertained an exaggerated notion of the extent of the power of the paramount chief of the Makalanga. This ruler they termed the Monomotapa, and his residence was held to be in the neighborhood of Mount Darwin. The actual political state of the region seems to have been that the chiefs of the various tribes acknowledged the religious suzerainty of the Monomotapa, but were far from being his vassals.

Although the Portuguese persisted in trying to establish relations with the current Monomotapa for evangelical and commercial reasons, for the most part they dealt with lesser tribal leaders — at Sofala, Sena, Tete, or the outposts they occupied elsewhere. These relations were usually rudimentary, the payment of subsidies for trading rights or a small percentage of the commerce passing through the chiefs' domains. Except for several large military expeditions into the backcountry, the Portuguese were content to put conquest or occupation to one side and save their arms and energies for the more formidable Arab foes to the north. When it was to their advantage the captains at Sena or Sofala would intervene in tribal struggles, but never in the sixteenth century did the Europeans exert the influence in Moçambique that they did in the Congo. It was really not until the late nineteenth century, when possession of Africa was held to be occupation, that Portugal made a determined effort to implant her rule in the backcountry.

In spite of the fact that Sofala, until the emergence of Sena on the Zambezi in the 1530's, was the nearest port to the most productive region of that part of Africa (and the only part where Portuguese traders moved into the interior), Moçambique island rapidly became the center of Portuguese authority below Cape Delgado and was, in fact, the most constant center of administration in all of East Africa. Although it is one of the anomalies of Portuguese overseas history that the town of Moçambique should have maintained itself for so many centuries as the isolated capital of the colony, reasons for its importance in the sixteenth century are obvious: the island was a favored port of call for Indies shipping and was closer to the Arab cities to the north. In 1507 the captain at Sofala, Vasco Gomes de Abreu, carried out his instructions to build a permanent post at Moçambique, which was to consist of a factory and fortress and a hospital for the sick arriving there on the transocean carracks. Moçambique became the most important point of call between Lisbon and India. Here the Sofala gold and ivory were transhipped to India and from here the Portuguese attempted to curtail Arab coastal shipping north and south. At the beginning, a tame sheik was left in nominal power over the local community, but as the town's importance increased, his token office disappeared and the captain of the fortress assumed full responsibility for local as well as imperial matters.[7]

With Hormuz and Malacca, Moçambique island was one of the key bastions of Portugal's far-flung mercantile empire. Yearly ships from the Indies fleet rode at anchor in her harbor; through the port passed viceroys, convicts, poets, stray foreign visitors, all drawn eastward by the lure of sudden fortune. A few stayed in Moçambique, some to die of malaria and others to swell the European population which came to leave its impress on "this most Portuguese of colonial cities." As investment in the East developed so did Moçambique in the first half of the sixteenth century. The island port generally prospered as a depot for men and goods and became the center of a local trade from which the Portuguese in the Indian Ocean derived more profit than they did from the commerce between the East and the metropolis. The captaincy of the island fortress became one of the plums of the colonial service. Originally trade was handled by the king's factor, who had his agents selling the royal treasury's goods wherever possible to the African people. Later the captain received privileges of trade in certain products or areas not reserved by the crown, and finally the whole area of Zambezi trade was delivered over to the captain of Moçambique for a certain (usually quite high) sum on his taking office. In return the captain assumed responsibility for the maintenance and administration of the fortress and for the protection of the people on the island in case of famine or inflation in food prices — events of some frequency since the island was far from self-sufficient, as shown by the frantic pleas sometimes sent to Lisbon for shipment of provisions by the next annual fleet. The practice of leasing the trade monopoly (at times the treasury reverted to its earlier practices of working exclusively through its factor) resulted in considerable scandal and charges of dishonesty, but no fewer charges were made against the factor and his agents in their day. Into the storehouse of the island were piled the beads and cloth for the Bantu trade; beside them lay the gold, ivory, and ambergris for the markets of Goa or the holds of the Lisbon-bound liners. In other arsenals were the ships' supplies, arms, and provisions.

The captaincy at Moçambique, for both its commercial and military implications, was an important one. The distance of Moçambique from Goa and Lisbon increased the autonomy of the commander, but his authority was not without checks and balances. He held office under the jurisdiction of the Indian viceroy, as did the captains at Hormuz, Ceylon, and Malacca. On some matters of administration he was obliged to act in consultation with his subordinates and others of the king's officers, such as the factor or magistrate. His political and judicial powers were circumscribed by the *regimento* and he was required to submit periodic reports to the viceroy and the Indies Council in Lisbon. Generally, the captains were chosen from men with years of military or administrative experience in the empire, although such caution sometimes resulted in an efficiency in corruption as well as in administration. The indiscriminate accusation of dishonesty against Portugal's officials in the East is a commonplace of that nation's colonial history, but such accusations have been sometimes motivated by the desire to find a scapegoat or convenient excuse for the decline that occurred, and in the sixteenth century one may find examples of the disinterested official, like Diogo de Almeida, who refused honest profit, saying that his honor forbade him to make money at his country's expense.

Because of the nature of the occupation of Moçambique province in the first seventy years the captain had no influence over the African population except at points of contact along the coast or in the bush. He was instructed to respect the rights of the African chiefs, especially those who from time to time proclaimed themselves vassals of the Portuguese king. The reality of Portugal's tenuous position in Bantu Africa carried more weight than royal instructions, to be sure, but the intent of the crown was still manifestly clear: its representatives should attempt to work in alliance with African leaders and not pursue a policy of terror or extermination. When in the seventeenth and eighteenth centuries this official attitude was overridden by the tyrannical plantation owners of Zambézia,[8] it was partly the result of the diminishment in Lisbon's rule over the area and of a neglect similar to that suffered in the Congo kingdom. And in Moçambique province, Portugal's most durable African policy, miscegenation, was carried out, in the absence of women from home, with the same ardor as in the Congo.

By the middle of the century the island town of Moçambique had achieved such importance that Dona Catarina, regent for her son

Sebastião, resolved to implement her husband's plan for the building of a massive fortress there. In the 1540's João sent materials and stone-masons to begin the work, but the project languished until ten years later when the distinguished architect Miguel de Arruda — who contributed to plans for the Escorial — arrived in Moçambique. For the next forty years the great solid structure of the *fortaleza* São Sebastião was devised and armored into the impregnable bulwark that withstood the Dutch attack of 1607. Still in use today, the hulk of São Sebastião hovers in lonely fashion from its low white coral reef over the peacock sea. Within its walls were quarters for a thousand men, a gigantic cistern, a chapel, and a hospital; it was the most substantial Portuguese monument in the East. Befitting the scope of the fortress, the captain, or governor, as he was sometimes called, was granted wider privileges and power. He was permitted a small portion of government profits in the ivory trade and instructed to prohibit competition in his territories by ships from India. He had a predominant voice in the appointment of the captains on the Zambezi and at Sofala and Malindi. His responsibilities also increased. A population of about one hundred Portuguese grew to perhaps four hundred by the end of the century. This figure was multiplied many times when a large fleet wintered at the island before proceeding to India. The Portuguese, undismayed by fevers, food shortages, scandals, intrigue, complaints, made Moçambique town a rich bustling replica of metropolitan Portuguese towns.

In an effort to speed up the export of gold, the captain at Moçambique in 1531 founded a Portuguese fair at Sena, where there already existed a small Arab settlement. The town, now only a place-name on the banks of East Africa's greatest river, prospered intermittently but surely, and in the next two hundred years became the center of plantation and colonization experiments along the Zambezi. A few years later the town of Tete was created further up the river, some 260 miles from the sea. In closer contact with the lands of Monomotapa and the gold fields of Manica and Mashona, these two settlements supplemented with fair success the trade in gold that already trickled down the Save valley into Sofala. At Massapa, southwest from Tete and not far from Zimbabwe, the mysterious ruined stone city that sometimes served as the great chief's capital, a Portuguese adventurer set himself up about 1550 as a free-lance trader and adviser to the Monomotapa. Taking advantage of his presence, the viceroy conferred upon him the title Captain of the Gates (the gates being figuratively those to the

Mashona gold fields), making him a royal factor and the viceregal representative at the African court. Through him Arab and Portuguese traders paid duty to the Monomotapa's treasury. António Caiado was one of the first in a long line of frontiersmen who found it possible to live and prosper independently among the Bantu tribes of Africa, the most famous of the breed being the nineteenth-century explorer and merchant in Angola, António da Silva Porto. Caiado's success drew several countrymen to take up residence with him, and the office of the Captain of the Gates was passed down to numerous successors before it died out.

Still other small centers of trade, some ephemeral, others more permanent, were founded in the first half of the century. In 1544 a factory at Quelimane, a few miles inland from the coast, came into being. In the same year Lourenço Marques skirted the coast south of Sofala to Delagoa Bay where he made arrangements with the local chief for regular visits by Portuguese coasters to buy ivory. Although the present capital of the province bears Lourenço Marques' name, no permanent settlement was made in the area until much later. In like manner a desultory commerce at Inhambane was effected.

In 1568, Sebastião, moody, devout, and headstrong, ascended to the Portuguese throne at the age of fourteen. Although he earned the sobriquet *O Africano* from his ill-starred Moroccan campaign, Sebastião had a Rhodesian vision for southern Africa, the creation of a vast domain stretching inland hundreds of leagues from the Indian Ocean. Thus he conceived the idea of a large expeditionary force to the kingdom of Monomotapa. The main goal was an eminently practical one: seize the gold mines and make them produce as the Portuguese imagined they should. A self-righteous justification was offered by the murder of the Jesuit missionary Gonçalo da Silveira (whose fate will be treated in a subsequent chapter) at the hands of the paramount chief. Such a departure from the traditional policy of peaceful trade through alliance with the chiefs of the interior aroused serious opposition from a minority on the king's council. A legislative compromise was reached in the guise of an ultimatum to be delivered by the leader of the expedition to the African king. The gist of the message was that, in view of recent robberies and murders of Portuguese subjects in his lands, not the least of whom was Gonçalo da Silveira, the Monomotapa was requested to give free access to all Portuguese traders and missionaries and to yield reparations for past injuries. Since the presence of Arabs within his kingdom could only be considered prejudicial to Portugal's interest and inflammatory in their influence, they should be expelled.

To present his complaint to the chief, Sebastião chose Francisco Barreto, a former governor general of India. (Sebastião chose the opportunity to split his eastern government into three parts: the east coast of Africa, the territory from Cape Guardafui to Pegu, and the territory from Pegu to China. Each governor was to be supreme in his own jurisdiction; in point of honor each was the viceroy's equal.) Barreto had as his principal advisers the Jesuit Francisco de Monclaros for affairs of the soul and a grand master of the Order of Santiago, Vasco Fernandes Homem, for affairs of the military. One thousand volunteers, many from the nobility, were provided for by a generous grant from the royal treasury which was to be repeated each year until the task was done. In April 1569 the first African army took its thunderous leave from Belém bound for Moçambique.

Barreto did not set out upon his campaign immediately after his arrival, and even though part of the delay was warranted by the necessity for obtaining supplies, it still reveals the bad judgment that had begun to mark his actions which was in a major sense responsible for the mission's failure. He rejected his subordinates' insistence that they should enter the backlands up the Save valley, and in November 1571 Barreto's fleet of small vessels left the shelter of São Sebastião fortress for Sena. By the time the company reached the village, the rainy season, with its oppressive heat, had descended upon the land. The visitation of some eight hundred men on the tiny town, which boasted but ten European inhabitants, created tremendous difficulties of supply and transportation. Convinced that the fevers which were decimating his men and horses were the work of Arab poison, Barreto called for the shameless slaughter of the Mohammedan community. Many were disposed of with delicate savagery on the ends of pikes or in the mouths of cannon.

From Sena, Barreto sent an envoy to the Monomotapa asking for an embassy to come to Sena to discuss matters of mutual friendship. Unknown to Barreto, his man was drowned on the upper Zambezi. Impatient after half a year's wait, Barreto decided to use his large force to put down a rebellious chief, enemy of both the Monomotapa and the Portuguese. Barreto's decision did not run counter to his *regimento*, but it did to sound judgment. His men routed the chief with few losses, but the rigors of the march upcountry seriously diminished their numbers.

On his return to Sena, Barreto found a large embassy from the Monomotapa. He explained to them Sebastião's terms and left for Moçambique to counter intrigues against him there. In May 1573 he was back up the river, where only a handful of his men were able to greet him. The magnificent corps, with its subsequent reinforcements from India, was reduced to 180 men. Barreto himself died of fever and exhaustion two weeks later. In spite of an encouraging reply from the Monomotapa, Vasco Fernandes Homem, acting in consort with Father Monclaros and the remaining officers, decided not to press the advantage, and the remainder of the expedition was evacuated.

In Moçambique the old soldier Homem smarted under the comments of second-guessers on the failure of the famous expedition to accomplish its purposes. Homem resolutely collected another army of slightly more than four hundred men and in August 1574 departed for Sofala. In the interior he discovered that the two dominant tribes of the region were at war with each other. After several skirmishes the Portuguese reached Manica where they encamped near the present city of Umtali; here for the first time the Portuguese ascertained the actual gold-producing possibilities of the area. Their conclusion, substantiated in later years, was that without machinery and skilled labor the output of ore would be small. Homem concluded agreements with the local chief for the free passage of Portuguese and African traders before departing with those of his men not yet dead from malaria.

From Sofala, Homem went north to the Zambezi and up to Sena, where he decided to track down the persistent rumors of the silver mines of Chicoa. With a few reinforcements to fill the gaps in his company, Homem marched along the banks of the river beyond Tete. The silver mines did not come up to the usual naïve expectations, but the governor had a stockade constructed to house the two hundred men he intended to leave behind for further investigations. While Homem returned to Moçambique, the entire garrison was destroyed by African tribesmen. The fate of the two expeditions convinced the crown, now engaged in preparations for the far more spectacular disaster at Alcazarquivir, of the futility of trying to occupy the interior of southeast Africa. Shortly thereafter, Moçambique was reduced to its original status of captaincy under the thumb of India. Then, as even now, the difficulties of terrain and disease along the Zambezi defied the best efforts of Lisbon planners.

The most coherent source of information on life and customs — African and Portuguese — in sixteenth-century Moçambique is still João dos Santos' *Ethiópia oriental*, published in 1609. Dos Santos was a Dominican who was in East Africa from 1586 to 1597 and again in the early seventeenth century. His impressions, recorded during the decade of his first residence, spent mostly at Sofala although he visited Zambézia and the coastal regions of the province, are remarkably free from fanciful exaggerations. He wrote that Sofala was in the twilight of its importance. Its trade with the island of Moçambique was handled by small native coastal vessels, manned by Swahili crew and European officers. Two villages, one Christian, the other Mohammedan, were located near the fort. The Christian village had a mixed population of about six hundred people. Zambézia was divided into four tribal domains, usually at war with each other. To the chiefs of these kingdoms the Portuguese paid tribute or duty on goods. Thus the captain at Sena was obliged to give a supply of cotton cloth and beads to the embassy from the Monomotapa which visited the town with great flourish every three years. Sena was the core of Zambezi trade, boasting a fort, warehouses, church, and a population of perhaps fifty Portuguese and seven hundred and fifty Indians, half-castes, and African slaves. Tete was almost as large. In addition to its officials, some forty Portuguese and five hundred Asians and Africans resided there. The factor enjoyed the protection of a Bantu guard of honor, two thousand soldier-slaves presented to the fort by a generous Monomotapa after a victory over a neighboring tribe. South and southwest of Tete in the backcountry were three lesser factories at Massapa, Luanza, and Bukoto. At none of these outposts did the Portuguese have any influence over the African villages save that granted by the African princes. Dos Santos also gives a sketchy mineral survey of the territory somewhat less glowing than the reports Goa and Lisbon were accustomed to receive.

The pages of the *Ethiópia oriental* contain an account of the ravages by the Zimba who appeared along the Zambezi in 1570, one large party of whom turned seaward and scourged the coast up to Mombasa. Another group appeared soon thereafter and remained in the vicinity of the river for years terrorizing the Makalanga. In 1592 Portuguese forces from Sena and Tete were routed in a savage encounter with the Zimba, and a punitive expedition from the island of Moçambique met a similar fate the next year. In the last years of the century Portuguese fortunes on the Zambezi were at their lowest ebb.[9]

In the seventeenth century the monopoly which the Portuguese enjoyed in East Africa and the Indian Ocean was threatened and finally broken by Arab, Dutch, and English power. The Arabs, as we have seen, reasserted much of their former influence north of Cape Delgado. In the East, English and Dutch trading companies, encouraged by national policies of expansion, displaced or outflanked the Portuguese in their once unique position as European middlemen in the oriental trade. Only Moçambique remained firmly Lusitanian; so pronounced was Portugal's decline elsewhere that the African province was more than once referred to as Portugal's most prosperous colony. It had the virtue of costing the crown nothing to administer and little to protect. Its relative prosperity in the seventeenth century was partly the result of a change in imperial policy which favored African interests more than previously and partly the result of a lack of interest in the area by Portugal's adversaries. Even so, Moçambique did not escape completely from the turbulence of the age. Increased activity in the interior brought added tensions in relations with the African tribes. And there were the Dutch.

The French and the Dutch were the first European nations whose ships rounded the Cape of Good Hope in the wake of da Gama, but their sixteenth-century voyages had little immediate effect either at home or in the East. The Dutch presented the more serious challenge. Denied access to Indian products by Philip of Spain when he took over the Portuguese throne in 1580 and encouraged by the precise intelligence concerning navigation and trade in Indian waters gathered by Jan Huyghen van Linschoten, the Dutch sent a fleet to the Indian Ocean in 1595. There were other voyages, and the intruders were sufficiently bold in 1604 to blockade the island of Moçambique and disrupt coastal shipping. The impregnability of São Sebastião discouraged a lengthy siege, but the next two attempts on the fortress were more determined than the first. Eight Dutch ships arrived under the island's guns in March 1607. The Dutch entrenched themselves on the island and called upon the fortress to surrender. Malaria came to the aid of the Portuguese, and after six weeks of bombardment and insult, the Dutch withdrew. Before the inhabitants could repair their damaged town, a still stronger Dutch fleet of thirteen ships and possibly two thousand men under Pieter Verhoeff entered Moçambique harbor in July 1608. The second siege, similar to the first but marked by needless Dutch atrocities, was no more successful, and in the latter part of August, Verhoeff ordered his ships to weigh anchor. In 1663 a fourth futile attempt was made to capture São Sebastião.[10]

Moçambique island was not alone in her troubles. The whole Zambezi region was in turmoil from 1590 through the first two decades of the seventeenth century. A spate of African tribal disputes broke out, in which the Portuguese participated, either for political advantage or, as sometimes happened, against their will. Also, the Portuguese had fallings out among themselves as a series of royal edicts created a triple split of authority placing the viceroy at Goa, the captain at Moçambique, and the captain at Sena frequently at odds with one another. These squabbles were symptomatic of the confusion in Lisbon as to the real nature of the African colony and of a general Portuguese demoralization in the East. The prevailing unity of purpose characterizing most of the sixteenth century, when the Indian Ocean was a Portuguese sphere of action, disintegrated. Latent jealousies and corruptions, once subordinated or minimized in the course of a concerted exploitation of new-found worlds, now became vitally disruptive factors.

In 1608 Philip III, blinded by the glitter of gold and silver that streamed from the American mines and deluded by a recent sample of ore of high quality from Africa, decided to organize another expedition to extract Zambezi silver. The goal was again the alleged mines of silver in the vicinity of Chicoa, and the enterprise seemed sensible enough at the time if one overlooked the empty consequences of the Barreto-Homem expeditions. The moment was certainly auspicious. For fifteen years the Makalanga had been embroiled in wars during which much of the Monomotapa's power had been vitiated. The intervention of the captain of Tete, Diogo Simões Madeira, and other traders on behalf of their sometime ally — an intervention primarily to re-establish the security of trade — caused the grateful chief to cede to Madeira territories in the neighborhood of Tete and to grant Portugal mineral rights throughout his kingdom in return for continued European support. To bind the bargain he entrusted two of his sons to Madeira to be educated in the Christian manner at Tete.

Against this background King Philip reorganized the colonial administration. In a letter to the viceroy of India he ordered that a "Captain General of the Expedition" be named to supersede the captain at Moçambique. The appointee was to be supreme in southeast Africa and to name all regional officers. Key fortresses along the coast as well as in the interior were to be constructed or strengthened. The captain general was to dedicate his full energies to the pursuit of gold and silver; he was not to meddle in the Monomotapa's government, which might involve him in the distractions of African politics. The acting governor of India, Archbishop Menezes, was unable in those critical times to muster the five hundred men demanded, but he dispatched one hundred men under the command of Nuno Alvares Pereira.

On his arrival in Tete the new captain general appointed Diogo Madeira his field officer in charge of the mines operation. On his first journey to the Monomotapa, Madeira accomplished little except to help the African king complete the suppression of some troublesome tribes. Questions about the location of the mines were met with vague

gestures toward the horizon. Madeira returned to Sena to find that
Nuno Alvares Pereira had been replaced by Estavão de Ataíde, defender of Moçambique against the two Dutch attacks in 1607 and
1608. Ataíde ran into immediate difficulty with the Monomotapa, who,
seeing himself entrenched in power once more, demanded his traditional tribute for trading rights. Ataíde was unwilling and unable to
meet the demand, and the chief ordered all Portuguese goods in his
kingdom confiscated. Annoyed by the breach of faith, Ataíde made
plans to take the mines by force, but before the expedition could be
made ready he was called in 1612 to Moçambique island to reinforce
the depleted garrison there. When he returned to the Zambezi, a shift
in policy brought him orders to report to India; again the Chicoa campaign was delayed. Diogo Madeira was left in charge, although not
with the full powers of his predecessor, for complicated political ma-
neuvering had resulted in the return of civil authority in southeast
Africa to the hands of the Moçambique captain. Ataíde died in Moçambique before he could be tried for what Philip held to be his ineffectual action.

Diogo Madeira persisted in his pursuit of the mines. In 1614 he
erected twin fortresses — one on either side of the Zambezi — at Chicoa. He obtained several weighty specimens of ore which he sent to
Lisbon by two separate couriers.[11] But the antagonisms of various
merchants and officials at Sena and Moçambique and the many difficulties of maintaining the stockades forced Madeira to give up the project. Philip's advisers, however, were still intrigued by the chances of
African gold and silver and set up a governorship of the lands of the
Monomotapa, subservient to Goa, but holding jurisdiction over Moçambique. In the game of musical chairs, the office fell to Nuno Alvares Pereira, who was entrusted with the usual elaborate unrealistic
instructions for developing silver production. Pereira did his best, but
he obtained nothing of value. In 1622 the viceroy was told to drop
the project, and the administration of Moçambique reverted to its captaincy status.

The Chicoa silver hunt illustrates how poorly prepared was Moçambique province for imperial exploitation on a grand scale. Malaria,
unrest among the Africans, dispersal of authority, and the essential
poverty of the region conspired to thwart all ambitious plans for its
development. The most the Portuguese could hope for were the modest gains from commerce set up in the sixteenth century and the continuing trickle of gold from Manica. Through the sale of offices,

southeast Africa was a self-supporting and even modestly prosperous community within the empire. The island had recovered from Dutch devastations and was the most important Portuguese town in Africa with a Christian population (white, black, and brown) of several thousand and a fairly steady traffic through its port. Sofala, on the other hand, had entered the long final stage of its decay. The factory and fort remained for the export of gold, ivory, and ambergris, but the European population probably numbered no more than ten souls. Affairs on the Zambezi, after the recent frustrations, gradually took a different complexion with the rise of the *prazo*, or plantation, system and the influx of missionary priests. Sena boasted four churches in addition to its official buildings and a white population of about fifty people, a total that increased slightly. Tete had twenty residents in the shadow of its fort and a great many more scattered in the surrounding *prazos*. Up and down the river and in the lands of the Monomotapa, traders, soldiers, and priests carried on a solitary existence, as did a few others along the coast. A fair estimate of the Portuguese colony during this period would be one thousand people, a figure which did not show much growth until the twentieth century and even decreased from time to time.

Lisbon's discontent with the moderate profit shown by Moçambique was reflected in decisions other than hapless silver chases. In the early 1590's Agostinho de Azevedo submitted a proposal to the king that Zambézia be thrown open to free trade — free, that is, to Portuguese, not to Jews, Arabs, or Indians. He calculated that a customs rate of 20 per cent on all traffic in the area would bring in more money in six months than the sale of offices did in three years. He assumed that with a free passage of goods, prices would decrease and the indigenous inhabitants could be induced to work the supposed mines. The king's council submitted the plan for the approval of the viceroy and the governor of Moçambique, both of whom argued convincingly to the contrary; a side effect, however, of Azevedo's motion was an increase in the price of the Moçambique government. In another attempt to stimulate commerce, João IV, first king of the Bragança line, which had replaced Spanish sovereignty in Portugal, declared in 1643 that trade between Portugal and India, including Africa, was open to all Portuguese; but entrenched interests prevented the decree from taking effect. In 1671 a similar order concerning only Zambézia came from Lisbon and met with the same objections. A counterproposal, to which the crown assented, called for the creation of a board of trade as an appendage of the royal treasury. Its seat was in Goa with local governing boards at Moçambique and Sena. Governors and agents of the board were to receive salaries for carrying out all commerce in the area. Since the new organization had to buy out the monopolies already granted to local captains, it began in debt, from which it never emerged. Its administration proved costly and cumbersome; the inexperience and corruption of some of its agents responsible for buying and selling contributed to further inefficiency. In 1680 the board was discontinued and the whole region given over to free trade open to all Portuguese subjects in every part of the world.

Customhouses arose at African ports of entry, and the new governor of Moçambique was given additional men and authority to collect the anticipated added revenue and to prevent smuggling. The results were not altogether what had been expected. The queen regent of Portugal in 1661 had given England a handsome dowry with the hand of her daughter Catarina when the latter married Charles II; these concessions included Bombay and the right of free trade in Portuguese ports. The appearance of English ships along Moçambique's coast in the 1680's, though infrequent, still placed Portuguese merchants at a disadvantage, as in 1687 when four English vessels bought most of the year's ivory output. The consequences of the royal marriage, however, were felt more in another direction. With the passing of Bombay, much of Portugal's remaining mercantile position disappeared, and a number of Indian traders, generally referred to as Banians or Canarins, when not called harsher names, were thus attracted to Africa, where they gained a stranglehold on Moçambique commerce. One of the clichés still current in Africa has it that the only bush trader capable of existing on a lower standard of living in a hostile climate than a Portuguese is the Indian. In eight years the Portuguese merchant faced extinction, the market was glutted with cloth and beads, and the price of gold had risen to unprofitable heights. Heeding the local residents' desperate pleas for protection, Lisbon in 1690 placed a restriction on further Banian immigration and set up a chamber of commerce to regulate the traffic of goods. The latter move in effect canceled the decree of 1680, although by now a great deal of damage had been done to the white Portuguese subjects of Moçambique and a new element introduced into its population which was to play an active role for a century.

From 1690 to 1697 efforts were directed to the formation of a trading company similar to the ones operated so successfully by the Dutch and English. The company was in part subsidized by the home government, although shares were sold by general subscription. The company was required to pay substantial sums to the royal treasury for the defense of India in return for a monopoly of trade along the East African coast. After three years it collapsed because of under-subscription of its shares and the commitments with which it was burdened at birth. In 1700 the government again took over African commerce.

In the middle of the seventeenth century another commodity began to be exported from Moçambique, slaves. The Portuguese were here carrying on a practice the Arabs had initiated hundreds of years before them. From their earliest associations with East Africa, Portuguese captains and settlers had acquired African slaves, usually as gifts from native chiefs, and some had been sent to India, although the custom was to keep them as servants and soldiers. Now, however, a small trade with Brazil developed which was to grow slowly and fitfully until slavery became the principal commerce of southeast Africa. Ultimately it would contribute to the scandalous conditions of the nineteenth century and the final anarchic collapse of the whole Zambezi basin.

The native policy of the Portuguese crown — if the standard instructions incorporated in most *regimentos* on how to deal with African princes may be considered a policy — took on a slightly different aspect in the seventeenth century, although it may have seemed a problem in colonial dialectics to reconcile the earlier armed expeditions up the Zambezi with the traditional orders not to disturb the African's way of life. Certainly in the seventeenth century, when a larger number of settlers and missionaries joined the traders and officers already resident in the province, it became more difficult to comply with the spirit of royal dispositions. On the island, racial tensions were less than at Sena or Tete, for here the Portuguese were following a pattern of physical and cultural assimilation established by the Arabs, and much of the African or half-caste population adapted itself to the habits of its new masters, although many, to be sure, clung to their Moslem faith. The long history of this small community has been one of relative tranquillity in comparison with other parts of the province, even if still today the African there, in the majority, has not attained that degree of Europeanization of which the Portuguese boast.

On the Zambezi and in the lands of the Monomotapa where the Portuguese, in order to exist and carry on trade, were forced to deal with local chiefs, the course of native affairs took another turn. Unquestionably in the sixteenth century they sought nothing more than to be permitted to trade and search for gold in peace, paying tribute where necessary and allying themselves with the strongest African leaders for the protection of themselves and their business. In this they were not as skilled as the Arab, and there evolved a tangled skein of complications which were to plague life on the Zambezi until the present century. The Portuguese never had sufficient numbers in the region to implant their authority solidly, appearances to the contrary, and in many respects their increased numbers in the seventeenth century did more to compound the confusion than lessen it, since the area of friction with the African likewise increased. The *prazero* demanded laborers or slaves for his estates, the missionary sought converts among a people whose enmity often forced both to fall back on the use of arms. The material and spiritual inducements offered the African were seldom sufficient to win him over to the Portuguese cause; indeed the history of the Zambezi is more the history of the African assimilating the Portuguese than the reverse. Had not the African chiefs dissipated their strength quarreling among themselves and had not the converted Monomotapa given away his lands and people, it is not likely that the Portuguese could have survived the seventeenth century in the interior. That they did is more evidence of their tenacity than of their tact or the success of their colonial policy.

The whole population of Zambézia — trader, settler, missionary — was involved in the disputes of 1628. On the death of the Monomotapa, a son, Capranzine, had attained the chieftainship of his lands. Hostile to the Portuguese and jealous of the attentions given his nephew Manuza by the Europeans, the new king declared himself dissatisfied with the trading arrangements in his realm and ordered an *embate* (a combination blockade and warfare) and laid siege to several fortresses in the interior. To meet the attack, the Portuguese gathered together their private African armies and the tribes loyal to them and drove Capranzine deep into his kingdom, whereupon Manuza was proclaimed the new ruler. In the following year, Manuza formally put his mark on a lengthy document pledging vassalage to the king of Portugal; the agreement contained the customary promises to give the white men free access through his kingdom, permission for the construction of churches and missions, the expulsion of the Arabs, and the renouncing of all claims previously deeded to the captain at Tete. To each new captain of Moçambique he was to send three pieces of gold as token of his dependency on Portuguese arms. Shortly afterwards, Manuza became a Christian, taking the name of Filipe. For the first time in the history of the colony the Portuguese had achieved an uneasy dominance over the largest of the Makalanga tribes.

In 1631 Capranzine united a substantial number of dissident chiefs, including the paramount chief of Manica, and moved to retake his former lands. In the course of his onslaught he killed two Dominican priests and drove the rest of the Portuguese to the sanctuary of Sena and Tete. The captain at Moçambique, aided greatly by the Dominicans in the field who regarded war against Capranzine as a crusade for Christianity, got together a small army which dealt the pagan chief a crushing defeat. Now Manuza held his position more firmly. Lisbon was elated at the good news and foolishly revived plans to exploit the undiscovered mines, but the attempts were desultory and, as usual, unsuccessful. The first practical results of having a puppet as Monomotapa were a vigorous expansion of mission work and the breakdown of African resistance. Individual Portuguese through gift or purchase — but also as a result of bribes and threats — were able to gain possession of vast tracts of territory along the Zambezi which they ruled much in the manner of the lesser African chiefs they supplanted.

Manuza died in 1652 after a reign of twenty-two years in which he served Portuguese interests faithfully, realizing that without their support his tenure would have been uncertain. The rightful heir to the Monomotapa's stool, the son of Capranzine, had long since been carried to Goa where he entered the Dominican order; he died there, vicar of the convent of Santa Barbara, the holder of a diploma pronouncing him master in theology. The successor to Manuza in 1652 still held to his tribal religion, but under the guidance of missionary fathers he embraced the faith of his predecessor (taking the name Domingos), an event which caused rejoicing in Lisbon and Rome where the Dominicans held services to celebrate the conversion. In the next fifteen years, however, friction between the Monomotapa and the *prazeros* developed over disputed lands which the planters refused to restore to the African chief who claimed that they had been wrongfully taken from him. In 1668 open warfare broke out between Domingos and the now powerful land barons, in the course of which the chief was assassinated by a subordinate in his own army. The Portuguese replaced him with a relative thought to be safe, but the young ruler showed an independence which was responsible for renewed disturbances. He could not, however, weld together the demoralized African peoples, the majority of whom either succumbed to slavery or withdrew to parts of the country beyond Portuguese penetration, where they continued to harass individual traders and missionaries.

By 1700 the colony of Moçambique had entered a stage of decadence which was to last two hundred years. With the fall of Mombasa and the final passing of the eastern empire into alien hands, save for such dispersed remnants as Goa, Cochin, Macao, the flow of coastal and transocean commerce was considerably reduced, and the province was removed from steady contact with India and Portugal. At the beginning of the century the garrison at Sofala was abandoned. Portuguese subjects at Sena and Tete and on the surrounding estates lived in barbarically splendid isolation, squabbling with each other and with the Africans, creating a half-caste community which recognized no law but its own. Missionary services declined. In the last part of the seventeenth century a trading post was established at Zumbo far up the Zambezi on the present Rhodesian frontier, but its active life was short, and it was soon to be forgotten like many of the other smaller posts in the interior.

Portuguese imperial interests were now centered on Brazil whose agricultural and mineral wealth promised a renaissance of Lusitanian prosperity. India and Moçambique — Angola had value as source of slaves — were an exhausting distraction of national energies. In 1752 the administration of Moçambique was definitely separated from Goa, Francisco de Melo e Castro becoming the first governor of Moçambique, Zambézia, and Sofala. One hundred and fifty years earlier such a separation would have heralded a new phase of importance for the African province, but now it was only another indication of the fragmentation of the Indian Ocean empire and a belated attempt to encourage the colony along the road to greater self-sufficiency. The gesture meant little in terms of political result, and as one looks back across the two and a half centuries from 1752 to da Gama's voyage of 1498, one must conclude that tradition in Moçambique accomplished not much more than did experiment in the kingdom of the Congo.

III

ANGOLA TO 1858

ALTHOUGH the history of Angola in its early years may be considered a part of Portuguese activity in the Congo kingdom, the association is marginal, and the area held interest only in terms of coastal exploration and the projection of the Congo slave trade. Not until the foundation of Luanda in 1576 and the expeditions of that most celebrated campaigner in Portuguese Africa in the sixteenth century, Paulo Dias de Novais, did the lands to the south become a primary concern to the Lisbon court. For several decades thereafter, a declining Congo and a rising Angola shared equally as centers of Portugal's policy, but by 1600 the territory known as Angola had emerged as the more important sphere of influence. In contrast with her pacific policies of alliance and cultural assimilation in the Congo, here Portugal was disposed to implant her authority over the African *sobas*, or chiefs, by force and to govern directly — a shift in policy determined by various factors of which the two most important were the absence in Angola of a supreme chief of the stature of the Manicongo or Monomotapa and the need for military action to protect the blossoming slave trade. The first three centuries of Angola's history, from about 1550 to 1850, is a chronology of small wars and expeditions in the interior and of a dedicated commerce in black humanity, most of it with Brazil, which made up more than four fifths of total exports during this period. Angola still retains today some of the harsh frontier aggressiveness that has characterized its past and left its stamp upon the present; it is a quality which sets the province immediately apart from the more leisurely, perhaps more cosmopolitan, Moçambique. One of the most sparsely populated coun-

tries of Africa, Angola has not yet recovered from the terrible depredations of tribal conflict and a slave trade that, by conservative estimate, carried more than three million Negroes to the plantations of the
two Americas.

Diogo Cão in his voyage of 1482 reached a section of the coast
below Benguela before his return to the mouth of the Congo. On one
of his several landfalls he put in at the site of the future Luanda, at
the time the center of the Manicongo's cowrie-shell industry furnishing the coin of the great chief's realm. On his second voyage, Cão
sailed the whole length of the Angola coast whose inhospitable expanse seemed to hold little promise for exploration. In the early years
of the sixteenth century, ambitious merchants from São Tomé, dissatisfied with the Congo trade, made sporadic voyages to the island of
Luanda, although they gained little profit for their pains. Their activity tended to increase after 1512 when Manuel reserved for his
newly appointed factor the Congo slave trade, and more so after
1519 when another royal decree prohibited private vessels from
loading at Pinda.

The boundaries of the original lands of Angola are not definitely
known — nor were they in the 1500's. A fair estimate of the area
subservient to the Ngola (the dynastic title of the chief of the Kim-
bundu people inhabiting the region) would be the country lying between the Dande River in the north and the Cuanza in the south and
extending from the coast [1] back into the Dongo as far as the modern
city of Malange, although some scholars project the eastern boundaries all the way to the Cuango River. The Africans dwelling there
at the time of the Portuguese visitations were Southern Bantu people
who had moved into the area and formed one of several tribal divisions.[2] Over the petty chiefs of the Dongo country, nominally under
the thrall of the Manicongo, an invading chief from the lands of
Matamba (which lay to the west of the southern reaches of the
Cuango River) had gained dominance. This Ngola and several of
his successors continued to own informal allegiance to the Manicongo.
As was the case in the Congo, the Portuguese applied the name of the
local ruler to the country he governed.

In 1519 the Ngola, envious perhaps of the attentions received by
the Manicongo, asked Afonso to intercede on his behalf for an embassy of Portuguese merchants and priests. Since the request was
transmitted to Lisbon along with a sample of silver allegedly from
Angola, Manuel decided to send several representatives to evangelize
the people and search for metals. To lead the expedition he chose
Manuel Pacheco and Baltasar de Castro. The *regimento* given them

is typically Manueline in its careful considerations for the dignity of
the African chief. Pacheco was to pick up a priest at São Tomé and
proceed to the Cuanza, exploring en route the coast south of the
Congo, where he was to remain with African hostages until Castro
had made his way to the chief's *embala*, determined the sincerity of
his request, and returned. Thereupon, Pacheco and the priest were to
go into the interior to carry on the search for souls and silver. If the
Ngola refused to treat with the strangers, Pacheco was to release his
hostages and discreetly retire, afterwards sailing along the coast to
the Cape of Good Hope, bartering wherever possible along the way.

The first mission to Angola was not a success, although it did produce an interesting consequence in the long residence of Baltasar de
Castro at the chief's kraal. Apparently the captain general of São
Tomé saw no reason to assist in implanting royal authority in lands
where he could trade freely for slaves, and he refused to give Pacheco
a priest to accompany him. The Ngola himself underwent a change
of heart, possibly because of the absence of any missionaries in the
Castro expedition, and refused to discuss his conversion with its leader.
Castro sent Pacheco a message explaining the present situation as well
as the apparent mineral poverty of the region. Pacheco, on receipt of
this information, disobeyed his *regimento* by sailing off without Castro; nor is there any indication that he fulfilled the instructions calling
for the coastal survey to the south. Baltasar de Castro, either by order
of the Ngola or a personal desire to continue the search for the mines,
stayed in the interior, where he became a hostage for the chief's demands for a priest. At last tired of his captivity, Castro in a letter prevailed upon the Manicongo to send a missionary father. The paramount chief complied and the Ngola was duly converted, but Castro's
expectations were frustrated, for his captivity lasted until 1526 when
he showed up in Mbanza, tattered and gaunt. Although he brought
discouraging reports on the possible silver veins in Angola, Lisbon's
fancy had already been captured, and the legend was to be one of
the principal reasons for Portuguese expansion there later in the century.

If in the next thirty years Angola was forgotten by the crown —
save for an authorization to Diogo do Soveral to explore the areas of
the Longa River — it became a battleground for local Portuguese
and African factions. The issue, as always, was slavery; the antagonists, São Tomé and the Congo. Not only did the Congo partisans
control the trade through the only legal port below the equator,
Pinda, but they also sent their agents deep into Angola for the purchase of their product. To break the double monopoly, officials and

merchants at São Tomé intensified their own illicit traffic in Angola, hoping to create a situation which would force the Portuguese court to create a separate administration for the area. In the 1550's the cause of the São Tomistas was joined by the Jesuits who, rebuffed in their efforts to proselytize the Congo kingdom, sought other fields to conquer where they would have to face only the suspicion of the Africans, not the hostility of their own countrymen as well. They persuaded the governor of the island to send two missionaries to the Dongo country for the conversion of the Ngola, who resisted both, being now more interested in commercial dealings with the whites than their religion. The new recognition paid the chief of Angola wounded the vanity of the Manicongo and also drove the Portuguese and half-caste community to the desperate measure of getting him to attack his upstart vassal. Hence in 1556 a Congo army containing Portuguese subjects marched to the Dande River and near the modern town of Caxito was soundly trounced by an Angolan force also containing Europeans. The Ngola, inspired by advisers from São Tomé, declared his independence of the Congo and sent the appropriate embassy to João III asking for missionaries. Ambassadors from the Congo arrived to complain at the same time, a circumstance causing Lisbon momentary perplexity; but, João having died in 1557, the Jesuits were able to convince the queen regent, Dona Catarina, that the Society should be permitted to introduce into Angola the zealous missionary work already so successful in Brazil. The Congo ambassador could not forestall Catarina's decision; it represented the effective beginning of official Portuguese policy in Angola.

The small expedition of 1560 to Angola was pre-eminently ecclesiastical, a radical departure from previous policy which had viewed the missionary as a subservient or at most an associate arm of imperial design in Africa. Accompanying the four Jesuits (two priests and two lay brothers) was a grandson of Bartolomeu Dias, Paulo Dias de Novais. He was captain of the *caravela* and a glorified tour guide to see the missionaries to their destination; larger decisions were reserved to the Jesuits. After their arrival at the Cuanza in May 1560, the Portuguese party waited for the traditional welcome to the chief's *embala*, some sixty leagues in the interior (in the vicinity of Ambaca), but they received instead disquieting reports from Portuguese residing there. Sensing that this advice was not altogether altruistic, Dias, after a five-month delay, during which one father and a number of sailors died of fever, undertook the journey inland. The moment was indeed not favorable. The chief had recently died and been succeeded by Ngola Mbandi, who looked upon his visitors with suspicions un-

doubtedly implanted by Congo slave traders. He turned aside suggestions of immediate conversion and sent all the Portuguese (some
thirty-odd) except, Dias, Father Gouveia, and two other men, back
to their ship. Whether the chief held the four men as hostages for
further commercial relations or was merely displaying royal caprice
is uncertain. After undergoing initial discomforts and brutalities, Dias
and Gouveia were treated more tolerantly. Gouveia built a small
church in the village, which contained five to six thousand huts, by
his estimate; and Dias helped the Ngola gain victory over a rebellious
petty chief. By 1565 Dias had so ingratiated himself that he was sent
to Lisbon with slaves, ivory, and copper. Gouveia, however, was not
permitted to leave and ultimately died a prisoner, albeit a very es-
teemed one whose life the Ngola tried to save through the ministrations of his favorite witch doctors. The expedition had been a manifest failure and dispelled any notions Lisbon may have had of pursuing a policy in Angola similar to the one attempted in the Congo.
The captivity of Dias and Gouveia was held to demonstrate a lack of
good faith which could be most suitably met by military occupation.

Dias arrived in Lisbon in 1567 to find the court indecisive on the
future direction of its African investment. The difficulties that beset
the Congo kingdom and the murder of Gonçalo da Silveira in Moçambique indicated that a policy of hopeful temporizing and modest
missionary efforts would not further Portuguese interests in Africa
below the equator. On the other hand, the supply of slaves available
in Angola and the expectations of gold from the lands of the Monomotapa militated against the abandonment of either territory. Accordingly, the ill-fated Barreto expedition up the Zambezi was conceived and sent to southeast Africa. For Angola a different approach
was proposed, one which had already made Brazil the most prosperous
of Portugal's overseas dominions. Paulo Dias de Novais, as a result of
the concerted Jesuit support, was granted in 1571 the *donatária* (territorial proprietorship) of Angola. By this move Lisbon hoped to bring
about the conquest, colonization, and evangelization of Angola at an
inconsequential cost. Through such a grant the Society foresaw an
extension of its authority in Africa comparable to the position which
it enjoyed in Brazil as protector and guardian of the indigenous people.

The system of *donatárias* was a sixteenth-century colonial practice
having its origin in the medieval feudal organization of Portugal,
when the king, in the course of conquest over the Moors, gave jurisdiction over sections of the newly won lands to his victorious lords.
In the fifteenth century Prince Henry introduced the system into
Madeira for purposes of colonization; the *prazo* in Moçambique, and

its later-day derivation, the land company, were modifications of the same system. The terms *capitania* and *donatária* frequently have the same connotation, although in many cases the captaincy implied only an administrative jurisdiction over an area (as in Moçambique in the sixteenth century) and carried with it no privileges of territorial proprietorship. The proprietors favored by the crown accepted the responsibility to settle and defend the extent of their lands out of their own pocket. In return they received administrative and fiscal authority over the area. Usually the king reserved the monopoly of trade in certain commodities such as, in Africa, slaves. Otherwise, trade within the *donatária* was open to Portuguese subjects. The grant was not always hereditary and on the death of the proprietor (or when the terms of the grant had not been met) the *donatária* reverted to the status of crown captaincy, administered by Lisbon through an appointed captain general.

The title conferred upon Paulo Dias read impressively: "Governor and Captain General of the Kingdom of Sebaste in the Conquest of Ethiopia." Under the terms of his grant he received as hereditary patrimony thirty-five leagues of coast south of the Cuanza and all of the lands inland as far as he could possess. This land could be divided into various parcels and rented or awarded by Dias, with the stipulation that it should be cultivated within fifteen years or forfeited to the crown. Dias was also awarded for his lifetime the governorship of the lands between the Dande and the Cuanza and one third of the king's income therefrom. Lesser privileges included the salt monopoly and the untaxed export of forty-eight slaves a year. The governor accepted as obligations: to take and supply a small fleet and explore the coast to the Cape of Good Hope; to garrison his captaincy with four hundred men including technicians; to bring into Angola one hundred families, some of them farmers to whom he was to give seeds and implements, within six years; to build three fortresses between the Dande and the Cuanza; to build a church and take three priests with him.

The terms of the grant were specifically concerned with a colonization similar to that being carried out in Brazil. The questions of slavery and mining are implicit in several of the instructions, but what precisely Dias and the Society hoped for in Angola is not quite certain. Dias had spent enough time in the area to be familiar with its potentialities, as well as with its fevers and harsh terrain, and it would be illogical to assume that he accepted the financial burdens of the captaincy only for the sake of personal glory. He could not foresee, of course, that three years after his arrival he would become entangled in local wars; these continued until his death in 1589 and made impossible the success of any agricultural venture. Nor could he foresee that one part of his company would return to Portugal after the first glimpse of Angola and that another part would die of fever.

The only significant deeds accomplished by Dias were the foundation of the city of Luanda and several forts along the Cuanza. His military campaigns accomplished less than they were worth in terms of lives lost, and they had the effect of arousing the African population against the Portuguese. The slave trade continued to expand, but for such commerce the appointment of royal factors would probably have been sufficient. (Felner argues that the *donatária* was intended by those who promoted it — the Society of Jesus — as nothing more than a guise for the extension of their power in Africa by force of arms and that, given these circumstances plus the geography and native situation, the expansion of the slave trade was a logical sequence.[3])

Dias spent three years in Lisbon accumulating the necessary funds and personnel. The majority of his company, some four hundred men, were soldiers and craftsmen; neither in 1575, when his fleet arrived at Luanda island, nor later did Dias fulfill the requirement of settling one hundred families in Angola. Dias found that the island was already inhabited by nearly half a hundred Portuguese — agents from São Tomé or refugees from the Congo. Neither these men nor their compatriots scattered through the interior had much cause to welcome an authority or restrictions they had come to Angola to escape. Nevertheless, on Dias' arrival many made their way to the coast to greet him, dressed in forgotten finery and accompanied by their slaves and half-caste sons. Shortly thereafter a large embassy from the Ngola appeared to pay their chief's respects and renew the ancient friendship.

For three years Dias remained on the coast. In the middle of 1576 he moved his camp to the mainland and on the bluff over the sea began the construction of São Paulo de Luanda, erecting a fort, church, and hospital. Meanwhile pressures on the captain increased. The Jesuits complained that they were making little progress in their evangelical work and accused Dias of being tender-hearted in matters where the "best sermon was a sword and iron rod." Slave traders fretted that the supply was never consistent and that frequent local uprisings harmful to their business went unpunished. The murder and robbing of Portuguese subjects by insurgent tribes in the interior made it difficult for Dias to maintain that, in a country where the Portuguese were militarily inferior to the Africans, the best policy to pursue was one of friendship with the Ngola. Dias was also reminded of his obligation to build several fortresses and that he had not yet investigated the tantalizing rumors about the silver country of Cambambe (near the present town of Dondo). In 1579 Dias began a slow peaceful advance up the Cuanza, his ultimate goal being Cambambe. The Ngola, alarmed at the maneuver, which seemed to be a threat to his kingdom, and probably influenced by jealous Portuguese advisers, killed the twenty or more European traders in his kraal and confiscated their goods. Dias withdrew with his men to Anzele (near Caxito) where fewer than three hundred auxiliaries withstood an attack from the Ngola's army. When reinforcements from Portugal, requested the year before to aid in the occupation, arrived in Luanda, Dias returned to the coast to organize a second expedition.

The proprietor of Angola was now committed to a campaign which was to last ten years. Its only positive result was to raise Paulo Dias de Novais to the highest echelon of Angolan heroes, immortalized in a dozen street names and commemorative stamp issues. His innermost point of penetration on the Cuanza was only a few leagues beyond the fortress of Massangano, about seventy miles up the river. Intermittent successes in the vicinity of the fortress brought the local chiefs under Portuguese rule, but Dias never had sufficient men to inflict a crushing defeat on the Ngola and in a number of skirmishes the governor's lieutenants were routed. Almost two thousand Portuguese were lost to fever or enemy spears during the ten years of his governorship. Needless to say, the Jesuit fathers in Luanda, the most persistent voices for an occupation of Angola, profited little from the state of disorders prevailing in the 1580's; nor did the crown, which, anticipating the discovery of silver at Cambambe, had sent officers and engineers to organize the mines. Only slaving continued to burgeon. Through capture, robbery, or trade with petty chiefs, the Portuguese kept the caravans of humanity moving to the port of Luanda.

On the death of Dias in 1589, his aide Luís Serrão succeeded to his military offices. During his brief tenure, Massangano was made a municipality with appropriate civil administrative officers; with Luanda and Benguela the town was to be one of the three major points of Portuguese occupation in the seventeenth century. Serrão died a year later, after having failed in a fresh attempt to reach Cambambe. A successor was elected, but in 1592 a governor general, Dom Francisco d'Almeida, arrived in Luanda to supplant him and inaugurate a new epoch in Angola's troubled history.

In the creation of a colonial government in Angola, a status that has continued with almost no modification for three and a half centuries, imperial counselors relied upon a report they had ordered made in 1590 by the lawyer Domingos de Abreu e Brito. After visiting Angola, Abreu e Brito made a number of recommendations consistent with the situation there if not with Lisbon's ability to implement them. He urged the methodical occupation of the region by a thousand men to be recruited in Portugal, São Tomé, the Congo, and Brazil, the Brazilian contingent to be made up of five hundred *Mamaluco* (part Indian, part Portuguese) criminals.[4] Other recommendations were that twelve fortresses should be built and staffed; Angolan campaigners should be rewarded by the crown for their services as were those who fought in North Africa; governors should be appointed in the Congo, Luanda, and Benguela to carry out the king's design on these three fronts; the governor, or viceroy, of Angola should be of illustrious family; and for moral supervision of the colony, the Inquisition should be introduced. To facilitate communication with Moçambique and India, Abreu e Brito revived the proposal of an overland connection between the east and west coasts of Africa. His financial proposals were a tightening of export control over slaves; freedom of mineral exploitation, subject to payment of the royal fifth; a crown monopoly of salt and pitch; expropriation of the Congo's cowrie-shell fisheries; a factory to be put at Benguela for several years to ascertain possible income from that quarter.

How seriously the crown attended to Abreu e Brito's master plan is not definitely known but certainly the king's financial advisers were not prepared to underwrite the initial cost of such an extensive program, and it is unlikely that Governor d'Almeida's personal fortune was adequate for the extensive task. But the possibility of silver was attractive, and the governor was accompanied to Angola by four hundred soldiers and fifty cavalry and, more significantly, by a mining technician, a metal founder, a carpenter, and a blacksmith, whose collective presence indicated serious intention to conquer and work the mines of Cambambe. In spite of the success of Brazil's plantation economy in the sixteenth century, the Portuguese government remained unconvinced that southern Africa offered the same opportunities and clung doggedly to its hopes of uncovering a hidden wealth of precious ore.

D'Almeida did not reach Cambambe. His overtures in that direction were cut short by disease and the enmity of the Portuguese lords of the land, principally the Jesuits, who regarded the governor's presence as a threat to their own plans. Paulo Dias had made generous grants of land, including the inhabitants thereof, to his lieutenants and the priests. The Portuguese soldiers were busily engaged in slave commerce, buying, or collecting as head-tax payment, the local chiefs' people for export to Brazil; the Jesuits had thoughts of establishing a theocracy in their territories. The conflict of interest was inescapable, since any move that the governor made to implement royal authority, no matter how trivial, seemed a curtailment of the license enjoyed by the old inhabitants. The Jesuits and the *conquistadores* refused to be despoiled of their hard-won gains. When d'Almeida fulminated against their arrogance, the priests promptly excommunicated him. The following year, 1593, he was forced to retire from Angola.

The clash between entrenched interests and the vacillating policies of the crown characterized at an early date a confusion of authority and purpose in Angola which helped to blight the province's development for the next three centuries. The African tribes existed in a state of turmoil, resisting Portuguese intrusion and warring among themselves. Neither the missionaries nor the governors, even when working in accord, were strong enough to reconcile the diverse ambitions of the Portuguese population. A succession of governors after d'Almeida made a superficial peace with both the Jesuits and civilian landholders — by making no serious effort to interfere with their prerogatives — but their attempts to occupy the hinterland were almost as inconclusive as those of Paulo Dias de Novais. Another fortress, Muxima, was erected on the Cuanza, and the Africans of that area brought under Portuguese persuasion; penetration beyond was blocked by the armies of the Ngola and his allies. In the middle of the 1590's the population of Luanda was increased by twelve feminine immigrants from a royal orphanage, but their presence did not perceptibly alter the social life of the growing frontier town of soldiers and adventurers. Food was scarce, the climate debilitating, the Portuguese chronically weak and sickly. The most common traffic in the streets was half-naked slaves, many of them in chains.

The town's importance in 1602 was revealed in the instructions given the incoming governor João Rodrigues Coutinho, who was empowered by Philip III to bestow royal honors on the most worthy citizens of the colony, the crown's first recognition in Angola of services for the empire. Governor Coutinho could not have been unaware that the distribution of honors might make easier the fulfillment

of two important tasks he had been given by the monarch: the supplying of 4,250 slaves a year to the Spanish colonies in the New World
and the exploitation of the mines at Cambambe. The two projects
were related, since in the conquest of Cambambe one could assume
the capture of Africans to help meet the Spanish quota. What Coutinho had been granted was a virtual monopoly on Angolan commerce, and to carry out his program he took with him the largest
force sent to the colony up to that time: over eight hundred men
and many horses and cannon. At the head of this impressive array
Governor Coutinho marched up the banks of the muddy Cuanza,
but before he had gone many leagues he died of malaria. The title of
acting governor went to Manuel Cerveira Pereira, who in 1604 at
last reached Cambambe and founded there a blockhouse. At last the
silver bubble burst. There were no productive mines at Cambambe.

Cerveira Pereira was vain, brave, ambitious. He turned his attention to other matters. His contemporaries complained that he exploited his countrymen as ruthlessly as he did the African petty
chiefs. The first act of the new governor arriving in Luanda in 1607,
Manuel Pereira Forjaz, was to arrest the acting governor and send
him off to Portugal to stand trial. Forjaz was also instructed to carry
out a decree sent to Angola earlier but overlooked by Cerveira
Pereira: revoking the land grants made by Paulo Dias and putting
the local chiefs and their people, whom the Portuguese residents had
been mercilessly exploiting, under the protection of the crown. The
transfer held only a dubious advantage for the African leaders; they
were required to pay a tax to the royal treasury in return for the
theoretical protection given by the government. In reality the authority of Portugal did not replace that of the proprietors and another
burden was placed on the hard-pressed native peoples inhabiting the
pocket of Portuguese penetration in back of Luanda, and the revenues
from the new tax enriched the governor more than the treasury.

Manuel Forjaz also formed a private trading syndicate which
brought Portuguese and other European goods (mostly wine) into
Angola where the syndicate traded them for slaves who were then
sold to contractors for the Brazilian and Spanish markets. Realizing
that an overland route to the lands of the Monomotapa would widen
the scope of his business, the governor resolved to send an expedition
eastward. He chose Baltasar Rebelo de Aragão, an old African hand
and founder of the fortress at Muxima, to carry out the first serious
effort to link the two spheres of Portuguese occupation in southern
Africa. Rebelo de Aragão had proceeded inland over four hundred
miles from the sea and over two hundred from the fort at Cambambe

before he was forced to return to assist in the protection of the stockade. The explorer encountered few difficulties, according to the account he left of his exploits in Angola, and believed that he could have accomplished his goal without incident.[5] The other aspects of Forjaz' administration were not so imaginative. His tax policies did nothing to allay African unrest, and at his death in 1611 the spirit of rebellion against the Portuguese was unabated.

During these early years in Luanda and its environs two occurrences north and south of the capital presaged important developments in the history of the colony. In the beginning of the century, the Dutch set up a factory at Pinda for the export of slaves. French and English ships were also attracted to the area of the Congo and the southern coast where they found Portuguese ready to trade with them in spite of the royal ban. The Dutch factory was a more serious threat to Portugal's interests, however. It was met with characteristic indecision. The king of the Congo was asked to expel the foreigners, but in spite of proddings from the Portuguese bishop in São Salvador, the Manicongo dragged his heels, apparently preferring to let the enterprising Hollanders share the monopoly previously held by the Portuguese (the respect the Portuguese still maintained for the sovereign rights of the Manicongo is manifest during all of these negotiations). The failure to act more decisively also reveals that the center of interest in the whole area had passed to Luanda. Portuguese inaction proved a grievous mistake. In the next decades Dutch vessels roamed the Angolan coast capturing and burning merchant ships, and openly attacking the port of Benguela. In 1638 the worried inhabitants of Luanda laid the foundations of the tremendous fort of São Miguel on a bluff over the sea; it was not sufficiently finished in 1641 to turn back a Dutch invasion.

The founding of São Filipe de Benguela in 1617 by Manuel Cerveira Pereira opened another chapter of Angola's history. In the previous century, Benguela Velha (near the modern town of Porto Amboim) had figured occasionally in Portugal's plans, when half-hearted efforts had been made to build a permanent factory there. When Cerveira Pereira, having confounded his critics by winning his case in Lisbon against the charges made in Luanda, arrived in Angola in 1615 as governor of the province, he carried also special instructions as captain of the conquest of Benguela. He had convinced himself — and sponsors in Lisbon — of the existence of copper and silver mines in the interior south of the Cuanza, and after attending to the more urgent demands of Luanda's administration, he set out in April 1617 with two hundred and fifty men, a goodly number of them convicts and exiles, to seek out the source of the rumors. Unable to land at Benguela Velha because of sand bars across the harbor's entrance, he continued to Bahia de Santo António, where the company founded the capital of the new dominion of Benguela.

The first years of the settlement's life were ones of disorder and tribulation. An angry African population, the virulent fevers, and a mutiny against Cerveira Pereira's notorious brutality brought the project to the brink of disaster. The tyrannical governor of Benguela could not count on assistance from Luanda where a new governor of the dominion of Angola, Luís Mendes de Vasconcelos, jealous of his energetic rival in the south and influenced by old-time residents who had more than one score to settle with Cerveira Pereira, blithely ignored his royal instructions by withholding reinforcements for the Benguela campaign. On his incursions into the near interior Cerveira Pereira had discovered small samples of copper — in addition to valuable salt deposits — but these successes could not counteract the effects of his greed and brutality. A small group of men, including a Franciscan friar and an African priest, took advantage of a serious illness which left Cerveira Pereira helpless, to take him prisoner. They carried him to a small boat with one rotten sail and a container of water and left him to the mercy of the open sea. By his indomitable will the governor reached Luanda, where the Jesuits nursed him back to health.

In Luanda, Cerveira Pereira directed a letter to Philip asking for more men. With the forces sent from Lisbon and other young men whom the Jesuits helped him recruit in Luanda he returned to Benguela in 1620. He obtained samples of ore for the assayers in Lisbon, but they proved disappointing in their mineral content, and although the crown did not see fit at the moment to merge the dominion of Benguela with Angola, continued support for the southern region was not forthcoming. Cerveira Pereira remained in command of the new colony, ruthlessly exploring the vicinity and combating the intrigues of Luanda. At the time of his death in 1626, the garrison at Benguela had diminished to sixteen ill-clad soldiers. In the next fourteen years Benguela came more and more under the dominance of Luanda, whose governor participated in the choice of Cerveira Pereira's successors. Neither Luanda nor Lisbon bothered to encourage the development of territories so improvident in metal and slaves. In the late 1620's Governor Fernão de Sousa urged that the fortress at Benguela be dismantled, its garrison and arms taken to Luanda. He argued that Ben-

guela had little promise for the future and that its distance from Luanda and the difficulties of maintaining there an adequate force made
it virtually impossible to defend against the Dutch. And in 1641 the
port fell easily to Dutch invaders after a brief resistance by the inhabitants of the town. That year marked the effective end of the independent government of Benguela.

The small group of outcasts in Benguela who withstood the lustful
ambitions of Cerveira Pereira, the scheming neglect of Luanda, and
the Dutch occupation have a unique position in the early history of
Angola. The combination of renegades from the Congo, exiles and
convicts from Portugal, criminals from Brazil, with their wives and
children, were the first genuine colonizers of Angola. Frustrated in
their search for mineral wealth and unable to compete at first with
the slave marts of the north, they were driven to gain an existence
from the soil and the sea. The settlement of Benguela was from an
early date the home of traders, farmers, and fishermen, a strange contrast from the bustling mercantile center of Luanda. Only at Sofala
after the decline of the gold trade may one find a parallel in Portuguese Africa to the situation in São Filipe de Benguela in the middle
of the seventeenth century. Benguela was no showplace of Lusitanian
colonization and remained for the next several centuries a haven for
undesirables and the extreme element of Portuguese society, but at
the same time it became an almost self-sufficient agricultural and
fishing community. On a very limited scale its pattern of existence
exemplified the traditional Portuguese way of life better than other
more flamboyant centers of expansion in Africa and the East.

Many details of Angola and the Congo at the turn of the century
are found in the account of a captivity in those regions by the Englishman Andrew Battell of Leigh, whose extraordinary narrative has long
fascinated African historians and anthropologists.[6] In 1589 or 1590
Battell, a sailor, was captured by Brazilian Indians and delivered to
Portuguese authorities who sent him to Angola. In the next twenty
years, as soldier and prisoner, he visited every part of the Congo and
Angola known to the Portuguese: the Cuanza valley, the Congo and
the lands of Matamba east of the Cuango, Benguela and the Jaga
territory inland, the kingdom of Loango north of the Congo River.
The most sensational part of his story is a description of a twenty-one
months' captivity among the savage Jagas as hostage for a Portuguese
pledge. Although Battell's account casts little additional light on
Portuguese activities, it verifies the extent of their trade and conquest.

The larger contribution of the work is the much curious information it offers of African lands and life in 1600. Comparing the Angola of Battell's day with the accounts of Livingstone two hundred and fifty years later, or even with those of a twentieth-century observer like Alexander Barns, one is confronted with the seemingly time-resistant quality of native life in Angola and the small visible changes which have been wrought there in almost four centuries of Portuguese presence.

In Luanda the colonial administration of Angola proceeded into the second decade of the seventeenth century with scarcely any deviation from the established pattern. The limits of territorial occupation in the interior were reached with the erection of a blockhouse at Ambaca (on the Lucala River) in 1616, although Portuguese, half-caste, and African traders made their way throughout the area east of the Cuango River. Lisbon's reluctance to finance the costs of the Angolan government made the correction of abuses impossible. From the governor down, the administrative officials and soldiers received a trifling compensation for their services, and the slave trade represented the logical and only means of supplementing their income. Attendant irregularities were the steady increases in the head tax demanded of the African chiefs and the provoking of local wars to stimulate the flow of captives seaward. More than one seventeenth-century Portuguese critic denounced the course of action in Angola, maintaining that the colony would never be inherently prosperous as long as the so-called campaign of conquest and pseudo-conversion of the indigenous peoples was pursued. But these advocates of settlement and organized trade did not have a receptive audience. The few Portuguese who attempted to settle in the interior or to carry on business at the scattered fairs were chronically harassed and found themselves caught up in the periodic turmoil that swept the country, and the development of Angola died for lack of order.

In 1617 Luís Mendes de Vasconcelos arrived in Luanda as governor and almost immediately became embroiled in a war with the new chief of Dongo, Ngola Nzinga Mbandi, who was outraged that the Portuguese should have moved the Ambaca fortress several leagues up the Lucala River without consultation. For three years, Vasconcelos, assisted by a company of lawless slave traders, ranged through the Dongo and Matamba on punitive expeditions against the Ngola and his allies, taking an important number of captives to be branded, converted en masse, and sent to Brazil and New Spain. When Vasconcelos' successor João Correia de Sousa, took office in 1621, the African chief considered the moment auspicious to arrange a treaty of peace.

His sister, invariably referred to by the Portuguese as Queen Jinga, arrived in Luanda at the head of an imposing embassy. In her dealings with Correia de Sousa she showed intelligence and pride, and the treaty signed between the Portuguese and their African adversary was more of a friendship pact of equality than one between victor and vanquished. Jinga remained in Luanda for a year, and was baptized with great pomp in the cathedral as Dona Ana de Sousa.

Christianity rested easily on the soul of this impressive virago. The year following 1623, she adroitly poisoned her brother, who had been chased from his kraal by a Portuguese column after breaking the treaty his sister had signed with the Europeans. In a barbaric ceremony Jinga declared herself queen. With the aid of Jaga tribesmen she undertook a war against her former co-religionists. For the next three years she and the Portuguese were engaged in a series of conflicts. Meanwhile other Jaga tribesmen took advantage of Portuguese embarrassment to raid tribes loyal to the Europeans and rob the *pombeiros* (Portuguese-African slave traders) of their merchandise. These attacks in turn stimulated several lesser chiefs to throw off their vassalage to the distant white king. The frontier wars continued with bloody monotony until 1636 when emissaries from Governor Francisco de Vasconcelos da Cunha prevailed upon Queen Jinga to make peace.

The same governor attempted in 1638 to alleviate some of the evils associated with the head tax. An office of revenue collection was organized to regulate the fixing and collecting of the tax and to make it less of a personal spoils system handled by the governor and his aides. Several other events indicated a passing concern for an improvement in the prevalent morality of Angola. A Luanda philanthropist in the 1620's bequeathed his entire fortune to the Society of Jesus for founding a seminary for the education of African youths. Governor Correia de Sousa, much in need of money for his own less spiritual projects, strongly disputed the bequest but was rebuked by Lisbon. In 1626 the Inquisition appointed a Jesuit priest to represent its interests in Angola, although, in effect, neither then nor later was the Holy Office very busy in the colony. A hospital and a poor house went up in Luanda. An effort was even made to have the capital less dependent on the annual shipment of provisions from Brazil. In 1629 the governor ordered the cultivation of fruits and vegetables in small farms at the edge of the city. African conscripts were enjoined to work these lands.

In 1640 the eighty years of the Spanish Captivity came to an end,

and Portugal hastened to bring a halt to the drawn-out hostilities with
the Dutch which had been one of the contributions of the Hapsburg
dynasty to Portugal. Holland in this matter was faced with a politico-
economic dilemma: to recognize Portuguese independence would em-
barrass a mortal enemy, Spain; on the other hand, as the East and
West Indies Companies pointed out, to continue pressure on the Portuguese dominions in three continents might well bring the whole
empire into Dutch hands. A legalistic compromise was worked out
proclaiming a ten-year armistice. Officials of the Indies companies
urged their officers overseas to seize as much Portuguese territory as
possible before the truce was ratified. By 1640 the Dutch had come
into possession of an extensive coastal expanse of northeast Brazil. To
secure a steady supply of labor for their Pernambuco plantations, the
Dutch in Brazil determined to capture the source; such a stroke would
also cut off slaves for Portuguese Brazil and much of Spanish South
America. With the taking of São Tomé, Luanda, and Benguela, Johan
Maurits envisioned an absolute domination of West Africa's slave
market. For forty years Dutch ships had traded and harassed the coastline, setting up temporary factories, bombarding Portuguese towns,
and taking her ships on the high seas. The next maneuver in the long
undeclared war was the seizure of the territory.

In August 1641 an armada of twenty-one Dutch ships appeared
off Luanda. The Portuguese garrison was not caught unawares, but
the invaders found the narrow entrance into the harbor and brought
their ships to beach where the Portuguese cannon could not carry.
Suspecting that the intruders had come only to plunder, although the
size of the fleet must have caused some serious misgivings, Governor
Pedro de Menezes called for the evacuation of the city. Thus Luanda
fell into the hands of the Dutch, who marveled, as successive travelers
have done down through the centuries, on the spacious air of West
Africa's most beautiful city.

In December a smaller Dutch fleet rendered the fortress of São
Filipe de Benguela, where the neglected inhabitants, soldiers and town-
folk alike, gave a livelier account of themselves than their more prosperous countrymen in Luanda. But the town fell, and the defenders
made their way forty leagues into the interior where a number of
them perished from hunger. After nine months of privations they returned to the port to wait impatiently for reinforcements from Portugal to help them evict the conquerors. In Luanda the Portuguese who
chose to return to the city and sell slaves to the Dutch were permitted
to do so, but few accepted the invitation. The Portuguese had withdrawn to Massangano to plan a counterattack, but their task was made

more difficult by alliances the Dutch had made with neighboring chiefs, the Jagas, and the redoubtable Queen Jinga, all of whom welcomed an opportunity to settle old scores. In 1643 Governor Menezes attempted to recover the city but in a surprise attack the advancing Portuguese force was dispersed and two hundred men, including the governor, were taken prisoner.

Portugal, involved in a military struggle with Spain to insure the independence declared in 1640, was not able to aid directly her oppressed African colony. In 1644 the Overseas Council called upon Brazil to help in the campaign against the Dutch, an appeal the American colonists were willing to answer, since the loss of Angola had caused more hardships in Brazil than in the metropolis. The first expedition sailed from Bahia in 1645 and landed at Quicombo (about one hundred miles south of Luanda). En route to Massangano the relief army was overwhelmed by a Jaga horde. A second expedition sailed for Angola in the middle of the same year. Brazilian soldiers reached Massangano just in time to help the defenders of the fortress inflict a rousing defeat on Queen Jinga and her Dutch allies. In the two years after 1645, the Portuguese position became more tenuous, but the defenders held on. "The men who held out so stubbornly at Massangano despite an almost unbroken series of crushing reverses," Charles Boxer observes, ". . . were inspired by something more than the expectation of securing slaves. The crusading spirit in its good and its bad aspects was still far from dead in Portugal, and war against the Moslem, the heathen, and the heretic was still regarded as a sacred duty. Despite the violence, greed, and cruelty with which the history of Angola is stained, the fact remains that they sincerely believed that they were fighting God's battles and saving Negro souls from the fatal infection of heresy." [7]

In a desperate effort to retrieve her African colony, the government in Lisbon called upon her most distinguished colonial leader, Salvador Correia de Sá e Benavides, wealthy Brazilian landowner, former governor of Rio de Janeiro, and general of the Brazil fleets in the campaign against the Dutch in Pernambuco. In 1647 Salvador de Sá was appointed governor of Angola with instructions to retake the province. Such was the prestige of the new governor — and such was the need for slaves for the sugar plantations — that he was able to raise in Rio de Janeiro the funds and men for the third Brazilian armada, for which the crown furnished only five ships. In May 1648, fifteen ships and 1,500 men departed from Rio. On August 18 an unsuccessful assault on the fortress of São Miguel was made. Salvador de Sá was seemingly left with the prospect of confronting the Dutch when their numbers were swelled by the return of expeditionaries from the interior and the African troops that would accompany them. To his great surprise the Dutch commander that same morning agreed to a conference on the surrender of the town. The reasons for his eagerness to capitulate are not clear; overestimation of the Brazilian army, reluctance to suffer a long siege, shortage of munitions all must have contributed to his decision. It is also very possible that most of the officers and men of the Dutch contingent were sick and tired of Angola. Under the terms of the settlement, the Dutch would be permitted to withdraw with their slaves and property, the Portuguese supplying sufficient transportation to evacuate them. Some of the Roman Catholic mercenaries, mostly French and German, were permitted to remain in the colony. Shortly after the fall of Luanda, Benguela and São Tomé were relinquished.

When the jubilation in Luanda had subsided and the Dutch had departed, Salvador de Sá set about the reconstruction of Portuguese authority. The disloyal chiefs were punished for their lack of allegiance. The king of the Congo, Garcia Afonso II, had sought to profit from Portugal's troubled position in the 1640's by reasserting his independence. Although he had not joined the Dutch in military adventures, he had encouraged non-Portuguese Catholic missionaries, Italian and Spanish Capuchins, to take up residence in his realm, and had petitioned the Pope in 1646 to send him priests free from Portuguese influence. In a new treaty forced upon the fearful Garcia Afonso, Salvador de Sá specified that no foreign missionaries, save Spanish Capuchins whose activities were to be directed by Lisbon, were to be permitted in the Congo kingdom, a resolution overturned in Lisbon. Several harsher provisions were also eliminated from the treaty by João IV who held to the fiction that the Manicongo was nominally his vassal, but in reality an equal. A more serious problem was the reopening of the slave trade to Brazil and Buenos Aires. No difficulties, apart from the raids of Dutch privateers, were encountered in reviving the flow of Africans to Brazil. Commerce with the Spanish colonies was more difficult to implement, even though it brought much-needed silver to the royal treasury; but by 1650, Angolan slaves were again reaching Buenos Aires. The governor's suggestion that licenses be issued to foreigners for trade at Luanda, in particular for sailing directly from Spain, was immediately rejected by Lisbon whose traditional fears of outside competition and influence in her African provinces have always determined her colonial economic policies. The slave trade must remain substantially in Portuguese hands. To recompense the governor and the Brazilian colonists for the expenses incurred in liberating Angola, an additional tax was placed on each adult slave leaving the colony. Still another task was to see to the defense of the coast and provide protection for Portuguese shipping in the area. In 1652, Salvador de Sá relinquished his governorship to Rodrigo de Miranda Henriques and embarked for Brazil, his work completed.[8]

Salvador Correia de Sá, in addition to delivering Angola from the Dutch, gave the colony in his three-year tenure a momentum that was to carry it through the rest of the century. Angola now entered the most prosperous period of her history, excluding the last twenty years of the present century, although frictions among the Portuguese themselves continued as differences between the governors and the old-time residents and the ubiquitous Jesuits flared up again and again. Native wars were endemic, but such disturbances were accepted as part of Angola's pattern of life and even contributed to its flourishing. Portuguese authority was entrenched at Luanda, where the fortress of São Miguel was finished in 1689, and in the south at Benguela. In the backcountry smaller forts at Massangano, Muxima, Pungo Andongo, Cambambe, and Ambaca kept open the slave routes crisscrossing the province and provided centers of military strength to keep troublesome chieftains from seriously interfering with that all-important commerce. By the end of century Portugal held nominal control, according to Ravenstein's estimate, over fifty thousand square miles of Angola and the Congo. European population decreased proportionately with the distance from the coast, but traders and soldiers could move with relative freedom within the whole vast area.

The prosperity of Angola was irretrievably attached to the development of Brazil, a fact recognized by the crown itself, which was content to collect its tax on slaves and let matters run their eventually ruinous course. Angola's debt to Brazil was unquestionably great. Her salvation had come from the American colony, not the metropolis, and it was fitting that in the years following 1650 (until 1668 when Francisco de Távora was sent directly from Lisbon), the governors and functionaries responsible for the West African territory should also come from Brazil. It was equally fitting that these administrators should hold the interests of Brazil paramount. Portugal was still involved in a tiresome struggle with Spain which consumed her leaders and finances, and it was a useful and inexpensive device to reward the heroes of Brazil's war against the Dutch by giving them the prized and profitable governorship of Angola. Unlike Salvador de Sá, these men

The sixteenth-century fortress at Sofala, Moçambique

Avenue of the Republic, Lourenço Marques, Moçambique

The seventeenth-century church at Muxima, Angola

Luanda, Angola

contributed little to the welfare of the colony. They and their lesser officials received but a pittance for their services; their military and administrative budget was inconsequential. Their remuneration came from participation in the slave trade, either through association with resident slave merchants or by personal initiative.

The military and civil management of the kingdom of Angola was entrusted to the governor, whose local authority, if he chose or was able to use it, was substantial. He had the power of appointments to his own staff and a voice in the naming of the captains of the fortresses, although the latter, once in office, were not always ready to heed the instructions of the governor, and he, correspondingly, was usually loath to persevere in the face of their opposition. The affairs of justice and the treasury were also in the governor's charge. On matters concerning the general defense of the colony or those of broad general interest, he acted in consultation with his council, composed partly of colonial officers and partly of local inhabitants. The second most important official in the province was the *ouvidor*, or chief justice, who was responsible for juridical authority. How effectively the governor ran the affairs of Angola depended on the forcefulness of his personality and his skill in dealing with the Portuguese living there. The majority of the governors were content to accept the situation as they found it, realizing that in the balance hung the opportunity for personal gain. The system of administration in the seventeenth century did not undergo basic modification until recent days.

The permanent residents of Angola did not always look with favor upon the *parvenu* administrators, especially when they spoke of policies which threatened to restrict the residents' power over the lesser African tribes. These veterans of a score of campaigns formed a feudal caste resisting change and authority. As captains of fortresses, landholders, members of the city councils, they constantly asserted their entrenched independence. Many of them led lives of splendor, constructing palatial homes in Luanda, marrying or taking as mistresses African or mulatto women with whom they created generations of children who came to form a considerable proportion of Angolan society equally resentful of the prerogatives of the governor's court. The population of Angola was augmented by exiles, ambitious second sons from Portugal, and freebooters, who, if they survived the first devastating bout with fever, enlivened the colony with their many genial talents. These first and second citizens of the land had allies in the Jesuits, still powerful though their dreams of an African theocracy had disappeared, who brooked no interference with their traditional masterful jurisdiction over the well-being of the Portuguese and African population. It was a courageous governor who came to grips with the formidable citizenry of Angola.

The three large African tribes, all too powerful to be brought to permanent submission, were those of Matamba, where Queen Jinga still reigned, the Dongo with its Ngola, and the Congo. Each was theoretically a vassal of the king of Portugal, but actual Portuguese relations with the three tribes normally consisted of a state of truce, broken by sporadic hostilities resulting from the intemperate acts of individual slave traders. From 1665 to 1685, however, the interior was torn by a series of wars. No longer did the African tribes rise up one by one; they now joined together in a united front against the Portuguese. It was not practical for Portugal to try to maintain peaceful relations with the chiefs of the Congo and interior. Treaties with England and Holland in effect allowed these two nations to participate in the Portuguese slave trade by opening the ports of Brazil to their ships. At the same time the depleted treasury brought new demands on the colonies. These two factors had a profound effect on the Angola slave trade. From an estimated seven thousand slaves exported each year the figure began to rise sharply, with violent and deleterious effects in the colony. A number of incidents, real and imagined, led to a Portuguese invasion of the Congo kingdom, which, with the death in battle of its paramount chief, António I, lost the remnants of its former power. In 1670–1671, the Dongo was overrun by a force under the twenty-three-year-old Governor Francisco de Távora, and in the late 1680's, the area of Matamba was brought more or less effectively under Portuguese influence. At Benguela also the Portuguese expanded into the interior, to Caconda and beyond, and by the end of the century they had scattered the Jaga tribesmen and set up an outpost one hundred and fifty miles from the coast to help swell the supply of slaves from the highlands. The best intentions of the missionary orders could not withstand the disorderly state of affairs. In 1694 only thirty-six priests were active in the interior; most of their churches and schools had fallen into ruins.

To co-ordinate the administration of the occupied countryside, the first administrative code, or organic charter, for the colony was drawn up in the 1670's. It defined the responsibilities and obligations in particular of the captains of fortresses, especially in matters of revenue and justice, but like most Portuguese colonial legislation of the period it was an afterthought in African policy, and as such was not taken seriously by those to whom it was directed. A theoretic concern for the welfare of Angola accomplished little in the absence of steady encouragement to colonize and develop the wealth of the soil as was being done in the Americas. "Angola was becoming the colony which most betrayed the adventurous nature of Portugal's expansion, diverting its people from their ancestral ways which tied them to the soil and inciting them to covetousness, to an uneasy trivial existence, more disposed to risk all for easy immediate gain, instead of to a slow and legitimate profit from their sober hard work." [9]

Even the assaults of French ships on West African ports — a consequence of Portugal's involvement in the War of the Spanish Succession — did not seriously disturb the monotonous course of Angolan history in the first years of the eighteenth century. In addition to keeping the *sobas* in sullen submission the governors were presented with the cares of a coastal defense, but Angola had weathered far worse storms without drastic disruptions in her economic life. Nor did the appearance of the ships from other nations at Congo ports, in direct violation of treaties with the Congo king and the instructions given the governors, do more than ripple the surface of the prosperous and negligent country. Lisbon's concern for the slave monopoly was not always Angola's; foreign gold was as welcome as Portuguese. Local squabbles were more important than international disputes. The conflicts which flared up among the participants in the slave trade — governors, captains, citizens, clergy — led the crown in 1720 to prohibit its colonial administrators from engaging in any aspect of the commerce, but such distant pronouncements did not unduly burden the conscience of many. The material splendor of Luanda in the early 1700's was the admiration of foreign and Portuguese visitors. The mansions of the established settlers, the ecclesiastical edifices, the palace of the governor made it seem as though part of Lisbon had been transferred to African soil. The gardens at the city's edge were overgrown and rank, however; once again foodstuffs reached Luanda in the holds of empty slavers.

In 1765 the vigorous reforms the Marquês de Pombal had clamped on the metropolis echoed in Angola when the extraordinarily determined and farsighted Francisco de Sousa Coutinho arrived as governor of the colony. It was at once apparent to Sousa Coutinho that a commercial and pseudo-military occupation of Angola resting solely on slaving held no promise for the future natural development of the territory. One hundred years of expediency, prosperous though Angola was, could not be called a colonial program. Already voices in Portugal and abroad were being raised against slavery, an institution which clearly could not endure many years longer. What Sousa Cou-

tinho envisaged was a systematic occupation of the country; the settling of colonists in the healthful plateau regions; a curb on the vast
number of Africans being exported annually, which now threatened
to depopulate the land; and the self-sufficiency of Angolan agriculture. In some respects Sousa Coutinho was the first modern colonial
administrator in Africa.

As such he was a man out of his century. The wealth of Brazil was
one of the foundations of Portugal's national policy and Brazil's security continued to rest on Angolan labor. Pombal was no more receptive
to ideas which would jeopardize the *status quo* than were the slaving
interests in the African colony. The result was that many of Sousa
Coutinho's plans for improvement were never realized. Some of the
reforms he attempted to inaugurate are still fundamental to the
province's development in mid-twentieth century. He encouraged
local industry: sulphur, copper, asphalt could all contribute to the
colony's welfare. Under his guidance a shipyard was put in operation.
His greatest industrial dream was an iron foundry on the Cuanza, and
this was in small-scale operation in the year of his departure. Another
vision was a colonization scheme for the southern plateau. He suggested that the government bring settlers from Brazil and the Atlantic
islands to take up residence as small farmers in the fertile regions of
Bié and Huíla. Such settlers, he argued, would do more for the well-
being of the colony than the hundreds of wastrels, exiles, and convicts
whose only gift to Angola was a perpetuation of tyranny and scandal.
He also threatened to expropriate the large uncultivated tracts in back
of Luanda unless their proprietors used them to advantage. To his
own civil administration Sousa Coutinho brought temporary order.
From his subordinates he demanded propriety and strict honesty. In
Luanda he had built large warehouses for food reserves to be used in
years of famine or when the ships from Brazil were delayed. He built
a technical training school for young men. Of his work, Lopes de
Lima writes: "He was the first governor to civilize this semi-barbarous
colony and during his tenure he did more than all his predecessors had
ever thought of." [10]

The example of Sousa Coutinho was hardly infectious. Of his immediate successors only Barão de Moçâmedes partook — to a limited
degree — of his dedication. Moçâmedes organized a campaign of exploration of the lands south of Benguela to the Cunene River. Two of
the expeditions sent by him — one by land, the other by sea — made
careful examinations of the coast and interior, compiling much useful
information for expansion there in the following century. To the
spacious bay at Angra do Negro the explorers gave the name of their

sponsor. Not until the government of Tovar de Albuquerque in 1819 was Angola shaken again by a strong-minded personality. In his short-lived term of office, Albuquerque temporarily roused Angola from her somnolent condition. He encouraged the planting of cotton and coffee, overhauled the colony's fiscal apparatus, established a regular mail service to the fortresses in the interior, and instituted a modest public-works program. Unfortunately, the governor was deposed in an uprising.

As Sousa Coutinho had sensed, Angola could not count forever on being the slave market for much of the New World. Although Anglo-French differences at the turn of the century lessened temporarily the competition and benefited the Portuguese trade, the gain was neutralized by the disruption of Atlantic shipping. More significant was the growing humanitarian protest against the institution itself. These voices would eventually have, in diplomatic language, their effect on Portuguese statesmen. In the same years many Portuguese themselves argued against the practice. The Brazilian Elias da Silva Correia in his *História de Angola* (Rio de Janeiro, 1782) wrote moving pages describing the dismal procedure by which the African was bought or captured in the interior, marched to the coast, and shipped in *tumbeiros* to Brazil. He argued that as long as traders and their agents were permitted to pursue their fortune at the expense of the native population, Angola would never have a prosperous tranquil development. Only the free man working in harmony with his society could bring a lasting prosperity to the colony. Angola must cease to think in terms of expanding the slave trade; instead, she must direct her efforts first to curbing its abuses and then to its elimination.

By the beginning of the nineteenth century the surface splendor of Luanda had begun to tarnish; the fine buildings were falling into disrepair; its streets were unattended; transportation into the interior was in a state of neglect. Mission work in the colony still declined, and attendance at mission schools was apathetic. The population of Luanda and Benguela was made up predominantly of social castaways. Some went to live in the backcountry, there either to prosper as local merchants or to be absorbed into the African world — and in many cases, both. The countenance of the colony, in the first years of the century, was apathy on the coast and indiscipline in the interior.

A European spirit of progress and reform had made its impression on several Portuguese governors proceeding to Angola in the first three decades of the 1800's. Some, appalled by the condition of the colony, submitted lengthy proposals for its regeneration; others despaired of its salvation, claiming that its decadence defied all hope of spiritual or economic redemption. The more positive idealists, however, made concrete proposals. The prospects of a fishing industry, which would also make use of local salt, seemed encouraging to António de Saldanha da Gama, who also urged that the production of native cotton be expanded. Another governor tried to create a class of craftsmen and mechanics — smiths, tanners, shipbuilders, carpenters, tailors — to provide employment for the scorned and shiftless elements of Angolan population. The assertion was made constantly — as it is today — that few residents were willing to make capital investment in the country, content to employ their fortune in the purchase of necessities from Brazil and Portugal at a high price instead of attempting to establish local production. What was needed, these practical idealists insisted, was a dramatic reorientation in policy which would strengthen the colony's economy and give direction to its administration.

The same spokesmen also referred to the conduct of native affairs, ranging from charges that the African lived under the very real fear of abusive exploitation to the more familiar claim that the Portuguese were the only European people in Africa who had gained the loyalty and affection of the Negro. The critics decried the use of the African as a beast of burden and added their voices to the ancient chorus of protests against setting the chiefs against one another for the purpose of capturing slaves. Defenders of Portuguese custom in Africa extolled the work of the missionary fathers and the readiness of their countrymen to take African women and mulattoes as their wives. Such arguments were completely academic. In the early nineteenth century the Angolan was still viewed as a commodity; the chief was useful in obtaining this commodity, either through peaceful tribute or through warfare. This had been Portugal's native policy in Angola and, to a lesser extent, in Moçambique. It is true that the African woman, in the absence of Portuguese females, offered an outlet for the sexual impulse. Miscegenation in Portuguese Africa, however, although admirably free from the sense of shame which accompanied it in English colonies, still must be considered primarily as erotic expediency; it has become colonial policy only in retrospect.

As a consequence of the Napoleonic wars in the Peninsula, the Portuguese court removed in 1807 to Rio de Janeiro where, as many Portuguese in Angola believed, it had always been as far as Angola was concerned. Brazil declared its independence in 1822. Portugal herself was involved in a struggle between the constitutionalists and the monarchists which, though it ended in victory for the Liberal forces, set the stage for a turbulent political century. The effects of metropolitan unrest came quickly in Angola. A popular uprising in Luanda in 1822 and a mutiny among the troops deposed the incumbent governor, who was replaced by a provisional junta headed by the Bishop. Brazil, in order to guard her own economic ties to West Africa, proposed a federation with Angola and Moçambique, an overture rejected in Luanda but supported in Benguela, which had a separatist uprising. The chaotic decade came to an uneasy close with Governor Santa Comba having established a precarious peace among the colony's dissident elements. Santa Comba's program for the revitalization of Angola was of the commendable pattern outlined by several of his predecessors, but such efforts had been successfully resisted in quieter times, and his suggestions remained suggestions. When the news of the final constitutionalist triumph in 1834 in Portugal reached Luanda, the governor was replaced by a provisional junta with attendant disorders. Only with the arrival of Governor Bernardo Vidal, a champion of the Liberal cause, was a semblance of tranquillity restored.

The Liberal's colonial policy in Africa was idealistic and confused. The Portuguese Constitution of 1822 made no special provision for the colonies, for the constitution was to be applicable to all national territory, whether in Europe or overseas. The Ministry for Marine and Overseas was abolished in 1821, restored in 1823, abolished again in 1834, and re-created in 1835 with diminished authority. Even though the 1838 Constitution provided for special laws to govern the overseas territories, the fact that all important legislation was reserved for the Portuguese parliament — where many deputies believed that special legislation was unnecessary since metropolitan laws would serve as well — precluded the creation of a consistent colonial policy. The free population of overseas territories were declared Portuguese citizens sharing the same privileges as their countrymen in Europe. In 1832, even during the Miguelist regime, these territories were given the name overseas provinces (the shift from colony to province to colony to province in the last hundred and twenty years is one of the vexing aspects of Portuguese colonial history, even though the transitions have implied little more than a change in terminology). To the enemies of the Liberal government these gestures toward an *assimilação uniformizadora* were pure farce, sins for which the Liberals have never been forgiven by conservative colonial philosophers. Much of their criticism is exaggerated, because as far as the African in Angola and Moçambique was concerned his status was not appreciably altered by any of the Liberal's ideals, if he was even aware of them.

With many of the reforms projected for the overseas provinces the name of the Marquês de Sá da Bandeira is intimately associated. Working in the midst of confusion, animosity, and an instability that brought on the overthrow of his government, Prime Minister Sá da Bandeira from 1836 to 1840 evolved a program, most of it never implemented, of colonial development. He spoke of a permanent civil service in the Overseas Ministry to guarantee colonial stability through ministerial upheavals. Portugal should now, he declared, dedicate to Africa the same energy that had made Brazil a thriving country. The keys to his program were capital investment and colonization: African ports should be opened to foreign shipping and all products passing between Portugal and Africa — this to remain a Portuguese monopoly — should be duty free. Angola must not be a place of exile for political and criminal undesirables; settlement there by honest industrious citizens should be one of the first orders of business for the new regime.[11]

In 1836 Sá da Bandeira delivered his boldest decision: all traffic in slaves from Portuguese possessions was to cease in December of that year. The decree, though long expected, met implacable resistance from residents in Angola. Governor Bernardo Vidal was not the man to enforce the suppression of the traffic; on the contrary, prior to his dismissal in 1838, he made a fortune in bribes by allowing it to continue and sent a cargo of slaves to Rio de Janeiro on his own account. So violent was reaction to the decree that no governor until 1845 was able to cope with the problem. The men who served as governors in the years between were obliged to close their eyes to the clandestine shipment of slaves from Angola in order to be able to carry out their other duties. Portugal herself had not the navy to maintain constant vigilance along the coast. Only the blunt and arrogant intervention of England and the effective co-operation of Angola's Governor Pedro Alexandre da Cunha in 1845 brought about a final suppression of the commerce by the middle of the century.

It has been the fashion since the last decade of the nineteenth century, when both Joaquim Mousinho de Albuquerque and António Enes documented the miserable condition of Portuguese Africa, for many Portuguese historians to hold the Liberals responsible for all the neglect and frustrations that beset the overseas provinces. Such assaults are manifestly unfair. Making the African a citizen of Portugal, ludicrous as it may seem to those who make this piece of legislation their principal target, had no practical effect whatsoever on the continued decline of Angola. As for the slave trade, by 1830 it had run its course in Portuguese Africa. In a sense its final suppression was a recognition of its failure to do more than enrich a privileged class and keep the colony in a state of chronic backwardness. It is true that the resistance of the disenfranchised traders to any program designed to benefit the province was a serious handicap, but this resistance had been present in the previous century. There comes a time in the study of Portugal's colonial policy in Africa when ideals that failed must be given equal consideration with the dismal realities they were meant to replace. The aspirations of men like Sá da Bandeira sprang from an enlightenment too frequently absent in European colonization in Africa. That certain Liberal ministers and governors were not content merely with phrasing eloquent legislation but also tried to implement it in the face of hostility in Africa and political chaos at home is a fact that should not be overlooked by contemporary critics.

The next move to shock the residents of Angola from their resentful lethargy was the complete abolition of slavery. Lisbon naïvely hoped by this legislation to promote the peaceful occupation of the interior, since the source of friction between the African and the European would be removed and the need for expansion created. The African would cultivate and sell the products of the land instead of his own kind, and Portuguese traders would develop a healthy commerce in manufactured goods. Many individuals — slave merchants and plantation farmers — would be distressed and the colony's economy would be disrupted, but the ultimate benefits to the province, it was held, would outweigh these inconveniences. The abolition of slavery would also exempt Portugal from the growing humanitarian criticism of her African native policy, a criticism which could have unpleasant international consequences. Accordingly, in 1858 a compromise decree, promulgated by Sá da Bandeira and his associates, was signed. Under its provisions all Africans presently held in slavery would become free men in twenty years, enjoying an interim status from 1869 as *libertos*, a classification not too clearly defined and less clearly enforced. During the twenty-year period no African could be enslaved and children born of slaves would be free. Even such a modest proposal was angrily received in Angola with manifestations and acts of violence. The spirit of slavery died hard in Angola, and many colonists refused to accept the decision of the government, resisting by both defiance and stratagem. At the beginning of the twentieth century their oppressions were to burst forth in a scandal which shook the metropolis and the province.

Nevertheless, the legal abolition of slavery severed the major link with a discredited past, and Angola turned reluctantly to a new and perhaps more difficult era. In 1854 David Livingstone reached Luanda. The consequences of his historic travels were to lead indirectly to the Conference of Berlin and were responsible more than any other single factor for drawing Angola and Moçambique into the complexities of the modern age in Africa. To protect her acquisitions in the southern half of the continent, Portugal, lacking military might and international prestige, was driven to asserting the values of her occupation in these lands during the previous three centuries. The present reality of Portuguese Africa offered less than convincing proof to the ambitious hard-headed statesmen of Europe that Portugal's colonization endeavors had been successful. Her claims of priority and of the ability of her people to adapt themselves to the African land and culture were empty arguments against the obvious devastations wrought by the slave trade, a score of moldering fortresses, and scarcely visible vestiges of missionary work. As proof of claims to large areas of the interior of the continent and the retention of territory linking Angola to Moçambique, three hundred years of Angolan history counted for little.

IV

COLONIZATION AND
SETTLEMENT

ONE of the most serious problems for Portuguese policy in Angola and Moçambique has been a chronic inability to establish a sufficiently large white population for the continuing Europeanization and
development of the two areas. Only in the present century — more
particularly in the last twenty years — has the number of white inhabitants in the African colonies visibly swelled.[1] That Portugal
should have been among the first successful colonizers from modern
Europe, having settled Madeira and the Azores in the fifteenth century and Brazil in the following two centuries, and have failed until
recently in her efforts in Africa has long disturbed both the men
responsible for the overseas possessions and her colonial philosophers.
In Africa Portugal's record as a colonizing force is in fact not much
worse than that of other European nations; nevertheless, the examples
of Brazil, the New World colonies, and what is now the Union of
South Africa have served as unhappy reminders of what some Portuguese feel might have been in Angola and Moçambique. This attitude is mostly nineteenth- and twentieth-century hindsight. The occupation of the pestilential coastal plains and deserts was uneconomi-
cal as well as virtually impossible, and the interior plateaus remained
largely inaccessible until the appearance of modern transportation.
Quite apart from these factors, the formidable opposition of African
tribes and the peculiar orientations of Angola and Moçambique
toward other distant Portuguese colonies forestalled, as I have
mentioned in previous chapters, a local development along the lines

followed by Brazil and the Azores, or even Cape Verde and São Tomé. Finally, the population of Portugal was inadequate. The nation's abrupt expansion around the globe created grave demographic strains. The capacities of small Portugal were equal to but one Brazil.[2]

The Portuguese conqueror in Africa was not a successful colonist, whatever the reasons for his failure, and when Portuguese theorists speak of the colonizing mission of the soldier in Africa they are dealing in psychic generalities difficult to defend.[3] The colonial historian Gomes dos Santos was closer to the reality of Portuguese rule in Africa during the previous centuries when he wrote bitterly in 1903: "We did not know, and we do not know, how to colonize. . . We are utopian dreamers, a race of inept sluggards who have always been content with national sovereignty." [4] That industrious and tenacious segment of Portuguese society, the lower-class farmer and worker, was conspicuously absent in the African colonies until very recently, unless he appeared in the guise of would-be conquerer in pursuit of slaves or gold. Without such vital reinforcement, the Portuguese communities in Angola and Moçambique remained stagnant or were absorbed, and the exploitative interests of a few administrators and profiteers prevailed.

A large portion of the white population in Portuguese Africa was made up, until the twentieth century, of "transported criminals and political exiles known as degradados. Each year a shipload of human flotsam and jetsam arrived [in Moçambique] from Portugal. Beggars, embittered by hardship, thieves, assassins, incorrigible soldiers and sailors, together with a sprinkling of men suffering for their political offenses, were dumped into the colony. Sometimes these men were accompanied by their 'wives,' girls from orphanages or reformatory schools whom they married at the moment of embarkation from Europe. These unfortunate people, who had already been degraded in mind and body by imprisonment at home and the rigours of the voyage, merely added to the misery and inefficiency of the colony." [5] Sentences for the degradados varied: four to six years of jail plus eight to ten years of exile or exile for life. Many were sentenced to work on public projects, others imprisoned in the fortresses of Moçambique island or Luanda. Most of them remained along the coast, and although it was not unknown for some to go into business, achieving a fortune and social status, their contribution to the African colonies was small.

The difficulties of persuading Portuguese men to reside in Africa were multiplied a thousand times with the Portuguese woman. After the shipment of twelve women to Angola in 1595 no further efforts were made to encourage a feminine immigration. Only in the last quarter of the eighteenth century was a governor to Luanda accompanied by his wife (however Cerveira Pereira took his wife to Benguela in the 1610's during his governorship of that kingdom). Travelers in Moçambique in the nineteenth century constantly comment on the scarcity of white women; the estimated population of Portuguese women in Lourenço Marques in 1887 was two. Nor were the women who resided in the colony renowned for their attractions. Henry Salt is most critical of the few he met on the Zambezi in 1810; he found them sallow, thin, slovenly, devoted to their pipes.[6] Most of the women brave enough to face the rigors of the two colonies died within several years of their arrival, usually in childbirth.

While Portugal failed to populate Angola and Moçambique with her own people, she was enormously successful, to the subsequent displeasure of most Portuguese colonists, in persuading Indians to come to Moçambique. A not unreasonable guess would be that in the eighteenth and nineteenth centuries these traders and colonists from the East outnumbered the Portuguese. Even in 1900 their number was such that Mousinho de Albuquerque considered their presence a danger to the nationalization of the province and urged that restrictive laws be enacted to keep more of them from entering.[7] There were two segments of Indian population in Moçambique. The Banians were Hindu traders who were usually agents for Indo-British houses in Damian or Diu; they generally secured their goods from the East India Company. These merchants were accustomed to live along the coast, did not settle in the colony or invest in it, and returned to India after a residence of some years. They were regarded with disfavor by the Portuguese who found it difficult to discourage, or match, their competition and sought satisfaction in hurling epithets: usurers, thieves, Jews of Asia. The Goans or Canarins were Roman Catholics for the most part and considered themselves, whether half-caste or no, Portuguese subjects. Some became traders, frequently in the interior, while others became civil servants or soldiers. They made their home in Moçambique, often marrying African women. Both Banian and Goan did more good than harm to the colony. The two charges that some Portuguese have made against their presence, that they made the formation of a white middle class difficult and that they held back, because of their rootlessness, civilizing influences, are patently ridiculous. For two centuries the Indian kept alive small trade in the interior and made eventual occupation by the Portuguese a simpler task. As colonists, or *prazeros*, along the Zambezi, the Goan was no better and no worse than the Portuguese and his Afro-Portuguese descendants. His estates were the last strongholds of Portuguese authority in Zambézia, and his resistance to the invading tribes from the south in the nineteenth century probably kept the region from being submerged and eventually lost to the crown. Writing in 1838, Torres Texugo defends the Indian as being the only industrious and respectable element in Moçambique society.[8] The Indian has never fitted into Portugal's plans for colonization, save for occasional fruitless suggestions in the middle nineteenth century that a small number be introduced into Angola (which today still has hardly any Indian residents), but he has been accepted as a reality of Moçambique's economic and social life. Certainly he is not the object of racial persecution that he is in the Union of South Africa.

The Goan-Canarins were associated with that remarkable system of feudal land settlement along the Zambezi, *o regime dos prazos*, and have been accused by some Portuguese observers of having brought on its decline. While it is true that some of the more notorious *prazeros* of the nineteenth century were partly of Indian descent, the chaotic breakdown of the institution had more deep-rooted causes than the aggressive behavior of Goan families and represented one phase of Moçambique's difficult passage into the modern African world. The *prazo* system was Portugal's most serious attempt to colonize her southern African possessions until the middle of the past century; that control of much of the territory passed into the hands of half-castes and Indians signified nothing more than the failure of the metropolis in its efforts to promote European settlement of the area.

In the middle of the seventeenth century, the alleged golden age of Portuguese occupation of Moçambique, the lands in an area determined by drawing a line from Quelimane to Chicoa and from Chicoa to Sofala, the lands of the Rivers of Sena, were divided into great estates, or *prazos*, ranging in size from three or four square leagues to eighty or ninety square leagues. The most prosperous were those bordering on the Zambezi from the coast to Tete. The owners of the *prazos* were powerful and independent men who either lived on their lands in great luxury and splendor or who, especially in the eighteenth century, were absentee landlords, residing in Goa, Lisbon, or Moçambique island. Theoretically responsible for the development of the land and the protection of its inhabitants, the *prazeros* in reality were mainly indifferent to any profitable enterprise except the collection of taxes and fines. A trickle of quitrent ran into the royal treasury, but in the absence of an effective Portuguese officialdom along the Zambezi the amounts were not high, and the financial benefits received by the crown were negligible.

The Moçambique *prazo* originated in the late sixteenth century when individual Portuguese soldiers and merchants infiltrated the interior up the great river. They found an African society not too different superficially from the semifeudal society of Portugal. The lands of the Monomotapa and other paramount chiefs were governed by lesser chiefs whose allegiance to the supreme ruler took the form of tribute, military assistance, and a declaration of fealty. Under such a system white adventurers with ambition and strong constitutions prospered. By helping the Monomotapa in his innumerable small wars with neighboring or rebellious tribes, they received grants of land in the paramount chief's kingdom and authority over the inhabitants. Having taken African wives, learned the language, and acquired small personal armies, they expanded the limits of their grants by absorbing the contiguous lands. The main allegiance of these early Portuguese settlers was to the Monomotapa; to their own state, or its isolated representatives at Tete, Sena, or Quelimane they owed and paid nothing.

When in the seventeenth century the Portuguese government attempted seriously to extend its jurisdiction over the Rivers of Sena, it was confronted with conditions it had no choice but to recognize; in fact, Lisbon saw in the established system a means of projecting its sovereignty into the interior. It recognized the rights and privileges the Portuguese pioneers had received from the Monomotapa or taken for themselves and sought only to give juridical form to an existing organization. At the same time the crown itself divided the captaincy of the Rivers of Sena, issuing *prazos da coroa*, or crown grants, to its subjects who had rendered distinguished service. Some of the *prazos* were hereditary, others limited to two or three generations. The concessionaires were to receive not more than three square leagues of land, were to reside in the province, marry Europeans also residing in the province, and cultivate and colonize the *prazos*. What the imperial counselors had in mind was a modification of the *donatária* system so successfully implemented in Brazil and unsuccessfully attempted in Angola with the proprietary land grant made to Paulo Dias de Novais in the 1570's. What happened in Moçambique was that the *prazos* seldom remained small, but swelled to tremendous proportions impossible either to cultivate or populate; the concessions often came into the hands not of deserving subjects but of speculators. Many *prazeros* refused to reside in the colony, and many *colonos*

(African residents of the *prazo*) refused to be enslaved and fled the region. There was no one on the Zambezi to enforce the terms of the grant; on the contrary, the captains at Sena and Tete often had to rely on the *prazeros'* private armies.

On his lands the *prazero* was absolute master. He arbitrarily established the tribute, a modified head tax, to be paid by the petty chiefs residing on his lands; of this collection the *prazero* paid from time to time a one-tenth quitrent to the Portuguese treasury. Further contributions were demanded of the Africans on such special occasions as the *prazo's* passing to a new owner. In default of payment in goods (usually ivory) of the *mussoco* (head tax), slaves were accepted from the petty chiefs by the master. The *prazeros* had taken the original power of the local chiefs and increased it. Acting together they were the strongest force in Portuguese East Africa, able to overwhelm the Monomotapa and bend the Portuguese captains to their will. Their great deep-walled residences attracted the admiration of seventeenth-century visitors. The lofty cool rooms were furnished with oriental luxury, tables were set with imported delicacies, scores of slaves served the white lords and their guests as the *prazeros* tried to outdo one another in displaying their wealth.

In the latter part of the seventeenth century complaints from missionaries and civil administrators emphasizing the state of barbarism in the Zambezi country moved the Lisbon court to try to check the excesses of the *prazeros*, many of them by this time mulattoes who lacked whatever national loyalties their fathers may have had. To introduce fresh Portuguese blood into the region, by which it was hoped the white population might be stabilized, Lisbon devised a plan whereby the inheritance of the *prazo* would pass to the eldest daughter, to be retained by her only on the condition that she marry a Portuguese born in Portugal. The government also gave new *prazos* to a scattering of orphan girls as dowries, these grants being subject to the same matrimonial stipulations. After three generations the land was to revert to the crown. These measures did not have wide application and enjoyed only limited success. Lisbon was distant, the rights of the *prazeros* too entrenched, and the way of life on an African tribal estate too strenuous for most European women. The *prazos da coroa*, totaling almost a hundred by the end of the century, remained under the control of Portuguese and half-caste males.

Constantly decried as a vicious regime, the *prazo* system continued through the eighteenth century with little modification. The traditional boundaries changed only slightly in spite of various decrees to reduce the size of the estates. The son zealously defended his father's land against the encroachments of his neighbors, the attacks of African tribes, and legislation from Portugal. The classic report of Villas Boas Truão, governor of the Rivers of Sena in the first decade of the nineteenth century, describes the stagnation of the area. In the three towns of Quelimane, Sena, and Tete and at the posts of Manica and Zumbo he found altogether about five hundred Christians, white and black. His conclusions on why the population did not increase and why such a fertile land was barren of people are: the lack of security for person and property; the excessive size of the *prazos*; inefficient administration and an absentee landlordship which drained the country and put nothing in; the flight of the African *colonos* from the slaving practices of the manor lords. No crops were cultivated save in African gardens. Religious morality was nonexistent, he claims, for the Dominicans had become so corrupted by their environment that they did nothing without payment. Education, commerce, and industry were not to be found.[9]

The report of another official holding office shortly after Governor Truão echoes the charges. Mendes de Vasconcelos e Cirne argued that the estates could have been rich and profitable if placed in proper hands — a category that did not include Indians. To improve the deplorable situation he suggested that the laws of inheritance be enforced; if no daughters were available, then the land should be given to a poor Portuguese man, on the condition that he marry an African woman within a year. He further suggested that no one be permitted to own more than one *prazo*, that the Dominicans be obliged to cultivate their lands and conduct themselves more like servants of the Lord or lose their grants, and that severe restrictions be placed on absentee landlords.[10]

The Portuguese government outlawed the *prazo* system in 1832. This legislation had no more practical result than did subsequent decrees in 1838 and 1841 and the elaborate diploma of 1854 which proposed significant changes designed to promote Portuguese expansion and settlement up the Zambezi. The abolition of slavery which, with the head tax, had been the financial support of the *prazeros* did not loosen their tenacious grasp on the most productive lands of Moçambique. The *prazero* could only be deposed by force, and even when he was chased into the bush by Portuguese troops he carried with him his court and chiefs and native army to carry on "the ancient and well-known struggle which closes out all periods of feudalism; the sovereign power trying to strengthen its authority and the feudal barons defending their traditional rights which are the very reason for their existence." [11] As late as 1880 when the Lisbon government declared all *prazos* to be the crown's property, Governor Augusto de Castilho, a bitter enemy of the system, could make no fundamental changes in its feudal nature. The head tax, the obligation of the native to work for the proprietor, the commercial monopoly within the borders of the *prazo* all remained intact even where Castilho's influence was most felt. By these oppressive measures (to be adopted soon by every other colonial power in Africa) the African was kept in a state of subjugation and exploitation. From this grinding imposition, Lugard observed, the natives "received no equivalent of any sort; for neither were they protected from their enemies nor was the country opened up by roads, bridges, railways, or any other works." [12]

The turn of events from 1885 to 1895, however, the urgent necessity Portugal now felt to occupy the hinterland of Moçambique, gave the previously discredited system a new significance as an instrument of colonial policy. The old-time *prazero* must go, but the system was to remain. Major Caldas Xavier, a contemporary hero-philosopher, called the *prazo* in 1888 indispensable for the native. Mousinho de Albuquerque, whose pronouncements are in part the basis for much of Portugal's colonial philosophies in the twentieth century, states positively that the *prazo* plan must remain and even be extended to the district of Moçambique; it is the only effective way of getting the Portuguese to dedicate themselves to agriculture. He scorns the arguments of the *negrófilos* who have protested the abuses suffered by the African *colonos*; whenever a strong race conquers a people as inferior as the Negro, Mousinho explains, abuse is a natural consequence. While it is true that the *prazo* is similar to medieval estates, this is not necessarily a deplorable condition, for the African, like the feudal serf, does not pass from slavery to full citizenship in one day. An intermediate stage of servitude is needed to bring him into contact with European civilization. Under the *prazo* system, according to Mousinho, this beneficent tutelage may best be exercised; on the *prazo* the African may be taught that only through hard work may he achieve an advanced state of civilization. [13]

Such reasoning pervades the 1888 "Report of the Commission to Study the Reforms to be Introduced in the Prazo System of Moçambique" [14] and the decree of 1890, drafted by António Enes, which gave the *prazo* the form it kept until its final abolition by the Salazar government when the leases granted in the 1890's and early 1900's expired. The *prazo* was held to be essential for the development of modern Moçambique once the estates were taken from the unproductive *senhores de terra* and rented to more responsible individuals or companies for a specified period. The estates were to be auctioned to the highest bidder, who would pay the government a rent consisting of a substantial percentage (about 30 per cent) of the tax revenue collected. The "Report of the Commission" outlined the responsibilities of the renter and the *colono*: in essence, the obligation of the renter was to cultivate and develop the land and protect the African resident; for these services the *colono* was obliged to pay the renter a yearly sum in either goods or labor, whichever was the more appropriate to the landlord. The renter was still the supreme authority over his lands. He could demand both taxes and labor from the African; he still administered justice and had a private police force of sepoys; he still had a commercial monopoly within the boundaries of his territory. The extension of these ancient privileges was considered necessary by the colonial government; without them the renter would have been powerless to recruit a working force for the large-scale agriculture which had now begun to flourish in the Zambezi region. The benefits received by the *colono* continued to be negligible. The positive achievements of the new regime of the *prazos* were two: some physical improvement in the lands of Zambézia and the introduction of capital investment in the region.

Generally the price for the twenty-five year concession was put so high that the renter could not make a profit by merely collecting taxes and was forced to cultivate part of the *prazo*. Many of the estates were taken over by the Zambézia Company or were part of the territory administered by the Moçambique Company.

In summing up the advantages and disadvantages of the system Vilhena in 1915 concluded that Moçambique had slightly profited from its continuation. He cites impressive figures to show that in Zambézia agricultural production was higher than in non-*prazo* lands. A second benefit was the fixing of the Negro to the land and obliging him to work. On the other hand, the traditional abuses continued: the state had little authority over the lands, and its normal administrative functions were implemented there with difficulty; many renters were concerned only with enriching themselves as quickly as possible and instead of obliging the African to work on the *prazo* they made contracts for the African's services in other parts of the province, recruiting and exporting him like a slave; the renter failed to fulfill his obligations to develop the *prazo*. Here Vilhena saw the weight of tradition and inertia; the best guide for the traveler to Zambézia was still, he suggested, the *Ethiópia oriental* of Father João dos Santos.[15] Throughout Vilhena's study is an implied criticism of a colonial policy which had failed either to promote the interests of Portugal in Moçambique or to bring civilization to the African tribes of the area.

The story of life on the Zambezi in the eighteenth and nineteenth centuries is told in the history of the notorious Cruz family. The founder of the dynasty, Nicolau Pascoal da Cruz, appeared on the river in the 1760's as sergeant of a company of Indian sepoys. Cruz himself was either Indian or Siamese. Settling in the vicinity of Tete, he prospered rapidly: he married one of the *donas* of the Zambezi, Luisa da Costa, half-caste proprietress of several large *prazos*. Nicolau subsequently became a factor of the royal treasury, a town councilor of Tete, captain of the fortress of Zimbabwe, captain of the Tete militia, and, on occasions, acting governor of the Rivers of Sena captaincy. He expanded the boundaries of his wife's *prazos* until the estate known as Massangano was one of the largest in the colony.

Nicolau's son, António, inherited many of his father's honors, but not his loyalty, and was hanged and quartered in Moçambique town in 1813 for having betrayed a Portuguese column under Governor Truão to the Monomotapa. From a union with one of the Monomotapa's sisters, António left a son, Joaquim José, who pursued a policy of aggrandizement on the Zambezi. His ambitions brought him into conflict with Pedro Caetano Pereira — son of a Goan *prazero* — who had overrun the left bank of the Zambezi from Lupata Gorge to Zumbo. Both men freely stopped shipping to Tete, claiming fees for right of passage, and both had their supporters in the desolate little town of Tete, which was practically at the mercy of the powerful *prazeros*. The rivalry between Joaquim José and Pereira broke into open warfare in 1853 when the latter attacked the Cruz fortress-compound at Massangano and was driven off after a long siege. The following year Joaquim José's private army scattered a small government detachment sent to punish him for insubordination, one of the first incidents in the so-called Wars of the Zambezi.

Joaquim's son, António Vicente da Cruz, the misanthropic Bonga, was a perfect specimen for a positivistic study of *prazo* life in the nineteenth century. Illiterate, thieving, cruel, barbarous, a drunkard, he represented the sum total of the vices which have been held to characterize life on the Zambezi in that period. But Bonga retained a shred of mystical faith in his Portuguese inheritance. He proudly displayed his insignia as major in the Portuguese army, a rank accorded most of the *prazeros*. He had several of his daughters baptized in the parish church at Tete. Like most of his contemporaries in the last desperate days of the hereditary *prazos*, he was miserably poor, for the slave trade was almost dead and the land produced little.

From the death of his father in 1855 until 1866, Bonga, though truculent and suspicious, lived in peace with the colonial government. At his informal customhouse on the edge of the river he did collect taxes on Zambezi traffic, but his demands were usually moderate, and as a reward for his restraint he was made in 1862 Sergeant Major of the Prazos of Massangano and Tipué. By conferring such honors the administration kept a semblance of public order in the district and delicately maintained a semblance of authority. By 1865, however, after Livingstone's two visits to the region, the time seemed urgent for an extension of permanent Portuguese authority over the independent *prazeros* and the creation of a new order along the river (Lisbon had even considered about 1860 subsidizing a colony of German immigrants on the upper Zambezi). One of the first steps under the new policy was to be the suppression of Bonga who, by virtue of living close to Tete, seemed the most vulnerable of the local potentates. He was accused of fomenting unrest and ordered to stand trial at Tete. When Bonga failed to appear, a column of almost one thousand men set out for Massangano in 1867. The force was defeated by Bonga's private army, and in the next three years three more punitive expeditions dismally failed to subjugate the *prazero*. An armistice was made in 1874, and when Bonga died in 1879 he was still a sergeant major and buried with appropriate ceremony by a priest from Tete. Not until 1887 was the stockade at Massangano taken in one of the decisive campaigns of the Zambezi wars.

The struggles between the Portuguese government and the Cruz family revealed both the resourcefulness of the *prazeros* and the pathetic weakness of Portuguese control in the interior of Moçambique. Bonga was neither a rebel nor a revolutionary; he fought in defense of his own — the traditional independence of the *prazero*. He sought no war with the colonial authorities and even refrained from pressing his military advantage after defeating the attacking armies. But he refused to submit to what seemed an arbitrary distant authority, and in his resistance he was joined by other *prazeros*, local tribes, and Zambezi adventurers. Against this array, the Portuguese forces, made up of *degradados*, India militiamen, and African soldiers who fled at the first opportunity, could do little. Portuguese authority, after almost two hundred years of neglect, could not be restored so easily in the turbulent estates of the Zambezi.[16]

To revitalize the ineffective *prazo* system and to stimulate the development of other parts of the province, the Portuguese government from 1885 to 1900 encouraged the formation of concessionary companies. The example of the newly formed British South Africa Company undoubtedly stirred Portuguese hopes that several large land companies operating in Moçambique would provide the necessary resources and administrative help for the colony's immediate future. Such help was most likely to come from outside Portugal and it was clear that Portugal must put aside her reluctance to allow foreign capital in the African provinces. Nevertheless, even though the charters of the most important companies were reminiscent of the powers granted under that most Portuguese institution, the *prazo* system, and even though the administrative councils of the companies had to contain a majority of Portuguese citizens, their formation touched off a lingering dispute. Critics of the companies had recourse to two arguments, that they introduced a dangerous denationalizing element into Moçambique and that they gave more profit to foreign investors than to Portuguese colonial interests. The most eloquent argument for the companies was the sad reality of the province in 1890. Something had to be done, even if it meant granting what seemed to be extraordinary concessions to companies capitalized outside of Portugal. Time has proved the government more far-sighted than its critics, for whatever progress was made by the companies until the expiration of their charters, it materially benefited the province more than it did foreign stockholders.

The three great companies formed in the last decade of the nineteenth century were the Moçambique Company, the Niassa Company, and the Zambézia Company, the last mentioned, however, not possessing a charter from the Portuguese government. Each of the companies subsequently granted subconcessions to other smaller companies. In 1900 the total area of land under the control of the three companies was more than two thirds of the area of Moçambique. The purposes of the companies were frankly exploratory, even speculative, as manifested by the meager working capital, in proportion to the tremendous size of the territories granted, put up in the first years of the charters. Their hopes lay in the discovery of substantial mineral deposits, the success of large-scale agricultural projects, and the letting of concessions within the territory. Portugal's hopes, of course, were equally speculative and were for the permanent occupation and colonization of the area.

The most important of these companies — the one that held the greatest promise for expansion into the interior — was the Moçambique Company, which grew out of a mineral-exploring concession along the Buzi and Pungué rivers. Initial reports were encouraging, and in 1889 the working capital was doubled to about $400,000. The rise of the British South Africa Company, however, in the adjacent territories made the formation of a richer, more powerful company imperative. In 1891, therefore, the Moçambique Company reincorporated the original society. The basic charter was granted in that year with modifying decrees issued during the decade. The new company found stockholders not only in Portugal but in other European countries and South Africa who bought shares to the approximate value of five million dollars.

By the terms of the charter the Moçambique Company was given sovereign rights to exploit and administer the more than 62,000 square miles which now comprise the modern district of Manica and Sofala. The concession was limited to fifty years, but could be withdrawn at any time the company should fail to fulfill the terms of the charter or become insolvent. The company was to be considered Portuguese with headquarters in Lisbon and the majority of the directors Portuguese citizens resident in Portugal. The government was to receive 10 per cent of the shares issued and 7.5 per cent of the total net profits, in return for which the government was to abstain from collecting taxes in the territory for a period of twenty-five years. The rights given the company included a monopoly of commerce; exclusive mining concessions; exclusive fishing rights along the coast; collection of contributions and taxes consistent with prevailing Portuguese policy (among these taxes figured the usual native head tax, the surest guarantee for a constant labor supply); rights for the construction of roads, ports, communication lines, and, with the approval of the government, the privilege of granting concessions to others for such construction; banking and postal privileges; and transfer of land up to 12,500 acres to other companies and individuals. At the termination of the concession all land under cultivation was to remain the property of the company. Also, the company was obliged to give land to the government for fortifications and military posts, and swore to hold allegiance to the Portuguese government and to protect Portuguese interests within its boundaries; it was required to maintain a police force and assist in internal struggles. The company was bound to respect the rights and customs of the Africans when these did not conflict with civilizing progress in the land. Municipal administration had to be maintained and schools established in towns of over five hundred houses. In the actual administration of the territory Portuguese citizens were to be employed, and all employees of the company residing in Moçambique were subservient to Portuguese law. At Beira, capital of the company's lands, were located the departmental offices of the treasury, port authority, customs, public works, agriculture and mines, and those of the secretary general in charge of native affairs, education, and health. Judicial matters remained within the colonial government's jurisdiction. The territory was to be divided into various circumscriptions, each with a Portuguese administrator. Finally, all points in dispute between the company and the state were to be referred to an arbitration board.

In 1891 a charter was given the Niassa Company, although it was not definitely formed until 1893; its principal source of capital was England. All the lands of the province north of the Lúrio River comprised the concession area. The terms of the concession were almost identical with those of the Moçambique Company, except that the period of the Niassa concession was for only thirty-five years. This part of the colony, still its most underdeveloped region, had neither the mineral nor agricultural expectations of Zambézia and Manica and Sofala, and a series of difficulties, not the least of which was a bad administration, prevented the Niassa Company from realizing any useful exploitation besides the establishment of Porto Amélia as a center of trade and administration. The dream of a railroad from the port to the lake, on which much of the territory's development depended, never came true in the company's lifetime; in its absence there was scant attraction for settlers and merchants.

The third great company formed in the 1890's was the Zambézia Company, whose history also has its origin in mining concessions granted in the previous decade. Some 80,000 square miles of land in the districts of Quelimane and Tete made it the largest of the land companies. Most of the area was made up of *prazos*. Its chief investors, more diversified than those of the Niassa and Moçambique companies, were firms and individuals in South Africa, Germany, France, England, and Portugal. The company was not responsible for the administration of the territory. The absence of this burden and the fact that it possessed some of the richest lands in the colony made the company's operations more profitable than those of the Moçambique Company. Many of the *prazos* in the company's domain were let as long-term subconcessions, the most important being those to the Boror Company, financed principally in Germany, and the Luabo Company. These two and two other companies formed independently, the Sena Sugar Estates (an English firm) and the Société du Madal (with headquarters in Paris) have contributed significantly to the development of sugar, sisal, and copra production in Zambézia.[17]

Although the *companhias majestáticas* ultimately proved a disappointment to their stockholders and even, to a lesser extent, to the Portuguese government, their contributions, especially those of the Moçambique and Zambézia Companies, during their short existence had greater significance for the colony than had the *prazo* in three centuries. To a large extent they initiated the transformation of the interior of the province from a wilderness to an economically productive region — a process still in its embryonic stage — and created conditions permitting the steady, albeit slow, settling of the area by a white population. The benefits the African derived from their presence seem less than negligible.[18]

Although few small-scale farmers subleased land from the companies, the great plantations brought in European personnel, some of whom remained in East Africa. New towns grew up and several old ones flourished again. The rebirth of commerce and the appearance of a modest transportation system also helped to fix a small permanent Portuguese population in that part of the province which had previously seen only administrators and garrison officers. Such gains may have appeared ridiculously small to the casual observer or to the impatient Portuguese citizen exasperated by his country's indecisive colonial policies, but viewed against the background of inertia and stagnation they represented an almost staggering advance in the development of Moçambique.

The restless state of Zambézia during the late eighteenth century and all of the nineteenth century was not always symptomatic of life along the coast, even in the city of Moçambique. Administrative independence from India after 1752, though accompanied by increased powers for the provincial governor and a plethora of legislative and commercial decrees, did not check the town's drift into an undisturbed sleep. In his thirteen-year governorship (1765–1779), Pereira do Lago applied himself to the colony's problems with Pombaline energy, reorganizing the local militia with Indian troops, encouraging the production of crops and waging constant war against rebellious tribes; but his efforts were useless, and in 1781, the Minister for Naval and Colonial Affairs, Martinho de Melo e Castro, admitted that Moçambique had reached the last stage of moral and commercial decadence. Perhaps an indication of the kind of hopes Lisbon held for its regeneration is seen in the shipment of thirteen prostitutes to Moçambique in 1782. Contact with the outside world was limited to the capital and the clandestine slave ports. To try to hold the province together, Melo e Castro ordered a military reorganization throughout the land and a strengthening of the garrisons with Indian and African troops. The commercial monopoly of Moçambique island was taken away and customhouses set up at Ibo, Quelimane, Sofala, Inhambane, and Lourenço Marques. An agricultural office was created to introduce new crops and European techniques. At the end of the century the famous scientific expedition of Dr. Lacerda de Almeida was dispatched to explore the upper reaches of the Zambesi — an accomplishment in which he was aided by *prazero* António José da Cruz. These activities had some temporary effect, but they were no permanent cure for the dilapidations and deep-rooted ills the colony suffered.

In the 1810's the extent of Portuguese coastal occupation was the same as in 1600 and consisted of forts and trading posts from Ibo to Lourenço Marques. Reports of travelers and governors record the apathy, disease, and neglect in these coastal towns. Lacerda speaks of the rotting humidity of Quelimane: "In such a place everything conspires to produce in the population fevers, malaria, bilious attacks, infections, dysentery . . . every sort of chronic disease coming from rottenness. . . All this contributes to another worse misfortune: the population does not increase; this year fifteen people died and three were born. . ." [19] Sofala was a collection of shanties huddled around a forgotten fortress garrisoned by convicts. Only the sparkling beauty of the town of Moçambique, its color and charm, saved the provincial capital from equally harsh descriptions. Other narratives, however, refer to its poverty, immorality, and degradation. Neither in the south nor in the north had the Portuguese penetrated appreciably into the interior; to the contrary, their coastal outposts sustained periodic onslaughts from bordering tribes. French vessels harassed local shipping, seizing ivory and slaves.

The Liberal revolution in Portugal briefly shook the colony much as it did Angola, plunging the island into a decade of anarchy. Throughout the nineteenth century an intensification of African hostility added to the chaos. The abolition of slavery cut off Moçambique's main source of revenue, although the trade itself had brought prosperity to only a few; a clandestine export of slaves continued for some years, first to America and then to the French islands off Madagascar. Arab slave traders continued to do business in the northern part of the province, as Livingstone discovered in the 1860's. Sá da Bandeira's antislavery decrees did result in several long-term advantages, for the colony's shaken economy was diverted into agricultural projects which by the end of the century constituted the major wealth of Moçambique. But the process of readjustment was slow, and the long years of the nineteenth century were for many Portuguese ones of despair.

Only in Delagoa Bay did fortune smile on Moçambique in this trying period. There the present-day capital Lourenço Marques emerged from its early stockade status to a position as one of the largest and most important ports of the East African coast by the end of the century. Once a temporary factory visited by coastal traders, the area meant little until Austria set up a small trading post and fort. The interlopers were easily expelled, but fearful of similar action by more formidable intruders, Portugal decided to keep a permanent post of some sixty men in Lourenço Marques. French corsairs destroyed the fortress in 1796; four years later a new stockade, with warehouses and administration buildings, was erected on the site of the modern city. The small town was forced to resist innumerable attacks from the Landin tribesmen, who finally in 1833, aided by some Zulu warriors, massacred the garrison. But fresh forces were sent to Lourenço Marques to occupy the post.

In the middle of the century the Boer republic in the Transvaal began to realize the importance of Lourenço Marques as a port of entry, and from the 1860's on, the flow of goods through Lourenço Marques steadily increased. Where there had been two houses of European construction in 1854 there were one hundred in 1877. Two years later Lourenço Marques was raised to the category of city. For more than fifty years, however, the port had the reputation of being a pest hole, and few visitors had kind words for the city that is now one of the loveliest in southern Africa. In 1857, the Englishman McLeod complained liverishly, "The town consists of a miserable square of squalid-looking houses . . . is filthy in every sense. . . It is impossible for anyone to see the town without being struck with the idea how it is possible for human beings to live there." [20] Even in 1890, Lourenço Marques was for another English traveler "the vilest, filthiest, and the most deadly place to white men I know of in all the hospitable world," [21] although by the end of the decade two other travelers treated the city more gallantly, referring to it as "cosmopolitan" and a "genteel prosperous town." [22]

The problems of colonization besetting Moçambique were duplicated in Angola, where conditions for permanent settlement were perhaps harsher — in spite of glowing accounts reaching Lisbon each year about the bounteous healthy plateau country. Traders lived in the deep interior far from the few military stockades the Portuguese maintained, but these men were not colonists; if they owned land, they generally used it to supply themselves with slaves. The contributions were slight; as a colonizing force they achieved, and could achieve, little in such isolation, and the fragments of Portuguese culture they may have imparted to their mulatto families usually disappeared within a generation. Without constant stimulation and support from Portugal, the task of colonization was an almost impossible one before 1900. Nowhere do the words of Professor Macmillan have better application than in Angola from 1600 to 1900: "The white man, if he would recognize it, suffers with all Africans the influence of a land which is deficient if not lacking in most of the essential means of civilization." [23]

The two centers of Portuguese occupation through the long centuries were Luanda and Benguela. Massangano's influence and size dwindled after its brief span as temporary capital of the colony during the Dutch occupation of Luanda. The two coastal cities were chiefly slave ports upon which converged the caravan routes from the dark interior, but Luanda was more than a slave port and provincial capital. For centuries it was the only white city south of the Sahara. Even in 1890, at a low point in Luanda's history, Mary Kingsley could write, "Say what you please, Loanda is not only the first, but the only, city in West Africa." [24] Commodore Owen in the 1820's calls it a large empty city. Winwood Reade, about 1860, speaks of the great fine churches and public buildings, "but the streets of Luanda are ankle-deep in sand, the public buildings are either decaying or in *status quo*; oxen are stalled in the college of the Jesuits. All that remains of the poetry and power is dying away in this colony. It is the Dark Ages in the interregnum between two civilizations. When will the second begin?" [25]

Benguela in 1845 had 600 houses, but only 38 white men and one white woman. The rest of the population was made up of 179 mulattoes and 2,200 Negroes, half of whom were slaves. A great number of the houses were in ruins, and grass grew in the middle of the streets.[26] Almost fifty years later, the waspish Daniel Crawford, an energetic champion of Anglo-Saxon enterprise, excoriates the drowsy little city: "Portuguese to the core, here you find a tropical town nearly fast asleep in 1889 — asleep, and no wonder. For most of these Portuguese have been boiling in this tropical kettle for many years, with the climactic result that many have a lethargic glaze in their eyes. . . Scarcely one Portuguese lady in the place. All their colonies have gone shipwreck by defying the foundation truth that whenever duty summons man, woman has a corresponding duty in the same place. . . A monthly steamer in these dismal days is the only distraction."[27] Even in their deterioration Luanda and Benguela were the most substantial European towns in West Africa. The English and French ports, by comparison, were poor factories maintained by a few fever-ridden men. In the struggle for survival in the most inhospitable regions of Africa the Portuguese pioneers need acknowledge the superiority of no other European people.

The wealth of Angola is of recent improvisation, for not until the 1900's has the heralded potential of the colony become a reality. Poverty and frustration faced the Portuguese who sought to gain a livelihood other than from slavery. In the seventeenth century that observant French voyager Pyrard de Laval called Angola the poorest country in the world. In 1810 Governor António de Melo sent the frankest of reports to his government. "I should like to be able to bring this colony to court so that your Royal Highness and his ministers could actually see the deplorable state it is in. . . Perhaps they will then believe that Angola is no Brazil. . ." The previous year Melo had written, "We who live in this country are always on the verge of dying of hunger in the dry years or being swept away in the rainy ones. In such a land what can prosper and who will dwell here?"[28]

Even in the celebrated highlands of Angola, Portuguese settlers did not prosper. In 1682, in from Benguela on the Bié plateau, they founded a fortress at Caconda near the rising of the Caporolo River. After a century of checkered history, the fort was transferred to the present site of Caconda by Governor Sousa Coutinho, who had the notion that in a healthier location Caconda could become the nucleus of a settlement and the center for trade in the region. "Since the fortress is situated in the best part of the province we must see that it is populated with industrious and hard-working people; to this end let all *degradados* and European soldiers who go there with a desire to work in agriculture and industry be free from military service and let them marry; the fortress may be garrisoned with natives who, although not capable of agriculture and industry, are very satisfactory soldiers."[29] He goes on to suggest that the African will be drawn into the community by the good example of the Europeans. Sousa Coutinho's vision was Utopian for Angola. Caconda did not fulfill its high expectations. The Portuguese intermarried and lived with their slaves and families in their compounds, but the colony did not progress. The fortress was one of the advanced points of Portuguese penetration and had a population of about 250 men at the beginning of the nineteenth century with as many as 15,000 Africans residing in the vicinity, but by 1840 the fields were abandoned and the inhabitants lived in poverty. Hermenegildo Capelo and Roberto Ivens found that Caconda had few Portuguese in 1878, although the community was impressive for its mixed population and shrewd Afro-Portuguese traders.[30]

Sousa Coutinho was not blind to the fact that *degradados* were not the ideal colonial stock and tried during his governorship to promote the immigration of farmers from Portugal and other colonies. He was aware that the exiles found the slave trade more attractive than tilling the soil or practicing a trade, and went so far as to suggest to the home government that foreigners would be more welcome. His pleas were renewed, without effect, by the Baron of Moçâmedes, who urged the subsidization of poor farmers willing to come to Angola.

Moçâmedes' correspondence played an important part sixty years later in the settling of southern Angola. In 1848 an antislavery nativist revolt in the Brazilian city of Pernambuco made recent Portuguese immigrants there fearful of their future, and they petitioned the Lisbon government for assistance in finding a salubrious area of Africa to which they could go. The Overseas Ministry, which for fifteen years had been unsuccessfully trying to promote the settling of Africa by making every kind of promise, was delighted at the unexpected inquiry and drafted a lengthy memorandum on the area around the port of Moçâmedes, taking much of the information from the Baron's reports. Pleased with Lisbon's response, which included the promise of financial aid, 170 Pernambucanos sailed for Angola the next year. In 1850 another 130 Portuguese sailed to join their friends. The new arrivals suffered incredible hardships; Moçâmedes was still too small to provide for even such a modest number of immigrants in spite of the best efforts of the governor general, who was on hand personally to arrange for their reception. Drought and the failure of the cane crop made some of the families decide to move to Luanda. Other families were sent to the plateau outpost of Huíla. But the settlement of southern Angola had begun. In 1853 a small fishing colony at Porto Alexandre was established along the coast south of Moçâmedes. From Portugal's province of Algarve a few fishermen and their families made their way, some in tiny fishing vessels, to Angola. They prospered and built up the fishing industry of southern Angola, today one of the most important segments of Angola's economic life.

Angola's accidental good fortune in finding colonists for Mo-çâmedes and Huíla did not last. In Lisbon the newly formed Conselho Ultramarino, or Overseas Council, tried to evolve plans of action to mitigate the economic devastations caused by the abolition of slavery. In decrees of 1856 the government was authorized to contract a loan exclusively for the purpose of "establishing colonies in Angola and Moçambique to be composed of citizens of Portugal and the adjacent islands." The loan was to be repaid from duty collected on the importation of wine into the provinces. The Council made elaborate studies of transportation, the regions to be chosen for the colonists, and possible methods of administering the settlements, but the plans never got beyond the drafting stage.[31] Frontiersmen like Silva Porto explored the plateaus of Bié and Huíla, but their solitary explorations did not have the effect of drawing Portuguese to Angola, and only a handful of colonists could be persuaded to go to West Africa in the next two decades. In the early 1880's the colonial office again had recourse to the penal colony system, setting up or expanding camps at Malange, Pungo Andongo, and Caconda.

In the year 1880, however, the largest band of settlers seen in Angola up to that time appeared in the vicinity of Humpata on the Huíla plateau. The group consisted of about three hundred Boers, the "Thirstland Trekkers," under the leadership of the patriarchal Jakobus Botha. On their arrival in Portuguese West Africa they were advised by Father Duparquet of the Congregation of the Holy Ghost to go to Humpata. There the district governor granted them extensive tracts of land. The story of the Boers is one of the most curious interludes in the annals of Angola. In 1875, to escape what they considered British tyranny, they set out from near Mafeking, journeying with their wagons and cattle across Bechuanaland and into South-West Africa south of the Etosha Pan. When the group finally made their way across the Cunene into Angola, over three hundred had succumbed to the rigors of the trek, but the three hundred who survived formed a startling number, by Portuguese standards, of willing colonists.[32]

The Portuguese government, traditionally sensitive to the presence of denationalizing forces in its African colonies, felt mixed emotions about the Boers. They regarded them, on the one hand, with natural suspicion; on the other, they welcomed the opportunity of gaining useful allies in the work of developing the *planalto* and pacifying the African tribes of the region. In the end, Lisbon made the gesture of nationalizing the Boers in 1882 as Portuguese citizens. Artur de Paiva, the young army officer who was made adviser to the new colony, was enthusiastic about the Boers, and his reports were in some measure responsible for Portuguese restraint. Paiva himself married Botha's daughter. His vision was for a union of Boer and Portuguese colonists from which would come the prosperous growth of Huíla. Paiva principally admired their great courage and religious zeal. He admitted that they were selfish, argumentative, and violently intolerant of the African, but these drawbacks, he felt, were outweighed by their promise of becoming industrious farmers and ranchers.[33] The journalist Henry Nevinson, who loathed every aspect of Angolan life, regarded them with scorn and admiration: "A slovenly, unwashed, foggy-minded people, they are a strange mixture of simplicity and cunning, but for a knowledge of oxen and wagons and game, they have no rivals. . . They trade to some extent in slaves, but chiefly they buy for their own use, and they almost always give them their freedom at the time of marriage." [34]

The contributions of the Boers did not measure up to Paiva's anticipations, although traces of their presence are still felt around Humpata. Some of them did become successful farmers, and their well-tended farms were welcome havens for weary travelers. But more than farmers the Boers were, as Nevinson noted, hunters, fighters, and wagon drivers. They gave the Portuguese valuable assistance in the systematic pacification of the Ovimbundu in the years around the turn of the century. With their massive carts drawn by ten and twelve pair of oxen they penetrated the hinterland in all directions, following native trails or blazing new ones, some of which have become the principal roads of southern Angola. In the country which they at first referred to as the land of milk and honey, the Boers multiplied and prospered moderately, their numbers augmented from time to time by small groups of countrymen from the Transvaal or South-West Africa, but their inveterate restlessness kept them from sinking their roots too deeply into the soil of Huíla. Some went down to the coast; others migrated beyond the Hungry Country to the Belgian frontier and disappeared. The majority who remained in the *planalto* grumbled more and more about their grievances, real and imagined, with the Portuguese. The approach of the Moçâmedes railroad, new restrictions on firearms licenses, a growing sense of isolation in a Catholic, Portuguese-speaking community made the Boers receptive to overtures from the Union government for a return to South-West Africa where, among other things, the Union wanted to counteract the influence of the German population. In 1928–1929, some 1,500

Ox-drawn Boer cart, Angola, 1937

The docks at Lourenço Marques, Moçambique

Car ferry, Cuanza River, Angola

Modern bridge, Moçambique

Boers left Angola; thirty-five families remained behind, some of whom left in the next few years. But the Boers did not forget their fifty years in Angola and the graves they left behind. In 1957 four hundred descendants of the original colonists came back to Humpata on a pilgrimage to the promised land of their fathers.

The presence of the Boers in Huíla forced an intensification of direct Portuguese colonization in the early 1880's. Impoverished, generally ignorant families were recruited in all parts of the metropolis to be sent off at the government's expense to southern Angola to insulate the Boer community. At the same time the region was closed off to further shipments of *degradados*. Most of the colonists were from the Algarve and Minho districts of Portugal and from the island of Madeira. The rapid indiscriminate selection of settlers did not produce immediate results, and the colony, half forgotten in the distractions of the Conference of Berlin and the immediate necessity for a military pacification rather than civilian occupation of the African provinces, did not receive the continuing assistance it needed. To neutralize the influence of the Boers was an easy task, since Botha and his men were not empire-builders or even acquisitive, but the union of the two white cultures, anticipated by Paiva, did not come to pass. Paiva himself complained that the new Portuguese colonists were a poor lot whom the Boers, proud of their Dutch and French inheritance, disdained to marry, even when the differences of religion could be removed.

In spite of the government's neglect, the privations of a frontier existence, the native wars at the end of the century, and the isolation, the stubborn peasants hung on. In a sense Huíla is today the most Portuguese region of Angola, its small farms replicas of those in Portugal and Madeira. So intensely did these conservative immigrants entrench themselves in the province that they now consider themselves Angolan, not Portuguese. Like the Boers whose influence they were sent to counteract, they do not take easily to change and are suspicious of new agricultural techniques and political schemes originating in distant Luanda or more distant Lisbon. Not only did these tenacious people survive, but they increased their numbers. By 1913, Sir Harry Johnston estimated 2,500 Portuguese to be residing in the vicinity of Lubango (Sá da Bandeira).[35]

In 1900, when Portugal gave up her efforts for the direct colonization of Angola the white population of the province was about nine thousand, a substantial part of which was administrative personnel.

To this reality it is hard to adjust the image of Portugal as a nation of colonizers. In four centuries she had built coastal towns in Angola and Moçambique and erratically maintained stockades in the interior. Tete, Sena, and Massangano were the only towns in the interior worthy of mention. The Portuguese who went to Africa went for trade or gold or administration. Those who stayed did so as masters of the land or of the African; the land they seldom worked and the African they often sold. It is a curious, though explainable, commentary on the divergent patterns of Portuguese expansion that for a Brazil and an India with their agricultural and commercial development, there should have been an Angola and Moçambique, productive only in terms of human beings.

Yet it would be a mistake to assume that Portugal's occupation of East and West Africa in these years achieved nothing. If her role as a white colonizing force was scarcely visible in many parts of the two provinces, she accidentally rendered valuable service to the African people she found there.

In three centuries Portuguese administration had apparently done little to justify any rights based on effective occupation, and it has become usual to dismiss the Portuguese with contempt — as if all were said when it was sorrowfully recognized that they intermarried freely with Africans and, therefore, "degenerated." Wayside gardens in Angola are witness that members of the little Portuguese garrisons still throw in their lot with the adopted country as completely as the Dutch or British have ever done. Between them the Arabs and the Portuguese introduced most of what are now the staple African crops, maize, yams, manioc (cassava), the sweet potatoes, besides sugar-cane, pepper, ginger, citrus, tomatoes, pineapple, and tobacco . . . Africa as the Portuguese found it was useless even as a port of call to supply the East Indian ships with fresh supplies in their long voyage to the more important East. There is much to be said, therefore, for the Portuguese who made this momentous contribution, and also succeeded in getting their African pupils to adopt these new crops as their own.[36]

V

THE MISSIONARY EFFORT

T HE role of the Christian missionary in Africa is a difficult one
to define. For some he is a relic from a Victorian past trailing memories
of discredited policies of white imperialism. For others he is a
dedicated individual who has made real contributions to the welfare
of the African. In most of Africa the age of missionary political influence is past. Only where the Christian missionary has been able to
reconcile the traditions of his Western European culture with a genuine sympathy for the political, as well as the spiritual and physical,
advancement of the African does he not stand in humanitarian isolation. The simple direct relationship of earlier days between the missionary and the African population has now been complicated by the
rise of the city in some parts of the continent, by divergent colonial
and national policies, and by the spirit of nationalism, and it may be
that the missionary dream of the past century for Christian Africa
is a dead letter.

But generalities which can be stretched to include most of Bantu
Africa seldom apply to the Portuguese colonies. By a curious circumstance the situations prevailing in another part of Africa at a given
moment are usually ones which prevailed in Angola and Moçambique
several centuries before or will probably prevail there a hundred years
hence. It is always dangerous for a student of African affairs to assume
that what may be true in Nigeria and the Belgian Congo and Uganda
and the Union of South Africa (a most unlikely hypothesis) will also
hold true in Portuguese Africa. No other colonial power on the continent is more bound to traditional ways, but these ways are not Bel-

gian, English, or French. Today Angola and Moçambique, save for their busy ports, are still among the least known parts of Africa. A knowledge of the superficial aspects of the colonies may be revealing, but it is not sufficient for an adequate understanding of past and present problems. In the course of Portuguese history, in Iberia and overseas, certain attitudes and traditions have become part of Portugal's reality and deeply influence her policies and conduct in Africa. A case in point is the missionary endeavor in the two colonies.

It is hardly necessary to say that Portugal is a Catholic nation. More significant, perhaps, is that a number of Portuguese spokesmen have proclaimed her on occasions the *most Catholic* of nations, a distinction she may well share with her neighbor Spain. Centuries of combat against the Moors, a religious as well as a political enemy, forged a Christian nationalism which has given a fundamental identity to Portugal's personality. Her insularity has tended to impart to Portugal's Catholicism a provincial dogmatic quality which, ironically, an ultramarine expansion has strengthened, not weakened. Portugal has long considered it her unique mission to implant her faith among heathen peoples. The concept of the cross and the sword has had a very real significance in Brazil, Africa, and the East, and the time-worn remark attributed to Vasco da Gama, "I seek Christians and spices," contains more truth than rhetorical fancy. That the history of Portuguese Africa is closely bound to missionary efforts there is a logical expression of national character.

In native affairs the missionary to Portuguese East and West Africa has always occupied a pre-eminent position. Since 1500 he has made himself responsible not only for the spiritual welfare of the African but also for his educational and physical welfare. With certain Protestant missions in Africa it is sometimes difficult to say whether the social or religious aspect of their program is more important, but in justice to the Catholic missions in Portuguese Africa there has been until very recently no such problem. First things first. Historically this has meant the conversion of the Negro. While it is true that such orders as the Jesuits and Dominicans maintained schools and hospitals in the two colonies, their social conscience was generally that of their age. The African clergy educated in the colleges of Africa or Portugal were created in the image of the European priest and often showed less concern for the material welfare of the native people than did their teachers. Nevertheless, whatever cultural advantages the African in Angola and Moçambique achieved from 1500 to 1900 were gained through the guidance of the Catholic missions. Only in recent years has the Portuguese government been able to accept growing responsibilities for assistance to the African, and in the task of bringing modern civilization to Africa, the church and state still work in common accord. Article 24 of the Colonial Act of 1930 reaffirms the traditional relationship. "The Portuguese Catholic missions overseas, instruments of civilization and national influence, shall have juridical personality and shall be protected and helped by the State as institutions of education."

The co-operation of church and state in Portugal's African provinces has not always worked to the best interests of the church. The African's acceptance of Christianity for reasons of political prestige was seldom rooted in sincere convictions (in spite of the example of Afonso I) and brought the church little profit in terms of lasting Christian influence. Furthermore, the example of white Christians manipulating their black Christian brother, often turning him against his own people, was not lost on the African.

Nor has the close identification of church and state always meant harmony in the Portuguese colonies. Long before the Liberal interludes in the nineteenth century, which are sometimes held responsible for most of the evils and decay associated with the African missions, missionary fathers were denouncing colonial officials for corruption and brutality, a charge answered in kind when the priests were accused of greed and mundane interests.[1]

Although Portugal in the nineteenth and the early twentieth century was torn into two camps on religious issues, as far as the colonies were concerned there has seldom been a *fundamental* split between the government and the church over the need for missionaries. The most outspoken Liberal, frequently anticolonial and anticlerical, was usually willing to admit the necessity of missionaries, albeit secular priests, for the task of civilizing Angola and Moçambique. Mousinho de Albuquerque's accusation that when Portugal most needed the missions in order to advance her claims in Africa they were lacking and that, when other countries were expanding evangelical work in Africa, Portugal's Liberals were smothering hers in only a half-truth.[2] The decline of the church's program in Africa coincided with political and economic declines, and the collapse in the nineteenth century was the inevitable result of conditions originating one and two hundred years earlier. In the corrosive atmosphere of Africa few European institutions have survived without fresh inspiration from the metropolis. In the Congo, for example, an early scene of some of the most fervent missionary work in all of Africa until the last one hundred years, practically no trace remained in the late nineteenth century of Christian presence.

There are, of course, reasons other than climate. One Portuguese historian says that the early missions failed to sink permanent roots in Angola because of the slave trade, the failure to educate African women, and the chronic lack of clergy.[3] Oliveira Martins attacks the method of evangelization, arguing that "the idea of introducing Negroes to civilization by means of Catholic metaphysics is an illusion."[4] In 1773 the Bishop of Angola complained of the urgent need for missionaries and the low quality of those who came from Lisbon. "Some come to seek their fortunes and pursue their own interests . . . others satisfy their passions . . . others flee from the discipline of their prelates. . . And from these greedy, lustful, expatriate, rebellious, and libertine men what else can be expected than the spread of vice and scandal in which this land is already buried."[5]

The shortage of missionaries was a constant problem in Angola and Moçambique. Even in the years when Portugal herself had a surplus of clergy, few were willing to risk ending their days, suddenly, in most cases, in Africa. The dedication of the Italian Capuchins in the Congo, of the Holy Ghost fathers in southern Angola, and even of the Protestants in the interior of Angola has been a cause for shame and envy — and sometimes inspiration — to many Portuguese.[6] But while the record of Portuguese missionaries as spiritual leaders of the African people and as educators has admittedly been spotty, where they have had sufficient funds and personnel, as in Moçambique at the end of the sixteenth century and in Angola in the first part of the seventeenth, their record compares favorably with what has been done in other parts of Africa.

In Moçambique the trajectory of Catholic mission work ran parallel to the political course of the colony, although in the period of decline along the Zambezi the clerical population suffered more acutely than the often opulent semi-independent *prazeros*. From 1506, and perhaps a year earlier, secular priests and representatives of various orders who had made their way from Portugal held services at Sofala and Moçambique. It was Portuguese custom to have, whenever possible, two priests at each large fortress in Africa and the East. The gradual penetration of the interior and up the Zambezi by Portuguese merchants and soldiers in the first half of the sixteenth century brought in its wake a small number of priests who began the work of evangelization among the Africans attracted to the European outposts. Until 1534 all fathers in Portuguese East Africa were under the jurisdiction of the Diocese of Funchal, but with the establishment of a bishopric in Goa in that year, supervision of the East African field now came from India. Among the celebrated names that have enriched the history of Moçambique was that of Saint Francis Xavier, who spent six months in 1541 and 1542 on the island, preaching and assisting in the relief hospital.

In 1560 two Jesuit fathers and a lay brother arrived in Moçambique. One of the priests was Gonçalo da Silveira, destined to become the most famous of Catholic missionaries in southern Africa. In 1556 his evangelical zeal had caused him to leave Lisbon where he had the reputation of being one of the city's most eloquent preachers. In India he waited restlessly for permission to lead a missionary expedition to the spiritually desolate lands of the Monomotapa of which he had heard on his journey east. Once back on the island of Moçambique, Father Silveira, disregarding suggestions from government officers, left for the mainland after less than a week. He spent seven weeks at the kraal of an African chief near the present site of Quelimane, where he converted the chief and five hundred of his subjects. But the great challenge for Gonçalo was still the lands of the Monomotapa, and leaving two fellow Jesuits in charge of the new mission he headed up the Zambezi. At Sena and Tete he resisted the blandishments of the Portuguese population and pushed on. Through the ministrations of Captain of the Gates António Caiado, he was extended a welcome to the Monomotapa's capital at Zimbabwe, which he reached at the end of the year.

Gaunt, fever-ridden, but driven by messianic intensity, Father Silveira set about his work. After twenty-five days of training in the Catholic faith, the Monomotapa, his favorite wife and his sister, and three hundred relatives and tribal leaders were baptized. Gonçalo's success with the royal family was his undoing. Swahili traders, seeing an end to their own influence over the impressionable chief, told the young African leader that Silveira had come to his territories as a spy, that he had secret powers of incantation and death. The potentate resolved to murder the missionary. Hearing of his plans, Caiado unsuccessfully tried to forestall them and went to warn Silveira. He found the missionary already aware of his fate. The priest held Mass for his Portuguese friends and went on with his work among the African tribesmen, baptizing on the next day some fifty villagers. That evening he was strangled in his sleep by seven men, who threw his body into the river. The impact of Silveira's death was enormous in Lisbon and the Catholic world. The subsequent Barreto expedition was in part designed to avenge his murder, and for a short while the attention of both Rome and Lisbon was centered on a distant African river.

Discouraged by the death of Father Silveira and the reluctance of their converts to put aside their native ways, Silveira's two companions returned to Goa in 1562. Seven years later two priests and two lay brothers from the Society took part in the ill-starred Barreto expedition, Father Monclaros being Barreto's principal adviser. When the expedition failed, so did the mission. Monclaros had little hope for effective work among the tribes of Zambézia, characterizing them as committed to their own tribal customs, unable and unwilling to understand the affairs of the soul. He saw clearly that missionary work on the Zambezi was a difficult and perhaps useless enterprise, and after 1570 the Jesuits temporarily abandoned their plans for Moçambique.

The Jesuits returned in 1607 more hopeful than the far-sighted Monclaros of converting the African. In that year two Jesuits came to Zambézia, and seven more priests arrived in 1610. Within five years they had constructed eight churches along the river up to Tete. For the rest of the century a handful of Jesuits were along the Zambezi; as explorers of the *sertão* and in trying to carry their faith to the remote recesses of the region they performed feats of exploration unequaled in Portuguese mission history. At their headquarters on Moçambique island they maintained a college from 1610 to 1760, although as a training center for local clergy it did not achieve the success of the famous Jesuit seminary at Goa or the college at Luanda. More than a theological center, it became a hospital and asylum.

It was inevitable that soon after their return the Jesuits would be in conflict with the Dominicans, who had come to dominate the mission field in Moçambique during the last thirty years of the previous century. The Dominicans angrily demanded that King Philip keep the Jesuits from Zambézia and the lands of the Monomotapa, asserting that they would only serve to confuse the work of conversion. Lisbon briefly entertained the notion of splitting the colony into various missionary districts, but since this solution was not viable the rivals were instructed to work in different parts of the province and avoid prolonged encounters. Since there were only three centers of Portuguese influence in Moçambique — the capital, Sena, and Tete — this instruction had little effect.

From the middle of the sixteenth century the Dominicans had moved through East Africa with great speed and energy. Along the coast from Sofala to Mombasa and throughout the lands of Zambézia and those in back of Sofala, in dangerous and pestilential country, they spread faith and empire. The Dominicans of this first impulsive stage were dedicated selfless men chosen carefully by the Congregation in

Lisbon. Wherever they could, the Dominicans adopted the tactic of working with the African chiefs; they tried to make each conversion a permanent decision and to this end educated the Africans in the faith they were to accept. By 1590 they stated they had baptized some twenty thousand Africans, a small figure only when compared with the ridiculously grandiose estimates from other Portuguese possessions and the New World. The Dominicans were entrenched at the court of the Monomotapa, into whose territory the headquarters of the order at Sena sent a steady flow of missionaries. The late sixteenth century was the brief apogee of Dominican work in Moçambique.

The church activities in Moçambique were periodically inspected by a *visitador* from Goa, but in 1612 the churches of the colony were removed from the jurisdiction of the Diocese of Goa and an independent ecclesiastical administration set up suffragan to the metropolitan see. The administrative vicar for Moçambique had all the secular powers of a bishop, although he remained a simple priest. The seat of the ecclesiastical government was at Sena until 1780, since the Zambezi was the scene of the most wide-spread mission efforts. In 1783 Moçambique was made a prelacy with a bishop *in partibus infidelium*.

The beginning of the missions' decline in Moçambique occurred about 1590 with the temporary debacle of Portuguese fortresses around Sena and Tete resulting from the raids of the Zimba. Several Dominicans were brutally murdered, and the rest abandoned the area. Once the panic had passed, the Dominicans, as well as the Jesuits and secular clergy, returned, but the impetus of the 1570's and 1580's was broken. Clergy from Portugal were now reluctant to go to a colony beset by both disease and hostile Africans. Goan Dominicans and secular priests were dispatched to help carry on the work; many of the new arrivals lacked zeal and scruples, and the Dominican authorities in India were openly accused of unloading their undesirables and failures in Africa. In spite of financial grants from the crown subsidizing in part the evangelical program, many of the missionaries devoted themselves more to personal gain than to the work of the church. Village churches had to be abandoned for lack of personnel and the churches in the larger towns were understaffed. In 1630 there were probably less than fifty priests in the entire colony. African villagers, without the guidance and encouragement of the white fathers, quickly lost the veneer of Christianity they possessed and reverted to their traditional ways. Some priests sorrowfully concluded that converting the African was a well-nigh impossible task. The inception of the overseas slave trade in the middle of the century was perhaps a final blow to the ambitions of the demoralized Portuguese clergy in Moçambique.

But the years were not without recompense, in terms of prestige at least, to the Dominicans. Responding to clerical diligence and political necessity, various African chiefs, the most important being the Monomotapa, submitted with their families to baptism; through most of the century the missionary fathers could count on the half-hearted support of the paramount chiefs, although the relationship was frequently jeopardized by the acts of the Zambezi *prazeros*. It was impossible, however, to take full advantage of these conversions, which were often a compromise with tribal traditions and not based on any genuine understanding or acceptance of Christianity. The Goan Dominicans, furthermore, were often content to use their association with the Monomotapa for their own devices. A number of the Monomotapa's sons, as well as other African youths, however, were persuaded to prepare themselves for the priesthood at the Dominican seminary in India. The majority of them, captivated by the cosmopolitan glitter of Goa or Cochin, remained in India; others who returned to upcountry Moçambique did not, from contemporary accounts, contribute notably to the anticipated spiritual progress of their land.

It was hoped that the arrival of missionaries from other orders and the addition of African priests would serve to bolster the diminishing number of Dominicans and Jeuits in the seventeenth century. Several small groups of Capuchins came to Moçambique in the first half of the century, but they were not able to withstand the colony's climate and withdrew. In 1681 eight friars from the order of São João de Deus took over the care of the Moçambique hospital from the Jesuits. At about the same time a royal decree ordering the establishment of a seminary on the island for the training of African youths was received; a conflict of interests between the Jesuits, Dominicans, and the Augustine administrator doomed the project to failure, even had it been possible at that late date to obtain sufficient staff and students. One of the main arguments in favor of the seminary was the need for bi-lingual priests, since only a few Europeans with long residence in the colony were prepared to carry on the work of Christianity without the doubtful services of a translator.

The decay which spread through Moçambique in the eighteenth century had its effect on the clergy as well as on the administrative and civilian population. The influx of Indian traders, Lisbon's erratic economic policies, and a general lack of interest in the colony threatened to eradicate European presence. The Portuguese in Moçambique, demoralized by the uncertainties, appeared to seek whatever security was contained in the accumulation of wealth. Few governors during the century were not accused of corruption and easy financial dealings, and lesser officials made their fortunes at the expense of the government or in violation of the law. In this milieu of laxity, the conduct of the Dominicans hardly offered a refreshing contrast. "Scandalous" is one of the milder epithets used against the order's conduct in the eighteenth and nineteenth centuries. "The Dominican friars [at Sena] . . . are violent and oppressive in their behavior. . . The promulgation of knowledge is most strenuously opposed by the priests as utterly subversive of their power, its strongest support being the ignorance of the people." [7] In violation of their vow of poverty, Dominicans in Zambézia held great tracts of land which they administered like any *prazero*, collecting head taxes and dealing in slaves. In addition to their commercial activity some Dominicans took over civil and administrative responsibilities. Although the dearth of Portuguese men in the interior resulted in the Dominicans' accepting such charges, and they did help maintain Portuguese sovereignty there, these activities were not always consistent with their missionary obligations. Some Jesuits also participated in agricultural and mining ventures along the river to the detriment of their one-time evangelical zeal. Missionaries from other orders and secular priests responded to the tenor of the times. The church was in effect confronted with a moral crisis in Moçambique; the occasional pompous processions which dazzled the African did not disguise the fact that the missionary spirit had been largely replaced by material values. The tumble-down churches at Sena and Tete and Quelimane attested not only to decline in missionary work but to the disappearance of its inspiration.

The Marquês de Pombal's quarrel with the Society of Jesus had its repercussions in Moçambique in 1759 when the nine Jesuit priests there were banished from the colony. The Jesuits in Moçambique deserved better of Pombal. Although they too had succumbed to the pervasive moral climate, the Jesuit fathers were more active than those of any other order. Their property was confiscated and sold at auction; the *prazos* reverted to the crown; the college at Moçambique became part of the governor's residence; their churches along the Zambezi were abandoned.

Toward the end of the century an ecclesiastical census of the colony revealed the following: Moçambique island had a cathedral, one parish church, two chapels, the monastery of São João de Deus, the Dominican monastery, the former Jesuit church of Saint Francis

Xavier, and a clergy of six priests and five lay brothers; Mossuril had three parish churches and two priests; Sofala, one church and one Dominican; the parishes of Quelimane and Sena, six churches and three priests; Manica, one parish church and a chapel entrusted to the care of two Dominicans; Tete, three churches and two clerics; Zumbo, Lourenço Marques, Querimba, and Amiza, each a church and a priest. Such was the physical extent of Christianity in Moçambique, and the spiritual influence of the church did not extend far beyond these points. An estimate of some years earlier had put the total number of Christians in the province at 2,141, a figure which slowly decreased as the century came to its close, since priests were now baptizing only those Africans in mortal danger. Not even the slaves on the estates were being indoctrinated.

If mission affairs were bad in the eighteenth century they were calamitous in the first half of the nineteenth. Along the Zambezi only a vestige of Christianity remained, and on the island the situation was not much better. In 1825 the number of clerics in the province was ten, seven of whom were Goan. The Liberal government's decree of 1834 abolishing religious orders had little meaning for Moçambique, since by then they were virtually extinct in the colony. The lands of the Dominicans, who had more *prazos* than priests to manage them, were confiscated and handed over to local captains major.

In 1843 the Portuguese government had some second thoughts on the traditional role of the church in African affairs and set about shoring up the dilapidated missionary program. Aware of the unwillingness of the metropolitan clergy to serve in Moçambique, the government sent an urgent appeal to the Archbishop of Goa to speed priests to East Africa, but the archbishop was obliged to reply that a similar reluctance prevailed in India. In some years there was not a single missionary in the interior and only three or four along the coast. In the 1850's the government by a series of recommendations attempted to collect ten African youths to be educated at seminaries in Santarem and Goa, but the measures failed for lack of candidates. Bartle Frere, writing to the Archbishop of Canterbury in the early 1870's, remarks on the scarcity of Portuguese priests in the colony; of the few he encountered he could not "learn that it was considered any part of their duty to attempt Missionary work among the Africans." [8]

The slow upturn in the ecclesiastical fortunes of Moçambique came in 1875 with the arrival of three priests from the College of Portuguese Overseas Missions at Sernache do Bonjardim. The college had been organized in the 1840's to train missionaries for the colonies to replace those from outlawed orders. The college functioned until

1911; more than three hundred of its graduates went overseas. Its graduates faced difficulties in the early years of their work in Moçambique. The atmosphere was hostile, and the task of repairing the desolation wrought by two hundred years of negligence and decay almost impossible. At first they lived among the Europeans in the colony, helping in the several hospitals and teaching rudimentary letters to the children of the towns. In the last decade of the century, under the driving inspiration of António Barroso, prelate of Moçambique, the religious reconquest of the interior was cautiously undertaken, although a large-scale campaign for converting the African population was to be delayed for many years by the usual lack of funds and clergy and by the delays in the military pacification of unsettled areas. In spite of the frequent animosity of governors and district officials, the number of missions and parishes increased. By 1910 seventy-one Catholic missionaries were engaged in Moçambique, thirty-six from the college at Sernache.

The remainder of the priests were either secular or from various orders, once again in legal operation. In 1881 the Jesuits made a reappearance; four members of the Society accompanied Paiva de Andrade to Moçambique. From then until 1910, when the establishment of the Portuguese Republic produced a wave of anticlericalism resulting again in the dissolution of religious houses in Portugal and the second deportation of the Jesuits, more than one hundred members of the Society, Portuguese and foreign, were active throughout the colony. They were joined in 1898 by the Franciscans, who made important contributions to Moçambique's primitive, almost nonexistent educational system.

When the Jesuits left Moçambique they turned over their missions to German Friars of the Divine Word who ran them until the First World War. The Germans were but a part of a number of foreign Catholic missionaries invited or attracted to Portuguese East Africa at the beginning of the twentieth century. Among the first were five White Fathers who were subsidized by the Portuguese government. A few Salesian priests brought their educational talents to the colony from 1907 to 1913, when their schools in the Moçambique district were given to civilian teachers. Several Trappists from Natal briefly served in the province. After the end of the war, to Niassa came — uninvited — French fathers of the Monfort Congregation and a few Consolate Italian friars. The nationalism of the Portuguese was sorely tried by the abrupt appearance of these missionaries, but the need for priests and teachers of any nationality to aid in the occupation of the country was too great for them to be rejected.

The fifteen-year span of the Portuguese Republic was not the easiest period for the Catholic missionary. From 1911 to 1919 Catholic missions were banned in the colonies, but the Republic never got around to setting up more than a handful of its lay mission schools, and in 1919 the need for their services was such that they were allowed to return. The Catholic priests sometimes had the experience of being subjected to administrative harassments. Brito Camacho, High Commissioner of Moçambique in the 1920's, accused them of selling themselves, making ridiculous teachers, and even of running a lottery in Lourenço Marques, "bought by a father from a Durban Jew." Camacho vowed that he would never give the assistance of his government to a mission program which did no more than catechize the African.[9]

Where the Dominicans dominated the mission scene in East Africa, in Angola the Jesuits were all-powerful, and in the Congo kingdom, the Italian Capuchins. As the way of life on the Zambezi *prazos* counteracted and corroded the aspirations of the missions, so in Angola the demands of the slave trade made a sincere evangelization of the African impossible, although on neither coast could the *prazo* or the slave trade be assigned full responsibility for the collapse of the church's work. Another difference was that Angola had a much higher percentage of African clergy than did Moçambique — in part a testimonial to auspicious beginnings in the Congo. On the other hand, there were no Goan priests in West Africa; missionaries arriving from Brazil were exclusively Portuguese.

Long after Portugal had dismissed the Congo as a major area of interest in Africa, the missionary activity begun there before 1500 continued with undiminished, perhaps increased, fervor under the charge of the Capuchins. Even before their arrival in the 1640's the Portuguese Catholic Church had not given up entirely. After 1570 the Dominican order kept three to five fathers there; several Franciscans and Discalced Carmelites carried the gospel to the Congo until the first decade of the seventeenth century, when the bad humor of the Manicongo forced them to abandon the field. The Jesuits, after their initial disappointments in the middle of the previous century, returned to São Salvador in 1614. In 1624 the college sponsored by a Luanda philanthropist began operation, but in the morally turgid climate of the Congo capital its contribution was slight. Young African men were slow to enroll, and by 1640 only two priests were left at the college. In 1669, following spasmodic attempts to invigorate its program, the Society left the Congo in order to concentrate its efforts in Luanda.

The creation of the Diocese of the Congo and Angola in 1596 was intended to bolster sagging Portuguese influence. The honor, it was hoped, would impart new luster to the Manicongo's court, draw him closer into the orbit of Portuguese influence, and help reconcile his quarrels with the great chiefs of the land. The principal offices of the bishopric were held by European clergy, the majority of the lesser offices by African priests educated in Lisbon or São Salvador. The elevation of the Congo, like so many other projects for the region, did not achieve its desired goal. Bishop Manuel Baptista, writing to the king in 1612, complained of the profitless sacrifice made by European fathers in the unhealthy climate amidst a people so variable in their faith. Many there were who labored for evil purposes, few for the good. He reproached the African canons who, allying themselves with Spanish and Dutch alike, opposed the work of the Portuguese priests and undermined Portugal's prestige.[10] In the abandonment of São Salvador by Europeans in the first part of the seventeenth century the Bishop and his aides participated. More often than not the actual seat of the bishopric was Luanda, and after 1676 no bishop sat at São Salvador.

One of the consequences of the Manicongo Dom Alvaro II's embassy to Rome in 1608 to plead for more missionaries was the creation in 1620 of the Apostolic Prefecture of the Congo. This the Vatican entrusted to Italian Capuchin friars who were to work under the authority of the Bishop of the Congo. The first mission leaving Rome in 1640 was blocked in Lisbon by the newly proclaimed government of Portugal. But another mission bypassed Lisbon, obtained authorization from the king of Spain, and arrived in the Congo in 1645 — an act of defiance to Portugal's priority in the Congo. Impressed by the great number of baptisms made by the Capuchins shortly after their arrival (calculations ran as high as fifteen thousand a year, the distinction between baptism and true conversion being somewhat blurred), the Pope sent a new group of missionaries to the Congo in 1648, fourteen friars, mostly Spaniards and Flemish, the latter chosen because of their ability to communicate in Dutch to the captors of Luanda. In the same year the proposal was made by the Propaganda Fide in Rome to send, at the expense of the king of Spain, an archbishop, two bishops, and thirty missionaries, all Spanish or Italian, to follow up such auspicious beginnings. Portugal had resented the earlier violation of her traditional rights of Catholic patronage in the Congo, and quite naturally João IV protested this new infringement of Portuguese privilege. The victory of Salvador de Sá restored João's sovereignty over Angola and the Congo at a timely moment; now he had more persuasive arguments. The following year João bluntly ordered the Capuchins to declare their fidelity to Portugal or be expelled. Under duress the Capuchins yielded, and in 1650–1651 several of them took up residence in Luanda and Massangano to begin mission work in Angola.

The relations of the Capuchins, the majority of them Italians, with Portuguese administrators were reasonably harmonious. They talked enthusiastically of a Christian Congo kingdom, envisioned more than a century before by Manuel and Afonso I. By 1655 about thirty friars, divided almost equally between the Congo and Angola, maintained eight mission stations in the two regions. A short five years later, the inevitable reaction had begun. Only fifteen priests now remained, many of them having a decided preference for the more civilized, reputedly healthier lands of Angola.

Since reinforcements from Europe arrived slowly, the Capuchins began to think in terms of an African clergy, but plans for the establishment of a seminary collapsed and plans to send likely African candidates to Rome were regarded skeptically by the Portuguese, who have always held that, whenever possible, African youths should be educated in Portuguese by Portuguese. But Portuguese opposition was not primarily responsible for the Capuchins' failure to bring large numbers of Africans into the priesthood. Principally the failure was the result of their inability to create Christian communities in the interior which might have supplied the candidates necessary for the success of their plans. Isolated stations in the bush run by several priests whose strength was sapped by malaria and dysentery were not enough. Mass baptism added only to impressive statistics. Intertribal wars and the ravages of the slave trade produced chaos where there should have been tranquillity. Against such a background it was not surprising that neither Italian Capuchins nor Portuguese Jesuits could create an adequate African clergy in a European image.

The fortunes of the Capuchins ebbed and flowed during the rest of the century. A number of stations were maintained in the back country, and there were usually several Capuchins in Luanda, but the mission work did not expand. The eighteenth-century missionary endeavor of the Capuchins in Angola and the Congo is a familiar story. For whole decades the work was abandoned or entrusted to one or two fathers. The arrival in the 1770's of a dozen Capuchins did not stay, and scarcely postponed, the final attrition. The Franciscan monk, João de Miranda, who went to São Salvador in 1781 was shocked at its collapse and the spiritual impoverishment of its inhabitants. He remarks that there had been no priest there for eighteen years.[11] By 1800 the work of the Capuchins in Angola was, for practical purpose, at an end. For those who hold that the Portuguese have been inadequate missionaries in Africa, the results achieved by more than four hundred foreign Capuchin friars in the Congo and Angola during a period of almost two hundred years offer an interesting failure for comparison.

The Capuchins were diligent men usually selected with care by their superiors for West African assignments. Although they preferred Angola to the Congo, the Capuchins were willing to serve for long years of isolation in the heart of the Congo backcountry. They were known to deal in slaves and to work them; otherwise, their record was probably the best of any mission order working in Africa until the present century. The total of their baptisms was fantastic: 100,000 by one priest from 1645 to 1666; 1,750 by another in forty days; 13,000 by Friar Giacinto di Bologna in 1747; 340,000 baptisms and 50,000 marriages by the Capuchins together from 1677 to 1700. Critics scoff at these overblown figures, arguing that the Capuchins operated almost no catechism schools and that few of them knew the native languages. For these reasons and because there were no missionary sisters to educate the African woman, they say that the Capuchins built on sand. It is true also that the colonial government was not always helpful, although on occasions Portugal did provide subsidies. But the failure of the Capuchins — and the failure of all other missions in Portuguese Africa from 1500 to 1900 — rested on deeper reasons than these or climate, scanty personnel, and doubtful techniques of evangelization. The principal reason was that the missionary offered nothing to the African but a disembodied doctrine, many of whose disciplines were distinctly distasteful. Where were the superior advantages of European civilization which went with this faith? They were not found in the slave trade, in the armed incursions in the interior, in the example of the Portuguese traders who often led a life more African than European. Nowhere except in Luanda was Portugal able to transplant a European way of life, and only in a few other areas was her military power permanently convincing. Without other cultural stimuli the convictions of a few good men, haltingly expressed, and the example of monastic existence could never have prevailed against the suspicions and indifference of an African population having its own traditions, whose passing associations with other Europeans were largely violent.

When Paulo Dias reached Luanda in 1575 he found that a small chapel had been constructed on the island by the several score Portuguese who lived or traded there. Occasional services were held by priests from the São Tomé ships. When the city was moved to the mainland, a parish church and a Jesuit residence were among the first buildings to go up. Within the town itself the members of the Society accompanying Dias baptized numerous Africans, but possibly remembering their trying sojourn in the Congo they limited their activities to the area close to Luanda. Only with the spread of Portuguese arms up the Cuanza did the Jesuits penetrate the interior of Angola. But they remained, and about half of the twenty-five Jesuits going to Angola up to 1593 perished there.

The missionary thrust of the Jesuits into the hinterland was of short duration. Luanda offered excellent possibilities for the unique talents of the Society, and from 1600 they concentrated their activities there, dominating, in the eyes of their contemporaries, life in the capital. Their most notable contribution was the Jesuit college which educated many Africans, mulattoes, and Portuguese throughout most of the seventeenth century. From this college emerged both a native clergy and a half-caste administrative class. The educated mulattoes formed most of Luanda's lesser bureaucracy, to the discomfiture of the white residents who chose to hold them responsible for most of the colony's problems. The Jesuits became the center of controversy. They tried to create for themselves the role they played so successfully in parts of South America, that of protector of the indigenous peoples. The economy of Angola being founded on the slave trade — in which the Jesuits participated — their pretensions brought them into immediate conflict with both governors and local residents who considered the Jesuits as meddlers and hypocritical trouble-makers. Frequent were the recriminations to Lisbon against their arrogance. Enemies of the Jesuits argued that members of the Society were often more engaged in commerce than in catechizing Africans and that although they received a substantial royal subsidy, they were getting rich from real-estate transactions, from the lands under their protection, and from the slave trade. The Jesuits *were* active in the shameful traffic; most of those in Angola subscribed to the prevalent belief that the best way to convert the Negro was to sell him so that he might be introduced to Christianity through work on American plantations. Several ships belonging to the Society were engaged in the Angola-Brazil commerce.

The Jesuits were joined in Luanda by Tertiaries of Saint Francis who assisted in educational work and hospital care. In the interior secular priests generally attended the spiritual needs of the fortresses. In the seventeenth and later centuries evangelization in the Angola hinterland was entrusted for the most part to secular priests — and the Capuchins — in contrast to Moçambique where the Dominicans dominated Zambézia.

The Dutch occupation of Luanda brought a halt to Portuguese missionary labors. In the capital, schools and monasteries were closed; in the interior, many posts had to be abandoned in the face of resurgent African enmity. After the liberation the restoration of the program offered many difficulties, which the colonial and metropolitan governments tried to help overcome by financial assistance. The shortage of priests was in part met by the influx of Capuchins and eight Discalced Carmelites. The Jesuits extended their activities up the Cuanza and sent several of their order further into the interior. Dominican friars appeared in Angola from time to time, but it was Portuguese and African secular priests who continued to bear the main responsibility for the Angola hinterland. By the end of the century the situation was barely equivalent to that existing in 1640. The sixty missionaries in the colony, half secular and half from various orders, appeared to have lost some of their ardor, and complaints about their conduct began to mount.

In 1716 the seat of the bishopric was officially transferred to Luanda, thus confirming the reality of the past sixty years. At this time there were in Angola, excluding the Congo, about twenty-five chapels or parish churches scattered through the interior each with a priest of its own. The Jesuits continued to be the most influential order in the colony. Their college was again in operation, and on their enlarged estates they sought to train their African charges in the simple ways of Christian society — although it was not unknown for some of their pupils to be dispatched to Brazil in the hold of a slaver. Most of the craftsmen in Angola now came from the small Jesuit factories and training schools. The Capuchins were going through another critical period. Their enthusiasm for life in the distant bush had begun to wane, and there were but six friars in Angola in 1693. Other orders also shunned the deep interior, preferring to make their contribution in the vicinity of Luanda, where they kept schools and a hospital. The colonial government continued to make valuable grants of land to the various orders to supplement the royal subsidy, and in a financial sense the missionary orders in Angola did not come upon the hard times suffered by their colleagues in Moçambique. But the work of the secular clergy in the interior did suffer from lack of funds. In many years the royal treasury gave nothing, and without the land which provided a fairly steady income to the orders the secular clergy were hard pressed — unless they chose, which happened with increasing frequency, to take part in the commerce of the region.

In the middle of the eighteenth century the deterioration accelerated. As the wealth of the congregations grew, their zeal flagged; hardly a Jesuit or Franciscan left Luanda for the backcountry. So the loss to Angola with the expulsion of the Jesuits was educational; their evangelizing was scarcely missed. The college, however, and the training schools were of some value to Angola, since they were the only centers of enlightenment, albeit dim, in the colony. Whatever failings the Jesuits had, it may be said that they were on occasions the conscience of Angola and the only mitigating force between the African and his oppressors. Even that harsh critic of Catholic practices in Portuguese Africa, David Livingstone, had praise for their accomplishments.

By 1800 there were nine or ten fathers and perhaps twenty-five parish priests, half of them Angolans, in the province. The sixteen churches standing in the interior were for the most part not regularly attended. The African clergy was half-educated, although more dedicated than the old-time Portuguese who had succumbed to inertia and spiritual sloth. Missionary functions were by now a formality, the continuation of a habit started long ago and kept alive through an ill-defined passive sense of responsibility. The African, if he paid any attention to the vague gestures toward his conversion, was progressively less influenced by the presence of itinerant fathers, even when they were of his own people. Nevertheless, Angola, principally because of a constant small number of young African men taking vows, was in a better position than Moçambique when religious orders were disbanded in 1834. But by the middle of the century in all of Angola there were to be found five priests, two in the capital, two in the Luanda parish, and one in Benguela.

Unable to obtain Portuguese priests to go to Angola, the Lisbon government made overtures to the Capuchins, who refused to return to the familiar scene. The offices of the Propaganda Fide in 1865 proposed French fathers of the Order of the Holy Ghost. Aware of the growing European interest in Africa, Portugal reacted coolly, as she had done in the seventeenth century to the Capuchins' request, to the suggestion of accepting priests who, although avowedly responsible to the Holy See, were probably more French than Catholic in their sentiments. Portugal spoke of the arrangement whereby the Capuchins had remained in Angola as dependents of the Holy See but under the jurisdiction of the Bishop of the Congo. On these conditions the first

Holy Ghost missionaries were admitted to Angola. After fifteen years of Portuguese suspicion and French truculence, rife with minor incidents and recriminations, a fruitful association began to develop. The Portuguese government gave the order free transportation to West Africa, free entry privileges, and later, direct financial help. For its part, the Holy Ghost mission has probably done more for Angola than any other missionary group, with the possible exception of several Protestant boards. Outspoken defenders of the African, they have had frequent brushes with colonial administrators. They were among the first European inhabitants of southern Angola and have contributed to its development; most of the schools and infirmaries in that part of the colony were established by the Holy Ghost mission. Their trade schools have helped produce the small nucleus of African artisans. On another front the Holy Ghost fathers, under the gifted guidance of their most famous Angolan missionary, Father Duparquet, took over the training of African secular clergy in the last two decades of the nineteenth century. Although the number of graduates was not large then, or afterwards, from their main seminary at Huíla, they helped tide the church through its critical years.

From 1875 secular priests from Sernache do Bonjardin joined the handful of missionaries stationed in Angola. The graduates from the overseas mission college, most of whom served as parish priests, set about rebuilding the ruined churches and drawing the African into the European community. Their work was slow, complicated by extreme poverty, and limited at first to a few key spots in the province: São Salvador, Novo Redondo, Caxito, Dondo, Golungo Alto, Duque de Bragança. The most important work was done at São Salvador do Congo by that most remarkable missionary in Angola's history, Father António Barroso, to whose labors is owed the regeneration of Portuguese mission work in Angola and Moçambique. Arriving in 1881 at the scene of one of Portugal's greatest overseas religious triumphs — the court of Afonso I — he patiently swept away the neglect of centuries in preparation for the spiritual and political reoccupation of the Congo. At São Salvador he erected, in addition to the chapel, a school and hospital, an observatory, and a work farm. Out from the ancient Congo capital he established small village schools run by Africans whom he had trained. What Father Barroso accomplished in the few years of his residence in the Congo was, by previous standards of missionary efforts in Angola, miraculous. An energetic man himself, Barroso saw no inconsistency between Christian teaching and the obligation of the Negro to the work. Reverting to one of the classic defenses of slavery, that through labor the savage may achieve a state of Chris-

tian civilization — a notion once more becoming popular in Portuguese colonial thought — Barroso saw the emergence of the African
coming not from a literary education, but from a practical training in
agriculture and manual crafts. In preparing the African for his role in
Angolan society, Barroso believed that the missionary was of primary
importance both to his church and the state.

Several orders, notably the Benedictines, sent a few fathers to
Angola in these years. In 1881 sisters of Saint Joseph of Cluny went
to Luanda and later to Moçâmedes where they operated schools for
the instruction of women. Other nuns followed to assist in the health
and educational programs in the larger Angolan towns. In 1900 there
were more than 125 priests, nuns, and lay brothers working in Angola,
and by 1911 missionary activity was sufficiently revitalized to withstand the effects of the war and the legislation of the new Portuguese
Republic. The lay missions intended by the Republic to replace the
religious missions had only faltering existence from 1913 to 1919, and
since the latter date the church evangelical has had steady expansion
throughout the colony.

When the writings and personality of David Livingstone dramat-
ically centered the popular attention of Europe and America on
Africa, the response of the Protestant churches to the apparent need
for an extension of missionary services in southern Africa was almost
immediate. Angola and Moçambique, scenes of much of Livingstone's
travels as well as targets for his antislavery sentiments, attracted their
share of European and North American evangelists. The first contacts between the Portuguese and members of what many of them
regarded as an alien, if not heretical, faith were not always pleasant.
In the troubled years of the late nineteenth century the Lisbon and
colonial governments looked upon the Protestants as advance scouts
for territorial adventures by her neighbors in Africa, principally the
English. The Portuguese were not without justification in their suspicions. The Universities' Mission to the Shire highlands had resulted
in the loss of a part of Niassa which Portugal had long held to be
hers. Rhodes had made adroit use of missionary penetration to push
his claims in doubtful areas. Even the Holy Ghost fathers in Angola
had made ambiguous remarks about French sovereignty in regions
bordering the Congo River which were traditionally in the Portuguese sphere of influence. These incidents, plus others real and
imagined, and Portugal's inherent insularity — a sentiment also present in the empire — hardened her attitude toward foreigners in her

African provinces. The period 1885–1890, the years of the Conference of Berlin and the British ultimatum of 1890, were the worst. The Portuguese were overcome by such a hysteria of suspicion that they distrusted their leaders and distrusted themselves. The sense of self-conscious weakness of this period further contributed to Portugal's preternatural fears for Angola and Moçambique.

Nevertheless, Portugal has honored in substance her obligations under those international or bi-lateral treaties to which she was party. The Berlin Act of 1885, the Brussels Act of 1890, the Anglo-Portuguese Treaty of 1891, and the Treaty of St. Germain-en-Laye of 1919 all contain provisos for the freedom of religious movement in the African colonies, subject to national security and order. This does not mean, of course, that Protestants in Portuguese East and West Africa have always been free from annoyances, legal obstructions, and occasional sharper conflicts with the colonial administration (in fact, the Protestant missions in Moçambique today are suffering what may only be called religious persecution). One of the most vexing issues in the early twentieth century was a series of decrees establishing Portuguese as the required language in all mission instruction. On the other hand, some Protestant missionaries misused their position during the early years of their residence in Portuguese territory by fomenting disaffection among the Africans. Even the period when the Republic was in power did not completely reduce the friction between the two faiths, in spite of the fact that the Lisbon government made a startling offer to help subsidize Protestant mission work. Friction still exists, in part because the Portuguese have chosen sometimes to set up Catholic churches and missions near Protestant centers, and is bound to increase when an African consciousness becomes a serious factor in Angola and Moçambique. Up to now, it has created problems but not impossibilities for the Protestants, the majority of whom have earned the admiration of the local administration for their services and dedication, although they have not dispelled the basic antagonism toward their faith.

There have been a variety of Protestant groups engaged in the two provinces since 1880.[12] The most important work in Angola has been done by the group formed of the American Board of Commissioners for Foreign Missions and the United Church of Canada, by the Methodist Episcopal Church, and by the Brethren's Mission. The distinction of being the first, however, is reserved for the English Baptist Missionary Society. The Society, stimulated by Stanley's explorations of the Congo River, sent two men in 1878 to investigate the area as a possible mission field. Finding it hard to pass beyond São

Salvador toward Stanley Pool, Messrs. Comber and Grenfell set up a small station at the old Congo capital. Because of its poverty and the keen competition of Father Barroso, the Society's progress has been relatively slow. By 1930 they had three stations in the Portuguese Congo, a hospital, and numerous schools.

In 1880 three members of the American Board, one of them a Negro, arrived in Benguela from Lisbon to begin a meritorious missionary program among the Ovimbundu of the Benguela highlands, work in which they were joined six years later by the United Church of Canada. The first station was at Bailundo. Their initial years in this unoccupied part of Angola were uncertain because of the turbulence resulting from the military pacification of the *planalto* and from the rubber boom which kept the upcountry in a state of unrest until the period of the First World War. From that time onward, the growth of the combined missions has been phenomenal. The headquarters at Dondi has become the largest mission station in Angola. In 1930, over 90,000 African Christians were carried on the missions lists and the number was being swelled by 5,000 a year. Five hundred and fifty schools, including two theological and training schools on a secondary level, taught 25,000 students. The school for boys at Dondi, Currie Institute, founded in 1914, is famed as a model institution for the education of African youths.

Throughout the highlands at main missions and outstations the almost one hundred members of the joint American and Canadian Board have worked with the Africans, helping them build modest churches and schools and training an African staff to maintain them. As opposed to most Portuguese Catholic missionaries in Africa, who tend to view the African as a child, the members of the Board, like most Protestant missionaries in Angola, approach him as an adult citizen of his own world. He is treated with equal respect, not good-natured tolerance. Mutual participation in the work of the missions involves mutual responsibility. In this respect it is possible that the Protestants are building more solidly than did the Jesuits and Capuchins and that in the total absence of white leadership the work of the Protestant boards would continue.

In the field of education and scholarship the missionaries of the combined Board have made outstanding contributions. Men like Dr. Walter Currie, Dr. John Tucker, and Dr. Gladwyn Childs have added signally to African pedagogy and anthropology. Members of the Board have created a small Christian literature in Umbundu translation. The hospital at Dondi attracts patients from every part of the colony.

The work of the Methodist Episcopal Church in Angola is noteworthy for its early struggles and for the remarkable growth the program has undergone in recent years. Begun in 1885 by the extraordinary Bishop William Taylor of Africa, it has been located in Luanda and the interior toward Malange. In all of Angolan history no missionary group suffered more than the members of Bishop Taylor's self-supporting missions. To read the Angolan correspondence of the 1880's and 1890's in Bishop Taylor's *African News* is to realize again how cruel Africa could be to the foolish and unprepared. Not all of the Bishop's missionaries had his stamina (when over seventy, he averaged eighteen to twenty miles a day traveling through the bush on foot), and the missionaries and their families died with pathetic monotony, in spite of the reportedly healthful air of Malange and Pungo Andongo. Self-supporting missions, though ardently championed by Taylor for their economic opportunities, were folly in Angola — as they were along most of the coast. They made a little money but few converts, since the major exertions of the missionaries went into lumber mills and farms.

In 1897 the Methodist Board of Foreign Missions took over what remained of the Angolan mission personnel and stations. Possibly because of its impecunious beginnings, the evangelical work of the American Methodists was discouraging for a number of years. In the first third of the century there were instances of considerable friction between some of the missionaries and the Portuguese administration, the issues being based on Portuguese fears of denationalization of the African and the missionaries' resentment at government restrictions on their teaching methods. But these frictions have largely disappeared and with the emergence at the main station of Quessua of boarding schools, a hospital, and shops, and with an increase in the number of outstations, the progress of the Methodist program has been rapid.

In terms of numbers of missionaries in Angola, the Brethren have been the largest in the Protestant field. Under the leadership of Frederick Stanley Arnot — whose goal was to carry the gospel to Central Africa in the footsteps of Livingstone — the Brethren came to Angola in 1890. Within a few years they had set up missions in most of Bié. Later they pushed west and northwest into the Lunda territory toward the Katanga and Rhodesian frontier. Instead of constructing a large central mission like the ones at Dondi or Quessua, the Brethren preferred to maintain a number of smaller stations and schools in remote parts of the interior. James Johnston, who visited several of their missions shortly after the Brethren entered Angola, was not impressed with their techniques. He said the natives scorned them, that they held services only for themselves, and spent the rest of the time in their gardens or hunting.[13] The Brethren gradually lost their resemblance to Bishop Taylor's self-supporting missions of which Johnston was also critical. By 1932 they had fourteen central stations and about one thousand outstations or posts regularly visited.

Whether this type of missionary work or the central plant surrounded by lesser stations is the more effective way of reaching the African has been the subject of much controversy. Defenders of the small-mission program say that it is the only satisfactory way of making direct contact with the people. On the other hand, only in the large mission can there be a concentration of medical and educational facilities. One of the casualties of twentieth-century specialization seems to be the old-time bush missionary who went forth to evangelize armed only with the Gospel and a rifle, and it may be that the fate of the small mission will be that of these rugged individualists.

The other Protestant missions in Angola have been relatively small, with the exception of the South Africa General Mission which extended its work to Angola in 1914. Most of its efforts have been in the large isolated corner of the province bordered by Northern Rhodesia and South-West Africa. The Mission Philafricaine was an independent mission founded by Heli Chatelain, a Swiss scholar and linguist of international fame, in 1897. Chatelain had worked with Bishop William Taylor and tried to keep the ideal of self-supporting missions, a task in which he was not spectacularly successful. After his death the three stations of the mission were maintained by artisan missionaries. In northern coastal Angola and the Cabinda enclave, the Angola Evangelical League (1897) and the Christian and Missionary Alliance (1910), both nondenominational, have prevailed in the face of Portuguese hostility and limited funds. The small North Angola Mission, also nondenominational, has built a model little Christian community near Uige to the admiration of Portuguese and Africans. Founded in 1925 by a Swiss and an Englishman, by 1932 it had built four outchurches. The Seventh Day Adventists have also been active in Angola, principally in the Benguela plateau. Their well-known reserve has kept them out of the informal Protestant missionary alliance, a co-ordinating council created to deal with the Portuguese government, and they are distrusted by the colonial government.

The Protestant missions have served the general welfare of the colony. Any hospital or school is a welcome addition in underdeveloped Angola; when these are first-rate institutions, as several of the mission establishments are, they perform inestimable services to the African community. By European or American standards the proportion of hospitals and dispensaries, for example, to the needs of the population of the province is discouragingly small, but when one realizes that in the 1920's and 1930's over half of all such medical services available to the African were run by missionaries, and of this total more than 30 per cent by Protestant missions, one begins to understand the nature of their contribution to at least a small part of the indigenous peoples. The same percentages will hold true of schools, although a higher proportion of schools are in Catholic hands, the Portuguese being generally more apt to subsidize the salvation of the soul than of the body. In these two fields Protestant labors have wrought impressive results.[14]

On the troublesome issue of contract labor the Protestant missionaries have stood in not always silent rebuke to the extreme practices of the colonial administration, becoming involved more than once with angry Portuguese authorities who felt their hospitality outraged by this improper interest in the African's welfare. It is possible that the presence of the Protestant missions has helped soften to a slight degree these abuses. Certainly their attitude toward the problem has been one of the reasons why the official reception of their work has been politely reserved. The main reason is of course the historic animosity of the Portuguese Catholic Church toward those of any other persuasion, an attitude that has strengthened during the Salazar regime. This sentiment has made impossible any substantial co-operation between the two churches in Angola.

Protestant mission work in Moçambique has not been as successful as in Angola. The inaccessibility of the highland regions, the priority of Catholic missions along the Zambezi, the hostility of Portuguese administrators in the 1880's and 1890's to any suggestion of English expansion, and the Moslem penetration in the north of the colony have limited Protestant efforts to the area between Delagoa Bay and the mouth of the Zambezi.

The American Board in 1879 decided to extend its Zulu mission into the Gaza district, but after many difficulties the project was abandoned in 1889 and the Board's representative, Mr. E. H. Richards, was transferred to the Methodist Episcopal mission which had just been established at Inhambane. The Methodist mission has been in existence since 1889–1890 and gradually pushed into the near interior from Inhambane. In 1885 the Free Methodists had begun working in the same town, but a temporary suspension of their program and a serious clash with the local government have curtailed any vigorous expansion. The Wesleyan Missionary Society operated in the Delagoa Bay area in the 1880's and 1890's under native African auspices; in the early 1900's a modest program directed by white missionaries was begun. The Anglican Church established several small stations in the vicinity of Lourenço Marques; on Likoma Island near the Portuguese shore of Lake Nyasa the Universities' Mission maintained an outstation which in 1911 was instrumental in precipitating a bitter dispute between England and Portugal.[15]

The most important Protestant group in Moçambique has been the Swiss Mission which came there in 1881. Its work has been mostly confined to the Lourenço Marques district. Members of the Swiss Mission have taken a keen anthropological interest in African culture; Henri Junod's distinguished studies on Moçambique tribes are the work of one of the Swiss Mission's foremost leaders. The Mission also has the distinction of being the Protestant group least admired by Portuguese officials in Moçambique. Outspokenly critical of Portuguese native policy, they have often brought down on their heads the charge that they stir up rebellious tendencies in the Africans. Mousinho de Albuquerque held them at least indirectly responsible for the revolts of 1894; for Mousinho all Protestants were to be distrusted because they confused the African by standing for something different, and their theories of equality and their support of black against white made them dangerous and untrustworthy.[16] A similar view was held for a long time by the Portuguese administration of the British-capitalized Moçambique Company which kept Protestant missionaries from most of its territory. Until recent years, however, the Moçambique government has treated Protestant missions in the province in much the same manner as they have been received in Angola — with discreet tolerance broken by sporadic unpleasant incidents.

As in Angola much of the limited medical and educational work carried on in Moçambique during the first third of the century was by Protestants. From 1919 to 1930, when the government forced them to close it, the Swiss Mission ran in Lourenço Marques one of the colony's two secondary schools. At Kambini the Methodist Episcopal board established a training school for African men; with its model village and agricultural school, the center has been hailed by Portuguese administrators as the best school of its kind in the province. The same mission has also maintained several schools for girls. The Free Methodists set up two boarding schools and several primary schools in the bush. Some of the major medical services have also been the work of Protestant missions. The Lembombo Mission has staffed a hospital on the coast south of Beira, and the Methodist Episcopal mission at Inhambane, a hospital with a nurse's training center. The Swiss Mission at Lourenço Marques and near Vila de João Belo have maintained two hospitals and several dispensaries. Other missions have also established small hospitals and dispensaries. As with schools, the number of medical centers has been pathetically inadequate, but even the slightest help has been a contribution to the woefully neglected hinterland of Portuguese East Africa.

The success of either Protestant or Catholic missionaries in creating an indigenous church in Angola and Moçambique is, as Dr. Childs observes, still debatable.[17] Statistics of baptism or membership do not give a truly adequate picture. One need do no more than compare the impressive figures sent to Rome by the Capuchins in the middle of the seventeenth century with descriptions of the religious state of the Congo one and two hundred years later. The greatest of all missionary teachers, the Jesuits, left only a trace of their influence on the African in Angola, the ability of a few to read and speak a fragmentary Portuguese. Of Dominican labors on the Zambezi nothing was left.

It is obvious that the work of the Christian missionary can no longer accomplish much either in a vacuum or proceeding antagonistically to the political and economic course of an area. In this respect the traditional Portuguese concept of a militant church and state has real significance, although like so many other colonial philosophies of Portugal its practice has been seen to differ from the theory. If, as has been suggested, a sense of personal insecurity drives the African deeper into his own culture, to a renewed belief in witchcraft, the need for a closer co-ordination of national and religious policies is evident. The Portuguese are presently determined to stay in Angola and Moçambique. While it is not yet clear that the African is determined that they shall not, it is also clear that the African has not been completely convinced of the desirability of a European culture. In the task of persuasion the missionary has a vital role in Portuguese Africa, but for his work to be efficient the Portuguese must resolve the dilemma of the past. If the African is to be drawn into a Christian community he must be treated with Christian dignity and understanding.

VI

THE SLAVE TRADE, SLAVERY, AND
CONTRACT LABOR

No questions have aroused greater controversy in the history of Portuguese Africa than those of slavery and contract labor, and on no question have the Portuguese been more sensitive. The last century and a half has been frequently marked by domestic and international polemics. With England in particular Portugal has had a lingering dispute over these problems. Nor is it by any means certain that the arguments have run their course, for the Portuguese colonial administration is obviously not yet disposed to abjure its repressive exploitation of African labor on which the present expansion of the economies of Angola and Moçambique is largely based.[1]

To meet the blunt accusations of slaving and improper labor practices Portugal has been forced in the past one hundred and twenty-five years to respond with the creation of an elaborate legislation, some of it genuine, as, for example, Sá da Bandeira's antislavery decrees, and other parts of it synthetic. If this legislation has sometimes failed to convince most foreign critics, it has probably convinced a majority of the Portuguese, even some of those who have been as critical as foreigners of the African labor situation in the overseas provinces, for many Portuguese seem to have an almost mystical faith in the solution of problems by reports and complicated legislation. Nor have Portugal's traditional policies on the use of African labor always been lacking for support from outside Portuguese territory, and it is not unusual to hear the cliché in many parts of Africa, "Only the Portuguese know how to treat the native." [2]

In recent years the Portuguese government has tried to soften the unpleasant implications of contract labor by emphasizing such terms as "the dignity of labor," "spiritual assimilation," "cultural evolution," and "black Portuguese citizens" when speaking of its native policy, but the reality is pretty much the same today as it has been for four hundred years: the indiscriminate use of the African for Portuguese profit.[3] Had this vision of the African shown any marked change in these centuries, beyond the final abolition of slavery and the creation of an ambiguous legal language to define the African's status vis-à-vis the colonial administration, a discussion of slavery and contract labor would be only a historical exercise; but there has been no such change, and a study of this aspect of Angola and Moçambique should contribute to an understanding of present tendencies. Whether the African has been an export commodity, a domestic slave, a *liberto*, *contratado*, or *voluntário*, his fundamental relationship with the Portuguese has remained the same — that of a servant. When the African is supposed to emerge from his centuries-old apprenticeship and tutelage into the role of responsible citizen of Greater Portugal cannot be known (historically, a few Portuguese Africans have always been able to achieve a position of economic and social responsibility in the clergy, commerce, and lesser administration, thus giving some validity to Portuguese assertions of racial equality; and in recent years the emergence of the *assimilado*, especially in the cities and larger towns, has shown a slightly encouraging progress), but the idea of an Angola or Moçambique for the African seems to have about as much significance in Portugal's colonial plans as the notion of a United States for the Indian has in American deliberations.

In none of her native policies has Portugal stood alone among the colonial powers. In comparison with the atrocities in the Belgian Congo at the turn of the century and with German repressions in East and South-West Africa, her conduct has been one of tolerance; nor would many Portuguese seriously defend the drastic subjugation of the non-European people in the Union of South Africa, which is essentially alien to the Lusitanian spirit of tolerance for the Asian and African. Portugal's record as a slaving nation is no worse — and no better — than that of other European and American countries, and her exploitation of the African has never been because he was an African, but because he was exploitable. Hence Portugal feels justified in her resentment against attacks on her policies from nations who have come all too recently to be moved by humanitarian ideals. In an age of atomic destruction, Buchenwald, segregation, slave labor camps, it is difficult for a foreign critic to maintain an absolute moral position on

Portuguese action in Africa. Nevertheless, in many parts of Africa there is today apparent a sincere recognition of past offense and a desire, undoubtedly prompted by African nationalism, to contribute to the future welfare of the African, even at the cost of colonial sovereignty. It has been Portugal's slowness to accept this trend and her reluctance to conform with the principles she professes which have brought down upon her the censure of others.

Nowhere has Portugal been on surer ground in her own defense than on the question of the slave trade. The responsibility for the horrors and outrages committed in the course of the trade was shared by many European countries, and the only distinction that may be legitimately attributed to Portugal is that she was one of the first nations of modern Europe to engage in the African commerce and one of the last to give it up. To her credit let it be said that the trade had almost as many opponents, ineffective though they were, among Portuguese subjects as it did elsewhere. That the major slave emporia were for a long time in Portuguese hands should not hide the fact that her early monopoly was ambitiously contested and in some areas broken by her more powerful European neighbors.

From the 1440's the Portuguese were engaged in the West African slave trade, first at Arguim (Cap Blanc) and by 1480 in the Gulf of Guinea. On the whole extent of coast from Arguim to the Congo, Portugal sought two products: gold and slaves. To promote and control the commerce in these two products the Portuguese in the second half of the fifteenth century established themselves in several well-chosen islands and mainland forts. More so than in Angola and Moçambique, Portugal's policy in upper and lower Guinea was commercial. The distances were too great, the climate too deadly, and the African too unfriendly for Portugal to do more than make a gesture of subjugating and evangelizing the African tribes of the mainland. Only in the vicinity of their factory-fortresses were the Portuguese constrained to make their presence felt through arms or alliance. Otherwise, they were content to let the flow of trade come from the interior to their coastal outposts. Until other nations of Europe were attracted to West Africa in the middle third of the sixteenth century, this commercially sensible and moderate system of trade functioned admirably. Even after the preponderance of influence in West Africa north of the Congo had swung to the Dutch and English, the Portuguese, though their trade was proportionately reduced, managed to maintain themselves in several parts of the coast. The Cape Verdes,

Portuguese Guinea, and the islands São Tomé and Principe are the twentieth-century remnants of the sixteenth-century enterprise.

The four main points the Portuguese occupied north of the equator were Arguim, Santiago (the Cape Verdes), São Jorge da Mina, and São Tomé. At one time or another all were intimately associated with the slave trade. The most important bases were unquestionably Mina, because of its gold, and São Tomé, for slaves and sugar. The island of Arguim, however, was the first post of consequence to be established. Shortly after its discovery in 1443, a factory was put up in hopes of tapping the wealth of western Sudan. Arguim soon became a center of Moslem-Portuguese dealings in a variety of mundane and exotic products. Gold was the primary desire of the Portuguese, who had hopes of diverting into their own hands part of the vaguely defined gold trade of Timbuktu. But they were forced to settle for slaves, a commodity which made Arguim wealthy for almost a century. In its heyday the island was reputed to have sent one thousand slaves a year to Portugal and was the leading Portuguese slave port of the fifteenth century. The rise of the transatlantic trade and the difficulty of holding the island against pirate attacks caused Portugal in the reign of João III to concentrate her interests further down the coast.

To a limited degree Portugal was obliged to share the West African trade with Spain in the last half of the fifteenth century. Although the extent of Spanish voyages has not yet been fully clarified, it is certain that Spain took a definite interest in West Africa until the discovery of America and the Treaty of Tordesillas in 1494 insured Portuguese priority. Spanish privateers continued to make their way to the Guinea coast in the sixteenth century, and Spain's associations with West Africa went on for centuries, for here was the major source of New World labor. Through the sixteenth century, slave contractors of assorted nationalities supplied the Spanish colonies with workers from the coast of Africa. By the middle of the sixteenth century more than four thousand slaves were shipped annually to fill the Spanish contracts; possibly another two thousand were shipped to America clandestinely aboard English, French, Spanish, and Portuguese contraband-runners.

In the supply lines to the Spanish colonies Lisbon for a while held special importance as the largest entrepôt of the trade. Some of the Africans remained in Portugal as domestic servants in Lisbon and Evora and as agricultural workers in the Ribatejo and Algarve. Slavery was by no means a novelty in Portugal. Extensively practiced by the Moors in the Peninsula and adopted by the Christians, the institution had received new impetus as a result of the North African campaigns in the first half of the fifteenth century. Moorish prisoners and, subsequently, Moorish and "Ethiopian" slaves purchased in Morocco were a common sight in courtly circles. These slaves, however, were disappearing when West African captives began to reach the country in considerable numbers. Their fairly sudden appearance and their concentration in Lisbon and southern Portugal led to some fanciful observations on the Negro population of Portugal in the early sixteenth century, and even two hundred and fifty years later travelers to Iberia commented with amazement on the number of black faces seen in Lisbon. Absurd claims that the Alentejo and the Algarve were almost entirely peopled by Negroes, that slaves outnumbered the white population of Lisbon, and that the royal family was mostly Negroid gained credence.[4] Neither the country nor the capital was overrun with Negro slaves; a census of 1554 fixed the number in Lisbon at about 10 per cent of the population, and there were fewer in the countryside. Evidence of the African's presence occasionally appears in the courtly and popular literature of the day,[5] and there are still African motifs in Portuguese folklore.[6]

By the middle of the eighteenth century, Negro slavery in Portugal was almost an anachronism, appearances to the contrary. The institution was never a fundamental aspect of Portuguese society. Substantial though it may have been, it was but a shadow of imperial slavery. When Gilberto Freyre speaks of a Portuguese slave consciousness (allegedly an extension of the Moorish system of domestic slavery) in Brazil, he is presenting a thesis difficult to substantiate in fact. There was more in common between slavery as practiced in Brazil, Angola, and Moçambique than there was between slavery in any one, or all, of these colonies and the metropolis. The rest of Freyre's argument that the Portuguese-Moorish brand of domestic servitude was less cruel than the Anglo-French-Spanish variety is equally problematical.[7] For the African working in the Brazilian sugar mill, at least, "life was hell on earth," [8] an observation equally valid regarding certain slavery customs in the African provinces.

The second center of Portuguese slaving activity in West Africa was Santiago — in the Cape Verde group — and the mainland opposite. The island itself, settled by Portuguese, Castilians, and Genoese, was the entrepôt for the upper Guinea trade. To encourage the settlement of Santiago the crown granted its inhabitants extraordinary concessions in the 1460's to trade the coast. As in the Congo, the Europeans, in the absence of any consistent royal authority and intercourse with the home country, made up an undisciplined community of adventurers and fugitives. Some made their way to the mainland, Senegal, Gambia, and Sierra Leone, where as lords of the land and traders they kept the flow of slaves to Santiago and coastal factories at a lively level. Since they had few compunctions about operating in areas restricted to the crown monopoly or about selling to unlicensed ships, their presence became a painful thorn to the government, which issued ineffectual decrees to curtail their activities.

Some of the traders were authorized representatives of slave companies. The Guinea coast was let for a yearly rental by the crown to Portuguese, Spanish, or Italian contractors. Exclusive rights for four to five years in the five coastal divisions (Arguim, Senegal, Gambia, the Rivers of Guinea, and Sierra Leone) were put up at public auction in Lisbon. The contract for Gambia was generally the most profitable and brought the highest fee at auction. At times several districts would be rented to a single contractor or company, and after 1521 one such group held a monopoly for all of upper Guinea. Each contractor employed factors, some of them permanent residents of the area, to conduct their affairs. Although upper Guinea superseded Arguim as the chief supplier of African labor, in the mid-sixteenth century its importance began to dwindle when English and French intruders appeared in the Gambia area.

São Jorge da Mina was the third point of Portuguese influence — and the most imposing with its great castle and fortified site of São Jorge poised magnificently over the sea. Here slavery was a secondary consideration until the Dutch capture of the city in 1637. Portugal was concerned with gold, which in the first fifty years of São Jorge's occupation (from 1482) arrived in encouraging quantities from the regions of Ashanti. With the Africans of the area the Portuguese had a tenuous relationship, bribing, intriguing, and, on occasion, fighting to keep the surrounding tribes from pushing them into the sea. São Jorge and the lesser mainland forts at Axim, Samma, and Accra made Portugal supreme on the Gold Coast. From Benin, São Tomé, and even Arguim the Portuguese brought slaves to trade for Mina's gold.

The most constant source of Portuguese authority in lower Guinea, and in fact in all West Africa, was São Tomé. In the last decade of the fifteenth century, the decision was made in Lisbon to populate this steamy fertile island. In the next few years young Jews, convicts, and exiles were sent there. The inhabitants were authorized to trade in slaves with the mainland, principally in the kingdom of Benin, although the commerce quickly spread southward and was carried on from the Slave Coast to the Congo. Few areas of the Portuguese empire have ever shown such rapid, tropically luxuriant, and decadent prosperity as São Tomé. The island has also possessed a puzzling vitality which has enabled it to withstand the vicissitudes of centuries. Its economy rested on slaves. From the shores of Guinea, the Congo, and Angola, black laborers poured into the island to culti- vate the sugar plantations and operate the refineries. Simultaneously São Tomé became Portugal's chief base for the slave traffic to the West Indies and, later, to Brazil. The contract for the island was the fattest Lisbon had to offer, and duties were a notable contribution to the royal treasury. Men like Fernão de Melo, who held the captaincy of the island until 1522 when its administration reverted to the crown, and the island planters were vigorous defenders of their prerogatives, which often put them into conflict with the Lisbon government. Slave rebellions in the second half of the century, the lack of white popula- tion, and the rise of Luanda brought a decline to the island's economy for a hundred years, and not until the last part of the seventeenth cen- tury did it reassert its position as one of the centers for the Guinea trade. The island had the distinction also of contributing to the rise of Brazil. With Madeira it helped to introduce the sugar economy into Brazil, and with it a way of life based on the labors of the African.[9]

The golden age of slaving on the Guinea coast extended roughly from 1650 to 1800. In this period the Portuguese played a lesser role in the systematic depopulation of the region. The devastation wrought under the sixteenth-century Portuguese monopoly must have been slight compared with the combined efforts of English, Dutch, and French traders. Reliable statistics for the earlier period do not exist, but five hundred thousand slaves exported would seem to be a gen- erous estimate for the whole coast from Arguim to Benin until 1600 — a modest figure against a calculated five to eight million for the next two centuries.

By 1600 Portugal's monopoly had already begun to fragment un- der the growing competition of European interlopers. The Dutch West India Company was the principal adversary in the years 1625– 1650, and by 1642 the Gold Coast was in Dutch hands. In the 1660's French and English companies engaged the Dutch in a triangular struggle for the whole West African slave trade. Portugal managed to hold isolated sections of the coast. In the Cape Verdes and Portuguese Guinea she resisted pressures from north and south as the French came to dominate the trade in Senegal and the English in much of Gambia. Though Angola remained the chief source of supply, the Portuguese were not finished on the Guinea coast and by 1700 had recovered sufficiently to consider forming a Lisbon company to take over the Spanish contract for the New World. But the negotiations fell through and the French gained the contract, yielding it to the English after the Peace of Utrecht. In 1677 a Portuguese slave port was established on the coast of Dahomey to expedite shipments to São Tomé and Principe and later to fill the vessels arriving directly from Brazil in the eighteenth century.

By 1700 Brazil demanded more than ten thousand slaves a year, a number that could not always be met by Angola, which was furnishing Africans for other parts of Latin America as well. The need for workers in the newly discovered gold and diamond mines was an additional factor in bringing a large part of Brazil's trade back to the Guinea coast. Hoping to acquire slaves accustomed to mining work, Brazilian financiers dealt with Dutch contractors on the Gold Coast. Subsequently, their demands contributed to the devastation of Dahomey. The Companhia de Cacheu e Cabo Verde was founded in 1690 for exploiting the upper Guinea coast. The company had only limited success in the face of efficient competition from the English and French, and in the middle of the eighteenth century the powerful Grão-Pará and Maranhão Company, in which Pombal held interest, financed the rebuilding of Bissau into an important slave center. During certain periods of the eighteenth century Guinea surpassed Angola in the number of slaves sent to Brazil. Slave ships from Brazil bought indiscriminately along the coast from English, French, Dutch, or Portuguese factories. By 1790, however, the English, exporting 38,000 slaves annually to the New World from fourteen posts, and the Dutch, exporting some 26,000 slaves from fifteen posts, were the principal suppliers. Portuguese traders hung on at only four factories, from which they yearly dispatched some 10,000 Negroes.

The rise of the Congo-Angola trade, though primarily a natural consequence of expansion below the equator, was stimulated by several other conditions in the early sixteenth century. First, there were the ambitious intentions of São Tomé to tap a rich new area of supply. Second, there was the tempting relationship with the Manicongo, whose obvious desire to please his European friends led him to open the Pandora's box of the slave trade. Third, the Guinea trade, subject as it was to the vexations of Arab dealers of upper Guinea and the intrusions of foreign ships, could not produce a sufficient number of slaves.

It is impossible to overestimate the importance of the trade in the Congo during the first half of the sixteenth century. Everyone engaged in it: merchants, priests, ships' officers and men, the king's officials. The importance achieved by the Congo commerce was recognized in Manuel's decree of 1519 forbidding any save ships of the crown to load Congo products at Pinda. In vain Afonso complained that the Portuguese who scattered through his realm like locusts were depopulating his lands, collecting and selling his subjects as well as legitimate *peças*. His efforts to regulate the excesses were, as we have seen, ineffective. The example of the Congo, which was to set the tone for Angola, shows that wherever slaving was allowed to become the dominant interest, policies of diplomatic alliance produced the same conditions as did policies of military occupation. By 1600 the Congo kingdom was a shambles; the trade through the mouth of the river had probably averaged over five thousand slaves a year throughout the century. The Congo trade went on for another two hundred years; during much of the time the only European contact with the interior was through the slave trader and his half-caste and African agents.

For the first seventy-five years of the sixteenth century, the island of São Tomé was a predominant influence in the affairs of the Congo and Angola. São Tomé was the chief consumer and distributor for most of the slaves brought from below the equator. Ships from the island, frequently unable to acquire sufficient slaves from the lands of the Manicongo, traded sporadically at points near the present ports of Ambriz and Luanda and at the mouth of the Cuanza. By 1550 these ships may have been carrying up to three thousand slaves a year to São Tomé. But with only a few Portuguese traders and their assistants to organize the trade in the backcountry, the commerce was often uncertain and inadequate. Without some sort of Portuguese occupation Angola was not a wholly satisfactory source of slaves.

With the arrival of Paulo Dias de Novais in 1575, Angola became the Black Mother. From Luanda in the twelve years from 1575 to 1587 the yearly average of slaves exported was about 2,500; with the letting of the contract to Pedro Sevilha and António Mendes Lamego, the yearly average tripled in the next four years. These figures are for slave cargo from Luanda alone and do not include the covert commerce from other ports. The usual estimate for the century 1580–1680 is a million slaves from Angola with perhaps another 500,000 from the Congo.[10] Of the annual total, about 8,500 went to the Brazilian ports of Bahia, Rio de Janeiro, and Pernambuco (Bahia was the largest port of entry in South America), some 5,000 to the Caribbean area, and about 1,500 to the Río de la Plata region. In the early years of the seventeenth century Brazil's sugar economy had become absolutely dependent on Angolan labor. A remark of the day was, "Without sugar there is no Brazil and without Angola there is no sugar." The price for the *peças de Indias* — one of the exotic commercial labels for the slaves — was high and the profits great. Angola and the Congo became and remained the largest concentrated area of slave supply in West Africa.

Luanda from the days of its first contract was the most important port south of the equator, supplanting the ports at the mouth of the Congo, although the Congo territory, let on separate contract, had a more international clientele, attracting ships of Dutch, English, French, and Spanish flags. Even before the silver and copper mines of Angola proved imaginary or unworkable, the slave was the only real article of commerce in the colony. The principal dealer was usually the governor, whose interest in the trade was not necessarily his own capital, but the power and facilities of his office plus whatever privileges were contained in his *regimento*. Then there was the contractor, working for himself or, more frequently, for a corporation of investors who had purchased the licenses permitting them to export an appointed number of Negroes in a certain period of time. Through the offices of the governor or his staff the terms of the contract were often discreetly changed during the actual operation to allow more slaves, on whom no taxes were paid, to be exported. Working for the contractor or for themselves were local merchants living in Luanda, or sometimes in the interior, whose *pombeiros* scoured the country bringing in captives from the most remote sections of the colony. On the margin of this legal activity adventurers and residents promoted the clandestine trade.

Slaves were acquired in various manners. They were obtained at fortresses in the interior where they were brought by African chiefs or their agents to be traded for manufactured goods. In Angola this method was less successful than in the more commercially advanced Guinea coast. A surer way was for the merchant to send his *pombeiros*, or African traders, into the interior. Accompanied by a number of domestic slaves bearing the merchandise to be traded (cloth, wine, metal goods), the *pombeiros* ranged through the countryside for more than a year bartering with local chiefs. The slaves acquired were then marched to Luanda. It was not uncommon for the *pombeiros* (or for free-lancing Portuguese traders) to stir up a local war with the hopes of being able to buy the prisoners. In the many so-called wars of conquest the Portuguese administration waged against the great chiefs or petty *sobas* in the interior a substantial number of captives were taken, many of whom were sold to slave contractors and dispatched to America. Such procedures were not above criticism by the humanitarians of the age.

Still another source was the well-populated lands granted by the governor to deserving soldiers and clerics. The taxes demanded of the chief could be conveniently paid in slaves; many of these *sobadas* were in effect slave farms. Curiously, the word *resgate* (hostage or ransom) and *resgatear* (to ransom or liberate) were the terms used to describe the process of acquisition, the original notion being that the African was received in hostage to prevent his slaughter by his fellow Africans and to liberate him from his pagan state through the teachings of Christianity. The original significance of the terms, going back to medieval Portuguese-Moorish relations, had no reality in the African trade, and may have been unconsciously used as a euphemism to hide the trade's unsavory character.

In Luanda the slaves were held in barracoons, large warehouses or sometimes open corrals. Since many slaves came from the deep interior, they arrived on the coast emaciated and exhausted. So that they could withstand the incredible rigors of the transatlantic voyage, here the slaves were fattened and attended. Their services were used, should their departure be delayed, in municipal and agricultural tasks. Before they embarked into the slave ships they were baptized wholesale. English polemicists have perpetuated the story that on the wharves at Luanda stood a great marble chair, the Bishop's Chair, where the Angolan prelate officiated at embarkation baptism ceremonies. The scene is evocative — and partly true — but usually the slaves were baptized prior to embarkation, and it is even possible that captives leaving lesser ports and neglected estuaries along the coast were not bothered at all with last-minute ceremonies.

No single step in the slaving process, not even the dreadful Arab slave-gang marches through East Africa in the nineteenth century, was more terrible than the voyage to the New World. The sickening conditions under which the Negro was transported, the brutal unconcern of the officers and crew of the slaver were the most dramatic examples of slaving horrors cited by European antislavery factions in the eighteenth and nineteenth centuries. Portuguese historians have made much of remarks by several Dutch observers of the seventeenth century to the effect that the Portuguese were more efficient and humane transporters of live cargo than other nations. Contemporary Portuguese accounts, however, revealed no such distinction.

It is also known that in Angola where they carry the prisoners to the ships, those on land weep copiously, horrified and fearful of the violence that is done them, seeing that in addition to taking them against their will, they treat them very inhumanely on the ships, whence a great number die suffocated by their own stench and from other bad treatment. There was one night in which thirty died on one ship in port because they would not open the hatch for fear they would escape, no matter how loudly those below shouted for them to open because they were dying; the only response they received was to be called dogs and similar names. And in another ship carrying five hundred from Cape Verde to New Spain after only one night at sea 120 were dead, suffocated in the hold because those carrying them were fearful of an uprising.[11]

Stories richer in detail may be found in countless reports and tracts on the trade. The Portuguese ships were generally smaller than the Dutch ships and carried proportionately more slaves in the narrow lower decks. To Brazil the Middle Passage was comparatively swift, from five to eight weeks. But much of the cargo never got to Brazil, or died shortly after being unloaded. Through disease, suicide, suffocation, 20 to 30 per cent of the slaves embarking in Angola perished. Whether, as critics of the practice argued, conditions grew worse from the seventeenth to the early nineteenth century or popular reactions became more imaginative and vehement is a needlessly tortured point. At no time did the voyages of the *tumbeiros* have anything to recommend them.

In Angola and Moçambique until 1845, local slavery was subordinate to the export trade. The reasons have already been suggested in the lack of economic life in either colony to support resident slavery on a grand scale. The African was more profitable sold than kept. Slaves, however, were retained. There were the Jesuit work camps in Angola and the *prazos* in Moçambique, and many colonists had a corps of slaves as domestic servants or making up a small private army. The Angolan slave dealer and the Moçambique *prazero* each had a company of African soldiers, some free and some not, for his business and defense. In both colonies slaves were employed in clearing the land around the towns and fortresses. They were farm laborers on the manioc plantations and the scattered farms of the Portuguese. In Angola particularly the slave formed part of an African craftsman class, since few Portuguese in the colonies engaged in such tasks. Africans trained by the Jesuits in carpentry or at the forge were in constant demand. Slavery in both colonies was perhaps a more indolent affair than in Brazil, closer to African tribal slavery than to the servitude of American plantation life. But it was not without its brutalities and excesses; on the estates and *prazos* cruel masters were not unknown, and those who kept a seraglio of African women were even more common. Generally, however, the abuses of slavery in the African colonies were a nineteenth-century phenomenon.

In the last one hundred and fifty years of the legal slave trade (1680–1836) an estimated more than two million slaves were shipped from Luanda and Benguela. The illicit trade and the unknown quantity of Negroes sent from the Congo ports would increase this figure by at least another million. In its last desperate convulsion, Angola sent perhaps a quarter of a million slaves to Brazil in the ten years before the trade's suppression. The ports of the Congo had a new burst of importance in the last quarter of the eighteenth century as native chiefs found foreign traders who paid them more than the Portuguese from Luanda or Benguela, but after the termination of the English trade and the Treaty of 1815, the Angolan ports, with annual shipments of 18,000 to 20,000 slaves, reasserted their leading position. By 1800 it was only the initiative of the *pombeiros* which kept the caravans descending from upcountry to Luanda and Benguela. By then the Portuguese in the towns and fortresses had sunk into a satisfied inertia, playing out the final minutes of the game, indifferent to everything save their prerogatives and the profits of the trade.

The attitude of England toward Portugal in the nineteenth century was frequently characterized by pious cant and on occasions by hypocrisy; nowhere is this more evident than in the slaving questions arising in the first half of the century. Having come upon virtue late in life, England felt constrained to rebuke Portugal for her inhumanity and her reluctance to follow in the paths of righteousness taken by her European neighbors in the early nineteenth century. In her defense Portugal has often done herself a disservice by failing to emphasize the stern attitude taken by some of her citizens against the institution and by stressing instead the collective guilt of European and American nations and advancing arguments of canonical justification. The example of Sá da Bandeira, whose antislavery pronouncements sprang far more from nobility of character than from British pressure, was not unique. In the tradition of Las Casas and the Spanish Jesuit Alonso de Sandoval, isolated Portuguese clerics spoke out, in vain, against the sophistry of defending the Amerindian and closing one's eyes to African slavery. Several Angolan slave merchants realistically criticized the abuses of the trade.[12] Royal *regimentos* repeatedly stressed to no avail the necessity of treating the Negro with Christian kindness. In the middle and late 1700's tracts like the Brazilian Ribeiro de Rocha's *Etíope resgatado, instruído, libertado*

(1758) took their place in a growing antislavery literature in Europe. Governor Sousa Coutinho sought during his Angolan governorship to mitigate the atrocities committed against the African. In a series of *portarias* he condemned and, in some cases, corrected temporarily the arbitrary conduct of men in the slave business. Noting that chiefs were robbed of their people by captains in the interior, that the natives were forced to work, often at great distances from their villages, that free men were enslaved, he threatened dire punishment to all those who perpetuated these cruelties. He ordered the captains to stop slaving and protect the African from the greedy attentions of clerics, *degradados*, and *pombeiros*. Although he did not condemn slavery, he set his face against the wholesale exploitation of the colony. Sousa Coutinho's fulminations, it should be noted, were not predominantly humanitarian. In his vision for a healthy progressive colony, the slave trade was sorely out of joint. He was an early advocate of obligatory labor, a modified form of slavery, a proposition for which he was to be much admired by Portuguese colonialists one hundred and forty years later.[13]

The end of the slave trade came for most European nations with almost abrupt suddenness. In 1790 it was still flourishing; by 1820, most nations had abolished it; and by 1850 it was practically dead. Denmark, once a prosperous slave-trading nation on the Gold Coast, banned the traffic to her citizens in 1792. Antislavery sentiments in England brought that country to take similar action in 1807. A Napoleonic decree became French law in 1818. At the Congress of Vienna the participating nations agreed to abolish the commerce as soon as possible. In the same year the Dutch moved for suppression. Spain in 1820 formally renounced the shipping of Africans to the Caribbean, although the Spanish-Cuban trade did not completely disappear until after 1860.

Portugal and Brazil dragged their feet in joining the general condemnation. The dependence of the overseas economies on the commerce and the domestic difficulties arising from the Peninsular wars made any decisive action impossible. England's close involvement, however, with both the Lisbon and Rio de Janeiro governments gave her a privileged position from which to bring influence on Portugal, and on Brazil after that country's independence in 1822. In 1810 Portugal agreed to work toward a gradual abolition of the slave trade, and as a first step she limited traffic to only those areas belonging to her. When in the early 1810's it was apparent that the flow of Negroes from West Africa, instead of decreasing, had shown an increase, Foreign Secretary Castlereagh urged greater co-operation on the Portuguese government. Stating that the British colonies had been amply stocked with slaves before suppression while Brazil had not and furthermore that some of her ships had been taken while in legal pursuit of the trade, Portugal agreed only to enter into further negotiations. In the treaty evolved in 1815 Portugal guaranteed that she would restrict her activities to south of the equator and to refuse to allow her flag to be used except for trade with her own possessions (*i.e.*, Brazil). In return Portugal was granted indemnities and concessions totaling about five million dollars.

In 1826, as a price for recognition of Brazil's independence, England demanded of Brazil a similar treaty. Such a treaty Brazil accepted and further agreed to make the slave trade piracy for her subjects at the end of a three-year period. Although the piracy clause was not strictly observed, in 1831 measures were taken to punish captured slave traders and confiscate their vessels. This treaty and the independence of Brazil in theory brought an end to the Portuguese slave traffic. But it showed no signs of dying, and no Portuguese government was strong enough until 1834 to cope with the problem. In 1835 Foreign Secretary Palmerston pointed out that Portugal had not observed a single restriction in the 1815 treaty and that her subjects continued to buy and transport slaves, although she no longer had a legal market for them. "The ships of Portugal now prowl about the ocean," he claimed, "pandering to the crimes of other nations; and when her own ships are not sufficiently numerous for the purpose, the flag is lent as a shield to protect the misdeeds of foreign pirates." [14] Portugal apologetically temporized, presenting as a counterclaim that British naval vessels had captured her ships and that it was not unknown for English slavers to fly the Portuguese flag.

Sá da Bandeira's decree of 1836 prohibiting the slave trade did not have the immediate effect desired by him and the British government. Angola and Brazilian slave dealers fiercely resisted it, and in the absence of Portuguese authority to enforce the law, scores of slave ships yearly left Ambriz, Cabinda, even Luanda, for Brazil. Negotiations between England and Portugal continued, now with obvious good intent on the part of the Portuguese government. But popular humanitarian sentiment in England was impatient. Thomas Buxton, one of the founders of the English Anti-Slavery Society, demanded ". . . a declaration that our cruisers will have orders to seize, after a fixed and early day, every vessel under Portuguese colours engaged in the slave trade, to bring the crew to trial as pirates, and to inflict upon them the severest secondary punishment our law allows." [15] In the same tone the British government plainly told Portugal her flag would no longer be respected. Three years of raids along the Angola coast and the seizure of Portuguese ships practically brought an end to the West African traffic. In 1842 a final treaty was concluded with Portugal wherein that country declared the trade to be piracy. With England and the United States she participated in mixed commissions, contributing a squadron of ships for the coastal vigilance. By 1850, after three hundred and fifty years, the Congo-Angola slave trade was virtually finished.[16]

To the exasperation of the English, Portuguese East Africa was more dilatory than Angola in bringing the traffic to an end. In the 1880's there were still complaints about Moçambique residents trafficking in Africans. In 1888 Lugard wrote with disgust, "These Portuguese are inveterate slavers."[17] Much of the English literature of the century is the natural exaggeration produced by the intense humanitarianism of an uneasy conscience and by British missionary and imperial politics in East Africa, but there was unquestionable evidence as late as 1890 of practices in Moçambique which could only be called slaving.

Although the Portuguese in Moçambique joined in the transatlantic slave trade relatively late, "black ivory" was an established commodity of Arab trade long before 1500, and the Portuguese, occupying only coastal sections and the Zambezi basin, never completely kept Swahili slave merchants from their trade in the interior. From the days of the Sofala captaincy, Portuguese ships carried Negroes from Moçambique to India and even in small numbers to America and Portugal. The main trade was eastward. Moçambique was too distant and the Cape passage too hazardous to make East African slaves an economical article in America. Only in 1640, with the relaxing of certain restrictions on Indian commerce and the loss of Angola to the Dutch, did the area become important, and ships from Rio de Janeiro arrived in Moçambique ports. Once begun, the Atlantic trade never entirely disappeared, even though there was no question of Moçambique's competing with Angola and the Guinea coast. Portuguese ships returning from India put in at Moçambique island and Quelimane to fill their half-empty holds with human merchandise. Neither in the seventeenth nor the eighteenth centuries was the trade in Moçambique organized, save for the Arab caravans north of the Zambezi, to exploit the population of the interior. Governor Lacerda was pleased to note in the middle 1790's that slave dealers made no money on their ventures, which, he observed, must have been punishment from the hand of God for making slaves of men created in his image.[18]

Although slaves formed the bulk of Moçambique's exports by 1800 — not a surprising situation given the defunct state of the colony's economy — slavery as a domestic practice was more important here than in Angola. Many a *prazero* had an army of captive Africans in addition to the usual large number of house and field workers, for the more slaves a man owned the greater his prestige in the Zambezi community. There was still in 1800 an academic distinction between slave and *colono*, the latter being the tribesman dwelling on the *prazo*. Allegedly a free man, the *colono* paid a head tax, was obliged to work without pay, and was subject to his landlord's caprice. In reality the difference between the two categories was indistinct and in some areas, nonexistent. Both were cheap labor in Moçambique. In the bustling period of the nineteenth century, many *prazeros* did not examine too closely the legal condition of the Africans they sold down the river. Sometimes at the coastal factories the captives were classified as *brutos* (those from deep in the back-country) and *ladinos* (domestic slaves who knew a little of European ways), the second group being much the more valuable.[19]

The nineteenth-century boom in the Moçambique slave trade was the usual result of supply and demand. Abolition decrees and restrictive treaties narrowed the source of labor down to Portuguese Africa without a commensurate decrease in New World needs. The Congo and Angola were not sufficient, and Moçambique, which had previously enjoyed its modest, though growing commerce, was called upon for larger quotas. Correia Lopes estimates that from about 10,000 slaves exported each year (5,000 in national ships and 5,000 in those of foreign registry) from 1780 to 1800, the figure rose to 15,000 a year and soared for a decade to perhaps 25,000 annually before spiraling downward after 1850. There was only a small decrease after abolition. England, her attention concentrated on the West African coast, neglected Portuguese East Africa until the 1840's. The commerce had a distinctive international flavor. For goods of British and American manufacture, Portuguese, Arab, Banian, and half-caste traders purchased African slaves in the interior for shipment on Spanish, French, Brazilian, and American ships, mostly of American construction, to various parts of the globe. Although most of the population was involved in one way or another, a few merchants, the contractors, and key officials garnered the profit, and the colony remained backrupt. It is unreasonable, on the other hand, to propose, as some writers have done,[20] that the trade destroyed Moçambique's

economy by diverting the healthy energies of the country into speculative channels, for from about 1700 on, Moçambique had shown very
few signs of healthy energies or legitimate commerce.

The abolition decree of 1836 had a reception in Moçambique
similar to the one it received in Angola: consternation, resentment,
and grim determination not to comply. Governors and captains of
fortresses, ill paid and often corrupt, rightly figured that they had
nothing to lose by permitting the practice to go on and to participate
if necessary. Some officials made sincere efforts to destroy the traffic,
but the means at their disposal were pitifully inadequate, a handful of
soldiers and several ships to watch the lengthy coastline in order to
prevent the shadowy Arab dhows from slipping from their secret
estuaries. Underpaid officials and *degradados* were not the best civil
servants and soldiers to confront the problem. The majority of them
found it more convenient to close their eyes.

The strong intervention of England in the middle 1840's, carried
out with the full co-operation of the Lisbon government, had good
effect in reducing the number of slaves (7,000–8,000 a year) then being shipped out of the colony. Vessels of the Royal Navy blockaded
strategic stretches of the coast, burned barracoons, and destroyed
factories suspected of participating in the sale of Africans. Their
activity and a declining demand brought the commerce to a low ebb.
After 1850 the Atlantic trade from Moçambique was past its peak of
the previous two decades. Vessels flying the flags (usually spurious)
of various nations still put in at Quelimane or lesser ports, but their
appearance was more and more infrequent. Ibo was the last port to
go under; from 1860 to 1865 the town became a center for the Cuban
trade which had briefly flared up again. Also from Ibo, Arab traders
shipped their cargo up the coast to Kilwa and Zanzibar.

The Moçambique trade, however, died hard. Now it took another
direction. From the beginning of the century French slavers had
called, openly and secretively, along the coast to acquire slaves for
transport to the New World or, a bit later, for France's island possessions in the southwest Indian Ocean. When the Zanzibari could not
deliver sufficient quantities of *émigrés*, the French began to rely
more on Moçambique in the early 1850's to supply indentured
laborers. Africans were brought from the interior, in most cases by
the same merchants and agents who had formerly supplied the slave
ships, crammed in barracoons until the arrival of a French vessel,
hauled aboard and asked if they were willing to serve as voluntary
workers on Réunion and the Comores for five years. The ceremony
was a farcical formality, and the practice nothing less than slavery.

The main ports in this infamous traffic were Ibo, Delgado, and Quelimane. Life in the interior, which had just begun to take a peaceful turn, was again upset by the violence of local slave capture, wars, and kidnapings in which Portuguese captains openly connived. Livingstone found the country around Lake Nyasa almost depopulated by the Arab traders.

In 1855 and 1856 the Portuguese government in Lisbon issued decrees prohibiting the system. Encouraged by Britain's sympathetic attitude, the government in 1857 sent out the vigorous Governor General João Tavares de Almeida to put a stop to the free labor emigration. Almost immediately after his arrival, de Almeida seized a French barque, the *Charles et George*, with over a hundred *émigrés* on board. A commission appointed by the governor brought in a charge of slaving, condemned the vessel and sentenced her captain. The French government had long argued that the system was a legal acquisition of African labor and ordered the vessel to be released.

A diplomatic crisis ensued, which England could not mediate, and in October 1858 two French warships entered the Tagus. Before such a display of force, the Portuguese, in the absence of visible support from her antislavery ally England, was obliged to capitulate and free the *Charles et George*. Lisbon was bitter over the British betrayal, and the government's efforts to suppress the emigration flagged. Although Napoleon III abolished the system in 1864, rapacious smugglers sailed the coast for another twenty years.

The implications of the latter-day traffic in *émigrés* went beyond Moçambique. Reports from the colony by British consuls and missionaries, though clearly not lacking in partiality, contributed to the hardening of popular and diplomatic antiPortuguese sentiment in England and, to a lesser extent, in Europe and the United States. The incubus of the slave trade rested heavily on the soul of the English humanitarian, who now sought to atone for his country's excesses by bringing the benefits of enlightened commerce and civilization to ravaged Africa. It became the fashion to view Portugal's occupation in Angola and, especially, in Moçambique as a relic of a barbaric and backward age; any diminution of her authority or territory could be only a triumph for enlightenment. This attitude, which more or less characterized English policy toward Portuguese Africa up to the First World War, came to serve the purposes of blatant English imperialism in southern Africa and was the most important single factor influencing Portuguese Africa's relations with the outside world.

Livingstone was not the first or only traveler to raise his voice in protest against the crimes committed under the Portuguese flag, although he was the most influential. It was not enough for the Portuguese government to claim — indeed, it was a tactical mistake — that she had no control over what went on in some parts of her colonies. As early as the 1820's Commodore Owen roundly condemned the actions of Portuguese officials in Lourenço Marques who captured free African tribesmen for sale. In 1857 the first British consul to Moçambique, Lyons MacLeod, an ardent abolitionist, spent nine hectic months in the colony, at the end of which he dedicated one of the two volumes in a work on the Arab slave trade to a neurotic indictment of the Portuguese in East Africa. That MacLeod was chased from his residence one evening by angry citizens of Moçambique island (one of the very few occasions when the traditional Portuguese hospitality, extended even to severest critics, did not prevail) and that he failed to gain the confidence of colonial officials for his unyielding campaign against the slave trade may have influenced his judgments. Nevertheless, such corrosive accusations as the following could only have made the blood of righteous Englishmen boil the hotter: "The slave-trade thrives only in the African dominions of the King of Portugal; and the late Portaria [a Luso-French agreement of 1854 on émigré labor] of that monarch at once places His Majesty foremost among the advocates of slavery. Until slavery is entirely abolished in the African dominions of Don Pedro the Fifth, the slave-trade will flourish, while outraged humanity and suffering Africans exclaim to that potentate, 'Thou art the man!'"[21]

Another contemporary account, by Reverend Henry Rowley, of the first Universities' Mission, contained incidents reminiscent of *Uncle Tom's Cabin.* Young children were described staggering under chains weighing not less than fifty pounds. When Rowley rebuked a Portuguese master for striking a Negro child with a whip, he evoked this most curious response:

You see, in order to live out here, I must have slaves, and in order to keep slaves I must have a whip. My whip is no worse than any other whip I know of, but I do not justify it as right, I simply defend it as a necessity. Wherever slaving exists discipline must of necessity be brutal. You English, because you do not keep slaves, take the philanthropic, the religious view of the question; we, who do keep slaves, take the material view, which regards the man as property . . . I admit the philanthropic view is the best, for in the eyes of God all men are equal; and, though the

African be a degraded man, I know enough of him to be sure that he can be raised by kindness and religion into a position not very inferior to our own. But, if you keep slaves . . . you must degrade them by the whip . . . until, like dogs, they are the unhesitating servants of your will . . . I know the philanthropic, the religious view of the question, is the best. I feel it is the best, but it will never pay me to adopt it. I am here. I must be here. What am I to do? Starve? Not if I can help it. I do as others do, I keep slaves, and while I keep slaves, I must use the whip.[22]

More than twenty years later Rhodes's agent, Frederick Selous, citing equivalent brutalities, wrote that slaving in the central Zambezi was by no means a thing of the past. On the other hand, the Portuguese were not entirely without defenders among the English: David Rankin, who lived and traded in the area for ten years, during the same period as Selous, wrote that at Tete it was not uncommon for natives to "voluntarily endeavour to make themselves slaves . . . for they are kindly treated. They have the best of food, they are clothed and well cared for, and have no more anxiety." [23]

Livingstone, in Angola shortly before the decree of 1858 abolishing slavery in all parts of the empire, and Lovett Cameron,[24] who visited the province while the slave was in the *liberto* stage, left a legacy of detail sufficient to stir the English imagination until the arrival of Henry Nevinson in 1904. Other travel and missionary accounts filled out the familiar picture of a continuing slavery and traffic in slaves existing under less provocative names. If the number of works on Angola by outraged Englishmen in the last half of the nineteenth century did not reach the proportions of those in Moçambique it was only because English subjects had no great material or evangelical interests in Angola at the time.

English attacks, whatever their inspiration or purpose, were not without foundation. Rather than a problem in African affairs, emancipation created a problem in semantics. The status of the African was not suddenly changed; his relationship to the European was not perceptibly affected; the unhealthy atmosphere in Moçambique and Angola did not clear away. Only the legal apparatus was different. Slavery became tutelage, forced labor, obligatory labor, contract labor. Those who take the Liberal government of Portugal to task for thrusting emancipation upon the colonies and thus, by indirection, creating an economic climate which bred these unsavory forms of African exploitation [25] beg several questions: that emancipation came abruptly and that Portuguese habits in the colonies, after three hundred years of slavery, were subject to substantial change. Slavery had been the ruin of the colonies; now, perversely, it was held to be its salvation.

The roots of tradition had grown deep in the African soil; they were not to be torn out by the earnest efforts of humanitarians. The time-calloused concept of the Negro as a working hand to be bought and sold prevailed over distant ideals. The involvement of Portugal in international disputes over the exploitation of the native population only reinforced this medieval, allegedly practical, vision of the African. By 1900 tradition became dignified as colonial policy and was given legislative form. Portuguese colonialists began to talk like European imperialists. In London in 1895 the Portuguese delegate, Sr. Ferreira do Amaral, at the Sixth International Geographical Conference (attended by Lugard, Stanley, and Ravenstein among others) gave his views on African labor and high tariffs: "We hear people today talk about imported or forced labor and we equally hear the *gros mot* of 'slavery' which has been used so often to exploit the tender-hearted people of Europe. For me, the Negro will never work willingly, and the only way to oblige him to work is to make him pay dearly for the satisfaction of his few necessities. This has been the economic policy of Portugal in Africa." [26]

The abolition of slavery came slowly in Portuguese Africa and was foreshadowed by a number of decrees and proposals. In 1845 it was proposed in parliament that the children of slaves be free; in 1849, a project for gradual abolition was presented. Five years later, a limited abolition decree by Prime Minister Sá da Bandeira became law. Its principal clauses dealt with government slaves and Africans imported from other lands: both categories were made *libertos* for a certain number of years (in other words, they were freed but obliged to work for their former masters). In 1856 slavery in the Ambriz district of Angola was abolished — to avoid certain diplomatic tensions — and in the same year Sá da Bandeira determined that children of slaves should be born free, although their parents' masters should have their services for twenty years. Finally, in April 1858, abolition of all forms of slavery was set for twenty years hence; [27] the reasons for the delay were to make the transition from a slave labor economy to free labor less painful.

The violent reaction in Portuguese Africa to emancipation has been noted. Colonists protested they would be bankrupt, and officials swore that the best means for the gradual exploitation of the interior had been taken from them. If the colonial governments had carried out a policy of using free African labor, instead of slaves or *libertos*, on their projects, the road to genuine emancipation might have been easier. But administrators clung to the *status quo*. Among the protests in Angola were the words of António da Silva Porto, one of the most respected frontiersmen in Portuguese African history. His beliefs have been advanced up to the present day in defense of the "We must go slow" approach to native policy.

It is much to be desired that our legislators had limited their patriotic love to the prosperity of the colony and not touched the matter of slavery, letting it continue at home and in the crown colonies, where there might be use for its assistance. Religion, progress, time, and, finally, the repression of the traffic to foreign possessions would bring about its extinction; with the advance of civilization slaves and free men would come to be so aware of its benefits that there would be created a love for work . . . In the absence of this process and with the law of April 29, 1858, the consequences will be the disrespect of the black for white men and, perhaps, assassination will be the final result! Unhappily, the present laws invite such an end.[28]

Although the English traveler Winwood Reade gave a jolly picture of affairs in Angola in about 1860 ("Those who know what slaves are will immediately infer that those of Angola are really the masters; and not only masters, but tyrants. Such is unfortunately the case with negroes, schoolboys, and all inferior beings. It is useless to appeal to anything except their epidermis"),[29] proponents of abolition in Lisbon were less convinced. Aware that little was being done in preparation for the final expiry of slavery, they promulgated the decree of 1869 whereby the state of slavery was immediately abolished throughout the empire. All slaves were made *libertos*, and although the ultimate connection with their master was not to be severed until 1878, in their future association with him they would be granted such privileges as remuneration for services and protection of person. Did this well-intentioned legislation plant the germ of an idea that a slave could be a slave in the absence of slavery? Certainly the equivocal position of the *liberto* could have been suggestive to the legislative mind concerned later in the century with devising laws which would simultaneously guarantee the African his independence and the European his supply of labor. Even more certain is that the condition of the *liberto* was maintained, in one guise or another, long after 1878.

In 1875 the state of *liberto* was abolished, effective one year later. However, the ex-*liberto* was obliged to contract his services, preferably to his former master, for two years. The 108 articles drawn up to implement the 1875 decree during the two-year period of tutelage have been called the first Portuguese native labor code. Among other points it introduced into colonial legislation the vagrancy clause, suggested by Sousa Coutinho a hundred years before, under which the nonproductive African could be judged a vagrant and made to contract for his services.

For residents of Angola the vagrancy clause was one of the loopholes in the labor code of 1878, *Regulamento para os contratos de serviçais e colonos nas províncias da Africa*, although it is doubtful that the rugged slave owners and traders of either colony needed a formal loophole, since many of them ignored the *Regulamento* completely. The Regulation of 1878 has drawn the heated attacks of conservative Portuguese colonialists, since it flatly abolished forced labor and endeavored to replace it with a system of free labor. Enemies of the measure protested that it sanctioned indolence and vagabondage and saw to it that future legislation, particularly the labor code of 1899, had an obligatory work clause. The Regulation was an advanced milestone in Portuguese native policy which has not been reached again. It was designed to protect the rights and interests of the African and sought to guarantee for him a basic human dignity. Impractical, possibly, but any labor policy which did not sanction slavery was impractical in the African colonies. Enlightened for its age, this Regulation is one of the refreshing moments in a colonial policy which all too often seems to have been characterized by intent to exploit the Negro in Africa and confuse Portugal's critics abroad.

But the measure did not condone vagrancy as it was defined in the metropolitan penal code and was based on the supposition that a labor contract between African and Portuguese would benefit each mutually. These were two flaws which would not have had such grievous consequence had the Regulation fallen on receptive soil. It did not, and African-Portuguese relations rested on hypocrisy and injustice. A series of techniques were evolved under which the colony's labor supply — which was also São Tomé's — remained relatively undisturbed. The simplest method was for the master to keep his former slaves under the pretense of contracted *serviçais*. In the interior, certain Portuguese, mulatto, and Negro profiteers operated as in the days of the slave trade, with the small difference that instead of buying the prisoners or subjects of a chief they contracted for them. For his part in gaining the contracts of workers, who remained in ignorance of the whole procedure, the chief was bribed with alcohol, powder, and guns. A third source of supply consisted of the so-called vagrants. In some areas Portuguese officials considered all Africans not under contract vagrants. Since certain colonial authorities, known as *curadores*, were empowered to use their office in drawing up contracts between employer and worker — and to act as guardians or protectors for the African, a notion put forth by the Jesuits in Angola in the seventeenth century — the door to exploitation was open: declare the native a vagrant, force him into the usual five-year contract, let the state, or its representative, pocket the revenue.

Practically, free labor did not exist in the colonies. The employer felt less obligation to the contracted laborer than he had formerly to his slaves. The *serviçais* were maintained at subsistence level. Many died or failed to return to their villages, especially those exported to São Tomé, and some parts of Angola were almost emptied of their inhabitants; from other areas the Africans fled into the deep interior. Some contract workers, driven to desperation by the distance from their villages and the inhumanity of the treatment given them, revolted and formed fierce little bands of warriors. Missionary literature of the 1880's and 1890's is replete with horror tales, which were promptly discredited by local officials, who have long held that foreign missionaries should give up freedom of conscience and speech for the privilege of working in Angola and Moçambique. But commentaries on brutality in the colonies came not only from foreigners. Belo de Almeida was a Portuguese soldier in Angola during that period, not a missionary.

It was the custom in those days to give them [*serviçais*] the rudest and most difficult work, in domestic service as well as in the fields and factories, above all in the matter of porterage, in which they took the role of humble animals.

For the slightest fault they were often cruelly punished by being beaten with the hippopotamus-hide whip which cut their skin horribly. Very frequently one heard in the late hour of a warm mysterious African night piercing shrieks of pain from the poor wretches who were being beaten by the company officers or head men, generally hard-hearted mulattoes.[30]

The rubber boom at the turn of the century intensified the scramble for workers. In the madness that swept over the rubber country in the Belgian Congo and Angola, whole villages were regimented and marched hundreds of miles to extract the precious latex. With the male population of the village frequently under contract in another part of the colony, the majority of the workers were women and children. The work was hard, the food insufficient. On the return trip the villagers acted as bearers. If not all of those who went returned, neither the chief nor the rubber contractor was unduly concerned. Nor was the Angolan government, which did not care one way or the other, pleased to collect the export duties on rubber which was the colony's major product in those years.

The principle of forced labor, denied in the Regulation of 1878, was the heart of a report submitted by a government committee which met in 1898 to study the problems of Portuguese Africa. The gist of the committee's recommendations was incorporated in the Regulation of 1899, the most complete native labor code until 1928 and the practical philosophy for much of the New State's African policy. The committee was dominated by António Enes, hard-headed imperialist and former royal commissioner of Moçambique. Enes had scored the previous labor code and was determined that muddled liberal ideas should not be the basis for another. Aware that Portugal was in a weak diplomatic position vis-à-vis her European neighbors because of the underdevelopment of her African colonies ("Portugal must, absolutely must, without delay make her African inheritance prosper, and prosperity can only come from productivity"), Enes maintained that this material development rested on the African's shoulders. Lest the bald implications of forced labor again draw the fire of humanitarians — and because they believed that what they said was sociological law — members of the committee sought to define these repressions in the language of the day, to wit, that it was the duty of Europe to promote the African's advancement into civilization: "The state, not only as a sovereign of semi-barbaric populations, but also as a depository of social authority, should have no scruples in *obliging* and, if necessary, *forcing* [italics the committee's] these rude Negroes in Africa, these ignorant Pariahs in Asia, these half-savages from Oceania to work, that is, to better themselves by work, to acquire through work the happiest means of existence, to civilize themselves through work . . ." [31] Tradition had reasserted itself in African policy.

Thus the first article of the Regulation of 1899 states that "all natives of Portuguese overseas provinces are subject to the obligation, moral and legal, of attempting to obtain through work the means that they lack to subsist and to better their social condition. They have full liberty to choose the method of fulfilling this obligation, but if they do not fulfill it public authority may force a fulfillment." The obligation was considered fulfilled by those who had sufficient capital to assure their means of existence or those who had a paying profession, by those who farmed on their own account a plot of land whose size was to be determined by local authorities or by those who produced goods for export in quantities judged sufficient by local authorities, and by those who worked for salary a minimum number of months each year, this number to be fixed by local authorities. Exempt from the obligation were women, men over sixty years of age, boys under fourteen, the sick and the invalid, sepoys, policemen, chiefs, and locally prominent Africans. "All others who do not fulfill voluntarily the obligation to work . . . will be compelled by the authorities to do so." To make sure that sufficient employment opportunities were available for refractory Africans the law permitted their services to be requisitioned from the provincial government either by government agencies or by private individuals and companies. To protect the African worker the Regulation specified that the employers provide adequate salaries for him and look after his health and living conditions. Finally, the law flatly forbade the employer to hold back any of the worker's salary or oblige him to buy from the employer's store.

The Regulation of 1911 continued almost intact the provisions of the 1899 code. It limited the term of the contract to two years and provided additional penalties for employers administering corporal punishment to the African worker. Three years later the Portuguese Republic issued a decree revoking all previous native labor legislation, replacing it with an extensive document designed to correct the abuses committed under previous legislation. The new code was a little softer around the edges but as hard at the core. "Every sound native in the Portuguese colonies is subject under this law to the moral and legal obligation of providing, by means of work, his sustenance and of progressively bettering his social condition" (Article 1). The obligation could be filled in some cases by three months' labor and in others by nothing less than a year's. Correctional labor penalties ran from a week to a year. Correctional labor could only be used by the provincial government or a municipality except when these bodies were unable to provide work for the men, in which case the forced laborers could be taught the dignity of work by an approved private employer requisitioning them (in Angola the use of forced labor by private firms or individuals was theoretically abolished by a decree of 1921). The government also reserved the right to requisition labor within each chief's jurisdiction for works of public utility within the area. The obligation of colonial officials to assist in recruiting was withdrawn, but the colonial government was to encourage the African by all legitimate means to contract his services. What this article tried to do was to curb, but not kill, the enthusiasm of administrators in the interior and to bring an end to indiscriminate recruiting. The good offices of the chief were to be used in persuading reluctant tribesmen to fulfill their obligation. Professional recruiters, individuals and companies, of established good character were permitted, within specified restrictions, to contract the services of Africans (the recruiters were usually hired by large land companies, although free lances supplying smaller farms and industries also practiced). Although contracts were not legally demanded of workers, they were required to possess a duly stamped record of gainful employment. The Regulation stressed increased obligations for employers in matters of transport, medical care, maintenance, salary, and instruction.[32]

It would be agreeable to observe that the reality was an improvement over the ideal, but this, of course, was not the case, and it would be bootless to dwell on the continuing exploitation of the African in Moçambique and Angola, although labor conditions in the first quarter of the twentieth century were a little better than they had been throughout the nineteenth. There is often a generous sensibility present in the Portuguese character, and in the face of the intolerable reality perpetuated by restrictive labor codes, a number of provincial governors strove to prevent excesses, and citizens of both provinces made repeated protests in the African's defense. The tragedy was not only that the primary intent of the legislation was carried out zealously, but that its positive side, which did contain a modicum of social justice and improvement for the African, was neglected. There is not much evidence that the African was "civilized through work," while there is plenty of evidence that he was degraded and exploited. That a similar exploitation went on simultaneously in French Africa, as readers of Gide are aware, in the Belgian Congo, in German East Africa, and even in the Union of South Africa should not give comfort to the Portuguese and less to foreign critics. The Portuguese have long boasted that they better than any other European colonial power understand the African, but if it is this understanding which is incorporated in the native labor codes of 1899 and 1914, one may conclude that understanding the African and exploiting him are often one and the same thing.[33]

The continuation of something very akin to slavery — and even the slave trade — in the late nineteenth and early twentieth centuries and the official sanction this activity seemed to find in the labor code of 1899 involved Angola and Portugal in a controversy which has not yet been forgotten and aroused resentments perhaps greater than those created by the problem of the slave-trade abolition. This was the São Tomé contract-labor scandal which grew out of the Nevinson and Cadbury reports. Once again a number of important vocal Englishmen took up cudgels against their country's ancient ally on the matter of improper labor practices in Angola and São Tomé.

The São Tomé scandal had been simmering for forty years before it boiled over. Had not the publicized atrocities from the Belgian Congo rubber forests drawn the attention of a shocked Europe to that part of the world, it is possible that Angola's neo-slave trade to São Tomé would have run its course without disturbing the world's conscience. It could not have lasted very long after 1904–1905, the years of Nevinson's visit, because Angola herself needed labor too desperately to permit its export to São Tomé.

As early as 1865, Commissioner Vredenburg, British member of the English-Portuguese Mixed Commission on Slaving, complained that Negroes were still being shipped from Benguela to the cocoa plantations of São Tomé and Príncipe. The efforts of the governor general of Angola to halt it were unsuccessful, and his special representative reported that the governor of Benguela was apathetic and lesser officials there were in open connivance with the traffic. In 1868 Acting Commissioner Hewitt and in 1869 Vredenburg again picked up the issue, noting that the slaves were now called *libertos* and classified on shipping records as steerage passengers to the two islands. The response of the Portuguese minister in London was sharp and indignant: he pointed out, incorrectly, that it was a question of the emigration of free labor and, correctly, that existing Anglo-Portuguese treaties did not deal with *libertos* but slaves.[34] The matter seems to have ended there, although subsequently the Earl of Mayo described in 1882 the system of recruiting labor in Angola for the islands, and missionaries (particularly those of Bishop Taylor's self-supporting missions) and travelers (Crawford, Harding, and James Johnston) published gruesome tales of slave processions from the highlands along the *via dolorosa* to Catumbela. Readers of Joseph Conrad's "An Outpost of Progress" (1898) were introduced to a fictional band of ten Negro traders from Luanda who had penetrated into the Congo in search of slaves. Responsible opinion in the Portuguese government and press demanded investigations and corrective action, and gestures were made by the colonial office in Lisbon and the governor general's office in Luanda; but without honest co-operation from minor officials and a stronger authority throughout the province than Portugal exerted, little could be permanently accomplished.

The most pointed presentation of the process was not written by an Englishman, but by a governor of Portuguese Guinea, Judice Biker.[35] The majority of the workers, Biker stated, came through the ports of Benguela and Novo Redondo. They were purchased in the interior from local chiefs by merchants, or their agents, from the two ports. When an order for laborers came down the coast, African villagers were taken before the *curador* (the officer in charge of native affairs), contracted as *serviçais*, and sent off to São Tomé. Generally the *curador* was as ignorant of their language as they of his, and the contract negotiations were reduced to a formality. The contract was for five years, but at the end of the period none of the Angolans returned. "Is this because the *roceiro* [plantation owner] makes their life so agreeable, dressing them and feeding them so well, instructing them, civilizing them, creating necessities for them so that he may have the satisfaction of satisfying them? Do they choose to continue to work there, renewing their contracts?" Biker asks. "Would that this were so." Biker goes on to describe the twelve-hour working day in the moist island climate, the high infant-mortality rate, the poor diet, the treatment of pregnant women. The main supply of workers came from Angola, increasing steadily after 1878, save for a few Africans from the nearby coast and a handful of Chinese peasants. The export figure for Angola ran from two to five thousand a year, men, women, and children. The greatest crime, concludes Governor Biker, was not the enslaving of the Angolan or his sufferings on São Tomé, but the refusal of the plantation owner to repatriate a single worker. Herein lies the strongest condemnation of the bad faith of planter and officials alike.

Henry W. Nevinson in *A Modern Slavery*, published in 1906, did nothing more than document in cold and angry detail the substance of the charges made by Biker and by both Portuguese and outside critics distressed by the brutalities committed in the name of contract labor. The difference was that Nevinson had a larger, more receptive audience. One of the most famous foreign correspondents of his time, having reported the Greco-Turkish and South African wars for the *London Daily Chronicle*, Nevinson was to be found in the vanguard of all social reform movements. On his return from South Africa he was approached by Harper's, asking if he would undertake an "adventurous journey" for them for one thousand pounds. After discarding Arabia and the South Seas as possible destinations, Nevinson consulted H. R. Fox Bourne, Secretary of the Aborigine's Protective Society and recent author of an exposé of the Belgian Congo rubber scandals, *Civilisation in Congoland* (wherein Fox Bourne implies that Portuguese treatment of Africans is preferable to the Belgian variety) and Travers Buxton, Secretary of the British and Foreign Anti-Slavery Society. Both spoke of dim rumors — contemporary reports from the British consul in Luanda were hardly to be classified as dim rumors — of appalling horrors reaching them from Angola and São Tomé. "My decision was taken, for here was a journey almost certainly ad-

venturous and with an object definite, inspiring, and possibly bene-
ficial." [36] Nevinson's presence in the Portuguese African provinces,
then, was not accidental, nor is it likely that his talks with Fox Bourne
and Buxton left him altogether without prejudice toward his subject.

At the same time Nevinson was neither a trouble-maker nor an international carpetbagger nor a hired hand for antislavery forces. It
has been a serious mistake for Portuguese officials to attempt to dismiss him, and others like him, such as Edward Ross and Basil Davidson, with hasty countercharges and personal invective instead of
trying to make a thoughtful and substantial presentation of the Portuguese case. In the first place, Nevinson was a good journalist. He got
his facts right. On the basis of travel, interview, and reading, Nevinson made a reasoned, if not impartial, presentation of slave-labor practices which Portuguese writers have denied but never satisfactorily
refuted. In the second place, he isolated the guilt to those involved:
the village chief, the contractor, the supplier in Benguela or Novo
Redondo, the planters on São Tomé, and the corrupt or misled officials
along the line who permitted the transactions. The Portuguese, Nevinson noted, were "as sensitive and kindly as other people" and didn't
like their province referred to as a slave state. He cited the *Defeza de
Angola*, an occasional newspaper which had exposed the system. He
also wrote that the old caravan shipments had been reduced in recent
years because of the shock of public feeling in Portugal and the stern
action taken by the commandants of several interior forts.[37] *A Modern Slavery* is inspired by a genuine humanitarian feeling; it is not
built on generalizations and innuendo. Its details are calculated to
shock, in the tradition of nineteenth-century antislavery literature, for
Nevinson wrote with passionate purpose. Even twenty years later, in
a volume of reminiscences, recalling a scene at Novo Redondo where
he had seen a young African mother try to scramble up a swaying
ship's ladder from a lighter loaded with *contratados*, Nevinson wrote:

> At last she reached the top, soaked with water, her blanket gone, her
> gaudy clothing torn off or hanging in strips, while the baby on her back,
> still crumpled and pink from the womb, squeaked feebly like a blind
> kitten. Swinging it around to her breast, she walked modestly and with-
> out complaint to her place in the row that waited the doctor's inspection.
> In all my life I have never heard anything so hellish as the outburst of
> laughter with which the ladies and gentlemen of the first class watched
> the slave woman's struggle up to the deck. It was one of those things
> which made one doubt whether mankind has been worth the travail of
> our evolution.[38]

Nevinson's accounts — in addition to *A Modern Slavery* he wrote a series of articles for *The Spectator* and *The Fortnightly Review* — set off a storm of indignation in England which had the effect of precipitating the controversy. In a series of lectures, Nevinson aroused public sentiment against "legalized slavery in Angola and São Tomé." He found support from many eminent Englishmen, among them Ramsay MacDonald, John Galsworthy, H. G. Wells, and Gilbert Murray, and from long-term Portuguese and foreign residents of Angola who wrote to him that he had understated the case. Nevinson urged his government to make representations to the government of Portugal and suggested that chocolate manufacturers in England set up a boycott of São Tomé cocoa. In particular he called upon William Cadbury of the chocolate firm to uphold his Quaker principles by refusing to buy from São Tomé and to publish a report his representative, Joseph Burtt, had made of conditions in the Portuguese African colonies.

Nevinson had met Burtt on São Tomé when the latter was on his way to Angola and had characterized him as a man who "appeared to despise 'the working man' and was inclined to reverence the working capitalist." Since Burtt confirmed Nevinson's suspicions ("The Portuguese are certainly doing a marvelous job for Angola and these islands. Call it slavery if you like. Names and systems don't matter. The sum of human happiness is being infinitely increased. And, after all, are we not all slaves?"), the journalist had scant hopes of converting him, although a Quaker, to the humanitarian cause and was agreeably surprised when Burtt sent back word to Cadbury, after a year in Angola and São Tomé, that Nevinson's report, far from being exaggerated, was an underestimate of the truth.[39] Cadbury was not immediately convinced and even tried to dissuade Nevinson from publishing an article in *The Fortnightly Review*. Thereupon *The Standard* took up the attack on Cadbury, on the occasion of the industrialist's own departure for Angola, and heaped satiric invective on his timidity, thus setting off one of the most celebrated English libel suits — wherein both parties were agreed that there *was* slavery in Angola — of the decade.

Cadbury was not as timorous as he was represented, although he had proceeded with supreme discretion. In 1901 Cadbury Brothers had called attention to unsatisfactory labor practices, and two years later Cadbury himself had gone to Lisbon where the São Tomé Planters' Association denied that such conditions existed and the Minister of Marine and Overseas made light of the matter. Acting in consultation with other English firms and a German company, Cadbury had sent Joseph Burtt to the islands, Angola, and Moçambique. On the advice of the Foreign Office, all controversy in the press was avoided until Burtt's return. Cadbury and Burtt then went to Lisbon to make further representations. The new Minister of Marine and Overseas, Aires de Ornelas, was frank and helpful, and promised immediate action; but three months later he was out of office, and Cadbury was again driven to correspondence with the Planters' Association, listing Burtt's allegations of contract-labor abuses. In his letter of November 28, 1907, Cadbury reviewed the charges of high mortality, non-repatriation of workers, bogus contracts, and concluded, "However much it may cost us to leave off buying your excellent cocoa and although we know it will cause a loss . . . we must say that our conscience will not permit us to continue buying the raw material for our industry, if we do not have the certainty of its being produced in the future by a system of free labor." [40] The Association responded that Mr. Burtt's figures were inaccurate, that workers died because of the climate, fled because of quarrels among themselves, and that they remained on the island because they wanted to and that it would be "illegal and inhuman to oblige them to go away against their wishes." As for the brutalities in Angola, the Association refrained from commenting particularly since they had no first-hand knowledge of the area, but they did observe that such inhumanity took place "in regions where no permanent government or police authority exists," and that the Portuguese government was taking energetic action in Angola. [41]

Cadbury then decided to verify the accusations by visiting the Portuguese possessions. The publication of his and Burtt's observations bore out in almost every detail what had been said by Biker and Nevinson. Labour in Portuguese West Africa was a temperate unemotional presentation of the facts. Numerous appendices contained recent decrees against forced labor and substantiating comment from Portuguese newspapers. As far as Angola is concerned, the most interesting section of the work is a presentation of the interview between Cadbury and Governor General Paiva Couceiro, during which the governor made the following points: Cadbury was free to go where he chose in Angola and see what he pleased; he could copy any published figures, but since Cadbury was not accredited by the British government, Paiva Conceiro was unable to give him any specific information; the Portuguese forbade slavery; Angola was a large province, and it was possible that sometimes breaches in the law took place; labor recruiting in Angola was done by the Labor Bureau of São Tomé, over which the Angolan government had no control; contracts made in the interior for native labor had to be examined on the coast, but the government was not responsible; a new law of 1908 had made minor changes, but the system of contracting labor was about the same as always.[42]

Shortly after Cadbury's return to England, Cadbury Brothers, two other English companies, and a German firm began a boycott of São Tomé cocoa. In the same year, 1909, the Anti-Slavery Society sent Burtt to the United States to convince chocolate manufacturers there to refrain from buying the island's cocoa. Burtt was received by President Taft, but no United States action resulted. Meanwhile the controversy in England fed on itself. In a letter to the *Times* (June 22, 1909) missionary Charles Swan, author of another study on contract labor, *The Slavery of Today* (London, 1909), claimed a twenty-three-year association with Angola and gave the results of an inquiry he had conducted — at the request of Cadbury — into forced labor in the interior. The statement was signed by all the missionaries in Angola Swan had been able to reach. The letter stated that Africans had been constantly bought and sold during the time each missionary had been in Angola, that although many Africans had been exported under the contract-labor system, they had not found one worker who understood the contract, and that they had never known one Angolan who went voluntarily to São Tomé nor one who had been repatriated.

In 1913 the most scalding condemnation of contract labor in Angola was published. John Harris' *Portuguese Slavery: Britain's Dilemma* reviewed what the author considered the blighted record of the past twelve years. Citing priests, colonial officials, Angolan newspapers, Harris made dramatic reference to skulls by the side of the old slave trail, shackles, murder, and a devastated land — details familiar to the reader of African slave-trade classics. On the Belgian Congo frontier, Harris charged, from 20,000 to 40,000 slaves were still sold each year. Regarding São Tomé, of the 70,000 to 100,000 Angolan workers shipped there in the thirty years preceding 1908, not a single one had been repatriated. "No amount of argument, no number of Pecksniffian decrees and regulations can alter these facts." [43]

Harris' work was the last important shot fired on the English side. The First World War, during which England and Portugal reaffirmed their friendship, diverted attention from the problem; in the meantime, Portuguese colonial administrators had taken a determined interest in mitigating the abuses of contract labor to São Tomé and saw to it that most of the workers returned to Angola on the expiration of their contract. The rigid attitudes taken by the British and Portuguese governments in 1910 and 1911 had made real co-operation in those years impossible, but in 1913 the Portuguese government agreed to accept a specially appointed British consul general for Portuguese West Africa, ostensibly to supervise consular posts there. Consular reports from the region from 1909 to 1916 reveal the vigor with which the Foreign Office quietly pushed the fight against the excesses of forced or contract labor. During these years conditions gradually improved, to the satisfaction of the English representatives, and in 1916 Consul Hall Hall, in the last report of a series, informed his government that conditions were such to justify the purchase of cocoa from São Tomé and Principe.[44] Two progress reports, one in 1915 and the other in 1917, indicate the changes that had taken place. From a total of four Africans repatriated in 1910 the number had steadily increased to the point where almost as many Angolans left São Tomé as reached there.[45] About the same time Joseph Burtt wrote that "a great human drama has been acted, and it has ended happily." [46]

The charges, countercharges, and recriminations growing out of the long debate came to have a certain sameness, but on some points there was fairly general agreement. Not even Nevinson found living conditions for the Angolans intolerable on São Tomé. Burtt found them quite satisfactory, and later observers classified them as excellent. As early as the 1890's the Portuguese on the island found a defender in Mary Kingsley, who refused to believe the story that some Krumen who had hired themselves out to planters there were not released when their contract expired. "I have seen too much of the Portuguese in Africa to believe that they would, in a wholesale way, be cruel to natives." [47] Both Portuguese and English were in substantial agreement that the labor-recruiting system in Angola was a cruel affair, breeding inequities and corruption, and both hoped, possibly with varying degrees of fervor, that they would soon be corrected. Nor was their any essential quarrel about the technical legality of contracting workers in Angola for the islands.

Quite apart from the popular and diplomatic pressures from England, members of the Portuguese government and many Portuguese citizens were disturbed about what was going on. Their distress was revealed in condemnations in the Portuguese parliament and press and in a number of legislative steps taken to control the practice. In 1903, 1908, 1909 (two decrees), 1912 (two decrees), the government set up restraints, in the words of a 1909 relatório, "to safeguard the prestige of the Portuguese name and to guarantee more effectively the rights of natives, as free citizens, granted by the national constitution."

When some Portuguese wrote, on the other hand, that the

Angolan went willingly to São Tomé and refused to return, that the labor contractor who brought him from the coast was saving him from death in the interior, they were less persuasive and seem to have been seeking to convince themselves. Nor did it further their defense to refer to the English critics as sickly sentimental philanthropists. They were on surer ground when they accused the chocolate syndicate of being motivated by economic reasons as well as humanitarian ones in discrediting the São Tomé producers. A second telling point was their invitation to Nevinson, Cadbury, and their colleagues to share their Christian concern with the Moçambique laborers contracted for the South African mines and to ascertain how many went voluntarily to serve English capital and how many returned from the healthful airs of the pits.[48]

The colonial administration of the Republic established in 1910, while maintaining the obligation for the African to work, bent its efforts to do away with these vestiges of slavery in Angola.[49] Governor General Norton de Matos, arrogant, blunt, and honest, refused to heed the complaints about the shortage of labor and the necessity to force the African to work. He overrode the resistance of local residents in a series of decrees and draconian measures designed to get the African to work for himself. He attempted to enforce those parts of the labor codes guaranteeing the contract worker minimum benefits. Corporal punishment was abolished, officials supervised, and the licenses of certain recruiting agents suspended. With the establishment of the circumscription (see Chapters IX and X) and regional civil administrators, Norton de Matos attempted to insure the rights of the Africans, to defend their property and to forbid violence and extortion. He tried to eliminate so-called vagrancy by promoting agriculture and persuading the African to produce more than he used. When asked where the European plantations and industries were to get workers, the governor replied that the economic development of Angola rested on the moral and material progress of the African, that it was the duty of Portugal to civilize, elevate, and instruct the African and to take advantage of his capacities as a farmer, to treat him with justice and equity. Matos held that the African had to be free, a property owner, and master of his skills; his administration had to have the courage not only to formulate this ideal, but to carry it out. On these principles were to be resolved the province's labor problems.

But the habits of centuries were stronger than the reforms of one man or one government, and after the governor general's departure in 1915 his programs for the Africans began to wither. When Norton de Matos returned in 1919 as high commissioner his concern for the welfare of the native population now conflicted with his grandiose dreams for Angola's development, and these projects demanded labor. The 1925 report of the American sociologist from the University of Wisconsin, Edward Alsworth Ross, gave a disturbing picture of African life in Angola.

The year before, Ross and a New York physician, Melville Cramer, came to Angola to study the native situation. In some ways Ross's visit (Cramer's contribution to the project was negligible) was typical of the whirlwind tour — followed by a superficial, often inaccurate account — which has brought so much ridicule on American travelers and journalists. Ross stated that he was in Angola from July 19 to September 3 and a shorter time in Moçambique. (Although Ross had some harsh words about Moçambique, his report dwells mainly on labor excesses in Angola.) His report was submitted to the Temporary Slaving Commission of the League of Nations, where it was given a careful rebuttal by the Portuguese delegation. With that the matter seems to have come to an official dead-end. But the resentments it stirred up linger on.

Had the Ross report been full of self-righteous indignation and generalities, one might discard it as the work of a hasty traveler who came to Angola knowing what he was to find and departing shortly after, having found what he was looking for. But this was not the case, and what Ross wrote was completely consistent with what others had been saying about labor conditions in Angola for half a century. Ross visited the interior, Malange, Bailundo, and Bié. That he spent most of his time upcountry with Protestant missionaries, who assisted him in his study and furnished him interpreters, made his work for Portuguese colonial officials not only worthless, but prejudicially false. One of the curious and troubling aspects of Ross's account is its unimaginative presentation. He makes no reference to what others have written about the abuses of contract labor. The work is a simple series of minuscule case histories on individuals and villages. Of an Ambaca village he wrote:

Their lot is getting harder. Things got abruptly worse from 1917 to 1918 [the year a number of European coffee planters arrived in this area of the province]. The Government makes them work, but gives them nothing. They return to find their fields neglected, no crops growing. They would rather be slaves than what they are now . . . Now nobody cares whether they live or die. The Government serfdom is more heartless than the old domestic slavery which was cruel only when the master was of cruel character. Now they are in the grip of a system which makes no allowances for the circumstances of the individual and ignores the fate of the families of the labor recruits.

There are 140 huts in this area . . . For fifteen months not less than 50 [villagers] have been required to work on the roads, and some months more than a hundred. The quota is maintained by shifts.

When a white man applies to the *Administrador* for workers a soldier is sent with him to the village who calls out the chief and notifies him that so many men must be forthcoming from the village. When the men are taken for distant plantations, they are provided with a thin jersey, a *pano*, and in the cool season a blanket. Two months ago thirty from this area were taken to an unknown area . . .

In 1922 twenty from this area were requisitioned to work as carriers between L—— and P——. Their taxes had already been paid. For six months service they got the equivalent of $1.80. They think that the Government gets twelve dollars for every man who works for the planter six months. Somebody keeps most of it so that the laborer gets no pay.

The law contemplates that the laborer shall enter into labor contracts with a free will. The *Ambaquistas* say that they put some thumb prints on some papers, but they do not know what the papers contain, and would be flogged should they dare refuse to sign them.[50]

Elsewhere Ross refers to work cards with thirty-six-day months, the terror inspired by the native sepoys, and the sense of hopelessness felt by the African villager. At several plantations and the mission farms he found the African well paid and contented, but his conclusions on the life of the African in 1924 bear the impress of centuries. The labor system in Angola is virtual serfdom, and the African spends so much time working for others that he cannot take care of his own crops. Wages turned over in trust by employers to the government seldom reach the African. Skilled labor is so misused that the African sees no point in learning skills. Needless roadbuilding places a crushing burden on him. Labor stealing is prevalent. Officials do not feel strong enough to stand up to farmers or traders in defense of the African. Sepoys are grossly brutal and abuse their authority. The government provides nothing in the way of schools or medicine or emergency relief. Parts of the interior are so bad that the Angolans escape to the Belgian Congo or Rhodesia. The amount of the hut tax and its manner of collection create severe hardships.[51]

Some of Ross's remarks might justly be regarded as inconclusive because of the choice of subjects he interrogated — almost exclusively from the vicinity of Protestant missions — and because of the usual difficulties encountered by a stranger working through an interpreter. But the district governor, F. M. de Oliveira Santos, who was given the task of making formal rebuttal to Ross's charges, did not pursue this line of argumentation. Setting out with an aide, Oliveira Santos retraced Ross's footsteps, collecting signed contradictions and additional statements from as many people as would admit having talked to the American. These documents, a vehement personal attack on Ross and the missionaries, and some eloquently vague declarations on Portugal's humane native policy formed the basis of the reply. Oliveira Santos' itemized conclusions indicated that the *Resposta* was as hasty a piece of work as the one it sought to correct: (1) Ross was not in Angola as long as he said he was. (2) He did not visit nineteen *embalas*, as stated, but only thirteen. (3) All of his information was furnished by Congregational and Methodist missionaries. (4) These missionaries insinuate themselves into the political and administrative life of Angola. (5) Some missionaries have carried out business and commerce in violation of their visas. (6) The vague cases of beatings and force reported by Ross have not been proved. (7) The violation of village women by sepoys was not proved. (8) His forced labor statistics lack foundation. (9) His charges of graft against local administrators are false. (10) Construction of roads reduces the necessity of using the Africans as bearers. (11) The Portuguese have a valuable native assistance program. (12) They have set up schools for the African. (13) The work done by the Protestant missions does not contribute to the welfare of the community. (14) Ross's conclusions, given him by the missionaries, are palpably false. (15) Dr. Cramer did not collaborate in the report. (16) His statements on native tools and primitive work habits are inexact and incomplete. (17) Portuguese abuse, when true, has been punished. (18) The crimes of sepoys, when ascertained, have been punished. (19) All laws regarding the African are faithfully followed. (20) The missionaries don't co-operate in getting the African to pay his taxes. (21) The Portuguese native policy is excellent. (22) The Protestant missionaries would be advised to act more circumspectly if they desire to remain in the province.[52]

In Moçambique the use of native labor, subject to the same general colonial laws and deriving from tradition, offered no sharp variations with practices in Angola, although Portuguese East Africa did not get embroiled in a São Tomé controversy. The French islands in the late nineteenth century and the Witwatersrand through the first half of the twentieth century received their quota of contract workers from Moçambique. (The *émigré* system was as reprehensible as the *serviçais* traffic to São Tomé, but the recruiting for the South African mines had almost from the beginning a framework of legality and was partly based on voluntary contracting by the African. By 1930 earlier methods of coercion had largely disappeared.) The effect of this annual emigration of workers left Moçambique with the same labor shortages as in Angola.

In 1906 the district governor of Inhambane, Almeida Garrett, suggested several changes in the native labor code to produce more workers. These included raising the exemption requirements for African farmers, obliging women to work, raising the fine for forçados (vagrants), and increasing the head tax.[53] Ross reported the same harsh conditions existing in Moçambique as in West Africa. But there were vigilant citizens in Lourenço Marques whose outcries acted as a check to the wholesale exploitation of the African. The contract made by High Commissioner Brito Camacho, for example, with Mr. Hornung of the Sena Sugar Estates in 1921 granting labor recruiting privileges to the company brought down a storm of protest — not all humanitarian, to be sure — around Brito Camacho's ears.[54] At the beginning of the century Freire de Andrade, governor general from 1906 to 1910, implemented reforms and held his subordinates to an accounting of their conduct in native affairs.

The flow of Negro workers to the South African mines was a pointed issue from 1900. Some Portuguese were disturbed for humane reasons, others by the drain of labor from the colony. The arrangements between the colonial government and the Transvaal which formalized the exchange of workers for commercial traffic were defended by the administration mainly on the basis of expediency. There was a certain amount of truth in the argument, for the Africans from Angola and Moçambique have long been drawn across the frontiers into the Congo, Rhodesia, and South Africa by the lure of higher wages. In the 1870's Africans from Delagoa Bay migrated to Natal to work on farms there for three or four years before returning with their earnings. Portuguese authorities put into effect a passport fee which the Natal farmers, eager for the labor, sometimes paid. Gradually a series of agreements were evolved which attempted to regulate the emigration. With the development of the Witwatersrand gold and coal industry, Africans from the Lourenço Marques district showed a distinct preference for working in the mines to working at home. Powerless to halt the yearly migration across the border and aware that the money the miners brought back stimulated Moçambique commerce, the colonial government sought to make formal arrangements with the operators whereby the interests of the province, the mine owners, and the African would be mutually protected.

After 1895 the Chamber of Mines tried to centralize recruiting of workers and to obtain a monopoly of labor in South Africa. They were not as successful at home as they were in Moçambique where, "according to the report of the Rand Native Labour Association, 'the services of every Labour Agent in Portuguese territory whose opposition was of any moment' were secured at a cost which did not 'materially affect the price of natives landed in these fields.' " [55] Within six years the importance of this supply led to a *modus vivendi* whereby the Transvaal mining industry was permitted to continue to recruit in Moçambique in return for a guarantee that a percentage of the Transvaal railway traffic pass through the port of Lourenço Marques. It is this naked exchange of rail service for human service which has given offense to so many people.

In 1909 the Transvaal-Moçambique Convention was drawn up. Subject to revisions, the Convention provided for labor recruitment privileges in Moçambique in return for the passage of 50 to 55 per cent of all railway traffic to and from the competitive area (the Johannesburg, Pretoria, Krugersdorp industrial area) through Lourenço Marques. The Convention was valid for ten years, after which it could be terminated by either party on a year's notice. With the formation of the Union in 1910 the Convention became applicable to its government. The agreement came to an end in 1923. In 1928 another convention was negotiated which, with some modifications, has continued to the present day. Part I fixed the maximum number of Africans from Moçambique to be employed in the Transvaal mines, stipulated working conditions, and provided that recruitment, allotments, and repatriation be entrusted to an organization approved by both governments. Part II dealt with railway traffic and rates, and Part III with customs matters. Five years later the maximum (80,000) and minimum (65,000) number of Africans to be recruited each year was fixed and the railway traffic through Lourenço Marques reduced to 47.5 per cent. No serious adjustments have since been made.[56]

The recruiting in Moçambique was entrusted exclusively after 1903 to the Witwatersrand Native Labour Association, except for the period 1911 to 1913 when all Africans from the territory of the Niassa Consolidated Company were recruited by the company for delivery on the coast to the WNLA's agents. (After 1913 men from north of the twenty-second parallel were prohibited from working in the mines because of a high incidence of tuberculosis and pneumonia among Africans from tropical zones, thus eliminating Portuguese Niassa as a source of labor. In the 1930's a number of Africans from north of the parallel were again permitted to go to the mines.) The WNLA was responsible for the Moçambique worker from the moment he signed the contract with the agent until he was returned to his village, although the colonial government does have native affairs offices (*cura-dorias*) in the Union. Within the province the WNLA maintained from ten to fifteen main receiving stations and over fifty substations employing more than twenty-five Europeans and about two hundred and fifty Africans. In the years after the Boer War recruiting was affectionately known as "blackbirding" by the agents, and one agent has left an account of how the WNLA beat the bushes for workers. He is at pains to contradict the prevalent notion that the chiefs were coerced to order their young men to the Transvaal, saying that for most of the young men of Sul do Save going to the mines was life's greatest experience.[57]

There is little doubt, however, that pressures were often put on the chief, if not by the agents, then by Portuguese officials, to procure workers, although there has been less indication in recent years that the WNLA has had to rely on anything more than its promises and the testimonies of men returning from the mines — with their boots and blankets and phonographs. Working conditions in the mines have improved, and the high mortality rate prevailing in the first decade of the century, 67.6 per 1,000 (another report states that from 1905 to 1912, 87,000 of 418,000 workers, that is, 26 per cent, did not return for one reason or another) has steadily declined. No longer are East Coast workers permitted to remain two and three years in the Rand mines. A one-year contract, with a possible extension of six months, is the maximum the African may serve before repatriation.

From 1904 to the present the Transvaal mines have taken from 60,000 to 115,000 Africans from Moçambique each year, the peak coming in 1928–29. For fifty years these recruits have been the backbone of the mines' labor force. The advantage of the Convention to the African has been the opportunity to work for wages higher than those he would normally receive in the colony. The monopoly given the WNLA, however, has made it difficult for the African from Moçambique to enter the Union to work elsewhere, as in the Natal sugar plantations and collieries (in the central part of the province the Rhodesian Native Labor Bureau has recruited a substantial number of Africans each year for work on farms and mines of Rhodesia). The sum of seventy-five to one hundred dollars withheld until the African's arrival in Moçambique has meant the beginning of economic security for some, although frequently the money has been spent on gaudy attractions. For the mining companies the Convention guaranteed a constant supply of unskilled, inexpensive labor — which would be used in areas and tasks where voluntary Union workers refused to serve. For Moçambique the advantages have also been large. In addition to the emergence of Lourenço Marques into an East African port of primary importance, the provincial economy has profited from the Rand wages spent in Moçambique (the withheld salary is paid in *escudos* to the returned worker by the government, which receives these wages in gold) and from the charges the government has established, such as $1.40 for a worker's passport, $0.70 for an extension, and $0.36 a month contract fee.

The controversy over the Rand labor system which went on until the recent years of the Salazar regime, when debate on such issues went out of fashion, turned on the single point of whether the province profited sufficiently from the Convention to make it worthwhile. A favorite theme in colonial studies was to blame Moçambique's slow progress on the lack of working hands. It was argued that the utilization of the available labor supply was subordinated to the needs of another part of Africa and that cultivation of large areas in Moçambique by African farmers consequently suffered. The Moçambique Company, for example, refused to permit the WNLA to recruit within its territories. It is true that the continuing absence of a large body of workers was a real loss to the province, but under a native labor code designed to exploit the African for the benefit of plantations and governmental projects, the argument that native agriculture suffered extremely from lack of workers was hardly convincing. Certainly no one should have been surprised that the young African, faced with the necessity of satisfying labor laws by contracting his services locally at an inadequate wage, or being shipped to a plantation a hundred miles away, should have chosen to go to the mines, adventurous and profitable. (In this regard, native labor regulations worked to the definite advantage of the Transvaal.) Others held that many miners did not come home, preferring to remain in the Union, and that others frequently returned ill.

For some opponents of the Convention the dignity of work in the Transvaal did not offer the same civilizing values as did the dignity of work in Moçambique, for the African came back to his village a vagrant and full of exaggerated ideas about wages and working conditions. A recent criticism by Professor António Mendes Correia, a sociologist and leading spokesman on African affairs for the present Portuguese government, suggests that in addition to the fact that the energy spent in the Transvaal could more profitably have been spent in the development of Moçambique, the African brought back customs and languages not his own, thus making it more difficult to assimilate him into the Luso-African community. He asks whether it is really right that the Portuguese Negro should waste his vitality, which would otherwise have benefited humanity, to dig out gold for the benefit of a few capitalists.[58] But these contentions, which show a casual disregard for the welfare of the African either at home or across the border, beg the essential question whether the labor lost would have been used for the genuine progress of Moçambique, for all of its inhabitants, not just the municipalities, the estates, and the European population. The encouragement of free labor and native agriculture from 1900 to 1928 was negligible. This being the case, the material advantages gained in Moçambique from the Convention could scarcely have been less than the theoretical ones which might have resulted from its cancellation.

In no sense has the recruitment of workers in Moçambique by the WNLA been the degrading spectacle that was the contract labor scandal in Angola. There were admittedly many wrongs when the chief was bribed to deliver a quota of workers and others when the returning men found that their deferred pay was held back by colonial officials under various pretexts. More disturbing than these abuses is the recognition implicit in the terms of the Convention that Portuguese colonial administrators regarded the African as a commodity, no longer to be sold as a slave, but still to be exchanged in the market of material values. Nor is the Chamber of Mines any less culpable in this regard. The Convention does not provide for the voluntary emigration of the worker from Moçambique into the Transvaal; in fact it seeks to prevent it by a series of controls. Nor, as Mendes Correia correctly suggests, can the classic proposal that through work the African is drawn into the Portuguese community be made to apply here. The Moçambique–South African Convention is an international projection of contract labor, and as such it is the step-child of a centuries-old policy in Portuguese Africa which, stripped to its essentials, has regarded the African as a working hand, call him slave, *liberto*, *contratado*, *voluntário*, or what you will.

VII

LIVINGSTONE AND THE
PORTUGUESE

ON June 28, 1854, this notice appeared in the *Boletim* of the Government General of Angola:

There has been submitted to this Government General by the most illustrious Sr. Edmund Gabriel a brief relation of a trip undertaken by the Reverend David Livingstone through the interior of Africa from the Cape of Good Hope to Luanda, which we publish as the preliminary of a more complete and detailed description which the traveler promises to write as soon as he has recovered from the discomforts which he suffered . . .

"On the 31st of last month the Reverend David Livingstone, an English missionary, arrived in this city, having left the Cape of Good Hope in May of 1852 with the object of exploring the interior of this continent, and at the same time establishing friendly relations with the different native peoples on the basis of which missionary stations may be in the future established among them . . .

"In April of this year Mr. Livingstone arrived at Cassange, having encountered many difficulties in this part of his trip among the tribes bordering Portuguese territory, but as soon as he found himself within the limits of the province of Angola, these disturbances ceased and he received the kindest and most generous attentions from Portuguese authorities at every fortress. He wishes to use this occasion to thank those gentlemen most sincerely and to express his gratitude for the courtesies and hospitalities he received from them and for the promptness with which they facilitated his progress to Luanda.

"Mr. Livingstone has the satisfaction of having been able, in spite of the deplorable season of the year and the great rain he encountered during his journey, to make various astronomical observations which helped him determine the exact position of the greater part of the places he visited. He intends, as soon as his health permits and with the permission of His Excellency the President of the Provisional Government of the Province, to publish the observations he made as well as vital information relating to the commercial activities in the interior, which may be of some interest to the inhabitants of this province. Loanda, June, 1854." [1]

On this amiable note was the first official Portuguese recognition given to the historic journey. It marks the beginning of an association between the first European inhabitants of black Africa and the most important European in the history of the continent. Unfortunately, it was an association which degenerated from mutual respect and friendship to painful recriminations.

One of the results of Livingstone's early explorations in central Africa was to speed the transition of Portuguese Africa from the past into the present, for it was now clear that the great expanse of land between Angola and Moçambique could no longer be considered the private, albeit uncharted, domain of the Portuguese crown. No longer would Portuguese contacts with her European neighbors be limited to coastal points and discussions on the slave trade. From now on, the lands and commerce of the interior would gain increasing importance in Europe's African policies, and Portugal, stirred by Livingstone's travels, sought with belated urgency to prepare to meet the inevitable challenge to her position in that part of the continent.

The significance of Livingstone does not ultimately rest on his travels, although his expeditions and geographic contributions were of primary importance. African explorers before and after him made equivalent geographical discoveries. Stanley was his equal, if not his master, in opening up central Africa to the eyes of the world; he had as well the distinction of contributing to the formation of Africa's largest private estate. But Stanley's exploits will always be a reflection of the achievements of Livingstone, and in the final analysis, the English-American remains a journalist who made a success out of exploration. The example of Livingstone is the example of faith and morality. The heroic solitary figure, fiercely determined and independent, yet humble and even gentle, best represents the positive aspirations of nineteenth-century Europe for Africa and of the English humanitarian tradition. If in the course of his experiences in Africa his hopes for the evangelization of the native population seem to have succumbed to fantasies for penetrating the secrets of the Nile's origin, Livingstone never yielded in his grim struggle against the slave trade and those who supported it. His dreams for a legitimate commerce which would replace this traffic in humanity and teach the African to develop his own resources did not fade. He could not foresee the ruthless exploitation of the African which ensued in many areas of central Africa which he opened to the world and in this regard, perhaps, his trust in European civilization was mistaken.

For ten years before he set off from the lands of the Makololo on the first of his historic journeys, Livingstone had prospected for mission stations in the Transvaal and Bechuanaland, pushing his way as far north as Linyanti, some one hundred and fifty miles west of Victoria Falls. It is apparent that as he went deeper into the interior, further from Moffat's station at Kuruman, the unexplored mass of south-central Africa, literally the great unknown, began to have a magnetic attraction on Livingstone's imagination. In the north, in Sebetuane's country, he came in contact with the Arab slave trade, which set his resolve more firmly to open up Africa to missionary settlement and legitimate commerce. In 1852 his decision was made. "I will go no matter who opposes." One year later, in November, Livingstone set out from Linyanti with twenty-seven Makololo porters. Following the upper Zambezi northward, he passed through Barotseland to Lake Dilolo, where he turned toward the sea through the hinterland of Angola.

Livingstone's goal was Luanda. At the start of his travels he wrote that "St. Philip de Benguela was much nearer to us than Loanda . . . but it is so undesirable to travel in a path once trodden by slave traders that I preferred to find another line of march."[2] This is one of the earliest references to slaving, one of the issues which later destroyed the friendship between the Portuguese and the missionary. Several months before, in the middle of 1853, while exploring Barotseland, Livingstone had met the Angolan trader Silva Porto who was trading in slaves and ivory. Earlier in the year Silva Porto had accepted the request of the Angolan government to make an overland journey from Angola to Moçambique but because of the turbulent state of the interior and illness Silva Porto had abandoned the project, although several of his African bearers did make their way to the coast of Moçambique. Livingstone wrongly regarded Silva Porto as a mulatto (this is one of Livingstone's common misconceptions of the Portuguese resident in Africa; it was almost willful, one suspects, on Livingstone's part to refuse to believe that any white men before him had penetrated this part of Africa) and seems to have considered him primarily as an ivory trader who was a possible rival for the honors of prior exploration, another issue on which Livingstone and the Portuguese were to part company. Silva Porto offered to take

Livingstone with him to Bié and in his account of the singular meeting, he characterizes the Englishman as an inquisitive, somewhat quarrelsome intruder.[3]

Livingstone's impressions of the country west of the Cuango River reveal his preoccupation with the subjects of slavery and priority. He found that the African in this region was regularly visited by slave traders, although he concludes that "there cannot have been much intercourse between real Portuguese and these people even here, so close to the Quango, for Sansawe asked me to show him my hair on the ground that, though he had heard of it, and some white men had even passed through his country, he had never seen straight hair before."[4] Livingstone's possessive pride on being the first European explorer through central Africa is more pronounced on his return to the Cuango from Luanda bound for the east coast. He refers to the native traders, *pombeiros* of Cassange, noting that "two of these, called in the history of Angola 'the trading blacks' (os funantes pretos), Pedro João Baptista and António José, having been sent by the first Portuguese trader living at Cassange, actually returned from some of the Portuguese possessions in the East with letters from the governor of Mozambique in the year 1815, proving, as is remarked, 'the possibility of so important a communication between Mozambique and Loanda.' This is the only instance of native Portuguese subjects crossing the continent. No European ever accomplished it, though the fact has lately been quoted as if the men had been *Portuguese*."[5]

But neither Livingstone's inherent sense of English superiority nor his distress, not yet articulated into the ringing denouncements of later years, over the slave trade in the interior restrained his gratitude to Portuguese officials and travelers, white or half-caste, who helped him in Angola. Ill with dysentery and fever, he was welcomed with the generosity and kindness which have made the tradition of Portuguese hospitality renowned throughout Africa. In the area of Lunda a young sergeant, Cipriano de Abreu, stripped his garden to nurse the sick traveler to health. In Cassange he was received with elaborate attentions and on his departure given letters of recommendation to the inhabitants of Luanda that they take him into their houses. "May God remember them," Livingstone wrote, "in their hour of need." In Luanda where the residents had little cause to extend a welcome to a man whose sympathies on slavery ran so counter to their own and whose nation was in part responsible for the decline of the city's fortunes, Livingstone was accepted with equal warmth. The governor offered the services of his medical officer and every facility at his disposal. Of his journey eastward through Angola, Livingstone wrote his wife that "though I speak freely about the Slave Trade, the very gentlemen who have been engaged in it, and have been prevented by the ships from following it, and often lost much, treated me most kindly in their houses, and often accompanied me to the next place beyond them, bringing food for all in the way." [6]

Of Portuguese success in getting along with the African Livingstone was also commendatory. "Some of the governors of Loanda . . . have insisted on the observance of a law which, from motives of humanity, forbids the Portuguese themselves from passing beyond the boundary. They seem to have taken it for granted, that, in cases where the white trader was killed, the aggression had been made by him. . . This indicates a much greater impartiality than has obtained in our own dealing with the Caffres, for we have engaged in the most expensive wars with them without once inquiring whether any of the fault lay with our frontier colonists." [7] Nor was Livingstone disturbed by the lack of color bar. "None of these gentlemen had Portuguese wives. . . It is common for them to have families by native women. It was particularly gratifying to me, who had been familiar with the stupid prejudice against colour entertained only by those who are themselves becoming tawny, to view the liberality with which people of colour were treated by the Portuguese. Instances, so common in the south, in which half-caste children are abandoned, are here extremely rare. . . The coloured clerks of the merchants sit at the same table with their employers, without any embarrassment. . . Nowhere else in Africa is there so much goodwill between Europeans and natives as here." [8]

For the iniquities of slavery, Livingstone had only mild rebuke for his hosts in Angola ("The Portuguese do not seem at all bigoted in their attachment to slavery"). His Makololo porters, possibly more sensitive than Livingstone to the extent of the trade in the province, were reluctant to enter Angola, fearing that they would be fettered and sold. Of his conversations with Commissioner Gabriel, the explorer was pleased to report: "The Portuguese home Government has not generally received the credit for sincerity in suppressing the slave-trade which I conceive to be its due." [9] At the same time he was aware that the legislation of humanitarian statesmen in Lisbon could not prevail against the economic interests of the trade or the actions of colonial servants whose wretched salaries forced them into the still profitable traffic. It was only after he had seen the cancerous conditions of the Arab trade in East Africa that Livingstone's charity toward the Portuguese disappeared.

Livingstone was less impressed with the spiritual and material development of the colony. Although he extolled the good influence of the Bishop of Luanda, he found little evidence of missionary presence in the interior and decided that what "this fine field" needed was a few Protestants. That the Christians he encountered had no notion of the Bible grieved him, but he concluded that it was better for the Africans to be "good Roman Catholics than idolatrous heathen." Traces of the Jesuits and Capuchins — he attributes to them the importation of coffee plants, yams, and various fruits trees — remained in Ambaca, where the early missionaries had so instilled the desire for literacy in the Africans that long after the priests' departure, the natives passed on from generation to generation their knowledge of reading and writing. Everyone spoke well of the Jesuits, Livingstone concluded.

The physical decline of the province had kept pace with the spiritual decline. Livingstone found Luanda a considerable city, but decaying, and many of its public buildings in disrepair or abandoned.[10] The capital was considered a penal settlement, but, he comments, a remarkably well behaved one where every night the bulk of the city's arms were in the hands of men who had once been convicts. Massangano he found in a ruined state. Sousa Coutinho's iron foundry was abandoned; there were neither priests nor teachers in the town.

The agricultural and commercial possibilities of Angola seemed abundant. At Cazengo Livingstone visited several flourishing coffee plantations. Sugar cane, cotton, and corn prospered so readily that they seemed "a providential invitation to forsake the slave trade." The merchants at Cassange and points in the interior struck him as being prosperous and eager to extend their trade southeastward into Makolololand. Portuguese merchants generally looked to foreign enterprise, "but as I always stated to them when conversing on the subject, foreign capitalists would never run the risk, unless they saw the Angolese doing something for themselves, and the laws so altered that the subjects of other nations should enjoy the same privileges in the country with themselves." [11] With rare exceptions Livingstone saw little being done to develop the country, residents and government officers being disinclined to do more than pursue their own small projects. Lawful commerce had increased since the abolition of the slave trade, but had the province "been in the possession of England, it would have been yielding as much or more of the raw material for the manufacturers as an equal extent of territory in the cotton-growing States of America." [12]

On September 10, 1854, Livingstone took leave of his friends in Luanda. He had been tempted to return home on one of the British ships of the Mixed Commission, but mindful of his promise to the Makololo and certain that the approach to central Africa from the west coast was impractical, he felt obliged to turn eastward in an attempt to find entry from the Indian Ocean. He declined the company of the learned botanist Friedrich Welwitsch, finding him of irritable temperament — and indecisive on the slavery question. The return journey to Linyanti, lasting exactly a year, was more tortuous than the expedition to Luanda. After a two-month rest there, Livingstone began his trek eastward along the Zambezi. After the discovery of Victoria Falls, he left the river to cross the Batoka plateau, picking up the Zambezi again a hundred miles above Zumbo. He arrived at Tete on March 3, 1856. On May 20 he reached Quelimane, where he waited six tiresome weeks for an English ship. In December he was in England.

The contributions of the Portuguese to his progress in East Africa were as unstinting as they had been in Angola. Nor did Livingstone withhold his praise. "I ought to speak well for ever of Portuguese hospitality. I have noted each little act of civility received, because somehow or the other we have come to hold the Portuguese character in rather a low estimation. This may have arisen partly from the pertinacity with which some of them have pursued the slave trade, and partly from the contrast they now offer with their illustrious ancestors — the foremost navigators of the world." [13] At Tete and Quelimane, a warm friendship developed between the Englishman and the Portuguese commandants. Major Tito Sicard at Tete gave the Makololo porters land to plant their crops, fresh clothing, and permission to join his own servants in elephant hunts, refusing all recompense. He subsequently wrote Livingstone in London to tell him that the Makololo had killed four elephants. Colonel Nunes at Quelimane did all in his power to restore Livingstone's health.

Nevertheless it is on the Zambezi that Livingstone's disenchantment with the Portuguese becomes noticeable. The friendly candor of his remarks on Angola now turns waspish in the *Missionary Travels*. In part this is the result of the man's exhaustion, in part the decadent state of Zambézia, and in larger part, perhaps, the natural impatience of an English imperialist ("It is on the Anglo-American race that the hopes of the world for liberty and progress rest") that the mighty waterway, which would later be as much of a disappointment to Livingstone as it had been to the Portuguese, had not been used by the Portuguese to pursue lawful commerce in the interior. The neglect at Sena and Tete evoked the comments usually made in this period by travelers up the Zambezi — ruin, immorality, and the failure of authority to suppress the lawlessness of the Goan *prazeros*. He could not see, as he had in Angola, the beginning of a transition from a slave economy to the orderly development of the colony's resources. The slave trade had rendered commerce stagnant, and the revenue from the colony was not sufficient to meet expenses. The quantities of grain, gold dust, and ivory previously exported had vanished, for the Portuguese had found it more profitable to sell the slaves which produced these commodities. No vestige of missionary influence existed among the inhabitants of Zambézia. All was desolation. The panacea, of course, was free trade and free labor — to which the Portuguese were as receptive as was Livingstone to the slave trade. "All the traders have been in the hands of slaves and have wanted that moral courage which a free man, with free servants on whom he can depend, usually possesses. . . If the Portuguese really wish to develop the rich country *beyond their possessions* [italics mine], they ought to invite the co-operation of other nations on equal terms with themselves. Let the pathway into the interior be free to all; and instead of wretched forts, with scarcely an acre of land around them which can be called their own, let real colonies be made. If, instead of military establishments, we had civil ones, and saw emigrants going out with their wives, ploughs, and seeds, rather than military convicts with bugles and kettle-drums, one might hope for a return of prosperity to Eastern Africa." [14] Livingstone's easy tolerance toward the Portuguese was clearly changing into impatience.

In England Livingstone was honored and acclaimed as a national hero. The image of the lonely missionary doctor penetrating the dark heart of the continent stirred the imagination of his countrymen. When he spoke of colonization and settlement in the highlands beyond the lower Zambezi, when he spoke of the necessity for English action in central Africa, he was respectfully heeded. Without being aware of it, perhaps, he became the spokesman — and the conscience — for imperial designs in the lands he had explored. As a result of Livingstone's eloquence, although he did not propose it and was even reluctant to take charge of it, the Zambezi Expedition was hastily formed by the British government. The expedition was to consist of seven European technicians who, under Livingstone's direction, were to proceed beyond Tete, establish a central depot at the confluence of the Zambezi and the Kafue, and to explore toward the source of the Zambezi and the rivers flowing into it. [15] In its goal to find a water route to the upper Zambezi the expedition was a manifest failure (although it had a negative value in revealing the obstacles to be overcome in any program of settling the area), but the exploration of the

Shire River to the Shire highlands and Lake Nyasa had permanent effect in opening up this part of Africa to European penetration.

Portuguese acceptance of the expedition was indispensable, and Lord Clarendon early began to deal with the Portuguese minister. The background for negotiations was not good. Since his return to England, Livingstone had been speaking loudly about the African slave trade to a large and indignant audience. It was quite possible that an outraged English public, disregarding the hopeful antislavery decrees from Lisbon, might have its attention drawn to East Africa with fateful consequences for Portuguese sovereignty. As Professor Coupland has pointed out, "Portuguese ministers need not have been very conscience-stricken nor very faint-hearted to dread the passionate philanthropy of Britain, once it was on fire — they had felt its heat before — nor need they have been over-cynical to suspect that British philanthropy might be more fierce and predatory than it had ever been if it were now united with British commercial and colonial schemes and interests." [16] Livingstone's memorandum to the Portuguese government describing the expedition was not encouraging. He bluntly reaffirmed what he had written in the *Missionary Travels*: the scourge of East Africa was the slave trade; its suppression would best come through free trade and navigation; Portugal and Britain should act together.

So the Portuguese government was coolly receptive to the proposals for an expedition up the Zambezi. It was aware that Portugal maintained a theoretical jurisdiction over many parts of the continent Livingstone intended to explore, but how these claims would stand up against British demands egged on by an agitated public opinion was uncertain. But the Luso-British alliance was an old one and on it would probably rest the ultimate hopes for Portugal's position in Africa. In the end Lisbon yielded gracefully and promised to give the expedition all possible help in East Africa. On freedom of navigation up the Zambezi, Portugal balked and agreed to accept Livingstone as consul only at Quelimane, where foreign trade was already established, not at Sena and Tete, "which were not yet ready for foreign commerce." Anticipating on the basis of Livingstone's scornful description of its sovereignty along the river that frontier problems might arise from the expedition's passage, the Portuguese government in a decree of February 4, 1858, declared that Zambézia included all the territories traditionally held by the Portuguese in the Zambezi valley from the mouth of the river to beyond the fortress at Zumbo. Although just how far beyond Zumbo Portuguese territory extended was not specified, Livingstone and the English government were pleased at such modest claims, which approximated Livingstone's estimate of their occupation. Early March 1858, when the expedition left England, found Livingstone and Clarendon optimistic over the tenor of recent communications from Lisbon.

If the First Zambezi Expedition failed to achieve its immediate goals and fragmented into the well-known disappointments and resentments, the fault did not lie with the Portuguese government in Lisbon or its colonial officers in Moçambique. When repeated frustrations wore English tempers to the breaking point the blame was sometimes shunted to the Portuguese, but in 1858 and 1859 their attitude was courteous and correct, if not directly helpful. The same deadly conditions which had for centuries thwarted Portuguese enterprise on the Zambezi — heat, fever, native wars — also helped make the success of the English expedition impossible. There were other reasons: Livingstone's shyness and independent spirit kept him from assuming effective leadership over the group; the inefficiency of the steamer *Ma-Robert* and the difficulties of navigation on the Zambezi and the Shire; and the tensions which soon developed between various members of the party. Only when he shook himself free from the responsibilities of the expedition and reverted to the pioneering habits of his first journey did the genius of Livingstone reassert itself. The collapse of the first Universities' Mission — which had its inspiration in Livingstone's famous speeches at Oxford and Cambridge — arriving on the river in 1861 and the death of Mrs. Livingstone the following year made this the most heartsick period of Livingstone's life. In 1863 the remnants of the expedition, including the faithful John Kirk, sailed from Quelimane, with Livingstone to follow the next year.

It is not surprising, therefore, that the *Narrative of an Expedition to the Zambezi*, written by Livingstone in England in 1864–65, should have been tinged with bitterness "which is likely to affect his judgment. Where in his earlier book, a difficulty or threat was the will of God, it now became a plot by man against his purpose." [17] Nor is it surprising that this bitterness should have turned against the Portuguese, whose disinterested kindness Livingstone had once vowed never to forget. Unwilling to admit that part of the fault for the expedition's frustrations proceeded from circumstances and conditions which had long since beset the Portuguese — and produced the state of affairs on the Zambezi which was an open challenge to Protestant humanitarianism and imperialistic zeal — Livingstone turned against his former friends and protectors. Thus in the *Narrative* the English become more English (practical, dedicated,

humane) and the Portuguese more Portuguese (slovenly, selfish, in-
humane). "We could see plainly that we and our Portuguese friends
had different ranges of vision. We looked for the large result of benefit to all, both black and white, by establishing free commercial intercourse. They could see nothing beyond inducing English merchants
to establish a company, of which the Portuguese would, by fictitious
claims, reap all the benefits." [18] This is an English attitude toward the
Portuguese which had been taking shape for fifty years and here
received a definition which was to influence English action toward
the Portuguese for another fifty.

Livingstone's running quarrel with the Portuguese took several
directions. He was most sensitive to the apparent attempt in Portugal
to discredit his geographical contributions. He took particular um-
brage with José de Lacerda who had made it his task to prove that
much of the Africa explored by Livingstone had been previously
visited by Portuguese travelers. Most of these claims Livingstone dismissed contemptuously. "A vague rumor, cited by some old author,
about two marshes below Murchison's Cataracts, is considered con-
clusive evidence that the ancient inhabitants of Senna . . . found no
difficulty in navigating the Shire up to Lake Nyassa. . ." [19] The
polemic, which is still carried on in idle moments by Portuguese
geographers, was then more serious than an academic dispute. Unquestionably Livingstone's vanity was wounded more than he chose to
admit by Portuguese attacks, which accounts for the sharp tone of
his response. But Livingstone perceived that Portuguese protestations
of priority were meant to bolster their "pretense to power," and he
in turn lost few opportunities to deprecate their influence in Moçambique. "The Portuguese pretense to dominion is the curse of the
negro race on the East Coast of Africa." [20] At Zumbo he found desolation brooding; up and down the river only crumbling remains attested to the Portuguese passing. These were years of famine and
wars with the *prazero* Mariano, both being to Livingstone manifestations of Portuguese failure. Only by paying tribute to the tribes on
the right bank of the Zambezi did the merchants at Sena and Chupanga keep a semblance of the peace. Elaborate plans from Lisbon for
the regeneration of the region came to nothing when the only colonists were convicts. Indeed, as long as they pursue their present madness, Livingstone concludes, there is no help for them.

The madness was slavery. Livingstone was shocked by signs of
the traffic in Africans on all sides. Mariano he describes as a bully,
renegade, and slave trader. "The Portuguese at Tette, from the governor downward, are extensively engaged in slaving." The women

were sent to the interior to be traded for ivory and the men sold to the French as *émigrés*.[21] Quelimane existed only as a slave port. One of the results of Livingstone's penetration up the Shire valley was to make available a new supply of slaves; earlier, in 1860, he wrote of his journey to the upper Zambezi: "We were now . . . fully convinced that, in opening the country through which no Portuguese durst previously pass, we were made the unwilling instruments of extending the slave trade. . . . It was with bitter sorrow that we saw the good we would have done turned to evil." [22] Taking more vigorous action while conducting Bishop Mackenzie up the Shire, Livingstone and his company set free a gang of slaves, even though such interference could have proved prejudicial to the mission's passage through Portuguese territory. The explorer made remonstrances to Lisbon that the traders were dogging his steps, but unsatisfied with the response he wrote, "We regret to have to make this statement; but it was a monstrous mistake to believe in the honor of the government of Portugal, or their having a vestige of desire to promote the amelioration of Africa. One ought to hope the best of everyone, giving, if possible, credit for good intentions; but though deeply sensible of obligations to individuals of the nation, and anxious to renew the expressions of respect formerly used, we must declare the conduct of Portuguese statesmen to be simply infamous." [23]

Simultaneously the idea grew among members of the expedition that the Portuguese were guilty of double-dealing by issuing splendid public instructions for officials in Moçambique to give the English visitors all assistance and sending private instructions to thwart them at every turn. In view of Livingstone's denunciations against conditions in East Africa and the possessive gestures he seemed to be making toward territory nominally Portuguese, there may have been some truth in the English accusation. Secret instructions were not needed in Moçambique, however, and most of the obstacles Livingstone encountered were almost certainly thrown up spontaneously or were the result of local inertia. The Portuguese government was adamant on the matters of trade and political dealings with native chiefs, but their position in these matters was known by Livingstone before his departure from England and represented no change from traditional policies. In his reports to the Foreign Office Consul Livingstone made clear his suspicions, complained of open slavery, and urged that free trade be pressed on the Portuguese government, since the area could not be properly called a developed colony. The substance of his reports was sent to Lisbon with further pleas for the Portuguese to co-operate with Livingstone. Lisbon issued new decrees ordering such co-operation. More the British government could not do. The close relationship of the Prince Consort to the Portuguese royal family and England's embarrassing performance in the *Charles et George* controversy, mentioned earlier, precluded stronger backing for Livingstone.

The lack of forceful action by the Foreign Office and the decision of the British government to postpone any program of colonization in central Africa doomed Livingstone's aspirations for the area's salvation from the slave trade. In the last almost savage pages of the *Narrative* Livingstone was writing out of a six-year store of frustrations, going beyond the offices of diplomats to the public of England and America. The work in Africa must go on.

We ask with what face can the Portuguese shut some 900 miles of the East Coast from these civilizing and humanizing influences? Looking at the lawful trade which has been developed in one section of Africa, is it to be endured by the rest of the world that most of a continent so rich and fertile should be doomed to worse than sterility till the Spaniards and Portuguese learn to abandon their murderous traffic in men? When these effete nations speak of their famous ancestors, they tacitly admit that the same sort of mental stagnation has fallen on themselves as on the Africans and others . . . England would perform a noble service to Portugal by ignoring those pretenses to dominion on the East Coast by which, for the sake of mere swagger in Europe, she secures for herself the worst name in Christendom . . . Here, on the East Coast, not a single native has been taught to read, not one branch of trade has been developed; and wherever Portuguese power, or rather intrigue, extends, we have that traffic in full force which may be said to reverse every law of Christ and to defy the vengeance of Heaven.[24]

In the last years of his adventures in Africa, Livingstone had little contact with the Portuguese, since his explorations carried him for the most part north of the Rovuma River. He continued to condemn their practices of slavery and to defend the originality of his travels in central Africa against the claims advanced on behalf of earlier Portuguese travelers, but his humanitarian energies were now directed against the Arab slave trade from Zanzibar. He had brought the world's attention to East Africa. The Portuguese had discovered to their dismay that Livingstone the explorer could not be separated from the whole man. They had sanctioned the First Zambezi Expedition in the interests of science and had attempted to restrict its activities to this pursuit alone by decrees, tariffs, and fortifications,[25] but the philanthropic and imperialistic character of its leader refused to be contained, and Portuguese Africa was swiftly drawn, protesting and ill-prepared, into the realities of modern colonialism.

As in his way David Livingstone represented a particular attitude toward Portuguese enterprise in Africa which characterizes still an English view, so the response to Livingstone by Dr. José de Lacerda, a name now found only in the margins of Africa's history, was in its way a classic model by which defenders of Portugal's role in Angola and Moçambique seem still to be influenced. *Exame das viagens do Doutor Livingstone*, which appeared in 1867, is an angry, dignified, and dense reply to *Missionary Travels* and *Narrative of an Expedition*: its anger proceeds from an injured national pride; its dignity from a sureness in one's cause; and its density from a three hundred years' accumulation of detail. The *Exame*, there can be no doubt, is sentimentally and politically Portugal's official answer to Livingstone's claims and accusations. Replete with ancient maps and lengthy quotations, it is a synthesis of Portuguese activities in interior Africa, an effective and scholarly legal brief which did not fail to convince the Portuguese, at least, of the rightness of their case.

Although implicit in the *Exame* is Lacerda's suspicion that Livingstone was essentially interested in doing Portugal out of trade and territory in a part of Africa rightfully hers, he nevertheless meets the issues squarely. The main points of his six-hundred-page work — impossible to summarize satisfactorily — are these: on the matter of priority of exploration in central Africa, Lacerda produces extended documentation to prove that the areas visited by Livingstone had been penetrated or mentioned by Portuguese subjects. Barotseland and Makolololand were familiar territory for ivory and slave merchants who, though they surely knew the cataract Mosivatunya ("which Livingstone ostentatiously baptized as Victoria Falls"), were not primarily natural historians, for which reason the falls remained unpublicized. With regard to the crossing of the continent, Lacerda not only defends the *pombeiros* as Portuguese citizens, but suggests several other transcontinental journeys. The lands of Cazembe were reconnoitered by Francisco de Lacerda e Almeida in 1798 and again fifty-odd years later by Major Gamitto. The Shire highlands and the lands around Lake Nyasa were also the scenes of Portuguese penetration; if they remained unsettled, it was because the Portuguese were content to exploit their interests on the Zambezi.

To Livingstone's contention that Portugal had done nothing for the African, Lacerda cites the Jesuit and Dominican history in Angola and Moçambique and sarcastically asks what the Protestants had accomplished. "Protestant missionaries may perhaps be expert in history, mineralogy, geographical sciences . . . and to those who pay them they render more valuable services as explorers for industry or commerce than they do as truly sincere apostles for the Gospel and humanity, but what is the final result?" [26] He views Livingstone's repeated expressions of gratitude for Portuguese hospitality as an attempt to cleanse his conscience for committing subsequent intolerable offenses against his hosts. To prove that Moçambique had been throughout her history a productive center of Portuguese commerce, Lacerda arrays impressive statistics, including a contemporary census of the colony. He upbraids Livingstone for using a scientific expedition as a guise to suborn native chiefs loyal to Portugal for purposes of English exploitation. He questions Livingstone's antislavery sentiments, observing that the missionary was more concerned with alleged slaving by the Portuguese than he was with slave trading by the Africans themselves or with slavery at the Cape. If, in spite of Lisbon's stringent decrees against the traffic, it was still carried on in Portuguese Africa, such was the reality of African life, and Portuguese *prazeros* and traders were only conforming with the necessities of this reality. And, as Livingstone himself had admitted, no European people had better relations with the African [27] (although Lacerda is not concerned to any great extent with native policy as such, some of his remarks in this regard are significant as being the first specific elaborations of a Portuguese native policy). Such, broadly stated, are the points made in the *Exame das viagens*. Although Lacerda could not command the audience that Livingstone had, engaged as he was in debate with one of the most famous men of his age, his work is worthy of serious consideration by scholars and geographers.

Of all the discoveries and explorations alleged by Livingstone the one most hotly contested by Lacerda and his countrymen was the crossing of Africa. The *travessia* had been a goal of Portuguese policy in Africa since the days of Manuel and his hopes for an overland contact between the Congo Kingdom and the lands of Prester John. Repeated efforts had been unsuccessful; the result was that by the years when Livingstone went from Luanda to Quelimane the transcontinental journey had become as much a point of Portuguese pride as a matter of commercial expediency. There was the trip made by the two *pombeiros*, Amaro José and João Baptista, but in a candid

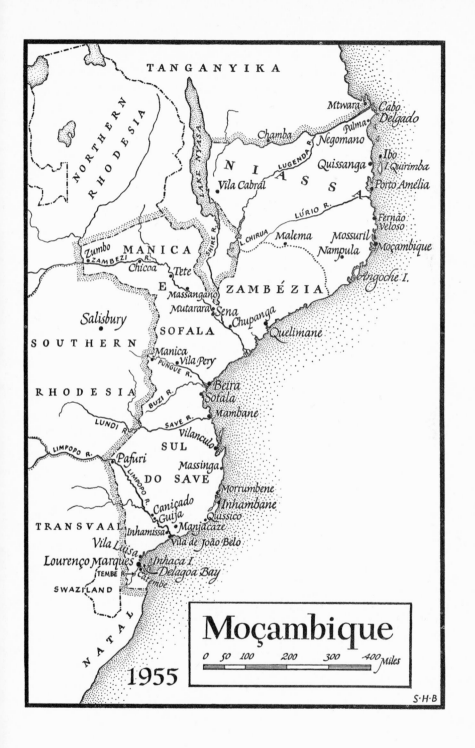

TANGANYIKA

NORTHERN RHODESIA

Mtwara   Cabo Delgado
Palma
Chamba   Negomano
LUGENDA R.
N I A S S A
Vila Cabral
Quissanga   Ibo
I. Quirimba
Porto Amélia
LÚRIO R.
Fernão Veloso
L. CHIRUA   Malema   Mossuril
Nampula   Moçambique
LAKE NYASA
SHIRE R.
Zumbo   MANICA
ZAMBEZI R.
Chicoa   Tete
Angoche I.
E
Massangano
Mutarara   Sena
ZAMBÉZIA
Chupanga
Salisbury
SOFALA   Quelimane
S O U T H E R N
Manica
Vila Pery
PUNGUE R.
R H O D E S I A
BUZI R.
Beira
Sofala
LUNDI R.   SAVE R.   Mambane
Vilanculo
SUL
LIMPOPO R.   Massinga
Pafuri
DO SAVE
LIMPOPO R.
Morrumbene
Caniçado   Inhambane
Guija   Qussico
T R A N S V A A L   Inhamissa   Manjacaze
Vila de João Belo
Vila Luísa
Lourenço Marques   Inhaca I.
TEMBE R.   Delagoa Bay
CATEMBE
SWAZILAND
NATAL

Moçambique

0   50   100   200   300   400 Miles

1955

S·H·B

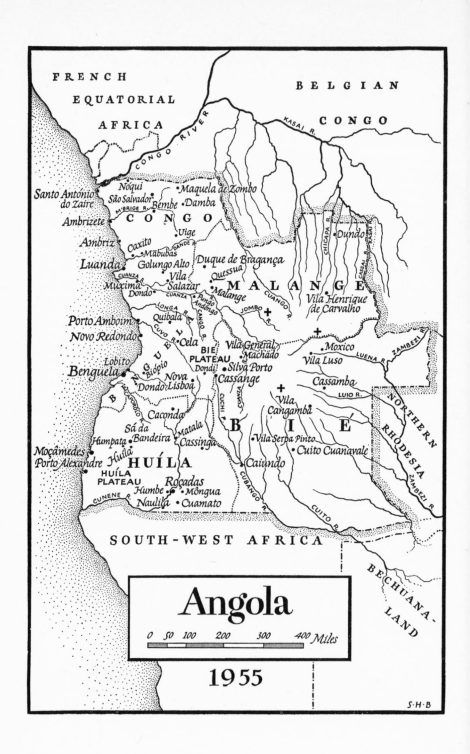

FRENCH

EQUATORIAL

AFRICA

BELGIAN

CONGO

KASAI R.

CONGO RIVER

Noqui

Santo António
do Zaire

São Salvador

Maquela de Zombo

M'BRIGE R. Bembe Damba

Ambrizete

CONGO

Ambriz

Caxito

Uige

Dundo

CHICAPA R.

KASAI R.

CASSAI R.

Luanda

Mabubas

DANDE R.

Muxima

Golungo Alto

Vila

CUANZA R.

Duque de Bragança

Quessua

Dondo

Salazar

CUANZA R.

Pungo

Malange

MALANGE

CUANGO R.

Vila Henrique
de Carvalho

Porto Amboim

LONGA R.

Quibala

Andango

CUANGO R.

JOMBO R.

Novo Redondo

Cela

CUVO R.

Vila General
Machado

Moxico

Vila Luso

LUENA R.

ZAMBEZI R.

Lobito

Biópio

BIE
PLATEAU

Dondi

Silva Porto

Benguela

Nova
Lisboa

Cassange

Cassamba

LUIO R.

CUCHI R.

Caconda

CUANZA R.

Vila
Cangamba

BIÉ

NORTHERN

Sá da
Bandeira

Matala

Humpata

Cassinga

Vila Serpa Pinto

RHODESIA

Moçâmedes

Huíla

Cuito Cuanavale

Porto Alexandre

HUÍLA

Caiundo

ZAMBEZI R.

HUÍLA
PLATEAU

Roçadas

CUNENE R.

Humbe

Môngua

Naulila

Cuamato

CUBANGO R.

SOUTH-WEST AFRICA

CUITO R.

BECHUANA-

LAND

Angola

0   50 100   200   300   400 Miles

1955

S·H·B

moment the Portuguese would admit to dissatisfaction in having to use the *pombeiros'* trip to substantiate their claims of priority. They hungered for something more authentically Lusitanian, and in lieu of fact, they relied on rumor and project. The rumors were little more than unsubstantiated bits of gossip, but since they appeared in authoritative works they contributed to the legend. In his *Colóquios dos simples e drogas da India* (Goa, 1563), the humanist Garcia da Orta refers to a secular priest who went from West Africa to India, passing through Sofala and Moçambique town, without using the sea route. Later in the century João dos Santos affirmed that there was direct communication between Sofala and Angola, for he had seen in Sofala a blanket come overland from Angola.[28] Projected crossings of the continent were easier to document. There was the expedition of Baltasar Rebelo de Aragão in the first decade of the seventeenth century. The Jesuit António Machado revived the Manueline ideal of a Congo-Ethiopia route in 1627. Salvador de Sá is reputed to have offered to link the realms of Angola with those of the Monomotapa. At the end of the century, Governor Aires de Saldanha sent off the frontiersman José da Rosa from Massangano, but he was refused passage through the lands of several *sobas* and returned. Among the thousand schemes entertained by Sousa Coutinho for the rejuvenation of Angola was a land contact with Moçambique, and with characteristic planning he began to collect information on the direction of the Cuango and Cunene rivers. Governor Francisco de Lacerda's expedition up the Zambezi at the end of the century was yet another serious endeavor, this time from the east coast. In back of all the attempts and failures were several misconceptions which were only cleared up in the nineteenth century. There was, first, the conviction that the continent was narrower than it is, one of the common guesses being that from Caconda to Tete was only a matter of some 300 to 450 leagues. The second erroneous belief was that the Zambezi was linked, either directly or by other river systems, with the Cunene and even the Cuanza. Finally, it was held, on the basis of Duarte Lopes's sixteenth-century account, that a great central lake giving rise to the principal rivers of Africa lay in the hinterland between Angola and Moçambique.

With the atrophy of Portuguese prestige in Africa by 1850 it was difficult for Livingstone to know the extent of historical penetration into the interior. Impatient with ancient maps, inaccurate for his purposes, and accounts hard to follow, Livingstone had respect for only a few Lusitanian explorers, chief among them being Francisco de Lacerda. The administrative limits of Portuguese Africa had been established for centuries by the line of forts through the interior of Angola and by the Zambezi penetration, but what of the traders and freebooters and campaigners who went beyond the fortresses to reside at the kraal of a distant chief, sometimes to return and sometimes not? Livingstone had met Silva Porto in mid-Africa, dismissed him as a half-caste, and gone on his way confident that he remained the European pioneer. It is certain that individual Portuguese traveled beyond the Cuango in northern Angola and in the south ranged well up-country from Caconda into Bié. In addition to the well-known trip of Gaspar Bocarro who went from Tete through a part of the Shire highlands, possibly skirting Lake Nyasa, before he reached the Rovuma and went down to the sea — the most extensive Portuguese journey in Moçambique north of the Zambezi — an almost forgotten captain at Tete, Sisnado Dias Bayão, led an expedition in 1643–44 into Matabeleland to a point deeper in Africa than any reached from Moçambique until the nineteenth century.[29] In terms of occupation the Portuguese had a short-lived mission station in the seventeenth century at Dambarare, some leagues up the Zambezi from Zumbo. In 1827, in the lands of Chief Cazembe, the Portuguese briefly occupied and garrisoned a town in what is presently the East Luangwa district of Northern Rhodesia.[30] Each is an isolated instance, for the Portuguese, like Livingstone, were at their best in acts of individual exploration, and together they made up a pitifully weak argument to meet the test of occupation (but, at that, stronger than the case of nonoccupation on which was founded the International Association of the Congo). Nevertheless, these scattered examples, and others like them, betray a greater activity in the interior than the improvident condition of the colonies indicated in the 1850's.

The unhappy 1798 expedition of Dr. Francisco José de Lacerda e Almeida was, in terms of scientific interest, the most important of the pre-Livingstone journeys made by the Portuguese. Lacerda was a kindred spirit to Livingstone. An antislavery advocate, he believed that through promoting trade and commerce, ignorance and cruelty could be dispelled and the material prosperity of the barbarous races advanced. The explorer, he felt, could do more than the conqueror. Lacerda was also a remarkable visionary. Alarmed by the British seizure of Cape Town in 1795, he addressed a letter from Tete to the Lisbon government, pointing out that this action could be the beginning of a great British empire in South Africa which would sweep northwards across the Zambezi splitting the twin Portuguese colonies forever. It behooved Portugal to fill the vacuum by extending her authority westward from Zambézia into Angola. Such a move would provide more protection for the Portuguese trading the interior, open an immense new area to commerce, and increase the speed of communication from Portugal to Lisbon. His proposals came to the attention of the son of another visionary, Rodrigo de Sousa Coutinho, in charge of the colonial office, who saw to it that Lacerda was named governor of the Rivers of Sena and authorized to undertake his expedition from Moçambique to Luanda.

Lacerda's expedition of perhaps twenty Portuguese and mulattoes, half a hundred African soldiers, and a number of porters made its way northwest from Tete toward the kraal of the great chief Cazembe, with whom Goan traders had dealt previously. Lacerda hoped to find the headwaters of the Cunene, or its tributaries, and thus establish an easy river route from the eastern colony to the western one. Both the Chambezi and the Luangwa were partially explored by Lacerda's men as he worked his way toward Lake Mweru. Desertions by African porters, dissensions among the Europeans, and the intrigues of Cazembe had slowed the expedition to an inching progress by the time the kraal was reached. Here Lacerda died from fever and exhaustion. A priest accompanying Lacerda, Father Pinto, was unable to reorganize the dissolving company, which returned to Tete in April 1799. Lacerda's legacy was a map of the area between Lake Mweru and Tete and a *Diário* of the journey's difficulties and disappointments. Richard Burton, one of the few English detractors of Livingstone, ranks Lacerda as one of Africa's great explorers.[31] Lacerda's greatest contribution to Portugal came sixty years later when his trip furnished abundant ammunition to defenders of Portugal's priority in central Africa.

The lands of Cazembe, roughly the territory between Lake Mweru and Lake Bangweulu, figured prominently in two more Portuguese expeditions in the first third of the nineteenth century. The first was the journey from Cassange in Angola to Tete by Pedro João Baptista and Amaro José. The two *pombeiros* were dispatched for Zambézia in 1806 by a pioneering Portuguese merchant of Cassange, Honorato da Costa.[32] The two bush traders were Negro, although they may have had some Portuguese ancestry. They should not be dismissed as lightly as Livingstone dismissed them. Since the early days of the Congo a select class of Ovimbundu traders had participated in Angolan commerce; they have been called the greatest traders of Bantu Africa. The leader, João Baptista, was sufficiently literate to keep a chronological journal of their adventures. From Cassange they headed east, reaching Cazembe's kraal, where they were detained three years by native wars and Cazembe's reluctance to let them return to Angola. With the restoration of trade between Zambézia and the lands of Cazembe, the two traders reached Tete. After a lengthy residence in the town, they returned to Cassange in 1814 with six hundred bales of merchandise. In Angola, João Baptista was honored by the Portuguese government.

What Amaro José and João Baptista had accomplished was denied two Portuguese officers in 1831–32. Majors José Correia Monteiro and António Pedroso Gamitto sought to follow the steps of Lacerda, exploring the headwaters of the Zambezi and crossing to Angola. Illness and the agitated state of the country prevented them from getting beyond Lake Mweru, whence they sent a letter to the governor of Angola by African messengers — which took seven years to arrive. Gamitto's narrative of the journey from Tete and back, *O Muata-Cazembe*, still offers valuable information on that section of Rhodesia.

No man in the history of Portuguese Africa comes closer to filling the role of folk hero than António Francisco da Silva, invariably known as Silva Porto. An adventurer in the grand manner — generous, shrewd, sentimental — his personality dominated the interior of Angola for almost fifty years. A father of several mulatto children, a confidant of local chiefs, and a spectacular suicide, he lived in a patriarchal relationship with the Africans of Bié; the characteristics of his way of life are what the Portuguese have most in mind when they speak of their ability to get along with the African. Born in Oporto, which name he later added to his own, Silva Porto set off at the age of twelve for Brazil. After a merchant apprenticeship in Rio de Janeiro and Bahia, he arrived in Luanda in 1839. For two years he traded in the backcountry of the capital, and in 1841 moved to Benguela. A few years later he was in Bié; in 1847 he built his home and stockade at a village he called Belmonte, less than a mile from the modern town which bears his name. From Belmonte he traded the countryside with his *pombeiros*, establishing a new route of commerce from Bié to Benguela by way of Bailundo and Chisanji.

Although full of uncertainties, commercial life in the plateau country of the Ovimbundu had existed for more than a century. *Pombeiros* and Portuguese half-castes dotted the area up from Benguela and out from Caconda with tiny forts and trading stations from which they brought out ivory and slaves. In the nineteenth century, with the abolition of the slave trade, which introduced a necessity for substitute products, and the cessation of the crown monopoly in ivory, commerce blossomed in this region of Angola. New Portuguese merchants took up residence in the Bié highlands, and the Ovimbundu came into their own as the most important African traders below the equator. With the opening of the ports of Benguela and Luanda to foreign ships, trade with the outside world took the encouraging upturn which so impressed Livingstone. Ivory and slaves were slowly replaced by beeswax and, after 1870, by rubber, as the principal items of export. Rum, metal products, and cotton goods remained the main import products and the staples of the inland traders.

Few, if any, Portuguese have known the interior of the colony as well as Silva Porto, and it is a pity that his journals and notes have yet to be published completely. His presence in the interior and his repeated warnings of its importance to Portugal helped keep a wavering colonial policy from entirely neglecting the hinterland in the crucial middle years of the century. When in 1852 several Swahili traders from Zanzibar appeared in Benguela after an overland trek from the east coast, Silva Porto responded to the provincial government's request to return with the merchants and carry messages to the governor of Moçambique. Leaving from Belmonte in the same year, he reached Lealui in Barotseland after a journey impeded by the rains and native wars. Here a spell of sickness and doubts whether a white man would be permitted to pass through some of the tribal lands lying ahead prevented Silva Porto from continuing, but several of his *pombeiros* did go on with the Swahili across the continent to the southern tip of Lake Nyasa and the Rovuma. Eventually the messengers reached Moçambique. It was on this expedition that Silva Porto met Livingstone and gave him valuable information on the state of the country the Englishman planned to travel through.[33]

On his return from Barotseland, Silva Porto settled down at Belmonte, where he was to remain, save for a visit to Portugal and a period of residence in Benguela, acting as captain major of Bié after 1885. He saw that Livingstone's visit had broken Angola's long isolation and that the days of considering coastal occupation tantamount to possession of the interior were numbered. Each year his warning grew more urgent. The interior must not be abandoned. Railroads must be built to the centers of Angolan commerce at Bié, Bailundo, Caconda. Neglect of Angola's richest district could only lead to infiltration by foreign agents and the increasing disrespect of the African for Portuguese authority. Missions and forts and communication lines were the only answer to Portugal's position of humiliating inferiority. In 1863 in scornfully rejecting the opinion of a provincial governor who held that coastal domination was sufficient, Silva Porto raged: "This is how it is in Portugal, where the only things that matter are pointless rivalries, while the foreigner mocks us and even, in his audacity, spits in our faces. Oh, misfortune! Damn the indifferent ones." [34] As it became more obvious that Angola would be encircled and union with Moçambique an impossibility, Silva Porto grew more distressed at Portugal's weakness and folly.

His suicide in 1890 was an eloquent conclusion to his now embittered life. In that inauspicious year, Portugal belatedly moved to prevent English annexation of Barotseland and sent Henrique de Paiva Couceiro with a small force to place the territory under Portuguese protection. The arrival of the expedition in Bié — the result at last of a policy he had advocated — placed Silva Porto in an ironically impossible situation: the *soba* of the region, Ndunduma (advised, many Portuguese believe, by the English missionary Arnot) refused Paiva Couceiro passage through his lands. Silva Porto, confident that his prestige and friendship with the chief would prevail, went to the kraal at Ecovango, but Ndunduma refused, insulting and threatening the old trader. Paiva Couceiro would not withdraw. Sensing perhaps that he was an anachronism and deeply wounded that the chief's trust in him had gone, Silva Porto gathered a dozen kegs of gunpowder (some authorities give fourteen) around his feet, wrapped himself in a handmade Portuguese flag, and blew himself through the roof of his house. Neither Paiva Couceiro nor Dr. Fisher of the Brethren Mission could save the horribly burned pioneer, who died the following day. A stronger force, including a contingent of Boer riflemen, returned later in the year, defeated the rebellious tribe, and shipped its chief off to the Cape Verdes. The new order had arrived in Belmonte.

Silva Porto's contemporaries in Angola included explorers and naturalists. Joaquim Rodrigues Graça in 1846–1848 traveled to the headwaters of the Zambezi and the territory of Lunda bordering Cazembe, obtaining treaties of friendship between the important chiefs of Lunda and the Portuguese government.[35] In 1852 the Austrian naturalist Friedrich Welwitsch was commissioned by Lisbon to make a botanical survey of Angola. For six years Welwitsch explored minutely the coast north of the Cuanza and the country in back of Luanda as far as Ambaca. His study, including reports on more than three thousand botanical specimens, was published in the *Anais* of the Overseas Council in the years after 1854. Welwitsch's health by 1859 was so bad that he was forced to spend more than half his time in bed; in hope of escaping the fevers of Luanda he sailed to Moçâmedes. After seven months in the highlands of Huíla, Welwitsch returned to Lisbon in 1861, his health ruined, but in possession of the most valuable botanical collection of tropical Africa.

The impressions made on the scientific world by the Welwitsch collection at the London Exposition of 1862 and the second Paris Exposition were so gratifying that the Portuguese government decided to maintain a naturalist resident in Angola, who would explore the province for zoölogical specimens for a collection to be formed in the Polytechnical Museum in Lisbon. The government chose José Alberto de Oliveira Anchieta, a Romantic with an intense enthusiasm for the phenomena of exotic lands who had already spent five years in the Portuguese Congo and another in Angola. In the first six years of his stay in Angola he explored most of the western half of the colony. From 1872 to 1876 he wandered up and down the basin of the Cunene; his equipment lost or stolen and himself almost forgotten by his government, Anchieta continued his work with that remarkable dedication which Africa inspires in so many Europeans. The last twenty years of his life were spent at Caconda where in a macabre museum he collected his specimens and notes for Lisbon. His extraordinary collection of Angolan mammals helped further the zoölogical knowledge of Africa.

Neither Angola nor Moçambique was as lacking in explorers and prophets as Livingstone had supposed, even though both provinces presented a discouraging countenance to Portuguese and foreigners alike. In the metropolis as well, scholars and statesmen hammered at a policy of colonial neglect which could only bear out Livingstone's declamations and increase the appetite of other nations. In the forefront of these colonialists were João de Andrade Corvo and Luciano Cordeiro, men schooled in the liberal tradition of Sá da Banderia.

As Portugal moved into the critical decade of the 1870's, it became apparent that the various committees appointed ten years earlier had been able to do nothing but make recommendations which were given passing attention and pigeon-holed. João de Andrade Corvo, a one-time history teacher and journalist who served intermittently as Minister of Marine and Overseas and Foreign Minister during the decade, in a series of candid articles and in speeches before the parliament defined the necessities of a practical colonial policy. About 1875 he wrote: "It is no longer possible to postpone the construction of roads, the navigation of rivers, the building of railroads, and, finally, the rewriting of tariff laws. We can no longer continue to live isolated, as we could when our African colonies were little more than parks for the production and creation of slaves. Today the world is one of work and not indolence; the earth is for men and no one can keep civilization from it. It must produce and produce well. . . The question of public works in our overseas possessions is not a political question. Our vast domains will be an effective force if we immediately bring civilization to them, if we bring to them education, work, liberty in its rational meaning, liberty in harmony with the moral and intellectual state of the population, if we attract capital . . . and permit the free exploitation of industry and commerce. . ." [36] In a speech in the Câmara dos Pares in 1879, he said: "Colonial problems must not be treated as political questions, but as questions of economics and administration. . . In my opinion, our country's interest urgently demands the development of our colonies. Only through these colonies will Portugal be able to take the place she deserves in the concert of nations; only on their preservation and prosperity does her future greatness depend." [37]

Such plain talk and the image of Portuguese incompetence in Africa — reiterated in the "calumnies" of men like Lovett Cameron — were not altogether without effect. In 1876 the government appropriated a sizable, if insufficient, sum for engineering projects in Africa. The year before a more important and less costly step was taken toward the rehabilitation of the colonies with the foundation of the Geographical Society of Lisbon. Growing out of a permanent geographical committee set up by Andrade Corvo and sponsored by the Overseas Ministry, the society made decisive contributions to Portugal's colonial cause during the last quarter of the century. Under the able guidance of one of its founders, Luciano Cordeiro, it undertook the difficult and often thankless task of creating an African consciousness in Portugal by sponsoring scientific exploration of the colonies and the publication of texts illustrating Portugal's historic role in Angola and Moçambique.[38] Cordeiro, who was subsequently a member of the delegation to the Conference of Berlin, made the society an effective force in combating the attitude prevalent in Europe toward Portuguese Africa. A special committee, the Portuguese National Committee for the Exploration and Civilization of Africa — more briefly called the African Committee — was created to study and report on foreign comments and attitudes on Portuguese Africa.

The Geographical Society shared in the promotion by the Lisbon government of expeditions which did far more than speeches and legislation to dramatize the presence of Africa and helped restore national pride in the traditional abilities of the Portuguese explorers.

The most famous of these was the Capelo-Ivens-Serpa Pinto expedition of 1877 which, though prepared in haste and having an uncertain purpose, was the most significant project of exploration since Lacerda's Zambezi journey of the previous century. The three men chosen by the government were young navy and army officers, all of whom had previous contact with Africa. Hermenigildo Capelo and Roberto Ivens were navy officers whose tours of duty had taken them to Angola and Moçambique. Lt. Ivens was the more ardent Africanist; on a trip up the Congo to Boma he had made a cartographical survey of the region. The striking personality of the group was Major Alexandre Alberto da Rocha de Serpa Pinto. Formerly a lieutenant in the Zambezi Brigade of 1869, Serpa Pinto had longed for seven years to return to Africa. When he heard that an expedition was being formed, he offered his services to Andrade Corvo, who referred him to the leader Capelo. Impressed with Serpa Pinto's zeal, Capelo welcomed him as a member of the expedition and asked him to accompany him on a trip to Paris and London to purchase equipment. The three men sailed for Luanda in July 1877.

The original plan of the expedition was to make a hydrographic survey of the Congo and Zambezi headwaters and to chart the territory lying between Angola and Moçambique. Subsequent instructions spoke of studying the Cuanza in its relation to the Congo and of following the course of the Cunene, two problems which had long defied Portuguese solution, but Andrade Corvo, realizing that plans made in Lisbon could not always be fulfilled in Africa, left ultimate decisions to the discretion of the expedition's leaders. After arriving in Luanda the three officers found it necessary to take advantage of this latitude in their instructions. It was impossible to get bearers in the vicinity of the capital. At the same time they discovered from Stanley, fresh from the heart of the Congo and in Luanda on Serpa Pinto's invitation, that one part of the original project had already been accomplished.[39] They thereupon decided to explore the Cunene, and Serpa Pinto sailed for Benguela to get bearers; but on the arrival of Capelo and Ivens some weeks later, plans were again changed in favor of a direct penetration into the district of Bié.

In spite of the assistance of Silva Porto, the problem of insufficient African porters again became acute after their departure from Benguela. At Caconda, Serpa Pinto, personnel officer for the expedition — Capelo was the meteorologist and natural scientist while Ivens served as topographer — went north to Huambo (Nova Lisboa) to recruit. In his absence, Capelo and Ivens, having found some willing Africans in Caconda, continued on their way. The reasons for their departure are not clear, but Serpa Pinto, lonely and sick, was deeply offended by the apparent desertion. At Huambo the idea of crossing Africa alone occurred to him. When he rejoined his companions at Belmonte, the split between them became final. Capelo and Ivens, after offering to accompany the exhausted army officer to Benguela, left him in Silva Porto's *embala* with a third of the equipment while they set off to the north.

On regaining his strength, Serpa Pinto determined to go through with his plan. Encouraged by Silva Porto, who promised to come to him wherever he was, should his aid be needed, Serpa Pinto left Belmonte in late May with twenty-three bearers. After three months of exhaustion and hunger, he reached the Zambezi at Lealui in the trading area of Barotseland known to the Portuguese. Now quite ill, he followed the course of the river down to Lesuma, where the fortunes of African exploration brought him into contact with two English zoölogists, Dr. Benjamin Bradshaw and Dr. Alexander Walsh. The two naturalists nursed Serpa Pinto for several days until arrangements could be made to transport him to the camp of the French medical missionary, François Coillard, some miles to the south. Through the patient ministrations of Coillard and his wife, the explorer regained his strength. After a side excursion to Victoria Falls, Serpa Pinto accompanied the Coillard family in their Boer carts due south across the western corner of the Kalahari Desert to Shushong, which they reached the last day of 1878. From there Serpa Pinto went on to Pretoria and down to Durban. His spectacular crossing of the continent had an immediate response in Europe; he was invited to address geographical societies in London and Paris, and in Portugal, where he was feted as a hero the equal of Stanley and Livingstone. His exploits did much to restore the confidence and reputation of Portugal in Africa.

The journey of Capelo and Ivens, less sensational though more painstaking, did not arouse the same popular enthusiasm as did the solitary passage of Serpa Pinto, but their journal *De Beneguela às terras de Iaca* was quickly translated into English, *From Benguella to the Territory of Yacca* (London, 1882). From Bié the two officers traveled in a northerly direction for two years to Cassange and Malange, then along the upper reaches of the Cuango, and from there back to Luanda. The expedition produced the first thorough survey of this part of the province. In 1884 the Portuguese government again called upon Capelo and Ivens, this time to lead an expedition from Angola to Moçambique. The ostensible purpose was to map the basin of the Cubango and investigate the commerce of the

interior. Fundamental to their exploration, however, was to discover
a trade route between the two colonies on the basis of which Portugal
could establish a sufficient connection to justify her claims for a
corridor across the continent. Departing from Moçâmedes, Capelo
and Ivens followed the by now familiar route to Lealui and then
swung northeast along the Kabompo River. Reaching a point slightly
north of the modern city of Elisabethville, they turned south toward
Zumbo and from there down the Zambezi to Quelimane.

Two other expeditions even more plainly designed to strengthen
Portuguese sovereignty were the Niassa explorations of Serpa Pinto
and Augusto Cardoso and the Cassai journeys of Henrique Augusto
Dias de Carvalho. Conceived by the ambitious overseas minister Pin-
heiro Chagas as further demonstrations of a Portuguese renaissance
in Africa, neither expedition was in any large sense one of geographical
discovery, since both areas had been penetrated and partially mapped
by previous explorers. Such African political excursions by the middle
1880's were generally explained as expeditions of scientific or commercial inquiry, a sacrosanct explanation which may have fooled some
scientists and businessmen, but which had a more cynical significance
for the statesmen of Europe. The Portuguese realized that if they
were to salvage the country east of Lake Nyasa and south of the
Rovuma, more persuasive arguments than ancient maps were needed.
In 1884 the government called upon Serpa Pinto, consul at Zanzibar,
to organize an expedition which would re-establish the traffic, though
not in slaves, of course, which formerly flowed between the lake
country and Ibo, thus offering indisputable evidence of Portuguese
rights to the area. Serpa Pinto suffered a recurrence of an old malaise
shortly after leaving the coast and was obliged to entrust Augusto
Cardoso with the responsibilities of the expedition. Cardoso fulfilled
his instructions perfectly; he raised the Portuguese flag on the shores of
Lake Nyasa and obtained signatures of fealty to Portugal from various
local chiefs.

Dias de Carvalho journeyed to the heart of modern Katanga with
the same purpose. At the kraal of the great chief of Lunda, the
Mutianvua, a treaty was signed wherein the chief recognized Portuguese sovereignty, asked Portuguese troops to occupy Lunda, and
agreed to prohibit slavery in his realm. This was the standard contract which every European explorer seems to have carried in his
boots on the offchance of running into a *soba* not signed to a rival
company; even in this eventuality, contracts were often broken. As
far as Lunda was concerned, by the time Carvalho reached the Mutianvua's capital beyond the Lulua River in early 1886 the diplomats

at the Berlin Conference had made other disposition of this part of the world. But the expedition was not made in vain. The occupation stations established by Carvalho had the effect of pushing the eastern frontiers of Angola to the Kasai, a formidable achievement if one considers that these territorial inroads were made into the private lands of that most rapacious humanitarian, Leopold II of Belgium.

By 1885 the record of Portuguese exploration in Africa, ancient and modern, was equaled only by that of the English. If the partition of Africa had been made purely on the basis of exploration, the boundaries of Angola and Moçambique would be different from what they are today, but this was not to be. Nevertheless, the contributions of Serpa Pinto, Capelo and Ivens, and Dias de Carvalho were not lost, for they served to give contemporary reality to traditional Portuguese claims and to fix Portuguese determination. And they were, ironically, the legacy of Livingstone.

VIII

INTERNATIONAL DISPUTES

For Portugal the significance of the Berlin Conference in 1884–85 was that European attitudes toward her position in Africa at that time hardened into policies. The conference grew out of the abortive Anglo-Portuguese Treaty of 1884 regarding sovereignty over the Congo basin — in fact, it was the Lisbon foreign office which first proposed a meeting of colonial powers — and it began a series of events, but few of them favoring the Portuguese, which extended to 1914. The conference decided little, and its importance, save for its symbolic significance of having fired a tardy starting gun for the scramble for Africa, has probably been exaggerated, since the principal regulations of the General Act almost all failed in their purposes. Its loosely worded philanthropic intentions furnished pretext and sanction for the use of power diplomacy and justification for unbridled imperialism. Of the major colonial powers taking part in the conference — France, England, Germany, Belgium, and Portugal — only the last failed to gain some sort of advantage. Nevertheless, Portugal, the European nation with the longest and most valid colonizing record in Africa (such a statement has value only in a comparative sense) was fortunate, in the view of some dispassionate observers, in not losing more than she did in the years after 1885.

The attitude in Europe toward the Portuguese colonies was predominantly the English attitude described previously, although on occasions both England and other nations, in moments of belligerence toward one another, found it convenient to defend Portuguese sovereignty in Africa and to pretend that what they had been saying yesterday about the low state of Angola and Moçambique was not really so or that affairs there had taken a sudden miraculous turn for the better. It is true that Germany, France, and Belgium in the 1880's found the accepted English view a handy club to beat the Portuguese with, but several nations of Europe, notably Holland and France in addition to England, had already had more than casual involvement with Portugal over the African territories and did not need to rely on second-hand prejudice. Nor had the issues been solely concerned with slavery. Commercial rivalries and Indian Ocean naval policies had their repercussions in Moçambique, and English arguments with the Boers also had effect there. Angola from 1650 to 1880, save for squabbles over the slave trade up the Congo and the interlude of the traffic's repression, escaped foreign notice, but Portuguese East Africa was from late in the eighteenth century either peripherally or centrally involved in international disputes.

After the half century (1600–1650) of Dutch attacks on Portuguese territories in East and West Africa, the two colonies were relatively undisturbed by serious foreign visitations until the late 1700's. English and occasional Dutch and French ships called at the ports of Moçambique, but these contacts were infrequent. Austria's Delagoa Bay adventure from 1776 to 1781 was important only for bringing that part of the coast under renewed Portuguese scrutiny. French activity, however, was a greater threat to Moçambique. Although by 1780 the only base in the Indian Ocean left to France was the Île de France (Mauritius), French vessels dominated shipping commerce from Mombasa to Cape Delgado and for the next twenty-five years seemed a constant threat to Portugal's possession of Moçambique.

Portugal, at home and in East Africa, vacillated in her affections between France and England; for the governor of Moçambique the situation was especially difficult. Although more attracted by the commercial prosperity of the Arab ports to the north, the French on the Île de France and Réunion still relied upon Moçambique to send them foodstuffs and a small number of slaves, and there was strong feeling in Moçambique that the insular French government, which made no secret of its contempt for Portuguese authority on the mainland, might at any moment decide to occupy the capital and the several worthwhile ports. Not being able to count on the assistance of the British navy, the governor of the province was constrained to follow a policy of hopeful neutrality, which became increasingly difficult as Portugal was drawn into the Anglo-French struggle. The French, for their part, were happy to accept a policy which continued the supply of food and slaves; officially they deplored the depredations of French corsairs which roamed the coast of Moçambique, disturbing coastal shipping and menacing the ports of Ibo, Inhambane, and the factory at Lourenço Marques where they forced the few Portuguese subjects to flee into the interior. To prevent the privateers' attacks the governor of Moçambique at the end of the century forbade Portuguese ships from going to the islands and opened Moçambique ports to French ships — under neutral colors — hoping in this manner to reduce the incidents at sea and to stimulate legitimate commerce. The new arrangement proved generally satisfactory. The trade in slaves and émigrés to Réunion in the nineteenth century, except for the five-year period of English occupation (1810–1815), was one of the province's most important economic props.

With Bonaparte's Egyptian campaign and his plans for a resurgence of French power in the Indian Ocean, fresh fears swept Moçambique. In 1799 the governor of Moçambique wrote his government that ". . . if the coast of Malabar fell into the hands of the French, they would immediately think of taking possession of the Portuguese establishments on the East Coast of Africa, as they depend entirely on these for their commerce in the two principal products, ivory and gold, which these two colonies furnish in exchange for their goods." [1] In turn, the Lisbon government warned the governor to be vigilant against possible French or Spanish attacks. These suspicions were not without foundation, in spite of English naval superiority in the Indian Ocean, and only after the blockade and capture of the Île de France in 1809–10 by British ships did Moçambique's fears of a French occupation subside. Even in 1810, Moçambique island might have fallen to French vessels sent from Brest to reinforce the Île de France; finding their base captured, the French captains resolved to take Moçambique instead, and only an unlucky encounter with English warships off Madagascar prevented the attempt.

In losing one suitor of doubtful character, Moçambique won another whose attentions were more persistent and no less improper. The presence of the French along the East African coast, the abolition of the slave trade, British expansion in South Africa, the financial plight of English commerce in India — all contrived to waken British interest in Moçambique. On the occasion of Bonaparte's invasion of Portugal in 1807, the desirability of taking over the Portuguese possessions in India and East Africa was seriously discussed by governing members of the East India Company and the British government; the discussion was motivated by considerations other than that of simply protecting the territories from French control should the pro-French faction in the Portuguese court prevail. In 1809 one of the earliest African scientific expeditions left the Cape to find out more about East Africa. But the two Englishmen and their bearers who made up the expedition disappeared in the vicinity of Sofala not to be heard from again. The next year two ships set out from Bombay to explore the coast south of Cape Guardafui in pursuit of information on the land, the inhabitants, and commerce. To these overtures the Moçambique government responded with matronly courtesy and reserve. At the same time England used its great influence on the displaced Portuguese court to obtain a commercial treaty in 1810 granting Britain a favored position in Portuguese territories, where duties on British imports could not exceed 15 per cent. British mer-chants were not to be restrained from buying and selling except in those products reserved for the crown monopoly.

The treaty did not alter the pattern of Moçambique's commerce, which was the slave trade. Ivory and gold dust were the only other important exports, both of these products being shipped principally to British India. Although more direct trade in Portuguese and British ships resulted from the treaty, the bulk of Moçambique commerce continued to be the small indirect trade carried on by Arabs, many of them so-called English Arabs, and Indian traders who went from India to Moçambique and back via Muscat and Zanzibar. The East India Company did not benefit from the carrying trade, but the increase in the flow of products between India and East Africa made the connection with the Portuguese colony a valuable one.

The point of friction between Portuguese and British interests in East Africa was not in commercial dealings, however, but in a British coastal survey and certain incidents at Delagoa Bay. In 1820 the British Admiralty, with assistance from the East India Company, decided to send several ships to investigate and survey the coast north of Algoa Bay. Command of the expedition was given to Captain William Fitzwilliam Owen, who from 1822 to 1825 surveyed and charted the coast from Guardafui to Table Bay. Important as was his scientific contribution, the consequences of the expedition were ultimately political.

Like so many Englishmen who visited Angola and Moçambique after him, Owen was a humanitarian and imperialist, scornful of the Portuguese and an advocate of dispossessing them of their colonies in the name of pious humanity and free trade. Delagoa Bay, one of the finest natural harbors in East Africa, seemed to Owen a logical place for his country to begin a policy of appropriation, since the Portuguese claim to the area was not clearly defined in terms of occupation and control over the African population. Owen's suggestions were one of the earliest examples of European conduct in nineteenth-century Africa which made the anomaly, "In grabbing land, no claim is better than a poor claim," a cornerstone of colonial philosophy.

From the sixteenth century the region around the trading station of Lourenço Marques represented the southern extent of Portugal's East African territories. Off and on, foreign ships had called there or set up short-lived factories (there were two Dutch posts and the Austrian fort briefly occupied in the eighteenth century), but by 1800 it was fairly well accepted by both the French and English that Portugal held jurisdiction over the great outer bay as well as the inner harbor where the fortress of Lourenço Marques was situated. The controversy which began with Owen and did not end until the arbitrated decision in 1875 turned on the matter of jurisdiction over the outer bay.

On his first visit to Delagoa Bay, where he presented his credentials to the fortress captain, Owen reported that the Portuguese soldiers there admitted to no control over the rampaging Zulus in the neighborhood, who alternated between attacking the fort and selling the local tribesmen they captured to the Portuguese. While Owen was visiting Moçambique island, a new district governor seized two British merchant ships in the Delagoa Bay harbor and claimed the whole bay area as a Portuguese possession. On his return Owen forced the return of the two vessels and made treaties of friendship and protection with several chiefs on the southern bank of the Tembe River. The following year (1823) the union jack was flown at Catembe (on the shore opposite Lourenço Marques), an action the Portuguese garrison could do little about, since in the same year their fortress was under assault by African warriors. But in 1824 a new Portuguese governor had the flag hauled down, raising in its stead the Portuguese banner. Owen did not give in easily, and in 1825 his warships captured in the bay a French slaver carrying Portuguese colors.

Owen constantly reminded his government that Delagoa Bay was of the greatest importance to the Cape colony, and nothing "would give him greater pleasure than to see ten thousand British of any sect occupy it." The Portuguese had no authority beyond their guns, and "Britain could arrange treaties with those independent chiefs and thereby destroy the slave trade, as well as establish factories for commerce where she could undersell the Portuguese 'and starve them out' without 'infringing on national or political justice.' " The Portuguese should be persuaded to move back to Inhambane.[2]

Subsequent British visitors to the region supported Owen's aggressive recommendations, stating that there was nothing to justify Portugal's claims. While an uncertain *status quo* was observed in Delagoa Bay, with rival flags fluttering on opposite sides of the river, the dispute was carried to London, where the case in point was whether the English ship *Eleanor* had been lawfully taken by the Portuguese garrison at Lourenço Marques in 1825. The argument put forward by England was that Portuguese authority did not extend to the south bank of the Tembe, that they neither held land there nor could claim the effective allegiance of the African tribes. Portgual countered with references to her historic position in Moçambique and held that various treaties she had made with Great Britain implicitly recognized her possession of the bay area and that prior to Owen's visit British trading ships had also respected Portuguese priority there. These contentions were the crux of the dispute arbitrated by President MacMahon of France fifty years later; in the late 1820's, however, England, while not formally acknowledging Portugal's position, failed to pursue a positive course of her own, and the affair was temporarily forgotten.

In the following decades Portuguese administrators reasserted their control over Delagoa Bay, charging for the right to trade there and closing the bay to trade when they chose. They did this without strong British protest. Toward the Boers local governors were more hospitable, in the middle 1840's regarding them as potential good neighbors and perhaps the salvation of the little town of Lourenço Marques. Lisbon was more skeptical of foreign instrusions and forbade any Boer settlement in the African port. Neither the English colony at Natal nor a Transvaal Republic to the west was viewed by colonial officials in Lisbon with any emotion except apprehension, and an effort was begun to fortify the town and bring local chiefs under Portuguese allegiance. The Boers, for their part, were anxious to obtain an outlet in the Indian Ocean other than Natal and entered into negotiations with Portugal in 1858 for the use of Lourenço Marques. A pact was proposed in that year providing for the recognition of Moçambique-Transvaal frontiers and for communication between the two countries, but it was not ratified. Portugal was still fearful about taking a step which might lead to the loss of Delagoa Bay.

The English in Natal were equally concerned about the Transvaal Republic's gaining an entry to the sea at Lourenço Marques. In 1861, they took Inhaca Island at the mouth of the bay, although no attempt was made to raise the British flag again at Catembe. Portuguese protests led to lengthy correspondence between Lisbon and London. In 1869 Portugal concluded a commercial treaty with the Transvaal which recognized the southern boundary of Moçambique at 26° 30′ S. latitude, well beyond the limits of Delagoa Bay, and provided for the use of Lourenço Marques by the Boers once effective communication was established. A new crisis was precipitated when Britain refused to recognize the treaty; finally she agreed to submit the dispute to arbitration. In 1873–74 both countries presented their cases to the referee, Marshal MacMahon, President of France. The English case was based almost entirely on Owen's treaties with the natives of the area and his observations on Portugal's doubtful sovereignty; Portugal's brief, five times as long, was a patiently detailed account of three centuries of Portuguese activities. In 1875 President Mac-Mahon admitted the justice of Portugal's claims and decided that her sovereignty in effect extended to the limits fixed by the 1869 treaty. Lack of occupation, he observed, did not violate her claims. No other border decision involving either Angola or Moçambique can compare in importance with MacMahon's ruling, for now Portugal indisputably held one of the finest ports in Africa, whose possession was to be the most influential factor in Moçambique's economic development.

The Delagoa Bay squabble, a prelude to the scramble for Africa, contributed to the deterioration of Anglo-Portuguese relations in Africa. English popular contempt for the allegedly sleepy degenerate Portuguese colonies found more than occasional response in the Foreign Office. Portugal, ever more apprehensive of Britain's designs in east and central Africa, nevertheless realized the folly of risking the loss of English support. With a realism not untouched by self-pity, Andrade Corvo defended the necessity for England's friendship if Portugal was to press her claims to great extents of territory for which she might seem to have, in modern eyes, slight justification.[3]

So low in esteem was Portugal held by other European powers that she was only belatedly invited to the Brussels Conference in 1877 — from which emerged the International Association of the Congo — to participate in a discussion of how best to open equatorial Africa to European civilization, although Portugal's historical contact with the area was greater than that of any of the nations attending. In the face of such disregard, the English alliance was vital for the preservation of Portuguese Africa, but it was a tricky problem of statesmanship simultaneously to maintain it and keep England from abusing it. Had not Portugal dragged her feet in suppressing slavery and had she spoken more convincingly of free trade in Africa, the English attitude toward Portugal would have unquestionably been different, but one can only speculate to what extent England would have been willing to subordinate her own colonial interests to those of Portugal in the last twenty years of the century.

At no time did Portugal need English support more than in the years immediately before and after the Conference of Berlin. Although the Conference was precipitated by an Anglo-Portuguese treaty on jurisdiction over the lower Congo, the issue of the Congo was an ancient one, dating back to 1600 when Portugal sought to prevent the Dutch from slave trading at the river's mouth. With the decline of Portuguese influence in São Salvador, the region was gradually deserted by its European inhabitants. At the mouth of the river, which in the centuries of slaving was an international port of call, the Portuguese usually maintained a small trading station. In 1784, mistrustful of French intent, Portugal built a fortress north of the river at Cabinda, but it was demolished by a French frigate — reportedly in the interest of the freedom of European trade along the coast — almost as soon as it was built. After the usual lengthy litigation, a treaty between the two powers was signed wherein France tacitly acknowledged Portuguese claims to the northern boundary of Cabinda, that is, up to 5° 12′ S. latitude. Portugal did not occupy this section of the coast, but in the treaties of 1810 and 1817 with England, the latter seemed to recognize Portuguese claims here by including this coastal section in the area where the slave trade could be legitimately carried on by Portuguese vessels. Afterwards, however, England, feeling that Portugal was making no efforts to put an end to the traffic north of Ambriz, refused to recognize Portuguese authority over any territory north of that port, which is situated at 8° S. latitude. Ambriz itself was not administered by Portuguese officials until 1855, and from then until the early 1880's the British resolutely forbade any expansion from there up the coast. Lisbon constantly protested the restraint and did not yield her claim to both banks of the Congo.

By 1882–83 England was ready to reconsider her position on Portugal's assertions of priority. The frenzied expeditions of Savorgnan de Brazza, in the service of the French government, and Stanley, who on behalf of King Leopold's International Association of the Congo had been scouring the Congo Basin and central Africa obtaining treaties of friendship and protection from African chiefs, alarmed both England and Portugal. Portugal foresaw that she might shortly lose territory she had been accustomed to regard as her own. Between the ambitions of France and of Leopold, England feared more the already known high-tariff policies which followed France's path down the coast. De Brazza's acquisitions posed the real threat that the river would be closed to international traffic and made England receptive to overtures from the Portuguese government in 1882 for a clarification of the latter's status in the Congo.

In choosing to treat with Portugal, England realized that she was dealing with a country whose notions of protective tariffs were more conservative than those of France, but the nineteenth century had proved that Portuguese statesmen were malleable. Portugal's dilemma was worse: she must decide which nation she less distrusted, England or France. Although England had been cool the year before to a new discussion of the Congo question, it was apparent that now in late 1882 the interests of the two old-time allies were closer. And it was obvious that France was moved by territorial ambitions along the Congo, while perhaps England sought only commercial advantages. Nevertheless, the idea of playing one against the other was an attractive possibility, and Portugal left the door open for negotiations with France through most of 1883, until it became evident that France had no intention of recognizing Portuguese claims north of 8° S. latitude.

In the Anglo-Portuguese treaty drawn up in 1884, but never ratified, England at last recognized the claims she had persistently denied for sixty years. This aroused very natural suspicions in France and Germany that the treaty was a prelude to English domination of the Congo coast. In return for the recognition Portugal agreed to charge a maximum duty of 10 per cent *ad valorem* on goods entering the area and to give British subjects a most-favored-nation treatment there. An Anglo-Portuguese commission would be established to control traffic. Britain, correctly sensing that a dual commission would create antagonisms among other powers, had favored an international commission, but gave way in the face of Portuguese reluctance. Portugal's sovereignty on both sides of the Congo would extend about fifty miles, up to Noqui, and she was to grant freedom of navigation on the river.[4]

A treaty which gave, as it seemed, commercial advantages to England in the Congo region and which placed control of the lower banks of the waterway in the hands of Portugal, regarded by her few friends as incompetent and by her enemies as backward and isolationist, was bound to meet with opposition. Jealousies of England in Europe and scorn for Portugal in England and Europe made such a disposal of equatorial Africa's principal waterway impossible. France's opposition was immediate. She made representations to Lisbon that both the 10-per-cent tariff and the dual commission were unacceptable, and that she was not prepared to recognize Portuguese claims to 5° 12′ S. latitude. Portugal seemed willing to compromise on the first two points, but clung doggedly to her territorial claims. Portugal also suspected that the English Foreign Office was not giving appropriate support to the treaty, a suspicion which grew when a considerable segment of Parliament voiced opposition to giving the Congo delta to a power whose "moral title was certainly no stronger than the legal title . . . whose customs systems were such as to fetter the activities of trade with shackles of a truly medieval type." [5] English popular opposition to the treaty must be viewed against a background of public opinion hostile to Portugal's role in Africa. The writings of Owen, Buxton, Livingstone, and Cameron had created a consciousness which made the English fear that some form of slavery invariably came on the heels of Portuguese occupation, a notion reinforced by Stanley's caustic anti-Portuguese comments in his many public denunciations of the treaty. Portugal's equivocal conduct from March to May of 1884 made the matter of amendments more difficult, but a diluted version of the treaty might have been salvaged had not Bismarck's blunt communication to the British government precluded all hopes of compromise. His note of June 7 was a flat rejection. "We are not in a position to admit that the Portuguese or any other nation have a previous right there. We share the fear which, as Lord Granville admits, has been expressed by merchants of all nations, that the actions of Portuguese officials would be prejudicial to trade . . . We cannot take part in any scheme for handing over the administration, or even the direction, of these arrangements to Portuguese officials." [6]

In the midst of the delicate negotiations Portugal had suggested that a new basis for the treaty might be reached at an international conference, a proposal rejected by England. But Portugal, her faith in England wavering, circulated the idea among other European capitals. When the proposal was taken up by Germany as an opportunity to seize the initiative from England, the Berlin West African Conference of 1884–85 was the result. At Berlin Portugal lost half of what she had sought to keep by her original suggestion for a conference.

Her role at the conference was not a major one, although she was one of the five major parties to the discussions. In the course of the negotiations Portugal discovered that she could consistently rely on the help of no other nation, although on some issues she collaborated closely with France, whose interests in the Congo now more nearly paralleled her own. That Portugal did not fare worse at the conference seems partly to have been the result of her secondary status (which did not bring her into essential political conflict with the great powers), of the skill of her delegation (which included Luciano Cordeiro), and of the jealousies of England, France, and Germany, which led these nations to use Portuguese claims as pawns to check their antagonists. Had not Leopold II skillfully manipulated these jealousies to advance the interests of the International Association of the Congo at the expense, in some cases, of Portuguese claims, it is very possible that Portugal's representatives might have kept her African colonies intact.

The various declarations set forth in the General Act of the Berlin Conference did not directly touch the substance of Portuguese claims, since such matters as the disposition of the lower Congo, though resulting from the conference and carried on while it was in session, were not within its framework. The first two tasks were to define the mouth and basin of the Congo and to assure free trade in the region. Without pressing her claims for the coast between 5° 12′ and 8° S. latitude, Portugal promised to permit free trade there if her claims were granted. Not even when the geographical limits of the free-trade area were pushed to the eastern watershed line of Lake Tanganyika and south to the watershed of the Zambezi, extensions taking in territory unquestionably Portuguese, did Portugal's delegation offer serious objections. Nor did she oppose the concept of free navigation on the Congo, but with France she demanded that along those sections of the river held by a sovereign power, pilot tariffs, navigation dues, and questions of general policy be reserved to that power. The subsequent division of the river revealed that Portugal and France had played into the hands of the International Association. In the third large problem taken up by the delegates, the conditions for the occupation of the continent, Portugal had little voice, although the purposely vague wording of the article ("The Signatory Powers of the Present Act recognize the obligation to ensure the establishment of authority in the regions occupied by them on the coasts of the African Continent sufficient to protect existing rights . . .") became a dangerous weapon against Portugal's interests in Africa. The interpretation given by Bismarck to the article, that the possessor of territory must within a reasonable time prove by practical achievements his will and power to exercise his rights and fulfill his duties there, became the convenient yardstick by which to measure Portugal's rights in Africa.

Before the conference was over, Portugal had been forced to make her first concession. Acting with the support of France, she attempted to hold the coastal sections north of the Congo's mouth as specified in the now dead Anglo-Portuguese treaty. The threat implied to the International Association (to be known as the Congo Free State on the termination of the conference) was at once apparent, and it became the task of Germany, later seconded by England and France, to convince Portugal to come to more reasonable terms. The first proposal made to Portugal was that she should accept the coast up to the southern bank of the river, the left bank of the Congo as far upstream as Noqui, and the right to lands stretching inland south of 14° latitude. Portugal refused, standing firm on her "historic rights" and leading England and Germany to believe that she was acting in collusion with France to bottle up Leopold's domain. In December 1884, however, France began to work with the Association toward a partition of the Congo, negotiations which were swiftly concluded. Leopold, suspecting that France was still secretly encouraging Portugal in her fixed attitude, held off his approval until France promised to use her influence on Portugal to reduce her demands. The Portuguese delegation gave way slightly: Portugal would grant an extension of the Association's frontier to Boma on the north bank and allow her to build a railroad through Portuguese territory along the south bank; but the river must remain under Portuguese control. These demands were untenable, and Portugal, now standing alone against the pressures of the impatient major powers, agreed to yield her claim to the north bank of the river provided she were given the enclave of Cabinda, a proposal the Association accepted after some hesitation.

In the meantime, political opinion in Portugal militated against such concessions, and before a convention could be signed, the Portuguese delegation asked for the port of Banana, at the mouth of the Congo on the north shore, and an extension of her lands on the left bank beyond Noqui to Vivi. It was felt at this stage of the negotiations that the Portuguese delegates, fearful of being accused at home of having sold Portugal's interests down the river, were seeking to produce pressure on themselves. Germany, France, and England obliged by delivering to Portugal on February 13, 1885, a note to the effect that if she persisted in her stubbornness, the territorial rights already recognized as hers would be questioned. Two days later a convention was signed. Portugal retained only Cabinda north of the river. She held the south bank up to Noqui and from there inland along the latitude of Noqui to the Cuango River, whose southern course was to form the boundary with the Congo Free State.

The final Angola–Congo Free State frontiers were fixed by treaties in 1891 and 1894, but not before the indefinite nature of the interior boundaries had caused several incidents. Portugal's claims again were extensive, but with the dissolution of her dreams for a trans-African colony, these lost some of their significance, and by 1891 she was willing to talk concretely. Following the Berlin Conference, Leopold's agents zealously carried on the practice of setting up strategic outposts and collecting treaties with native chiefs, techniques by which Stanley and his lieutenants had given reality to the International Association. The Portuguese government had not yet learned the lesson of moving decisively in central Africa, and by 1890 the two nations discussing territorial rights to the Katanga, where the Portuguese had been the first to trade and explore, were the Congo Free State and England. East of the Cuango the enterprising Baron Dhanis had persuaded Leopold to create the district of East Cuango. Portugal affirmed that Angola's frontiers had been violated and sent a gunboat up the Congo to Boma. But by 1891 Portugal was ready to begin formal and — from the Belgian point of view — realistic negotiations. The frontier established is the one, with small modifications, separating the two colonies today, with the southern courses of the Cuango and the Kasai forming the main lines of demarcation.

What perverse fortune drove Portugal in 1886 to attempt to reassert the trans-African schemes of Manuel, Sebastião, and Sousa Coutinho? Fifty, thirty, perhaps ten years earlier she could have claimed and occupied the land lying between Moçambique and Angola without threat of grave repercussions, but such a move in 1886 was an invitation to disaster. (Even in 1886 Harry Johnston submitted to the British Foreign Office a map partitioning Africa, in which he recognized Portugal's transcontinental claims.) Many factors, some rational, some emotional, precipitated the plunge into *Mittelafrika*. There was the very sound suspicion that the English would drive up the continent from the south, and with the grand disillusionment over the breakdown of the alliance at Berlin, there was no longer any necessity for Portugal to consider the loss of English assistance which might result from a conflict of claims. There is the possibility that Portugal mistakenly thought that the articles in the General Act referring to the establishing of authority back from the coast applied to the ambitions of minor colonial powers. Pique and vanity also helped turn the heads of Lisbon statesmen. Portugal considered herself humiliated at the Conference of Berlin, and in an effort to boost national confidence decided to try the blunt tactics of Bismarck which appeared to obtain such impressive results. Portugal, who had quibbled endlessly over a few acres of territory, now prepared boldly to embrace a piece of the continent larger than the accepted areas of both Angola and Moçambique.

Viewed in retrospect, the proposition to take over the country comprising most of Northern Rhodesia and Nyasaland seems a fanciful blunder, but Portuguese diplomats were not completely ignorant of the rules of African politics. If Germany, seconded by England and associated powers, legalized Leopold's empire in the Congo, why couldn't Germany and France do the same for a trans-African Portuguese empire? England had yielded on the Delagoa Bay question and by early 1886 had not pressed a claim to the Shire highlands; she might be persuaded by the unexpected boldness of Portugal's action and the lack of any definite policy of her own in this part of Africa to let the area go by forfeit. The two flaws in this reasoning were Portugal's unhappy reputation as a colonial power and Cecil John Rhodes. The intervention of Rhodes was perhaps difficult to foresee in 1886, but not to have realized that the distrust she inspired as mistress of African colonies was a pervasive and influential prejudice in English opinion was a grave mistake.

Accordingly Portugal began to execute her greatest colonial plan. For centuries the scheme had been the subject of tracts, speeches, and projects; now it was to be carried out with all the vigor of Portuguese diplomacy. Henrique de Barros Gomes, Minister for Foreign Affairs, was the guiding force in the early negotiations. From May 1886 to July 1887 omnibus treaties were signed and ratified with Germany and France covering the various frontiers between Portuguese colonies and those of the two powers. With France the frontiers of Cabinda and Portuguese Guinea with French territory were fixed without undue difficulty. Germany, however, by virtue of her explosive occupation in East and West Africa in the early 1880's, had come into territorial contact with the southern limits of Angola and the northern tip of Moçambique. Spheres of influence in East Africa, cause for later friction, were roughly demarcated by the course of the Rovuma River. In West Africa, Portugal was obliged to sacrifice to Germany her claims to the coast south of the Cunene to Cape Frio. In the treaties France and Germany recognized Portugal's privilege to exercise "the right of sovereignty and civilization in the territories which separate the Portuguese possessions of Angola and Moçambique, without prejudice to the rights which other powers may have acquired there."[7] Barros Gomes proudly announced that Germany was committed to the solemn recognition of Portugal's exclusive claims, and the following year the government presented to the Portuguese parliament the famous rose-colored map which swathed the interior of the continent roughly between the twelfth and eighteenth parallels in bright rose-pink.[8]

Portugal's African reputation was not good in the 1880's,[9] and England's refusal to recognize the transcontinental sections of the 1886 treaties was appropriate to the mood of the day. Barros Gomes may have erred in not negotiating simultaneously with England, but it is difficult to see what such negotiations would have produced. England was now following a policy of territorial acquisition in Africa; in 1885 Bechuanaland had been made into a British protectorate. The direction this policy would take was not yet clear, but obviously the Angola-Moçambique union could not be countenanced. The wisdom of England's rejection became apparent two years later. "The imperial destinies of Portugal required a solid block of Portuguese territory from Angola to Mozambique, while Rhodes and his followers, with that originality which is characteristic of the Englishman, decided that the destinies of Britain required a solid block from Cape to Cairo, running from south to north and therefore, necessarily, making all other nations' solid blocks — which ran from west to east — impossible."[10]

In his August 1887 memorandum to the Lisbon government, Lord Salisbury argued that under the General Act sovereignty came with occupation and that Portugal did not effectively occupy the territory claimed and was not able to keep order and protect foreign life and property there. Barros Gomes replied that the Berlin Conference spoke only of coastal occupation, and that if it were a case of occupation in the interior, German possession of large sections of East and West Africa, Leopold's holdings in the Congo Free State, and even some parts of British protectorates in the hinterland would be invalidated. He added that the frequent use of the term, "spheres of influence," in international documents was further proof that occupation, in the sense of permanently established authority, was not a criterion for possession. Finally, he summed up Portugal's historic claims in central Africa. Portugal's foreign minister did not remind Lord Salisbury that

three years earlier, in the Anglo-Portuguese treaty, England had recognized Portuguese claims north of the Congo which had less justification, either in terms of historical contact or of occupation, than those
made in the rose-colored map. But while Barros Gomes spoke of ancient treaties with the Monomotapa, ruined forts and factories in Mashonaland, of mining expeditions to Manica, missionary work, traders,
priority, the scientific journeys of Lacerda, Gamitto and Monteiro,
and Serpa Pinto, England needed only speak of Progress, the catch-
word of white imperialism, to eradicate all of Portugal's pretensions.

At several points in the ensuing negotiations a compromise seemed
at hand, but the intransigeance of the British missionaries in the Shire
highlands, Rhodes's gargantuan projects, and what Oliveira Martins
called Portugal's "stupidly patriotic insistence" frustrated any satisfactory compromise and brought on the British ultimatum of 1890.
Barros Gomes was to learn that the use of forceful diplomacy pre-
supposed an authority which Portugal did not possess.

But the fundamental conflict between Portugal and England was
between the past and the future. Few people in either the colonies or
the metropolis had yet acquired the determination or sense of necessity
which would have helped Portugal to compete with other colonial
powers. "There was born in the world a colonial spirit, the science of
colonization, a recognition of colonial rights; whereas in Portugal
there was still the idea of owning possessions for the benefit of a bureaucracy, of a few planters and importers, or of settlers of the metal
of the old-time heroes . . ." writes Eduardo Moreira. "Portugal had
been like some wealthy landed proprietor in Europe . . . who deemed
himself justified in exploiting imperfectly, or not at all, some portion
of the state he had inherited. . ." [11] The rules of the game had been
changed by players entering the game late, and no amount of historic
claims could prevail against Kiplingesque platitudes on progress and
duty.

In his memorandum of 1887, Lord Salisbury expressed his particular concern that Portugal should have laid claim to Matabeleland and
Mashonaland and to the missionary districts near Lake Nyasa. The internal situation in the two separated regions was quite different, but
as the controversy wore on, British interests in both became a common cause and it was events in the two areas which brought on the
British ultimatum. In the south, where Portugal hoped to restore her
former influence in Manica and lands to the west now under the rule
of the Matabele king Lobengula, the colonial party in Lisbon came
upon a *fait accompli* in 1888. Rhodes, who had three years before influenced the annexation of Bechuanaland, was set on the expansion of

British South Africa into the plateau country between the Limpopo and the Zambezi. Unable to convince his government either at the Cape or in London to undertake such an enterprise, Rhodes and several friends decided to work through a commercial company. In February 1888, Lobengula was persuaded by the missionary J. S. Moffat to conclude a treaty of friendship with the British government, placing most of what is now Southern Rhodesia under British protection, and in the following year a charter was granted the British South Africa Company for the purpose of operating and administering the vaguely defined region. Rhodes's ambitions in Mashonaland, to which English policy was soon committed, brought his Chartered Company into immediate conflict with Portugal, who even before the formation of the company had sharply reacted to the Lobengula treaty. She denied the African chief's right to place Mashonaland under British protection and dispatched in mid-1888 an expedition to East Africa to distribute Portuguese flags and conclude treaties with other chiefs in the area.

In the meantime a crisis was developing in Nyasaland, where British missionary and commercial interests had been slowly growing since the days of Livingstone. Portugal had never looked with any favor on the English colony expanding in lands she thought were hers, and from 1886 on she was determined to use aggressive tactics in pushing her territorial claims. Foreign shipping on the Zambezi was restricted and the importation of arms forbidden. Only when her sovereignty was recognized, she gave England to understand, would these frustrating tactics cease. While England was not ready to accept responsibility for Nyasaland, whose only communication with the outside world was then through Portuguese territory, neither was she prepared to deliver British interests there into Portuguese hands. Impatient with the inconclusive negotiations, the Portuguese government sent an expedition under António Cardoso to survey the Shire River and the western shore of Lake Nyasa and to implant Portuguese jurisdiction wherever possible through local treaties.

In October 1888 a tentative proposal was made to the Portuguese government that a *status quo* in Mashonaland and Nyasaland be maintained. The British ambassador in Lisbon suggested that perhaps if Portugal were prepared to recognize his country's rights in Mashonaland, England would probably recognize Portuguese claims north of the Zambezi. Such a possibility Barros Gomes would not consider. He did mention the possibility of arbitration by an international committee, but Salisbury, mindful of Delagoa Bay, declined. Throughout 1889 the argument became more heated. Missionary societies in England were vociferous in their denunciations of any scheme to place the Shire region under Portuguese control. Rhodes, in London to look after the founding of the British South Africa Company, pressed his government to regard the Nyasaland and Mashonaland questions as one and to let the company extend its sphere of influence to the southern edge of Lake Tanganyika. Portugal's claims he ridiculed, being of the avowed opinion that she should not even be allowed to retain the coast of Moçambique.

The intensity of the situation had created in Portugal a climate of opinion which made any concessions impossible; at the same time, England's appetite had increased enormously in the whole area from the Transvaal to Lake Tanganyika. In 1889 Portugal announced the establishment of a new district in the province of Moçambique, its center at Zumbo, which took in the northern third of modern Southern Rhodesia and the Luangwa valley. Such a move was designed to complete the isolation of Nyasaland and blunt any thrust northward by the South Africa Company.

The crisis was finally precipitated by a brush on the Shire between a Portuguese expedition and the Makololo, Livingstone's porters and their fellow tribesmen who had settled in the disputed area and dominated the local tribes. The presence of the Portuguese column, allegedly a scientific and peaceful treaty-making expedition, was a definite threat to British interest, and in August 1889, the Makololo were placed under English protection. The British Consul Harry Johnston, who was also in the employ of Rhodes, warned Serpa Pinto, commander of the Portuguese force, that he would probably encounter trouble with the Makololo if he proceeded further up the river.[12] But Serpa Pinto, having convinced Lisbon that a show of strength was necessary, continued up the Shire. The Makololo did attack the column and were turned back with heavy losses.

England complained of aggression. Barros Gomes replied that the shooting had taken place outside the limits of the protectorate and the Portuguese force was only defending itself. He again suggested international arbitration of all boundary disputes. Public opinion in England was now outraged by the murder of Livingstone's faithful Makololo by unprincipled Portuguese. Annoyed at Portugal's unchastened reply, Lord Salisbury in January 1890 called upon Lisbon to remove its troops from both the Shire region and Mashonaland and ordered warships from Zanzibar to steam to Moçambique. This sudden resort to an ultimatum over an exaggerated border incident revealed not only imperial impatience, but a basic doubt about the validity of England's claims in both areas. Nonetheless, Portugal's positive diplomacy came to an abrupt dead end. Faced with the naked fist, the Lisbon government complied with the terms and promptly resigned.

The reaction in Portugal was one of anguish and violence. At hardly any time in Portuguese history had the public taken such a close interest in African affairs, but during most of the negotiations it had been badly informed and led to expect the eventual triumph of their country's cause. "From chimera to chimera, madness to madness, we came to believe the romance of a rose-colored Africa, stretching from East to West. . . Nothing could satiate our stupid desire to look at pictures of these maps, with the result that, like the astrologer, we fell into the well." [13] A series of articles in *O dia* by António Enes, later royal commissioner in Moçambique, reveal the anger, humiliation, and self-pity that swept over Portugal.[14] Barros Gomes' house was stoned in one of the bitter demonstrations against the fallen government not only for backing down before the ultimatum but for having failed to occupy the disputed territory in 1887 and 1888. England's perfidy shook the nation as it had not been shaken since 1640. Around the statue of Camões — the poet laureate of European imperialism — the students of Lisbon took an oath to die in the defense of Africa. Public subscriptions were raised to send a cruiser with a squadron of men and arms to Moçambique to show that Lusitanian heroics were not yet dead. The country was in no mood to compromise, which made the task of the new government extremely difficult, for only through compromise and concession could Portugal salvage her African empire.

Portugal stood quite alone. Germany had no desire to disturb the talks she was carrying on with England in 1890 and advised Portugal to negotiate (by this date Germany had begun to formulate schemes of her own for the annexation of parts of Angola and Moçambique). France was polite, sympathetic, but offered only moral support.[15] The first step taken by the new foreign minister, Hintze Ribeiro, was to press once more for an international conference or arbitration — a step that led nowhere. A proposal that Portugal occupy the Shire highlands, create a common zone in upper Zambézia and Barotseland, and submit the boundary fixing of Mashonaland to a mixed commission was also turned aside in England where public opinion was as hostile to compromise as it was in Portugal. In the meantime several small incidents on the Shire further shortened tempers in both countries.

The expansion of the British South Africa Company in Matabeleland and Mashonaland, however, made protracted negotiations unwise for Portugal, since each delay meant the possible loss of more disputed territory. In July and August of 1890 the two nations worked earnestly on boundary settlements which would be acceptable. On August 20 a compromise treaty was signed in London which set the boundaries of Moçambique *very* roughly at their present limits, save for the region above Tete and the frontier with the southern half of Southern Rhodesia which extended further west. Nyasaland was irretrievably lost. In Portugal the treaty was greeted with a new outburst of vehemence. The government resigned and in October parliament rejected the treaty. In England there was strong imperialist sentiment that Lord Salisbury had sold out English claims south of the Zambezi; among Rhodes's supporters there was talk of annexing Beira and Gazaland. Nevertheless, both countries realized the necessity for a provisional arrangement, and the unratified treaty was accepted in November by Lisbon and London, without prejudice to either's claims, for a six-month period.

In the same month tensions exploded in Manica as a result of conflicting claims between the Moçambique Company and the Chartered Company. The area in dispute was the Manica kingdom of chief Umtasa (Mutassa) who had recently made a treaty with representatives of Rhodes similar to the one he had made with the Goan captain major Gouveia in 1873. Paiva de Andrade of the Moçambique Company, which had been formed in 1884, entered the chief's kraal with a small force and persuaded Umtasa of his error, but several days later the Chartered Company's police force took Paiva de Andrade and Gouveia prisoner and marched toward Beira. Another storm rocked Portugal; a Republican uprising took place in Oporto, and the government dispatched a volunteer expeditionary force to Moçambique. Rhodes left for London to convince the Foreign Office that Manica (including Umtasa's kingdom) was indispensable for the South Africa Company's expansion and that a formal treaty should move the frontier eastward from the Save River to a new line which would leave the Manica plateau in English hands ("The plateau for England, the lowlands for Portugal").[16] Meanwhile, Rhodes's agents approached the chief of Gazaland for concessions in his kingdom. Confronted with the potential loss of more territory here and apprehensive that a clash between the Portuguese expeditionary force and the Chartered Company's private army would create another disastrous crisis,[17] Portugal was in no position to bargain further. In return for additional concessions in the vicinity of Zumbo, she recognized the new Manica frontier, agreed to freedom of navigation on the Zambezi, and promised to build a railroad from the Rhodesian frontier to Beira. The treaty was signed in June 1891, and final frontier settlements were made in lesser treaties during the next five years. The agreement of 1891 was in every sense less favorable to Portugal than the treaty rejected the year before, but now all passion had been spent, and a serious financial crisis occupied the nation's attention.[18]

All that remained of the rose-colored map was a horrendous jig-saw puzzle which, when finally put together, revealed a crimson strip of British territory running north from the Transvaal to the Congo's Katanga province and German East Africa. Progress and enlightenment had prevailed, and for the moment Livingstone lay easy in his grave. Few will deny that the material development of the Rhodesias has proceeded more rapidly than it would have under Portuguese management, but one cannot be sure that the emergence of African interests has kept pace, for there remain in the Rhodesias today many visible traces of a conservative white imperialism. The triumph of progress over priority in Africa has not always brought corresponding benefits to the African.

There was, and is, no doubt in Portugal that England had treated her scandalously; her vanity had been hurt more by England's threats than by Germany's bad faith. But the ultimatum of 1890 served a practical purpose in Portugal, for not since the sixteenth century had the metropolis been so vividly aware of the African colonies; the feeling that something must be done united temporarily the many factions of Portuguese political life. It was commonly agreed that the miserable realities of Angola and Moçambique presented a challenge, since the threat of appropriation by other powers did not disappear with the treaty of 1891. It was apparent that exaggerated glories of the past, though admirably suited for speeches and for inspiring patriotic sentiments, and ancient documents would not be sufficient defense against another onslaught. For twenty years, Portugal was able to exploit the energies and anger stirred by the ultimatum for the occupation and development of the African provinces.

Financial problems were another factor largely responsible for a continuing sense of crisis centering on Angola and Moçambique whose ports (Beira, Lourenço Marques, Lobito Bay) were now being regarded by European powers as keys to the wealth of the interior. English imperial sentiment by the end of the decade was still strongly in favor of annexation ("Surely it is high time that a nation capable of managing the country and properly administering its affairs should obtain possession and control, and it now devolves upon the Paramount Power, with its pre-emptive rights, to complete arrangements whereby the cession of the bay and the Portuguese East African territory should be promptly made"),[19] but after 1891 Portugal had more to fear from her *quondam* sponsor of the rose-colored map. Already Germany, in a dispute over the northern boundary of Moçambique growing out of the Anglo-German East African settlement of 1890, had nibbled Quionga Bay, between the Rovuma and Cape Delgado,[20] as an appetizer to the main course of northern Moçambique and southern Angola, which would fall into German hands when Portugal defaulted on loans Germany was eager to make or when a bankrupt Portugal would be forced to sell her colonies.

Portugal's economic cares were complicated by the MacMurdo suit. In 1884 she had let the concession for the construction of a railroad from Lourenço Marques to the Transvaal to an American financier, Edward MacMurdo, who formed a British company to build the road. In 1889, as a consequence of the unsatisfactory turn of negotiations with England — and also as a result of persuasion by the Boer republic which feared British control over the road — the concession was rescinded and the line taken over by the Portuguese colonial government, which then concluded an agreement with the Transvaal fixing the rates for the Lourenço Marques–Pretoria–Johannesburg run. Reparations were demanded by both England and the United States, and although the case was submitted to Swiss arbitration, it was believed that a large award would be given MacMurdo's heirs. (In 1900 the Portuguese government was instructed to pay five million dollars.) There was much speculation in the 1890's about Portugal's ability to pay and which power would make her the loan and what the compensations would be for such assistance. England's strained relations with the Transvaal, who enjoyed Germany's sympathy, and her unpopularity in Lisbon made the obvious solution — a British loan — questionable, although in the early 1890's Rhodes made repeated efforts to buy for the Cape government all of Moçambique below the Zambezi or, at least, to obtain Delagoa Bay on a longterm lease. Germany's offer to buy the railroad was blocked by British pressure. Germany in this period was also toying with the possibility of obtaining Delagoa Bay. The landing of twenty British sailors in Lourenço Marques in 1894 to protect the British consulate during an attack on the city by African tribesmen was interpreted as an attempt to interfere with Portuguese sovereignty, and two German warships were ordered to the scene to protect German interests along the coast and in the Transvaal. Neither England nor Portugal welcomed the intrusion, although Portugal was led momentarily to believe that she had an ally, one whose motives were not, unfortunately, above suspicion.

In 1897 the British government offered to guarantee Portugal's possession of her African colonies in return for a promise that the Transvaal Republic would be given no exit to the sea except Lourenço Marques, whose port and railroad would be operated by an Anglo-Portuguese company. England further offered to pay the MacMurdo award and grant a loan on the security of the African provinces. Both these proposals and one the following year providing the same guarantee in return for the temporary occupation of Lourenço Marques in the event of war with the Boers were rejected. Portugal had not yet regained her trust in England's promises, nor was she fully disabused of Germany's intentions. The wisest course seemed to avoid financial entanglements with either power. Germany was still convinced that Portugal's perpetual economic straits would eventually force her to negotiate a foreign loan, and in 1898 the Anglo-German Agreement established, in a secret clause, a division of Portuguese territories south of the equator "should it not be possible to maintain their integrity." The German sphere of influence was Moçambique north of the Zambezi and southern Angola. To England would fall Delagoa Bay, and she also obtained, effective immediately, the promise that Germany would remain sympathetically neutral in the Boer crisis.

Portugal knew of the secret clause of this convention, which increased her determination to refrain from accepting any loans from Germany. But in 1899, German bullying of Portugal in Europe, where she tried to back her into a financial corner, and in Angola, where a small German contingent briefly landed at Lobito, created an urgent need for alliance. At the same time England was desirous of cutting down the flow of arms through Lourenço Marques into the Transvaal. Accordingly, in October 1899, two days after the outbreak of the Boer War, a secret Anglo-Portuguese pact (the so-called Windsor Treaty) was signed, reaffirming the earlier treaties of friendship between the two nations and underlining the promise contained in the 1661 treaty that England would defend and protect Portugal's colonies. In return, Portugal agreed to allow no importation of arms for the Boers through Lourenço Marques and to permit England the use of Moçambique ports for the landing of troops.[21] While the Windsor Treaty did not directly conflict with the Anglo-German Convention, which dealt only with the hypothetical disposition of Portuguese Africa, Lisbon statesmen felt that they had gained protection from direct aggression.

Germany's ambitions for the annexation of parts of Angola and Moçambique were revived shortly before the outbreak of the First World War. In the course of negotiations carried on by the German ambassador in London and British Foreign Secretary Edward Grey the

1898 agreement was amended and improved. Most of Angola, São Tomé, Príncipe, and northern Moçambique were assigned to the German
economic sphere of influence. The German ambassador regarded the
new agreement as much more advantageous to his country than the
old one.[22] He foresaw no serious impediments to creating a crisis which
would result in partition. Grey stipulated that the treaties of 1898,
1899, and the present one should be published, a point to which Germany objected, and war broke out before the treaty was signed. In
the course of the African campaigns both Angola and Moçambique
were the scene of occasional hostilities between German and Portuguese forces.

Not even Portugal's participation in the Great War placed her
African colonies beyond criticism, as this comment by Arthur Keith
in 1919 attests: "The weakness of Portugal and her poverty have rendered it natural to assume that her territories must sooner or later be
partitioned between the two Powers who have obviously the best
territorial claims to fall heir to her territories in Africa, the United
Kingdom and Germany. . . It is idle to suppose that the Powers will
indefinitely acquiesce in any regime which does not open the territory
of Portugal on the east and west coasts to freedom of trade." [23] In the
late 1920's among the rumors to the effect that Germany might be
compensated for the loss of her pre-war colonies were suggestions
that the League of Nations give Germany a mandate to administer
Portuguese East Africa and Angola. The usual references were made
to the backwardness of the two areas and an abusive native policy. But
the aggressive tactics of European imperialism in Africa had softened,
and no serious thought was given to despoiling Portugal of her colonies. With the construction of railroads from the east and west coasts
into central Africa, the use of ports in Angola and Moçambique were
made available, with mutual economic advantage, to neighboring territories, with whom diplomatic relations have been almost constantly
good. Minor boundary matters have been settled amicably with Belgium and England. One could still hear complaints about the lack of
initiative and progress in the Portuguese colonies, but these remarks
did not have the belligerency of old, and in the troubled, potentially
explosive political world of Africa below the equator, there was a
growing tendency for the white governments of the Congo, the
Rhodesias, the Union, and Portuguese Africa to find common cause.
It may well be that Portugal's greatest asset in Africa is today those
same neighbors from whom she once attempted to defend her possessions.

IX

A NEW ERA

T HE period between the abolition of the slave trade and the ultimatum of 1890 was the transition from one colonial age to another in
Angola and Moçambique, from the traditional to the modern or, possibly, as a contemporary Portuguese historian has suggested, from
the romantic to the practical.[1] The transition does not imply, in spite
of repeated demands for Portugal to follow the example of other
colonial powers, any fundamental change in African policy; rather it
is the intensification of Portuguese interest there and an attempt,
given urgency by political necessities of the hour, to carry out historic
programs of occupation and development. It is, in fact, the continuation of tradition in Angola and Moçambique which sets the two provinces so noticeably apart from the African colonies of English and
Belgian influence. The outspoken policies of Enes and Mousinho de
Albuquerque, which sometimes do not seem to be Portuguese because
of their very bluntness, were unquestionably influenced by the apparent vigorous success of Anglo-Saxon tactics, but they sprang from
the aspirations and realities of the Portuguese past. The deliberate if
not backward pace of economic and native policies in Portuguese
Africa has always been as much the result of customs and concepts
hallowed by centuries as of poverty.

The generation of 1895, those soldiers and administrators who
faced the task of reconstruction in the African colonies, well realized
that the problems were chronic and not brought on by the events of
the previous decade. They were also aware that the habits of neglect
and inertia which had led to the spoilations at the Conference of Berlin

and of the Anglo-Portuguese Treaty of 1891 could, if not corrected, lead to subsequent losses of prestige and territory. In 1892 a district governor of Moçambique wrote the Overseas Ministry that half-measures designed to meet each new crisis as it arose were not enough. For Oliveira Martins, Portugal's Cassandra in the fateful year 1890, the situation in Africa was not hopeless. "If, instead of declaiming, we face the colonial problem boldly and courageously, without politics and with a positive and practical spirit, it seems to me that sound legislation and a sensible and foresightful government will be worth more in the eyes of Europe than a hundred harangues against Perfidius Albion." [2]

Occupation of the interior, a reorganization of the provincial administration, and a colonial policy consistent with the present realities were the three compelling necessities of the 1890's. Although one could not be separated from the other, especially since the new generation of soldier-administrators in Moçambique and Angola were frequently the authors of treatises on colonial government, the most pressing problem was for the conquest and effective military occupation of the interior. Not only did this first step promise to accomplish what apparently was meant by the article of the Berlin General Act regarding occupation, but in a number of regions African tribesmen were now threatening Portuguese strongholds. A young Portuguese officer bitterly summed up the lamentable condition of Portuguese East Africa: "The province of Moçambique belongs without question to the blacks who live in it; this is neither a sophism nor a subtlety; right here in Lourenço Marques, in the streets, in the public squares, in the homes, the *preto* is the one who commands." [3] While the military and political value of the campaigns in the two colonies was thoroughly exaggerated by popular sentiment of the day, which desperately needed a show of national heroics, and later by the spokesmen of the Salazar regime, which has found it convenient to consecrate a hierarchy of colonial heroes, the psychological importance of Portuguese armed triumph over native forces cannot be minimized. At home and in Africa these victories stood for progress and positive policies; they meant that Portugal could now hold her head high with other great colonial powers who were busily implanting civilization in the hinterland at the end of a rifle.

Warfare with the tribes of Angola had gone on sporadically since the days of Paulo Dias de Novais. The campaigns grew out of the slave trade, intermittent compulsions to colonize the interior, the de-

sire to punish a dissentient chief, or, on many occasions, the necessities
of self-defense. In terms of ultimate pacification they served no very
useful purpose, for in 1885 African hostility in the backcountry was
as strong as it had been three centuries before. In spite of a population decimated by the slave trade and the superiority of European
arms, the Angolan held his own through most of the nineteenth century against the columns sent into troubled areas. The two regions of
most persistent opposition to Portuguese penetration were the Dembos (the country northeast of Luanda at the headwaters of the Dande
River) and the part of southern Angola west and south of Moçâmedes
to the Cunene River. The Dembos was in a state of almost constant
revolt after 1850, while in the south the attempted occupation of
Humbe at the end of the century was contested by the Cuanhama
tribes, some of the bravest warriors in Angola. In this period Portuguese forces were made up largely of *degradados* and native troops,
neither of whom distinguished themselves in the fighting.

The full-scale occupation of Angola began in the 1880's with the
campaigns of Artur de Paiva — Portugal's *chargé d'affaires* at the Boer
colony in Huíla — in the country between the Cunene and Cubango
rivers. On successive expeditions in 1885, 1886, and 1888 Paiva erected
strategic forts, the largest at Cassinga, and succeeded in establishing
Portuguese military authority to the right bank of the Cubango. His
expeditions had a more than local significance, for they were part of
Portugal's attempt to extend the rose-colored map across the Zambezi watershed to Zumbo. In the same area Paiva Couceiro in 1890,
following the suicide of Silva Porto, descended the Cubango from
Bié, imposing Portuguese sovereignty in his path. In that year also,
Artur de Paiva led an expedition north from Huíla to Belmonte for
the purpose of subduing Silva Porto's one-time friend Ndunduma. The
importance that the colonial government gave these campaigns of
pacification may be seen in the size of Paiva's column: twenty officers
and sergeants, five hundred and fifty regular troops and auxiliaries
(including Boers and formidable Damara tribesmen), fifty carts, two
Krupp field pieces, and two machine guns.

In the Humbe region it took Portugal twenty-five years in the
course of which she suffered several humiliating reverses, to establish
her authority. The fortress at Humbe was maintained by an inadequate garrison which had to have reinforcements from the north to
push into the surrounding country and subdue temporarily the Cuanhama. In 1897 an epizootic disease from South-West Africa infected the
cattle of the area. The African population refused to allow their cattle
to be vaccinated and massacred a squad of soldiers sent to convince

them. Artur de Paiva was again called upon to assert his country's dominance and with a small army — more than one thousand men — he conducted a number of operations to put down the unrest. In 1904, however, Portugal suffered one of the most serious setbacks of her African campaigns when an encampment at Cuamoto, located halfway to the frontier southeast from Humbe, was obliterated by the Cuanhama. Three hundred men, including one hundred and twenty Portuguese, perished in the ambush. To restore Portuguese prestige, Captain Alves Roçadas was sent south in 1906 with two thousand troops. From a fort on the east bank of the Cunene — which has since grown into a town bearing his name — Roçadas demolished the *embalas* of the Cuamato region. The Cunahama still continued their resistance, however, supplied with rifles bought from a Portuguese trader and donated by the Germans in South-West Africa. Following their disastrous encounter at Naulila in 1914 with a German contingent, the Portuguese were forced temporarily to abandon Cuamato, Roçadas and Humbe. Only in 1915 was the entire southern region of the Huíla plateau finally brought under Portugal's thumb when General Pereira d'Eça routed the Cunahama at Môngua, some thirty miles west of Roçadas, and left the area sufficiently fortified to prevent further uprisings.

The Bailundo campaign of 1902, which went beyond the limits of Bailundo to involve a number of tribes on the Bié plateau, is often regarded fondly by the Portuguese as the classic native war. This means that the Portuguese punitive columns were organized quickly, the Africans fought bravely but foolishly, every Portuguese soldier was a hero, and, finally, that thousands of Africans were killed while Portuguese losses were minimal. Since 1890 the backcountry of the Benguela district had been relatively peaceful, although with the increasing number of Europeans, many of them unscrupulous, frictions had developed. The dissensions caused by the rubber boom and the demoralizations of the rum trade brought the normally pacific Ovimbundu to the edge of revolt. In 1901–1902 native resentments came to a head over excesses committed in the conscription of contract labor, and the area of Bailundo was swept by a wave of murders, robberies, and burnings of trading posts. The contagion spread beyond Bailundo, and the Portuguese administration saw the danger of a general revolt throughout Bié. A column from Benguela joined at Caconda with the Moçâmedes Dragoons and Boer volunteers; these four hundred men marched north to Huambo. At a spot a few miles northwest of the present city of Nova Lisboa, the column defeated a small army of rebels entrenched in their rock fortress. A second column under Massano de Amorim proceeded up country from Benguela, burning African villages and scattering small groups of resistance. By the end of 1902 the *planalto* was reasonably quiet, although for the next two years the area northeast of Nova Lisboa remained openly hostile to Portuguese penetration. The improvements made in native policy by Massano de Amorim, who served briefly as governor of the district, were not permanent. The contract-labor trade was suppressed for several years during the course of an official inquiry — which led to the dismissal of the captain of Bailundo — but by 1905 only traces of the reforms were visible.

The Dembos campaign was the most trying one for the Portuguese in the occupation of Angola, principally because of the moist heat and difficult terrain in this virtually inaccessible northern region of the province. The Dembos (the word refers to the chiefs of the area) were not primitive people like the Cuanhama. Living less than one hundred miles northwest of Luanda they had been subjected to marginal European influences; many had Portuguese names and had constructed houses of a Portuguese type. By the last third of the century, the chiefs became exasperated by the extortions of the regional captains major, many of whom were African soldiers appointed by the Luanda government, and either killed them or chased them from the country. A two-year campaign established a precarious position for the Portuguese in the upper Dande country; nevertheless, in 1907 only a handful of Europeans lived or traded in the area, at the sufferance of the chiefs who demanded heavy taxes.

A haven for criminals, fleeing contract laborers, and white *degradados*, the Dembos resembled the sixteenth-century Congo and was an embarrassing example of the nonoccupation of Angola. In 1907 Captain João de Almeida, who with Artur de Paiva contributed most of the military pacification of the colony, made a remarkable journey through the region which convinced him that the power of the chiefs could be broken and productive lands made available for colonization. Obtaining a thousand men from Governor Paiva Couceiro, many of whom were exiles or convicts, Almeida moved through the Dembos, engaging the Africans in a series of skirmishes from village to village. As in campaigns in previous centuries, the main enemies of the Portuguese were heat, dysentery, fever, and the fatalities in battle were almost exclusively African. Within three years the Dembos was pacified and the way to the Congo frontier open to occupation.

By 1915 the Angola government could claim either the subservience or allegiance of most of the province's African population, although in 1917 it was necessary to conduct a small campaign in the

Moxico region. It had accomplished in thirty years what previously it had been unable to accomplish in more than three hundred. In part the success was the result of a determination born of necessity, in part the work of a cadre of resourceful military men. New weapons like the machine gun and new medicines for tropical diseases also contributed to the Portuguese victory. Of equal importance was that the spirit of African resistance had been eroded by slavery and contract labor; village leaders had been corrupted by rum-selling traders. Time and the maleficent by-products of European civilization were factors which contributed as surely to the outcome of the pacification wars as did officers, drugs, and arms.

The state of affairs in Moçambique in 1890 was, if anything, worse than that in Angola, and few Portuguese with knowledge of the province contradicted foreign assertions that their country's dominance rested tenuously on a few towns and scattered forts. Reviewing the situation, Mousinho de Albuquerque stated: "We controlled the capital of the province on the island of Moçambique; we also controlled the entire district of Inhambane; we occupied Lourenço Marques and exercised a more nominal than effective authority in the surrounding lands ruled by chiefs who were vassals of the crown; we had forts at various points in the province — Sofala, Tete, Sena, Quelimane, Ibo, Tungue, and a few more. This was the extent to which were reduced our royal domains in Portuguese East Africa; in the rest of our possessions in this part of Africa we had no authority of any kind." [4] Another official wrote: "The Negro is absolute master here . . . If we cannot dominate the Negro along the coast, how can we dominate him in the interior? . . . They say that the Negro is ruled by an instinctive respect for the white man, especially the Portuguese. But though this may be a lovely phrase for a speech, it is a cliché and absurd lie." [5] The need for a rapid occupation of strategic parts of the colony was more acute than in Angola, for although the boundary problems had seemingly been settled by the Treaty of 1891, the British South Africa Company still talked ominously of taking over Gazaland and what was left of Manica.

The wars of the Zambezi, the invasion of the Angoche Islands, and the frontier squabbles around Lourenço Marques had enlivened colonial life in Moçambique during most of the nineteenth century. Only the Zambezi wars could be called campaigns of occupation, and even here Portuguese attacks on the undisciplined *prazeros* and migrating tribes from the south were regarded as defensive measures. That Portugal enjoyed any prestige in the interior of the province resulted more from the efforts of a Goan immigrant than from those of the tattered companies of Africans, Indians, and *degradados* which sallied forth occasionally from the island of Moçambique.

Manuel António de Sousa, unusually known as Gouveia, had come to Moçambique at the age of eighteen and became an itinerant trader in Zambézia. He prospered rapidly and built himself a formidable kraal in the Gorongosa hills. In a short while he held most of the *prazos* south of Sena, and his army was the most effective fighting force in the colony. These soldiers he usually placed at the disposal of the provincial government, a favor for which he was appointed Captain Major of Manica and Quiteve and a colonel in the overseas army. Had Portuguese authority in the area between the Zambezi and the Púngue been more solidly implanted, Gouveia's ambitions would have conflicted with Portuguese interests, but until 1890 the former trader served Portugal best when he served himself. The line of forts he constructed did more to check the invasion of Vatua and Landin tribesmen from Gaza than all of the Portuguese columns. In 1873 the chief of Manica paid him homage, and ten years later the Barué tribes (in the area southwest of Sena) acknowledged him as paramount chief. For his assistance in the final suppression of the Zambezi *prazeros* the Portuguese government heaped honors upon him, including an audience with the king on his visit to Lisbon and the rank of commander in the order of São Bento de Aviz. In 1890 he was captured with Paiva de Andrade at Macequece by the Chartered Company's police force; he had gone there to remind the Manica king Umtasa of his 1873 vow of allegiance. In these last years of his life he labored principally for the Portuguese government, neglecting his own lands, which were overrun by several tribes. When in the early 1890's he tried to restore his former empire, he was killed by these warriors. With his death the Barué country and the lands south of the Zambezi reverted briefly to their quasi-independent state.

Gazaland, Niassa, and Moçambique district were also almost completely independent of Portuguese authority. The task of bringing permanent order to the province, however, had to begin in the south in order to vitiate the pretensions of the South Africa Company and to protect the swelling commercial movement through the port of Lourenço Marques, which was fast becoming the first city of the colony. In 1894 António Enes arrived in Moçambique as royal commissioner with vigorous plans for the occupation and regeneration of

Portuguese East Africa. The assistants he gathered around him were, among others, Caldas Xavier, Paiva Couceiro, Eduardo Costa, Aires de Ornelas, Mousinho de Albuquerque, and Freire de Andrade, who formed the brilliant generation of 1895, the group of soldier-administrators whose actions and policies have left a permanent impression on Portugal's colonial philosophy.

First to demand Enes' attention was the situation in Lourenço Marques. During 1894 a general uprising was sparked by a jurisdictional dispute between the Portuguese military command and local chieftains. The insurgent African armies attacked the city, chasing its inhabitants into blockhouses, and were only repulsed by the concerted efforts of the police and sailors from Portuguese vessels. With the arrival of an expeditionary force from Lisbon late in 1894, the colonial government was at last in a position to mount a full-scale offensive against the tribes which had so long beset the port. In February of the next year, the Africans were badly beaten at Marracuene (about twenty miles from Lourenço Marques) and their leaders fled to the protection of the great chief Gungunhana.

For five long years Gungunhana had been a serious thorn in Portugal's side. Chief of Gazaland (roughly the territory from the Limpopo to the Púngue), before 1890 Gungunhana had vaguely recognized Portuguese sovereignty and had permitted a representative of the provincial government to reside at his kraal in Manjacaze. More recently, however, he had discussed with Rhodes's men the possibility of making his kingdom a British protectorate. Although more inclined to intrigue than warfare, Gungunhana had an army of sufficient size to discourage any casual Portuguese expedition into Gaza, and for four years Moçambique officials fretted helplessly, anticipating either the cession of Gazaland to the British or a massive attack on Portuguese positions along the coast. After the victory at Marracuene and the arrival of the expeditionary troops from Lisbon, Enes decided to test the great chief's power. Three columns were dispatched against Manjacaze: one under Colonel Galhardo proceeded south after landing at Inhambane; another under Freire de Andrade penetrated north from Lourenço Marques; a third, amphibious, force was sent up the Limpopo. In August, Aires de Ornelas carried an ultimatum to Gungunhana which demanded the delivery of the rebel chiefs he had protected, annual tribute of about fifty thousand dollars in gold, free passage for Portuguese traders, the right to establish fortresses in Gaza and collect head taxes, and the recognition of Portuguese authority. After much deliberation and bargaining, Gungunhana declared that he was unable to accept all of the conditions. In early November, Galhardo's column of about a thousand men marched on Manjacaze. At Coolela, four miles from the chief's kraal, the two armies met, and in a forty-minute battle, the African forces, variously estimated from six to ten thousand men, were routed with the loss of only a few European soldiers. The legend of Gungunhana's prowess vanished. Several days later Manjacaze was burnt to the ground.

The final operations of the campaign Enes entrusted to the cavalry officer Mousinho de Albuquerque, whom he appointed district governor of Gaza. In December, on a daring raid with fifty men, Mousinho surprised Gungunhana at Chaimite where he had fled after the defeat at Coolela and made him prisoner. Gungunhana was shipped off to Portugal where in Roman style he was paraded through the streets of Lisbon before the admiring eyes of the populace. The Gaza campaigns had not only removed the major obstacle to bringing southern Moçambique under control, but they had provided the inspiration for the support of continued military action in both African provinces.

Although 1895 is regarded as the *annus mirabilis* in the occupation of Moçambique, twenty years more, as in Angola, were needed to dominate the African population. Enes' successor, Mousinho de Albuquerque, carried the war north to the mainland opposite Moçambique island in 1896–97, hoping to occupy the interior in three stages; but he was able to carry out only the first step of his scheme, the placing of a series of forts along the coast. In Gaza the chief who had taken the place of Gungunhana led various tribes to revolt in 1896. Caused by the apparent misconduct of sepoys in the Portuguese army, this conflict was sharper and more prolonged than the brief encounters of 1895, and only after Mousinho's defeat of a large collection of warriors at Macotene did Gazaland submit to Portuguese rule.

In 1897 the governor of the Zambézia district had to break up various centers of resistance on the lower river in the so-called campaign of the Sena *prazos*. As an extension of the same campaign Azevedo Coutinho invaded the coast north of Quelimane to suppress the troublesome Maganja tribes. By 1900 the only serious resistance south of the Zambezi was in the Barué region, which had fallan into disorder after the death of Gouveia. A haven for deposed chiefs, criminals, and resentful *prazeros*, Barué, especially the Gorongosa region, defied the attempts of the Moçambique Company to maintain order. An expeditionary force of some three hundred Portuguese under Azevedo Coutinho finally brought peace to the area in 1902;

the territory was then placed under the direct military administration of the colony.

North of the Zambezi, the Zambézia Company with the help of several government expeditions from 1902 to 1904 succeeded in extending its administration north of Tete and into Angonia toward the Nyasaland frontier. The last two districts of the province to submit were Moçambique and Niassa. In 1906 two columns from Mossuril and Fernão Veloso (near Nacala) reduced the tribes along the coast and in the near interior. To the south Arab tenacity in the captaincy of Angoche, a trouble-spot for centuries, called for an invasion in force; in 1910 a company of men under Massano de Amorim defeated the sheik and his African allies.

The last large region of the province to be pacified was the northwest section of Niassa, between the lake and the Lujenda River. Here the hostile Yao chief, Mataka, had beaten off small expeditions of the government and the Niassa Company. Four years were required to pacify the region. First the interior coast was occupied in 1908–1909; then a line of small forts was set up in the north along the banks of the Rovuma to keep the Yao and Macua chiefs from their source of German arms. In 1912 the main Portuguese expedition advanced on Mataka's kraal at Muembe (a few miles northeast of Vila Cabral). Mataka fled across the Rovuma into German territory, but the lesser chiefs submitted. Sporadic uprisings throughout the province — a serious one in Barué in 1917 — went on for a few more years, but the Niassa campaign marked the end of an active program of pacification in Moçambique.

More than in Angola the campaigns in Moçambique were of primary psychological importance, for the skeptical eyes of England and Germany were watching Portugal's attempts to occupy the interior that remained to her in East Africa. The actual battles were, in terms of white casualties, more like bloody squabbles, as High Commissioner Brito Camacho later observed, on election days in the metropolis. Five Europeans died at Coolela, an equal number at Marracuene, and in the Barué invasion of 1902 only one Portuguese soldier fell.[6] In comparison with the Zambezi wars or the struggles in Angola, these mortality figures were exceptionally low. The decisive military action, however, saved the province from eventual partition by England and Germany and brought to the forefront of colonial affairs the famous generation of 1895, the circle of António Enes who served as Royal Commissioner of Moçambique in 1894-95.

The men Enes chose for his staff, all military officers, were profoundly influenced by their associations with him — and with each other. It would be a mistake to call men like Mousinho de Albuquerque and Paiva de Couceiro Enes' disciples, but the generation of 1895 did find practical inspiration in his hard-headed policies and absolute dedication to Portugal's colonial affairs. Through the various members of his staff who later assumed responsibility for the administration of the colonies the influence of Enes was felt in Moçambique and Angola for the next quarter century, and his concepts were elaborated and redefined in a number of important studies by the men who had served under him.

The list of Enes' associates reads like an honor roll of Portuguese colonial history. Mousinho de Albuquerque succeeded Enes as Royal Commissioner; from his tenure came the classic study *Moçambique* (1899). Aires de Ornelas became Mousinho's chief of staff in 1896, governor of the Lourenço Marques district in 1900, and Overseas Minister for 1906 and 1907, during which period he was responsible for the Colonial Reform Act and the visit of the crown prince to the African colonies. Freire de Andrade, Enes' chief of cabinet, was governor general of Moçambique from 1906 to 1910. Henrique Mitchell de Paiva Couceiro, hero of the Angolan campaigns of the early 1890's and Enes' aide-de-camp, became the most vigorous governor general of Angola since Sousa Coutinho and was author of a number of colonial tracts, including the influential *Angola* (1898). Eduardo Augusto Ferreira da Costa was governor of Moçambique district in 1896, governor of Benguela in 1903, and governor general of Angola in 1906. Two of his works, *Ocupação e domínio efectivo das nossas colónias* (1903) and *Estudos sobre a administração civil das nossas possessões africanas* (1903) are key texts in the new colonial ideology. Pedro Francisco Massano de Amorim began his career in Moçambique with Mousinho, not Enes, but philosophically he may be considered of the same generation; of all his contemporaries his service in Africa was the longest. After ten years of campaigning in the interior, he became governor of Moçambique district in 1906 and subsequently governor general of Angola in 1910 and of Moçambique in 1918.

Although the product of a decade of disenchantment, the *círculo* of António Enes had spiritual forefathers in Sousa Coutinho, Sá da Bandeira ("To take advantage of the overseas provinces we must not consider only what they are at the present, but also what they are capable of becoming"),[7] and the generation of colonialists preceding the Conference of Berlin. What set them apart from the past, no matter how much their suggested policies may have had their roots in

the past, was the ultimatum of 1890 which proved to the new generation that former policies had been either wrong or ineffectual. Enes
and his followers had no responsibilities for these decisions, and in fact
they made it a point to abuse the Liberal governments for every
colonial failure in the nineteenth century. The Anglo-Portuguese
Treaty had now wiped the slate clean, and Portugal would, they
hoped, address herself to the problems of the African provinces with
new convictions.

First, there must be no politics in colonial affairs: at home and in
Africa the administration must be free from jealous intrigues, the
ambitions of selfish men, frivolous changes in policy. Second, the
colonies must be administered practically; if this meant free trade,
the admission of foreign capital, the open and systematic use of native
labor, then past prejudices should not stand in the way. The colonies
had to be run profitably, not for the benefit of a few officials or investors. The time had come to stop pampering the African, who
must be obliged to become a productive member of his society. Attainable goals must replace the extravagant dreams of the past, for
only by daily hard work would the colonies be saved. In an age of
supposed Anglo-Saxon superiority, the example of Rhodes was a
stimulus. More than Enes and his contemporaries feared Rhodes, they
respected him for his energy, his positiveness, his success, and it
seemed proper that the Portuguese colonies should be run with something like his single-minded ruthlessness.

António Enes was a child of his age, a Romantic turned positivist.
Dramatist, editor, polemicist, he was a member of the Portuguese
parliament in the 1880's, and in the many changes following the
English ultimatum served briefly as Minister for Marine and Overseas. His interest in the colonies was of long standing, and from 1890
on Enes became the principal agitator for colonial improvements.
He was sent to Moçambique in 1891–92 on a special mission to determine administrative reforms. The report of his mission bristles with
the truth as Enes saw it.

Moçambique (1893) has become one of the basic texts of Portugal's modern colonial policy. It is divided into three parts: a blunt
presentation of the realities of 1892, a thirty-six-chapter section on
proposed reforms in the economic and administrative organization of
the province, and a model budget. Enes' presentation is in itself so
succinct that it is virtually impossible to synthesize satisfactorily his
views on particular colonial problems. His judgments are consistently
pragmatic. Prejudice, tradition, ideals are all contemptuously swept
away unless, in Enes' eyes, they contribute to the welfare of the

colony. He defended the Indian traders as a valuable segment of the population who had helped keep the frontier open and stimulate trade. In spite of everything that had been said against them, they were honest and pacific, taking nothing from the state and contributing to its treasury. Where they settled and traded were the future centers of civilization.[8] With regard to capital investment in Moçambique, Enes clearly recognized the reluctance of his countrymen to invest in the provinces. "Therefore I say and I repeat: the colonial administration and public opinion must lose their fear of the foreigner, their jealousy of the foreigner, when they deliberate on what to do in Moçambique." [9] Her ports should be opened to ships of all nations, immigration restrictions eased, foreign capital sought. Portuguese fears of denationalization he considered grossly exaggerated. Indiscriminate immigration by would-be Portuguese colonists he held to be folly. If farmers from Madeira found life difficult in the highlands of Angola, existence for them in the low-lying territories of Moçambique would be intolerable under present conditions ("Let the optimists say what they will, there still has not been discovered in the province any region where white man can propagate himself").[10] If unscrupulous English adventurers seemed to be prospering in Rhodesia, it was because they possessed gifts of improvisation which the Portuguese no longer had. Let only the immigrant with capital come to Moçambique; let manual labor be reserved for the African. While the colony remained impoverished the institution of the *prazos* should be preserved in preference to large land companies. From the *prazo* the state could obtain workers and a steady income from the *mussoco* (head tax), but from the land companies with exclusive rights the state gained little.[11] Grants to chartered companies should be reserved for virgin territory where only an organization with abundant resources could penetrate. Missionary work must be judged in relation to its contribution to the province, and should be closely controlled by the colonial government. Enes realized the missions' value in education, medical services, and agricultural instruction, but felt that they should not be permitted to go beyond these activities.[12] Each overseas province must have its own administrative code. Uniform colonial legislation which had been only a copy of metropolitan laws was nonsense, for in each colony different problems prevailed. Within the province various districts should be empowered to deal with local conditions.

Nor would new laws alone be sufficient. New men would be needed, honest, zealous, prudent men, cognizant of the colony's economic weaknesses, prepared to suffer an intemperate climate, men who understood the African's temperament and could deal with native problems. The new administrators must be given more freedom of action, and their decisions must not be subject to petty individual interests.[13] Furthermore, it was indispensable for the colonial budget to be drawn up by the governor general and his staff for approval by the Overseas Ministry instead of being burdened with an unrealistic budget prepared by men in Lisbon with no knowledge of African affairs. The various suggested sources of income (taxes, licenses, customs, sale of land) are too extensive for presentation here, as are the thousand other details Enes' fertile mind conceived for Moçambique's development. Many of his proposals were attempted by later colonial governments; others proved impractical or were coolly received in Lisbon. But the *relatório* remains one of the most significant documents in Portuguese colonial history.

In one regard Enes was a traditionalist, although he himself seemed to believe that his ideas were at variance with the philosophy of his day, not realizing, or ignoring, the fact that the Liberal legislation he attacked had little or no reality in Moçambique. Enes was a forthright racist, and what he says about the African and his place in the colonies is a truism long accepted by most Portuguese colonialists. His views on the dignity of labor for the savage and the notion that through work he is led into the paths of a superior civilization were concepts espoused by Spanish and Portuguese defenders of slavery from the earliest days of discovery and conquest and in the nineteenth century reasserted by most positivistic champions of the philosophy of the white man's burden. Although Enes' remarks on native policy have more recently been clothed in ambiguous and humanitarian language, there is no real contradiction today between his views and those of the spokesmen for the New State who regard Enes as one of Portugal's foremost colonial statesmen.

With his characteristic honesty, Enes wrote: "It is true that the generous soul of Wilberforce has not transmigrated into my body, but I don't believe that I have in my veins the blood of a slaver; I even feel an inner fondness for the Negro, this big child, instinctively bad like all children — may all mothers forgive me! — although docile and sincere. I do not consider him something to be exterminated because of the necessity for the expansion of the white race, although I may believe in natural inferiority. Still I do not understand by what moral or legal doctrine our metropolitan legislators can justify their scruples in not obliging the half-savage African, innocent or criminal, free or captive, to work for himself and his society, to be forced to work when he refuses to do so voluntarily . . ."[14] Elsewhere, Enes wrote: "If we do not learn how, or if we refuse, to make the Negro work and cannot take advantage of his work, within a short while we will be obliged to abandon Africa to some one less sentimental and more utilitarian than we, less doctrinaire in legislating and more practical in administrating: and our final abandonment will not even benefit the native, because Portugal is, and will continue to be after imposing the obligation to work, the most benign and humanitarian sovereign of all those who have raised their flag over the African continent." [15]

The importance of António Enes is the importance of a doctrine. The importance of Mousinho de Albuquerque is the importance of a colonial hero. Mousinho's *Moçambique* is a more impassioned continuation of Enes' *relatório* and an account of his commissionership. Mousinho had few original thoughts on overseas problems. But his personality, aristocratic, stern, seemingly touched with the prophetic insight of the sixteenth-century Albuquerque, made him the most acclaimed Portuguese of his day. Quite apart from his dedication to the abstractions of duty and his mystical nationalism, qualities which have endeared him to the Salazar regime, Mousinho was more than a man on a horse. For Portugal he was the living link with the nation's past, a figure from another, more brilliant century who appeared miraculously in an age of Anglo-Saxon superiority to revive the historic Lusitanian values. Like Prince Henry, Afonso de Albuquerque, Pombal, men whom he resembles in so many respects, Mousinho seemed to give heroic direction to the necessities and aspirations of his age. His military campaigns were frontier scuffles and as an administrator he followed the lead of Enes, but in giving his country an illusion of greatness in a crucial hour, his contribution was almost without equal in Portuguese history.

Mousinho came naturally to the role. Born of a family tracing its ancestry back six hundred years to a bastard son of King Dinis, Joaquim Augusto Mousinho de Albuquerque grew up in a monarchal household which believed that moral force and prestige disappeared from Portugal with the revolution of 1820. It is completely in character for him to write of the 1895 campaign: "For us Portuguese, the task in Africa, at least, was to retemper the national soul, to revive the spirit of 'Awake, my steel,' engraved on the Toledo blade." [16] During a two-year illness which caused his withdrawal from the University of Coimbra, Mousinho became an ardent student of his country's history, an exercise which made the present even more intolerable. After several years at the royal military college Mousinho embarked on his colonial career, first in India as a civil engineer and later as secretary general of the colony. In 1890 he was governor of the Lourenço Marques district.

With his appointment to Enes' staff, Mousinho became the man of the hour and the inevitable choice to succeed Enes. As Royal Commissioner in 1896–97 he discovered that he no longer possessed the freedom of action he enjoyed as a cavalry officer. Considering himself thwarted in his plans for the occupation of the province and in extending the reform begun by Enes, Mousinho returned to Lisbon to press for financial and legislative support. After being borne in the royal galley from his ship to the shore of the Tagus where the royal family waited to embrace him, he was received with near hysteria throughout the country. But still he found it difficult to obtain from his government the extraordinary powers he sought. Feeling that he had finally convinced the Overseas Ministry, he sailed for Moçambique, but shortly after his arrival a decree of July 7, 1898, clipped much of his power as royal commissioner. Mousinho demanded that the decree be revoked or his resignation accepted. Men in the government whom Mousinho had scornfully dismissed as insignificant politicians and who feared his ambitions worked to see that the resignation was accepted. If enthusiasm for the hero had cooled in the government, he retained his popularity with the crown and the people, and on his return he was named tutor and counselor to the prince Dom Luís. In this post Mousinho's supreme arrogance increased the attacks upon him, which were eventually taken up by opposition newspapers. Whether he was rebuked by Luís for his cavalier behavior is uncertain, but during a fit of advanced despondency in 1902, Mousinho shot himself.[17]

Mousinho's authoritarian temperament is evident on every page of his *Moçambique*. In Lisbon's colonial policies of the early 1890's he saw only an extension of past idiocies, which he scorchingly described in this, the work's most quoted passage:

The administrative processes by which our colonies have been governed, or rather, disgraced, may be summed up as conventions and fictions. Vast territories conventionally ours where we exerted absolutely no influence; powerful chiefs tied to the Portuguese crown by fictitious vassalage; a system of government conventionally liberal in which improvised citizens elected in sham voting a fictitious deputy already designated by the minister, as unknown as he was uninstructed in the country he represented; conventional municipalities where there were no decently eligible town councilors . . . reserve officers without a reserve; battalions and companies without officers or soldiers; professors without schools and

schools without pupils; missions without missionaries; priests without
churches and churches without parishioners; even a medical service almost without doctors . . . And in the news that reached Europe not infrequently were mentioned glorious battles in which not a single Portuguese soldier had taken part, auxiliary troops of steadfast loyalty who on
the following day were declared rebels, notable patriots whose souls
worthy of ancient heroes were contained in the sooty bodies of black
bandits and mulattoes . . . And on top of all this, majors and colonels
and commanders, endless officers, bulky reports, countless laws, many decrees, a hundred unworkable regulations. Words, words, words.[18]

Such was the state of Moçambique in Mousinho's eyes. The solution he envisaged was that of Enes: direct forceful action and a policy
designed specifically for the colonies, not a bastardization of a
metropolitan administrative system. To the accusation that he planned
to establish an autocracy in Moçambique, he replied that no one was
more desirous than he of setting up a civil administration in the
colony. But, he asked pointedly, what purpose did roads, a rail system, ports, commerce, agriculture serve if they were at the mercy
of every native uprising. "My greatest goal is to establish royal authority throughout the province and to put an end once and for all
to the drove of native captains and other protected potentates." [19]
To defend his requests for additional appropriations, he wrote,
"These constitute my last attempt to obtain the indispensable means
to make [Moçambique] a province which will not bring shame to
my country, to the class I represent, and to my own name." [20]

Mousinho was more cautious than Enes about the introduction of
foreign capital into the colony, fearing that Portugal might compromise her own economic position. And in the rejuvenation of
Moçambique he felt that the missionary could play a more vital role
and should be permitted a wider scope of action than Enes prescribed.
He deplored the restrictions that had been placed on religious orders
at a critical time in Moçambique's history. Protestant missionaries,
however, especially the English and Swiss, represented a danger to
national interests with their theories of equality and their support of
the African in all his quarrels with the European. Such notions of
equality for the African Mousinho flatly asserted to be twaddle. To
pamper the African, to treat him well, was to make him believe that
the Portuguese feared him, for the African understood no authority
not imposed by force. The territories of the great chiefs should be
divided among smaller less powerful chiefs, none of them strong
enough to threaten either his neighbor or the white community. Dis-

respect of Portuguese rule had to be pitilessly punished.[21] Needless to say, Mousinho's views on obligatory labor were somewhat more conservative than those of Enes.

It was apparent to the generation of 1895 that to civilize the African provinces new administrative molds were needed. Armed occupation must be followed by civil government; the remnants of the ancient captaincies and the military commands over the regions of the interior had to be replaced by civil circumscriptions, and all entrenched colonial servants, Enes wrote, must adapt themselves to the spirit of reform or give up their posts. The first circumscriptions were established by Enes in 1895 in territories of the crown in the Lourenço Marques district, but not until 1907, following the administrative reorganization of the Colonial Reform Act, was most of Moçambique organized into circumscriptions — in those parts of the province where resistance to the Portuguese had been crushed. The system was not fully implemented in Angola until 1911.

The details of the proposed colonial organization are most clearly defined in Eduardo Costa's *Estudos sobre a administração civil das províncias ultramarinas*, a report submitted to the Colonial Congress of 1901. Costa's work is the basic study for the administrative reforms carried out in the African provinces in the twentieth century. His proposals, an elaboration of Enes' concepts, are the bases of present-day administration in Portuguese East and West Africa. Like Enes and Mousinho, Costa argued the need for decentralization, more autonomy for the colonies; the metropolitan government should have the power to inspect and regulate, the final right to approve or disapprove, but all essential matters of managing the provinces should be reserved for the local governments. What Enes and Costa sought above all else was the authority to initiate polices and make major decisions on matters of a local nature. The enhanced authority, legislative as well as executive, should be given to the provincial governors and their staffs, which would represent all classes and interests. The governor and lesser officials must be chosen for their experience, abilities, and probity. The existence of a local assembly Costa regarded as a grave inconvenience for the efficient operation of the colonies, given the backward state of their population.

Costa's contribution was not the discussion of the decentralization of the colonies, however; it was his perfecting the circumscription into a workable unit of colonial government, for with the serious occupation, or reoccupation, of the interior, the necessity for a firm control over native affairs seemed of first importance to the Portuguese.[22] Costa immediately disposes of any thoughts of equality for the African, pointing out that legal equality frequently produces the greatest inequality in practice. There must be two administrative statutes, one African and the other European, and the native code should vary from province to province and, where necessary, from region to region. Each district of the province should be divided into a varying number of circumscriptions, and the administrators of these areas must be for the native peoples administrative, judicial, and military authority at the same time, since the savage mind, according to Costa, does not accept any division in supreme authority. The *administrador* — in many respects a modern projection of the *pater familias* embodied in men like Silva Porto, the seventeenth-century *prazero*, and the responsible captain major — was a typically Portuguese creation; he was in effect a paramount white chief over the lesser chiefs and villagers in the *circunscrição*. Costa's policy implies no encouragement of tribal government; on the contrary, it envisions its eventual disappearance and the emergence of a single Pan-Portuguese community. The administrator was to be a more authoritarian figure than the British District Officer. According to Costa, "His purely administrative functions are very different from those of a metropolitan administrator, because, in addition to police and civil administrative services, he is charged with an important political mission, which is to maintain good relations with the native chiefs of the *circunscrição*, to assure their obedience and tranquillity, to intervene in their disputes over boundaries, rights of succession, and other complaints, in a word to acquire over his charges a dominating and respected influence." [23] Appointed by the governor general of the province, the administrator was responsible as well to the governor of his district — also an appointee of the governor general. In theory, anyone in the circumscription contesting his decisions had appeal to the same quarters, but the almost absolute local power wielded by the Portuguese proconsul made such appeals impractical. That the proposed system was despotic, Costa admitted, but only in this way could it provide "a just, humanitarian, and civilizing tutelage" for the conquered tribes of Portuguese Africa.

Among the members of the generation most responsible for the practical implementation of the concepts of Enes and Costa were Aires de Ornelas and Paiva Couceiro, both avowed monarchists who shared Mousinho's contempt for bureaucracy and colonial policies bound by legalistic — and contradictory — regulations.[24] Aires de Ornelas' work as Minister of Marine and Overseas has already been

briefly noted. As an administrator and a colonial thinker Paiva Couceiro is the more important of the two men. His studies on Portuguese
West Africa, *Angola, estudo administrativo* (1898) and *Angola, dois
anos de governo* (1910), are essential for a knowledge of the colony in
those trying years, although they do not differ fundamentally from
the works of Enes, whose practicality Paiva Couceiro shared, and
Mousinho, to whose messianic nationalism the Angolan governor
became more and more sympathetic. He had brighter hopes than
either Enes or Mousinho for the success of white colonization, believing that the development of Angola's agriculture was the answer
to the colony's chronic economic plight. An advocate of forced labor
for the African, he held that the system should not be spoilative and
must be accompanied by instruction designed to introduce the
African to the ways of the modern world. Paiva Couceiro was willing to accept a moral responsibility for the African's future — provided, of course, that this was coincidental with Portugal's future in
Angola. The African people had their place in a modern Angola,
not as a race condemned to perpetual servitude for the benefit of the
European but as assimilated citizens in a Portuguese African community, enjoying some day equal privileges and responsibilities. Only
if this were the goal of colonial policy in Angola, Paiva Couceiro
maintained, could Portugal consider herself a civilized nation in the
twentieth century. Finally, Paiva Couceiro reminded the Portuguese
people of their imperial heritage which offered inspiration for a renewed dedication to colonial problems. If they should forget the
lessons of their glorious past and permit mediocrity to triumph
over devotion to country and empire, then the future of the Portuguese in Africa would be meaningless.

X

PROMISE AND DISAPPOINTMENT, 1895–1930

I N the period 1895 to 1930, the year when the Colonial Act —
a statement of intent by the new Portuguese government — was
published and the African provinces became subject to the policies
of the New State, the present regime in Portugal, three problems
dominated colonial thought: consolidation of administration in
Angola and Moçambique, native policy, and economic development.
According to the emphasis given each of the problems, Portuguese
Africa seems to have passed through three stages during the thirty-
five-year period. First was the era of Enes and his followers, 1895–
1910, with its attempted administrative and economic reforms; this
was followed by the early years of the Portuguese Republic, 1911–
1919, and an increasing humanitarian concern for the African population; finally, almost a decade of semi-autonomy and economic uncertainties, especially in Angola, leading to the drastic controls and
a new centralization of authority in Lisbon imposed by the Salazar
government. But to divide the first third of the century into phases
serves only to indicate characteristic preoccupations. In fact, these
three unresolved problems had troubled the Portuguese for hundreds
of years, and they help to illustrate that curious timelessness which
even in moments of great urgency has seemed to envelop men and
events in Portuguese Africa. Crises, governors, decrees have been
ephemeral realities not seriously disturbing the colonies' measured
pace. This is not to say that Portuguese Africa, especially in the
twentieth century, has failed to show genuine, perhaps extraordinary,

material accomplishment or that colonial officials have been inattentive to schedules, deadlines, and five-year plans. It is only to say that from decree to fulfillment is a long, cautious, sometimes unfinished journey in the course of which the usual temporal distinctions like months and years are often blurred, often obliterated.

Of particular significance in the twentieth century was the realization by the metropolitan government that the African provinces were no longer untidy stepchildren who could be forgotten until they attracted the neighbors' attention. The modern colonial mentality which began with Sá da Bandeira's reforms and was later stimulated by the work of the Society of Geography and the expeditions of Portuguese explorers in Africa had been tempered in the critical years of the English ultimatum. The vigorous stamp of Enes' personality, Mousinho's overbearing pride, and the influence of both Aires de Ornelas and Paiva Couceiro kept Moçambique and Angola uppermost in public opinion as well as in the ministries of the government.[1] The importance given the colonies by Portugal's first republic is best shown by the men chosen to be governors general or high commissioners: João Norton de Matos, Vicente Ferreira, Pedro Massano de Amorim, Manuel de Brito Camacho, João de Azevedo Coutinho, men who were the country's most distinguished officers or statesmen.

Only by the late 1920's did interest in Africa begin to flag, principally as a result of Portugal's own economic difficulties, which reached a point of extended crisis, and of Portuguese Africa's failure once more to fulfill the rich promises it seemed to hold.

But in the first two and a half decades of the century, interest in the colonies was intense; possibly this was the age of Portugal's greatest preoccupation with the African provinces. Issues and policies became common discussion. Each week saw the publication of articles and books on colonial problems. Polemics dragged on in print and in parliament on the conduct of African affairs; whether the colonies should be prepared for independence or should be drawn closer under Lisbon's control, how to promote white colonization, directly or indirectly, whether the African should be systematically introduced to European civilization or should be allowed to follow his own cultural patterns were but a few of the issues. Portugal began to participate in colonial congresses with a vengeance and to promote congresses of her own at home and in the overseas capitals. In 1907 Prince Luís Filipe was sent off on a tour of Angola and Moçambique as a gesture of Portugal's solidarity with her African possessions. A few years earlier, under the direction of the Society of Geography, a training school for colonial officers, to be known as the Escola

Superior Colonial, was founded. Although not integrated with the colonial administration until 1926, the school provided a center of instruction and information for those Portuguese who desired to participate in their country's overseas activities.[2]

The administrative changes which took place in Angola and Moçambique from 1900 on represented, as Enes and his associates had urged, the beginning of a transition from military government to civil government in the interior and greater freedom for the provincial government from the supervision of Lisbon. These gradual changes wrought no miracles and the new order proved to be as controversial as the old. Some critics denied that anything had changed. For others the transition was slower than had been expected and was not accompanied by measures sufficiently draconian to break with traditions of the nineteenth century. Gomes dos Santos, writing in 1903, held that the most pressing needs were still for changes in the selection of personnel and a program of colonial education. First, a separate ministry for colonial affairs divorced from the navy had to be created and entrusted to a man versed in the problems of the overseas provinces. The governor general could no longer be a bankrupt or personally ambitious man who went to Africa to recoup his fortune or flee political embarrassment at home. The lesser positions should be filled from a civil service roster and not from the horde of clamoring office-seekers driven by desperation to take a job in Africa. All colonial officers ought to be instructed in geography, local customs, and administrative procedures before being sent abroad. Finally, he argued that care and planning must precede all important decisions.[3] But seven years later there were few signs of progress.

Carneiro de Moura wrote in 1910: "Portuguese colonial administration has been erratic and empirical. Military governors follow a pattern of colonial occupation characterized by violence, heroics, and great expense. Almost all our colonial statesmen are former governors like Mousinho de Albuquerque, Eduardo Costa, Paiva Couceiro, and it is not strange that they should favor a preponderance of military personnel in the administration of the colonies and a concentration of powers in the hands of the governors. Nevertheless, it is necessary to reduce expenses with an occupation more commercial and educational than military and destructive." He went on wistfully to point out that truly modern colonial powers tried to develop their possessions for the benefit of the Africans and white colonists, "while we draw up laws and regulations."[4]

Nevertheless, a slow transformation was underway in Portuguese Africa. While the first few years of the century were undoubtedly anticlimactic to the previous decade in their lack of furor, Angola and Moçambique made positive progress in the work of pacification and in opening up the interior by roads and rail lines. In 1907 the administrative reorganization of Moçambique was begun, a process not undertaken in Angola until 1911–1913. Incorporating the concepts of Enes, Mousinho, and particularly Eduardo Costa and giving juridical substance to changes already introduced, the reforms established the lines of authority by which the African colonies are, with small modification, still governed today. Not even the Republic's colonial laws of 1914 and 1920, which made extensive grants of autonomy to Angola and Moçambique, altered the fundamental context of the 1907 reforms. For the first time the responsibilities and limitations of the governor general were clearly defined, and although his powers were not as inclusive as they would be after 1920 — when the 1914 reforms went into effect — they were greater than those of his nineteenth-century predecessors and gave him a commanding voice in purely local decisions of administrative nature. The regional powers of the district governor in civil and military affairs were also expanded, although at the same time the district governments were to be more closely co-ordinated with each other and with the government general.

But the heart of the legislation introduced in 1907 by Aires de Ornelas was in the administration of the occupied territories. Only in a few places, around the larger towns of the province, was there a sufficient white or civilized population for the *concelho*, or council, system of government by local officials to be used. The rest of the province was divided, as Costa had outlined in 1901, into *circunscrições civis* and *capitanias-mores*, the latter to be gradually replaced by the former when the local inhabitants were deemed sufficiently pacified. The administrators of the circumscription, chosen by the district governor and the governor general, assumed paramount responsibility for the native population. In the Moçambique districts of Lourenço Marques, Inhambane, and Tete (Quelimane being under the *prazo* administration while the Niassa and Moçambique companies occupied the rest of the province), the administrator and his divisional assistants, the chiefs of post, were virtually white chiefs. In a certain sense the selection of an administrator was more important than the choice of a district governor, whose conduct was subject to supervision and scrutiny, while the administrator was frequently in charge of lands a hundred miles from a Portuguese settlement. Some administrators were incorruptible and others were not, but the dishonest or abusive administrator, isolated in the bush of Moçambique or Angola, possessed infinite opportunity for harm in these early years of the system.

In Angola pacification campaigns had gone more slowly than in the sister province, and it was not until 1911 that the regime of civil circumscriptions began to replace the old military administration in the interior, and not until the government of Norton de Matos two years later was the system widely put into practice. Nevertheless, the advantages of the *circunscrição* as a civilizing force were appreciated by Paiva Couceiro in his term as Angola's governor from 1907 to 1910; through the military captaincies, which, he believed, should not essentially differ from the circumscription, he undertook to place qualified Portuguese officers in close and sympathetic contact with the recently conquered African tribes. Paiva Couceiro felt that through the coexistence of two peoples, living and working side by side, the attainments of Portuguese culture could be progressively introduced into the primitive tribal life of Angola. He was an enemy of bureaucracy and its reports, plans, and recommendations. Energetic direct action characterized his administration, and he set a pattern which Governor Norton de Matos closely followed. But where Paiva Couceiro had frequently worked at cross purposes with the metropolitan government, Norton de Matos usually had the support of the Portuguese Republic's newly founded Overseas Ministry.

A man of enthusiastic and decided opinions on how to run a colony, Norton de Matos gathered a staff of administrators and district governors on whom he felt he could rely to carry out his programs over the resistance of the entrenched conservative residents of the province. His circular directive of 1913 to Portuguese administrators marks one of the most advanced steps taken in Portuguese Africa for the emancipation of the African and established the circumscription as the principal agent for Angola's regeneration. For a number of Portuguese this transition came none too soon. As late as 1912, two colonial theorists angrily wrote: "In our archaic process of colonial administration we began from a false point of view, that it was necessary to impose a military regime." Wherever a military post was set up, extortions and violence were practiced by the soldiers and their officers. Civil authority had to replace military authority immediately.[5]

The spirit of Norton de Matos' 1913 directive, *Regulamento das circunscricões da província de Angola* was contained in the Portuguese government's law for the administrative autonomy of the colonies, drawn up in 1914. Drafted by men like Norton de Matos and

Ernesto Vilhena, author of the study of the Zambezi *prazo*, the bill was based on the Aires de Ornelas reforms of 1907 and conferred upon the overseas administration, under the general supervision and broad economic control of the Lisbon government, the privileges and responsibilities of local autonomy. That part of the bill dealing with native affairs, apart from the continuation of a system of obligatory labor, was inspired more in the Liberal doctrines of the nineteenth century, however, than in the harsher philosophies of Enes and Mousinho. But the Republic had done little to modernize the ponderous machinery of Portugal's legislative processes, and before Angola and Moçambique could make from the principles contained in the Autonomy Act organic charters suited to the personality of each province, Portugal was embroiled in the World War, and the two colonies reverted to a quasi-military footing.[6]

In 1920 Angola and Moçambique were granted "financial autonomy and decentralization compatible with the development of each," in a series of laws later characterized by Colonial Minister Armindo Monteiro as an abdication of colonial responsibility by the home government.[7] In effect, practically unlimited powers were given to the high commissioners — a title commensurate with the increased authority — of Portuguese Africa. Colonial autonomy was in the air in 1920, and there was a feeling among Portuguese statesmen that with the work of pacification completed, Angola and Moçambique should be permitted to develop their resources more or less in their own ways. What ensued, however, was that the one-man colonial government in Angola, in the person of High Commissioner Norton de Matos,[8] brought the province to the brink of bankruptcy and that the government in East Africa passed into the hands of several high commissioners who swung from the extreme of using their great authority unwisely to the other extreme of making no decisions at all. Certainly the positive results in the two colonies were less than had been expected, although what the home government really hoped for in such a short time from these underdeveloped areas is uncertain. In 1926 the colonial minister for the dictatorship, João Belo, began to modify and curtail the legislation of 1920. The Colonial Act of 1930 flatly announced the necessity for solidarity and unity with Portugal and canceled most of the autonomous pretensions of the African possessions.

Although since 1885 Portugal was reconciled to the fact that her African colonies were liabilities more often than not, each new Lisbon government hoped that they could be run profitably by changing a few laws or tinkering with the administrative organization. The steps taken to grant them more local autonomy began in the 1890's when the idea gained currency that competent administrators like Enes ("What I am saying is that only with men, without one new law or the changing of a single existing law, will the province be re-generated, but there must be men to start and assist this regenera-tion"),[9] if freed from intrigues and petty politics, could somehow work a miracle. Portugal's own poverty, her economic and political instability, her lack of industry could be ignored, perhaps, but what of the equally sad reality that neither Moçambique nor Angola had any visible material assets to make them truly prosperous, whether they were administered and financed locally or from Lisbon? The most a skillful governor could do was to bring an order and stability out of which the provinces might make modest gains. This was the key to the limited success of governors like Paiva Couceiro, Freire de Andrade in Moçambique, and Norton de Matos in his first term in Angola. When the ambitions of the governor went beyond the ca-pacities of the province to absorb his programs, chaos followed; when the governor was negligent or overcautious, the colonies, lacking im-petus of their own, regressed. Whether the governor was a military man, as were most of the governors of Angola in this period, or a pro-fessional bureaucrat, as were many of the governors in Moçambique, the results were generally the same. In a final analysis neither laws nor men could work the expected changes in Portuguese Africa.

The divisive influences which Mousinho believed were responsible for the low state of the African provinces in the next-to-last decade of the monarchy and against which Paiva Couceiro never ceased to rail made the job of the governors and high commissioners appointed by the Republic equally exasperating and often fruitless. Brito Ca-macho, High Commissioner of Moçambique in the early 1920's, wrote that, "Intriguing politicians, those in the colony and those at home, can easily create for the governor or high commissioner insurmount-able difficulties, which keep him from realizing any useful work in his administration." Whenever he left Lourenço Marques, his enemies shouted in the streets for his withdrawal in the name of the province's salvation, and on his return he found that his authority had been undermined. "In every colony," he concluded, "there are always two groups or parties who fight for the governor's confidence. If he leans toward one, he has the others against him; if he leans toward neither, he has them all against him. I prefer to have them all against me to being the playtoy of any." [10]

In Angola, Norton de Matos suffered similar attacks during the same years. In what may be the most vituperative book in Portuguese colonial literature, *Calígula em Angola* (Lisbon, 1924), Cunha Leal accused Norton de Matos of being, among other things, a tyrant, murderer, and a singularly corrupt administrator. He charged him with closing down newspapers, chasing Protestant missionaries out of the colony, and shooting his horse "as an example to all other dumb animals." In such an atmosphere of distrust and antagonism only the most resolute governor could survive.

If corruption existed, as alleged, in the highest echelons of the provincial government, it was compounded on the lower levels where the pay of the administrator, chief of post, or military officer was inadequate and the profiteering traditions of centuries hard to suppress. A chronic complaint in Portuguese Africa until recent years was the moral inadequacy of much of the personnel to whom was entrusted the administration of the interior. Untrained in colonial affairs, sent to dwell in an unhealthy region in which they had no interest, and burdened with assorted responsibilities — legal, financial, technical — which would have tested the capacities of the most dedicated civil servant, many administrators gave up in despair and spent their time collecting taxes and African mistresses and tending their gardens, which were the admiration of the traveler.[11] In 1913 Norton de Matos emphasized the need for competent personnel, chosen competitively from a qualified roster of candidates. They should be paid well, have their families transported at government expense. Above all their work should be constantly supervised, for under no circumstances should the administrator be permitted to become "Africanized." [12] The effects of his reforms were transitory in Angola, and in the 1920's comments on administrative corruption there abounded.

In East Africa similar charges were heard. Moçambique's Jeremiah, d'Almeida Saldanha, compiled lengthy documents of misconduct, complete with names and dates. The most common crimes were overcharging on the African hut tax, accepting bribes for furnishing contract workers, and withholding the pay earned by Moçambique men in the Rand mines; more sensational charges included the one that the African girls' schools in the interior were often used to supply the white population, including the administrators, with concubines. Saldanha admitted that there was much truth in Professor Ross's "libel" against the Portuguese.[13] Official reports on the province, like those of Adriano de Sá and Viana Rodrigues, referred repeatedly to the inefficiency — and sometimes the dishonesty — of the administration in the *circunscrições*.

As an instrument of native policy the administrative circumscriptions were hailed by Norton de Matos in 1913 as "the beginning of a new epoch in the occupation and progress of Angola." By 1924 there were eighty-two such divisions in the province. But in the same year Ross gathered information on contract labor in Portuguese West Africa and discovered some administrators and *chefes de posto* to be culpable of either promoting or closing their eyes to irregularities in the contracting of labor in their regions. In 1924 when Norton de Matos abandoned the high commissionership of Angola the labor situation was little better than when he first came to the province in 1913. He still spoke with feeling of making the Angolan a free agricultural worker, for "if we don't do this, we fatally revert to forced labor, and we reduce the native in Africa to a condition worse than slavery and we destroy all our noble traditions of justice, love, equality, liberty, and protection of the races we discovered," [14] but at the same time the High Commissioner's ambitions for the material development of the province obliged him to follow a double morality. Forced contract labor — for the state, for the diamond company, for the sugar plantations, for the palm oil estates — existed in much of Angola, although small farmers and businessmen complained that the supply existed only for the large companies.[15] For the collection of laborers for these projects the administrator of the circumscription was the indispensable agent.

Norton de Matos in 1913 envisioned the administrator taking the place of the tribal chief, but using his powers wisely and paternally to draw the African into the ways of civilization. More sympathetic to the problems of the African in Angola than the generation of 1895 but less idealistically doctrinaire than the Portuguese humanitarians of the nineteenth century, he was, during his first governorship, Portugal's eminent example of the benevolent imperialist, firm in his faith in the white man's burden. His 1913 circular of instructions to administrators of circumscriptions is a reflection of the efforts made by the Republic to develop a new colonial mentality, to humanize the crude repressions of existing labor laws, and to mitigate the exploitations of the past. Written with the governor's usual candor, the circular referred to the administrative corruption presently corroding the work of moral improvement and economic progress in the province and to the necessity for the white man to maintain his prestige. The administrator was instructed to protect the native's rights, to insure his security and his property, to treat him not as a recently conquered enemy, but as a man of the same nation. The administrator's relations with the African must be founded on mutual esteem and justice; his customs should be respected unless they conflicted with national sovereignty. The Africans should be encouraged to work for themselves as farmers, proprietors, artisans. Colonial authorities were no longer to furnish workers to private concerns; the worker must contract for his services freely, and it was the administrator's duty to protect his rights (only with state projects was Norton de Matos inflexible; where free labor was not forthcoming, workers were drafted). To the anguished protests that arose, Norton de Matos made his familiar reply that the first concern of the colonial administration was the African. In a report he sent to the Minister of Colonies that same year, the governor stressed the primary importance of educational and medical services for the African if the Republic's program were to succeed.[16]

Norton de Matos was dealing with a problem perplexing other areas besides Portuguese Africa in the early twentieth century: he was trying to find a standard of administrative conduct morally compatible with the exploitation of an underdeveloped region. For Enes and Mousinho a practical colonial philosophy which rested on the idea of a white ruling race and a laboring backward people admitted no discussion. The African was to be obliged to work in the fields and mines at low wages, in return for which he received order, justice, and the privilege of buying manufactured goods. When labor was not voluntary, it must be coerced. Nor was there any thought that the African would progress through his labors to the positions of authority in the colony; he could aspire only to the spiritual benefits of white civilization.[17] This was the prevailing, though not uncontested, theory in Portuguese Africa in the early twentieth century and is summed by Freire de Andrade: "The education to give the native must be, above all, one which will make him a worker . . . who will contribute to the progressive richness of the country. . . We must not try to encourage him to put in practice the fable of the bull and the frog, in which the latter, trying to be as big as the former, blew himself up until he burst, for we should note that although in the fable when the frog burst he did no harm to the bull, this would not happen in our case. The mão de obra for agriculture, mines, and other industries can and must be furnished by the native. But how can we keep him from passing from a worker to a foreman, to an engineer, or, to put it bluntly, from being bossed to being the boss? Such a result may only be obtained by a labor law which, badly interpreted, will be called slavery." [18]

Neither Norton de Matos nor the Republic found any more lasting solution to the labor problem than has the Salazar regime whose own spokesmen belittle the Republic from time to time for its "well-intentioned follies." But unlike many legislators before and after, the Republic's colonial planners tried to evolve a series of programs which would coincide with the necessities of the African provinces and work toward attainable goals. Both Enes and the venerated Liberal traditions had their influence on the Republic's legislation of 1914, which was to be the basis for the native assistance laws of 1921 and 1930. It defined the civilized African, who could regard himself as a full-fledged Portuguese citizen, as one who could speak Portuguese, had divested himself of his tribal customs, and was regularly and gainfully employed. This is one of the early legal definitions of the *assimilado*. The rest of the African population were regarded as charges of the government for whom special laws and regulations were to be devised. An Office of Native Affairs was set up in Lisbon to administer all matters relating to these charges. Thus the *Lei Orgânica da Administração Civil das Provincias Ultramarinas* reversed the egalitarian concepts of the 1830's. At the same time, however, the Republic sought to protect and assist the African. The *portaria* (a sort of accompanying explanation) for the organic law stated that African workers had to be protected from exploitation either by the state or private companies. It also urged that infirmaries be established in administrative centers and medical posts in large villages. The *portaria* recommended that a system of public instruction be set up for the African as part of an over-all program of cultural assimilation and a means of bettering the African's social condition. Education for the African was to be useful, training in crafts for the men and in domestic science for the women. Administrators were to encourage native agriculture by providing seeds and technical advice, and by seeing that the farmer received a fair price for his crops. On these bases, a modified free labor system, medical and educational assistance, and the opportunity for the African to advance beyond what the Portuguese government considered his backward heathen state, the Republic rested its native policy.

In spite of inherent poverty in Portugal and in the colonies, which made the most modest program seem ambitious, there is the good possibility that the Republic might have gained limited success in some of its goals, especially in Angola where the dynamic Norton de Matos shook the province from border to border. But the history of Portuguese Africa often seems to be the history of what might have been and of what will be. The First World War postponed Portugal's plans until 1920, by which time the momentum behind the reforms had been lost in the numerous changes of government and colonial ministers, and new goals, principally relating to the material development of the provinces, took their place. The change is most evident in the behavior of Norton de Matos — champion of the African's rights and road-builder in 1913, road-builder and champion of the African's rights in 1920. Other factors were also responsible for the meager results obtained from the Republic's good intentions. Chief among them was the indifference or opposition of the European population in Moçambique and Angola to any proposals which might eventually lead to the African's emancipation. Many of the vehement attacks on Norton de Matos and Brito Camacho were against their reasonably enlightened gestures to alleviate the age-old abuses endured by the Negro. Social assistance, contract supervision, efforts at assimilation, all this was Lisbon's madness in the eyes of many local residents who, though they may have considered the African as a child, were never advocates of child-labor laws.[19] A second serious problem was the want of trained personnel, teachers, nurses, doctors, willing to work overseas in a questionable environment for a paltry governmental salary.

In the attempts made during the years 1895–1930 to evolve a native policy, two problems — apart from the labor question — primarily occupied Portuguese attention: education and alcoholism. As a concomitant of the slave trade, the rum trade had long been a reality of African commerce, and until the present century alcohol in one form or another represented in most of Africa the chief import commodity; the Portuguese were no more active in this trade than most other European nations.[20] Officials in both colonies were well aware of the ravages caused by the trade in rum and pure alcohol, even though Mousinho urged that Portuguese red wine be introduced as much as possible among the native population, arguing that Portugal could thus dispose of its yearly surplus and could reduce the consumption of German alcohol — which, he said, had a deleterious effect on the African — in Moçambique.[21]

In 1902 a law prohibiting the manufacture and sale of rum to Africans was enacted — to stimulate the sale of Portuguese wine — but district governors found the prohibition hard to enforce. Local sugar growers now sold their sugar directly to the African instead of the distillery, according to Governor Almeida Garrett of Quelimane, and bootlegging became the order of the day. "How can we claim to be a civilized nation when we adopt as a way of life getting our neighbor drunk?"[22] In Angola, Cadbury commended Paiva Couceiro for his determination in carrying out the clauses of the Brussels Convention relating to the sale of spirits in European colonies.[23] Four years later Norton de Matos, with his usual optimism, averred that "in no colony of the world has so much been done as in Angola in the repression of alcoholism. . . When I left Angola in 1915 alcoholic drinks for the natives had disappeared completely from the colony."[24] When he returned in 1921 he was chagrined to find that the free sale of liquor again flourished in the colony, a situation he says he set right with another vigorous prohibition decree. This one, like so many of the decrees promulgated by Norton de Matos in his demonic belief that a new law corrected every form of abuse, had equally short-lived effect, and in the late 1920's Alexander Barns — one of the few English travelers sympathetic to Portuguese problems — attributed the poverty of the Angolan to the fact that the father of the family spent his earnings on wine "which could be bought at most trade stores."[25] Frequently the wine was strongly fortified by local merchants who as a rule disregarded laws designed to control the sale and distribution of wine, such as restrictions on Sunday and evening sales. Many Portuguese officials, whatever their other shortcomings, condemned these practices; they realized that the only effective way to curb them and contingent excesses lay in a closely controlled system of importation and distribution, but such a step meant a curtailment of the colonies' leading import and article of trade. These were stringent measures which neither Portugal nor many provincial governors could bring themselves to take, and half measures were not enough.

At the beginning of the twentieth century, the few schools existing in Angola and Moçambique were almost exclusively run by missionaries. The Jesuits, until their expulsion by Pombal, had maintained a semblance of an educational system in Portuguese Africa, principally in Angola. With their departure and the continued decline of the colonies, instruction for African and Portuguese youth fell into a state of grand collapse. Random efforts by colonial governors proved fruitless because of the lack of teachers and local interest.[26] The Liberal regime made elaborate plans for colonial education: elementary schools were to be scattered throughout the provinces offering classes in reading, writing, arithmetic, Christian morality, teachers for these classes to be recruited, optimistically, *in loco*; secondary schools were to be set up in the provincial capitals with a faculty sent from Portugal. No distinction was made on the color of the student. But in 1865 the Minister of Marine and Overseas regretfully concluded that although the legislation "fulfilled an important service . . . local difficulties, negligence, and imperfect organization annulled or paralyzed its good effects."[27] In 1873, 456 boys and 33 girls were enrolled in

Angola schools. In the middle 1870's there were an estimated 400 pupils in Moçambique's primary schools. A reader of the *Boletim oficial* of either colony for the second half of the century is today struck by the pathetic inadequacy of instruction and student interest revealed in the official school reports. At Ambriz, for example, nine students ranging in age from three to nineteen were in attendance in 1879. Mousinho, with his characteristic disgust for all of the Liberals' programs in Africa, wrote at the end of the century that the education system was nonsense and folly. "Always answering their preoccupations of assimilation with the metropolis, they scattered along the coast, and even in the interior, government schools where improvised professors pretend to offer primary instruction to native children. Attendance at these schools was minimal even when they were turned over to secular priests. The profit derived, none. But, since it was similar to what Portugal had, the liberal spirit of symmetry was satisfied. The schools were a fiction. . . As far as I am concerned, what we have to do in order to educate and civilize the *indígena* is to develop in a practical way his aptitudes for manual labor and take advantage of him for the exploitation of the province." [28]

Improvement in the first years of the twentieth century was slow and erratic. In Moçambique about 1909, in addition to the few trade and agricultural schools, there were in the whole province forty-eight primary schools for boys and eighteen for girls, the greater part of them run by missionaries. Mulatto and African attendance had increased only slightly from the 1900 figure of 1195 (146 in government schools, 412 in municipal schools, 30 in private institutions, and 607 in missionary schools).[29] In Angola the increase from 1900 to 1908 was by 15 students, from 1,845 African pupils to 1,860; these attended 69 schools.[30] In the few municipalities of the two colonies the problem was not so great, because whatever educational facilities existed were available to African, mulatto, and white students indiscriminately. The task of bringing even a rudimentary education to well over a million potential students scattered through the interior was another matter. Neither the colonial government nor the Catholic-Protestant missions could undertake the task alone. There was also the need to decide what constituted the best education for the African youth.

What education should the African be given and why should he be educated if he was to be only a worker? How could the African be civilized without education? Should he be taught only the rudiments of reading and writing Portuguese or should he be encouraged to seek further knowledge? What about trade and agricultural schools, and did the African learn through working? Should Portuguese or the Bantu tongues be the language of instruction? What was the role of the state and of the missionary? Did Protestant missions contribute enough to offset what was suspected to be their divisive denationalizing influences? These were but a few of the questions which swirled through the air in the first part of the century producing argument instead of action. Some of the questions are still to be answered in Portuguese Africa today, but by the mid-1920's several facts and consistent attitudes were discernible amidst the rhetoric and contradictions. Elementary schools existed only, and inadequately, in the vicinity of the missions and larger towns, most of the teachers being missionaries; education in the bush was nonexistent. Agricultural and trade schools were deemed desirable, although only several were established in each province, again in the cities and at larger mission stations. Portuguese was to be the language of instruction (whether the use of the vernacular was absolutely forbidden by the many decrees touching this problem was not altogether clear) as the first step to nationalization. Protestant missionaries should be permitted to teach, although frequently under conditions of supervision which were nothing less than harassment.

The reports of the African Education Commission — which surveyed African education under the auspices of the Phelps-Stokes Fund and the foreign mission societies of North America and Europe and visited Angola in 1921 and Moçambique in 1924 — gave a generally dismal picture of conditions in the provinces. The commissions noted the hostility to Protestant missions, the practice of excluding native languages from the schools, misunderstanding and apathy in provincial government circles, lack of funds, and no encouragement of African teachers. Not only was the present state of education in Angola and Moçambique backward, especially in comparison with other colonial areas, but "observations in Portuguese Africa . . . offer practically no basis for hope of any essential improvements in colonial policy." [31]

The paucity of schools (Angola had no secondary education until the opening of the Luanda *liceu* in 1919) and teachers was also the result of indifference. Brito Camacho found that no one in Moçambique took education for the African seriously (one long-term resident remarked that education corrupted the African by helping him to read what he could not understand and that the only things the African needed to be taught were Christian morality and how to work),[32] that municipal schools, backcountry schools, and trade schools in the colony were empty and the teachers incompetent.[33] Arguments that the African rejected instruction were not entirely convincing. In 1895 Father Barroso wrote, "It is very easy to affirm that the black man is rebellious to instruction and work; this is a banal refrain which by force of repetition seems to be an axiom, and it is a lie; but it is a little more difficult to create schools for him which justify the name." [34]

But could education for the African hold a very important place in a developing concept of the African as a child who must be brought up slowly to civilized European adulthood? This view of the African, which is one of the keys to Portugal's modern native policy, began to emerge clearly at the end of the nineteenth century. It was derived from slaving traditions, which regarded the African as an article of commerce and a working hand, and from moralistic defenses of the trade, which conventionally considered him an irrational being (*i.e.*, a child) whom slavery saved and Christianity (*i.e.*, civilization) dignified. Even in the mid-nineteenth century, concurrent with the Liberal's policies of emancipation and the ideal of enfranchising the free African with rights of Portuguese citizenship, there existed a segment of Portuguese colonial thought which positivistically argued that the infantile capacities of the Negro made the work of civilization a slow one. In the writings of the hero-philosophers of the generation of 1895 this concept gathered authority and became a foundation of colonial policy. The significance of the various policies formulated from 1900 to 1930, including the moderate aspirations of 1914 and 1920, was that they reflected this paternalistic spirit. Thus when the authority of the chiefs was broken or dispersed it was replaced by the paternal authority of the Portuguese who tempered their indulgence with the rod and the hoe.[35]

How much of Portugal's failure to pursue productively an enlightened native policy, how much of her inclination to issue improbable decrees and evolve a meaningless colonial mystique has been founded not only on poverty and confusion, but also on an unconscious desire to maintain the past perpetually in the present? Was it not easier, if not to exploit the African further, to exploit the suppressed state in which he still existed? Contrary to their many pronouncements on the subject, the Portuguese have never made great efforts to understand the African or his culture; at no time was this more evident than in the early part of the twentieth century. What the Portuguese professed to understand was only his own image of the African and his culture, an image which summed up the African's psyche in platitudes and conventional superficialities and made native problems less complex and burdensome. His culture was relegated to the limbo of curiosa and folklore. The Portuguese have found it simpler to accept the African than to understand him. This is the key to their practices of assimilation and miscegenation. If the African chose to adopt the ways of the European, he was accepted more or less without prejudice. If the Portuguese chose to take an African wife or mistress he did so without shame.

As they found in a policy of paternalism a defense for their actions, past and present, in Africa, the Portuguese also began after the Conference of Berlin to philosophize on racial equality in Angola and Moçambique — although this was obviously not a characteristic of Portuguese behavior endearing to the white supremacy disciples of Mousinho. Vaz de Sampaio e Melo, one of the most faithful mirrors of his age, wrote in 1910: "For Portugal the problem of miscegenation in her colonies cannot fail to have the greatest importance, especially if the colonial system we adopt is one of political assimilation. . . In any case, however, miscegenation is the most powerful force of colonial nationalism. Given equality to the European under the law and admitted to administrative, religious, political, and military positions, the mulatto comes to adopt exclusively the customs and languages of the conquering nation, and they [mulattoes] constitute the most profitable and appropriate instrument for the spread of these ethnic characteristics in the native society, which they understand better than the European and to which they are closer by the affinities of heredity." [36] In a strict sense *mestiçagem* never became a colonial policy, but it was a reality to which Portuguese statesmen found it convenient to give moral dignity and egalitarian significance.

Anyone familiar with the pride exhibited by the Portuguese in all of their material triumphs in Africa — the building of a bridge, the extension of a railroad, an increase in coffee export — is aware that they still smart from a feeling of inferiority as a colonial power. One suspects that the Portuguese would much rather talk of financial success in Moçambique and Angola than of native policy, but in the absence of such continued success, they have frequently been driven to emphasize their moral contributions to Africa. While it is true that in parts of Portuguese East and West Africa astonishing gains were made, especially in comparison with those of the preceding century, neither province became the Cinderella colony which Portugal was led to anticipate by temporary upsurges in its economy. Capital was reluctant to invest in Portuguese Africa; mineral deposits eluded prospecting companies; the uncertainties of world trade during the war and the depression of the 1920's made agricultural ventures risky. Genuine progress was uneven, and although by 1930 the façade of both colonies had been changed by hundreds of miles of railroad track and bright new towns like Lobito, Beira, and Lourenço Marques, which gave manifestations of physical development, Angola and Moçambique were foundering on the verge of bankruptcy.

Since the sixteenth century Portugal's optimism over the potential wealth of Angola and Moçambique had bubbled up even in the most calamitous periods of the colonies' history, and with the emergence of a new era after 1890, hopes were brighter than ever before for the exploitation of this wealth. Studies like those of Francisco de Salles Ferreira, "Gold, Silver, and Coal in Golungo Alto and Cambambe" (Lisbon, 1896), revived legendary promises three centuries old. The enthusiasm was infectious; in the same decade the English consul at Luanda, Mr. Nightingale, concluded that "there is no doubt that the province of Angola is a very rich one." [37] All that needed to be done was to transform a trading post mentality into an agricultural and industrial mentality. The tariff system should be overhauled, white colonization sponsored, mineral surveys made, great land companies enfranchised, the African taught technical skills, and a network of roads and rail lines pushed into the interior.

It all seemed simple and logical. Somehow, the theorists of the day were sure, financial marvels could be accomplished in the colonies by a nation whose government in these years was passing from one crisis to another. When early success was not forthcoming, the system was at fault. "Our colonial economic system is very defective. No one has cared about the development of the colonies. . . In the metropolis the general laws governing colonization are unknown; there all they think about is obtaining favorable concessions which quickly enrich the concessionaires at the expense of colonial life. Our tariff system of 1892, with its blind protectionism, is only concerned with making various individuals and groups of people in Portugal rich. Various monopolies, like the National Navigation Company, the National Overseas Bank, and the Luanda Water Company, do nothing for colonial expansion." [38] In fact, the economic transition was slow. Apart from the monopolies, the great land companies — which did not flourish — and the transit traffic through the ports of Moçambique to the Union and the Rhodesias, colonial life retained many of its traditional characteristics: petty commerce in the hands of a few Portuguese traders, mulattoes, and Indians; subsistence native agriculture; and isolated communities of Portuguese farmers and fishermen.

After the founding of the Republic, the campaign in the colonies for economic as well as administrative independence from Portugal intensified. Before 1910 the national treasury controlled all colonial expenditure and income. The budgets presented by the governors general were subject to Lisbon's revision, and the annual profits shown by one colony were often used to defray the deficit shown by another. In each colonial budget were included the expenses of administration, costs of naval maintenance, and the upkeep of agencies and institutions in Portugal only indirectly associated with the overseas provinces. Reforms in 1907 and 1910 eased some of these restrictions, but not until 1914 was the system overhauled and not until 1920 was the new system completely implemented. Provisions in the new legislation allowed the colonies to administer their own finances subject only to broad supervision in Lisbon. The costs of administration were reduced to those incurred locally, and the colonies were no longer compelled to support programs beyond their frontiers. Most important of all, each colony could keep any yearly surplus and was empowered to contract loans for the development of its resources.

The funds available to the administrations of Angola and Moçambique came mostly from taxes and customs duties and from those communication services belonging to the state. The taxes included hut taxes, commercial and industrial taxes, various stamp taxes, and in Moçambique an emigration tax on labor going to the Rand mines. Modest property taxes and again in Moçambique, rent from the *prazos*, completed the sources of direct income for the colonies. The most important sources of revenue were customs duties and the native hut tax which, in Angola, sometimes constituted more than 50 per cent of the colony's income. In Moçambique the state-owned Lourenço Marques–Transvaal railroad was a third important contributor to the local treasury. In both provinces revenues were usually just sufficient to cover expenditures, so that any large-scale development program had to be undertaken on borrowed funds. The costs of maintaining an administration in Portuguese Africa were high — the number of people on government pay in the 1910's, for example, was a little under ten thousand in each colony — and most of the revenue received went to its support.

In the early 1920's the two provinces, particularly Angola, began to assert their financial independence. The prosperity of the war years and the feeling that now was the time to push through the programs of expansion which had been talked of for so long were the main factors responsible. The provincial governments floated large loans from the Banco Nacional Ultramarino. The bank itself gave extravagant credit both to the government and private firms. By 1923 Angola was in a state of full inflation, resulting, in part, from the grandiose schemes of Norton de Matos for developing Angola, and the provincial government was running a heavy deficit. Denied a loan by Lisbon, Luanda issued its own currency, which soon became worthless. The transfer of Angolan currency into foreign currency, chiefly pounds, to pay for the orders placed by the government and private firms, exhausted the bills of foreign exchange, and the price of the pound rose to fantastic heights. Each year Angola's deficit increased; by 1926, the most stringent measures had to be taken. As a first step, the Banco de Angola was founded exclusively as a bank of issue. In the next four years the metropolitan government had to assist Angola in meeting her foreign obligations; this help was prefatory to a renewal of Lisbon's close supervision of Angola's economic life.

The financial situation in Moçambique, which through its relations with Union of South Africa enjoyed a more regular income, was less volatile, but through the decade a fluctuating exchange and the manipulations of speculators created an instability which had its effect on the colony's development plans. By 1926 the economic situation had deteriorated to such an extent that Lisbon had to guarantee a loan of 100 million *escudos* to Moçambique. In neither colony were the expectations of 1920 fulfilled, although port facilities and communications were improved, especially in East Africa, and 1930 found both provinces discouraged and nervously facing a world depression.

The continuing low productivity of Angola and Moçambique, particularly Angola which from 1910 to 1930 had a trade deficit of from 10 to 12 per cent two years out of three, was the cause of lengthy controversies which sometimes had the effect of further stultifying commercial life. There were those who believed that careful surveys should be made of each province's wealth and capabilities and long-term plans formulated for colonial exploitation. Others held that Portuguese Africa was already overrun with planners and committees wasting their time writing reports when direct action — to be subsidized by the home government — was needed. There were proponents of more autonomy and of less autonomy. Some saw the colonies' ruination in the unchecked activities of foreigners, while others lamented that restrictive laws kept out foreign capital. Much of Portuguese impatience with African agriculture and industry was the result of overblown expectations and of the apparent success of other colonial powers on the continent. There was a disinclination to face the unpleasant reality that Portugal was a poor country and that the two colonies were — for the time being, at least — equally poor. Concluding his study on all of the Portuguese colonies, Elemér Böhm drew the obvious conclusion: the African provinces suffered from a want of capital and immigration and were mercilessly exploited by the metropolis. He raised the question whether Portugal kept her colonies only for reasons of tradition and prestige.[39]

Certainly Portuguese Africa had less success in attracting immigrants than it did capital. Plans, polemics, and promotion schemes yielded the same empty results as in the previous century. Brazil, because of tradition, its common language and customs, its expanding economy, remained the Mecca for Portuguese emigration, as the accompanying tabulation shows.[40]

	Total emigration	To Brazil	To Africa
1908	40,145	36,262	15
1912	88,298	74,860	90
1916	24,897	10,002	952
1920	64,783	33,651	1,153
1925	....	13,280	329
1928	....	27,705	189
1930	23,196	11,834	372

By direct subsidy, local grants, and publicity the Overseas Council tried to divert part of this stream to Africa, but only a few Portuguese workers and fishermen could be persuaded to face what they correctly sensed to be the rigorous pioneer life of Africa. Life in Africa was still hard and uncertain. The cautious Portuguese worker, though diligent, was neither imaginative nor adventurous, and of the handful that came to Angola or Moçambique most, confused and dissatisfied over the conditions of the bush and small villages into which they were plunged, returned to Portugal or went to live in the coastal capitals. Successful colonization of Africa by Portuguese immigrants demanded a constant campaign of education in the metropolis and sufficient capital and foresight in the provinces to create a community in which the immigrant could not only prosper but live contentedly.

The figures on immigration are somewhat deceptive for they represent only the number of Portuguese citizens who responded to the government's colonization programs for the colonies. Other Portuguese, technicians, employees on construction and agricultural projects, professional men and businessmen, and civil servants took up residence there. Of Angola's estimated 3,000,000 inhabitants in 1929–30, perhaps 50,000 were white or *mestiços*. Of Moçambique's population of about 3,500,000 in 1928, some 35,000 were non-African (17,800 whites, 900 Chinese, 8,500 Indians, and 8,350 *mestiços*). In addition to the Portuguese the white population in East Africa contained 2,000 Englishmen and 500 Germans, Greeks, and other European nationals. The non-Portuguese element of Angola's white inhabitants was lower, but some Germans and Englishmen were attracted there in the 1920's by the Benguela Railway construction and the large land grants offered to foreigners. Both provinces continued to be depositing places for *degradados* (for no other reason, comments Ferreira Pinto, than because his countrymen were great believers in preserving everything that was old and bad),[41] whose presence brought neither credit nor gain. That crucial segment of the white population, the Portuguese woman, showed a slow steady increase, but an equally vital segment, teachers and doctors, remained pitifully inadequate except in the cities and mission centers.

The growth of the colonies was most evident in the cities and towns. In Angola the ancient ports of Luanda and Benguela, it is true, seemed impervious to the transitions of modern progress, Luanda remaining, in Nevinson's words of 1905, "bankrupt and beautiful," while Benguela slept in the memories of better days, its importance passing to the upstart Lobito Bay, whose bright new buildings enhanced Benguela's tireless shabbiness. But in the interior the district capitals, Malange, Nova Lisboa, and Sá da Bandeira were all twentieth-century towns, centers of commerce and administration for the richest sections of the province. New little villages sprang up along the Benguela Railway.

The wonder cities of Portuguese Africa were of course Beira and Lourenço Marques. Lourenço Marques, boasting electric streetlights, a trolley system, a modern telephone service, was more than a port and colonial capital. With a golf course and the celebrated Hotel Polana the former fever-ridden fortress was now an international tourist center.[42] Beira, though not so large as Lourenço Marques, had also grown from a few hovels sinking in the marsh into a modern port city of 2,500 Europeans and perhaps 20,000 Africans. Its wide streets, parks, spacious villas, and native-propelled railcars gave Beira the Anglo-Portuguese air so startling to European visitors. Both Inhambane and Tete enjoyed a renaissance, and in the north the village of Nampula rose to challenge Moçambique as the capital of Niassa district.

Slowly the complexion of life in Angola and Moçambique was also changing for the African and Portuguese inhabitants. In northern Moçambique and southern Angola the two colonies had untrammeled frontiers, but modern transportation and an expanding colonial administration now made the provinces semicoherent units of government where before there had been only patches of authority in the wilderness. Almost imperceptibly, perhaps, but inevitably the colonies began to lose their heterogeneous personality and to become white men's colonies, estates to be administered and exploited efficiently by European techniques for the advantage of the European. The lines of contact between the African and the Portuguese — in the cities and in the *embalas* — which had often been imperceptible now began to separate. Not only were Beira and Lourenço Marques European cities, but in the interior the towns which sprang up along the rail lines had at their core white Portuguese communities. The African lived apart, in his village or in the city's sprawling slums. Still only a tendency in the early twentieth century, this characteristic of life in Angola and Moçambique has taken more definite shape with each passing decade. The mass of the African population, of course, lived as it had for centuries, in poverty, disease, ignorance — which Portugal could do virtually nothing to change — its chief contact with the Portuguese world being the necessity to pay the white man his tax and furnish his labor.

THE NEW STATE IN AFRICA:
MYSTIQUE AND ADMINISTRATION

T HE history of contemporary Portuguese Africa is as much a study of colonial philosophy as it is an account of administrative and economic action in Angola and Moçambique. On how well Premier Salazar's "New State" has been able to implement its involved and intensely nationalistic policy — in still another attempt to narrow the traditional gap between theory and practice — must be judged the success of modern Portuguese colonialism. Certainly no Portuguese government in the history of the empire has worked so diligently in planning and explaining its conduct overseas and in creating a colonial mystique from the values of the past and the promises of the future. The colonial effort which began in the early 1930's, partly as an attempt by the Salazar government to revive, for political reasons, an imperial consciousness, has been given urgent significance in mid-twentieth century by the anticolonial fervor penetrating Africa, since the Portuguese and the Afrikaner are the only white inhabitants of black Africa who steadfastly refuse to consider the possibility of some day yielding to the demands of the African population. Whether Portugal will be able to convince the African in Angola and Moçambique, as well as the Arab and Asian states who have replaced England as major critics of Portuguese presence in Africa, of the rightness of her cause is speculative, but for the present she seems at least to have convinced herself.[1]

The African colonies were but one of the problems the short-lived Republic passed on to the dictatorship in 1926, and during the next ten years the Portuguese government did little more than cancel most of the autonomy the colonies had received, institute stringent economic regimes in Angola and Moçambique, and hope for the best. But although Portugal's own economic plight precluded further direct action, colonial legislation and theorizing cost little and served to awaken a declining interest in the colonies. Much of this legislating and philosophizing was, and still is, a synthetic creation designed to bolster confidence at home and prestige abroad.

Paradoxically, at almost no time in their history were Angola and Moçambique greater liabilities or greater assets to the metropolis: liabilities because in those depression years they were a burden and a drain on national energies; assets because they were a living link with the past and formed the bulk of an empire which still made Portugal something more than a small and insignificant European power. Portugal, as much out of necessity as habit, was committed to keeping the African colonies — which are now one of the country's economic mainstays. No aspect of the country's history offered such abundant examples for nationalistic abstractions (Duty, Faith, Service) as the empire. A succession of colonial heroes from Prince Henry to Mousinho de Albuquerque, the Congo experiment, the work of the missions, and exploits of exploration and conquest all contributed to the reshaping of a Portuguese colonial mentality. Angola and Moçambique were simultaneously live exhibits in a museum of memories and a direct challenge to the capacities of the New State. Portugal was again determined to demonstrate — academically at first, through a barrage of legislation and publicity — that she was capable of re-creating what her spokesmen held to be the glories of her African past and to prove that the Portuguese colonial tradition was a vital and successful force in the development of Africa.

"It is often said," wrote Armindo Monteiro, Minister of Colonies in the early 1930's, "that we Portuguese have the vice of history. Some even say that we take refuge in the past to compensate for the smallness of the present — thus obeying the doleful law of Empire corroded by stagnation or decadence. In Portugal, however, we now feel that we are so much the legitimate heirs of a great tradition that the generation of today is entitled to invoke the past not as a remembrance of dead things, but as source of inspiration for the future." [2] Salazar, usually the least florid of government spokesmen, chose to address the Colonial Governors' Conference in 1933 in the same expansive terms used by his colonial publicists. "I have in mind now the great old figures of Portuguese colonization. They pass back and forth in my memory, these men of yesterday and those of today, the soldiers and administrators of the public trust in Africa and the

East . . ." Then, referring to recent colonial legislation, Salazar spoke of it as "a perfect expression of our national consciousness, and a close affirmation of the colonizing temperament of the Portuguese, [designed] for the aggrandizement of Portugal . . . and to make clear to the rest of Europe our position as a great colonial power." [3]

In synthesizing the speeches and writings of the early 1930's, the formative years for the colonial ideology of the New State, one can say that the government aspired to create a colonial mentality out of the maritime traditions of the golden age of Portuguese expansion, the historic realities of Lusitanian overseas policy, and the realities of the present. The new imperial mentality was defined by Jorge Ameal in terms of these essential characteristics. First there was the geographic element, "the notion of vast territories over which . . . our flag flies . . . It is the knowledge that our sovereignty as a small European state spreads prodigiously over three continents and is summed up in the magnificent certainty that we are the third colonial power in the world." The second characteristic was the heroic element, "the evocation of our epic as sailors and warriors, the ancestral memory of an astonishing gallery of discoverers and builders, who, moved by a sacred impulse, carried to the ends of the world our ships, our dominion — and our faith. In this heroic element is contained the most noble sentiment of our mission as a chosen people, as an evangelizing people, since the task of civilizing must have, above all else, a spiritual content. The Portuguese, like no other people, made their enterprises of exploration and conquest a transcendent campaign, a sharing of spiritual values." The third characteristic was the material element, "the sum of our efforts and the hardships of our expeditionaries to take from distant lands their hidden riches and the foundation in remote lands of centers of production and profit. It is the contruction of new cities where before there was only savage wasteland. It is the poetry of Portuguese labor in far and hidden places." [4]

Nationalistic sentiment found inspiration, as it had for centuries, in Camões' *Lusíadas*, the supreme exaltation of empire, and few official pronouncements have failed to make appropriate reference to the epic poem. During ceremonies in Angola in 1936, Marcelo Caetano, New State philosopher and in recent years Salazar's administrative assistant, spoke of "the supreme flower of the Portuguese language, the symbol of the moral unity of the Empire whose discovery and conquest for civilization it sings in imperishable lines . . . We are going to write a new epic in an aggrandized and renovated Portugal." In the following speech, the Governor General of Angola picked up the theme: "I am going to swear here, on this sacred book, the *Lusíadas*, on the Bible of our country, the loyalty of all the Portuguese in Angola. I swear that we, the Portuguese of Angola, will carry out, no matter what the emergency, or how difficult the sacrifice, our duty as patriots and that we know how to die, sacrificing our very lives for the lands of Portugal, which want to be and will always be Portuguese." [5]

In the fanciful elaborations of Lisbon colonialists in the 1930's the terms "neo-imperialism" and "Third Empire" recurred frequently as definitions of Portugal's policies and possessions. Portuguese imperialism, past and present, was held to be different from the garden variety of European imperialism, since it was characterized not by "exploitation, often iniquitous, by oppression of a vanquished people, or by systematic devastation," [6] but by altruism, abnegation, faith, and a historic responsibility of civilization. At the same time, however, the Third Empire was not to be the muddled humanitarian creation of the nineteenth-century liberals. "Empire and Liberty were incompatible concepts. Empire means Authority — and there is no Authority where Power is divided and diluted. It is the duty of the New State to re-establish the force of Power. With it will be revived all the power-concepts of the Past. One of these power-concepts was the unity of territory and of the Grail, as though there were no seas or races separating the constituent elements of the national Whole." [7]

Of all the theories publicized by the Salazar government in the evolution of its colonial mystique, none has been more consistently advanced than the vision of a Pan-Lusitanian community, geographically scattered over the globe but held together by spiritual bonds peculiar to Portuguese culture. Politically this concept is translated as one of identity. The idea of a Third Empire was mostly a paper concoction useful for purposes of propaganda and prestige, but the government's statements on the sense of unity existing between the colonies and the metropolis had genuine foundations in past colonial policy and in the national psychology. The feeling of solidarity of the Portuguese overseas with the home country is an amorphous sentiment, not the ethnocentric force so visible in Afrikaner culture; it grows out of his insular provincial personality and his celebrated sense of *saudade*. The close sentimental ties which still bind the Brazilian republic to Portugal are perhaps the best example of this feeling of attachment to the metropolis. This aspect of the Portuguese personality has been inflated, of course, to serve several political causes; emphasizing the spiritual cohesion of the colonies was originally an attempt to arouse interest at home in the overseas provinces and to convince the Portuguese overseas that the new regime did not consider them second-class citizens. It has also been an argument advanced in compensation for the slow material progress of the colonies, and more recently has been used vigorously by the government to confront the advocates of African autonomy. That the Portuguese are correct in asserting that the native peoples in her colonies share this psychic reality is doubtful, but for the moment it is sufficient if the white population maintains the attachment.

Language, religion, race, and tradition — or, in the words of António Leite de Magalhães, "one State, one Race, one Faith, and one Civilization" [8] — are the cement holding the colonies to Portugal. Thus, it has been said, the Portuguese colonies never seriously entertained thoughts of independence (Brazil excepted, of course, and separatist revolts in Angola and Moçambique in the 1800's overlooked). According to Sidney Welch, "Portuguese culture was so deeply rooted [overseas] that no combination of military and political power was able to destroy it altogether, where it had taken root." [9] The colonies were in effect an extension of Portugal, and for the practical Salazar they were more than a sentimental extension: "By the same national criterion . . . without distinction of geographic situation . . . we administer and direct the Portuguese colonies. Like the Minho or Beira [provinces of metropolitan Portugal] Angola or Moçambique or India is under the single authority of the state. We are a juridical and political unity, and we desire to go along the road to economic unity." [10] For many of Dr. Salazar's admirers his words meant the emergence of a new Rome.

It is difficult to gauge the extent to which the New State's colonial mystique has been a logical projection of Portuguese mentality and aspirations, for the Portuguese are not the least nationalistic of peoples and it has long been their custom to use hyperbole in discussing their colonial empire — even when urging that the colonies be abandoned. Unquestionably the government's propaganda machine produces its fair share of jingoistic claptrap and official cant, developed early in the 1930's, in which all linguistic contact with reality is suffocated. But to isolate the genuine from the spurious, the traditional Portuguese colonial sentiment from the synthetic abstractions sponsored by the present regime is a tricky task, for not only has the New State's mystique made its influence felt in all colonial legislation — in point of fact, it had its origin in the Colonial Act of 1930 — but it has also become the language of communication for most overseas administrators and has come to influence their conduct and thinking. In the popular mind as well much of the government's colonial credo has struck a responsive chord, although some Portuguese reject out of hand any government pronouncement, and there are old colonists in Angola and Moçambique who are cynical of a colonial administration which, in their regard, has been more concerned with verbalism than practical achievement in the African provinces.

In trying to popularize its colonial ideals and to arouse Portuguese interest in Angola and Moçambique, the New State was facing the same problem the government had faced in the 1870's. The impetus given colonial affairs by the nineteenth-century explorers, the English ultimatum, and the generation of 1895 did not survive the 1920's, and for many Portuguese the popular image of Africa was one of a far and dangerous place inhabited by Negroes and exiles. Statements emphasizing that Angola and Moçambique were merely distant fragments of Portugal did not detour Portuguese emigration away from Brazil to Africa. The new imperial consciousness could not be formed out of ignorance and lack of interest. Street-names, commemorative stamps celebrating overseas heroes, colonial fairs, and congresses were not enough. In the words of Vieira Machado, Colonial Minister in the late 1930's, "To colonize is, in the final analysis, to teach and to educate."

The number of periodicals dedicated to colonial matters which have appeared and disappeared in the last twenty-five years is enormous. Most of them subsidized by some government agency, either in Portugal or in the colonies, the more permanent titles include the valuable *Boletim geral do ultramar* (formerly the *Boletim geral das colónias*), the more general *O mundo português*, and the scientific journal *Garcia da Orta*, as well as such publicity handouts as *A voz de Angola* and the *Boletim dos portos, caminhos de ferro e transporte de Moçambique*. Some have been factual publications, while others, like *O mundo português*, have been concerned with keeping the public abreast of policy developments and with reinterpreting the heroics of Portugal's overseas past.

The government has also sponsored, principally through the Agência Geral do Ultramar, the colonial propaganda agency, a stream of publications on almost every aspect of the empire. Although all of these publications reduce reality to conformity and reflect the political ideas prevailing at the moment, they have made available valuable historical and anthropological material.[11] In recent years the Junta de Investigações do Ultramar has begun to sponsor a growing list of titles.

Only the metropolitan newspapers have maintained their customary disdain for the colonies, except on the occasion of a presidential visit or when the government provides a journalistic junket to Africa or India. While they no longer make such mistakes as putting Cabinda in Portuguese Guinea and do acknowledge the colonies by printing an overseas page in the Sunday supplements and running occasional news stories, the Lisbon dailies have not yet shown an overwhelming interest in Africa. Government spokesmen like Fernanda Reis have pointed out that great colonial problems go unnoticed in Portuguese papers and that editors are negligent in stimulating interest in the colonies and satisfying the public's curiosity about events there.[12]

The richest heritage of the past for the New State was a literary consciousness of the empire. Not only Camões, Europe's most eloquent poet of expansion and empire, and the Renaissance historians like Barros, Castanheda, and Couto, but successive generations of Portuguese writers, popular and courtly, found inspiration in Brazilian, African, and Eastern themes, even in periods when the Lisbon government was paying little attention to some of these areas.[13] Although contemporary scholars and publicists have been able to use this material in their research or for nationalistic justifications, the New State has been unable to encourage any significant additions to it. The failure has not been for lack of effort. The Agência Geral promotes an annual contest "to stimulate those writers who dedicate themselves to the study of overseas problems and those writers whose works are printed in the colonies." Prizes of 350 dollars are awarded to the writers of the best novel, the best poem, the best essay, and the best historical work. The response has not been overwhelming, and sometimes prizes in one category or another are not awarded for lack of satisfactory applications.[14] Other literary prizes, such as the one offered by the newspaper *Província de Angola*, have also failed to raise appreciably the level of Portuguese colonial literature. The three main deterrents seem to be a lack of interest in the colonies by the Portuguese intellectual, because of ignorance or disinclination, the difficulty of obtaining publication in Portugal for original literary works, and the stultifying intellectual climate created by the present regime's medieval attitude toward any artistic production. A semblance of a colonial literature does exist. Writers like Lopes Vieira, Hugh Rocha, Rodrigues Junior, Castro Soromenho, and Guilhermina de Azevedo have cultivated colonial themes with varying success. Contemporary Portuguese colonial literature almost invariably falls into one of two categories: a pseudo-epic poetry, alternately bombastic and nostalgic, and an impressionistic fiction, lushly exotic — and erotic. A purely African literature cannot be said to exist; in view of the official attitude in this century toward the use of vernacular tongues, the future promise that Heli Chatelain saw for a native Angolan literature has not been fulfilled.[15] A small number of mulattoes and assimiliated Africans in both provinces, however, have begun to write original works in Portuguese.[16]

The historical and scientific literature directly or indirectly supported by the government and various cultural organizations has been considerably more significant. The government has been attempting of late to co-ordinate historical research on the colonies through centralization of archives and materials. The quality of subsidized colonial research in Portugal is not consistently high, unless it is of a bibliographical or maritime scientific nature. Nonetheless, such works as Almeida de Eça's *História das guerras no Zambesi* and Silva Rego's mission histories have brought to light much new information on the African past. Anthropological teams have made cursory ethnographic surveys of Angola and Moçambique, collecting photographic and recorded materials, and there is a steady publication of scientific and semi-scientific works. A number of studies of native traditions in northeast Angola have been subsidized by the Diamond Company, whose museum at Dundo has what is considered one of the most important collections in Africa.

A peripheral aspect of the government's interest in literary and scholarly activity has been the cordial reception given most foreign investigators and journalists who express curiosity about the overseas provinces. Not infrequently extensive itineraries are arranged by the Overseas Ministry or the local government to permit the foreigner to visit the colonies at Portuguese expense. In Africa the impeccable Portuguese hospitality has stood the New State in good stead and served to soften what might have been intemperate remarks on the local state of affairs. Out-spoken visitors like Basil Davidson, A. T. Steele of the *New York Herald-Tribune*, and Brian Parks of the *Johannesburg Star* are in the minority. The majority of the visitors speak with enthusiasm and conviction of the wisdom of Portuguese policies, the harmony between the black world and the white, and the spiritual contributions Portugal has made to Africa. The bad-tempered English traveler of the nineteenth century is seldom seen now in Portuguese Africa.

One of the primary purposes of the government's propaganda campaign has been to educate a rising generation in colonial affairs. As a first step, the Escola Colonial Superior (now the Institute for Overseas Studies) was consolidated with the colonial administration. The announced intent of the Escola was to constitute a center for advanced colonial studies to instruct the elite of the nation in the special methods of Portuguese colonial action; to prepare bureaucrats and administrators to embody and carry out Portugal's philosophies; and to act as a center for scientific colonial investigation and orientation. Principally, however, the school has served to train colonial officers, and its graduates are coming to dominate the lower echelons of the colonial service.[17] Applicants for the four-year program must be high-school graduates. At the institute they receive instruction in colonial administration and theory, anthropology, the elements of Portuguese law, vernacular languages, and other subjects designed to prepare them for overseas service. Among the present distinguished professors at the institute are the noted anthropologist Mendes Correia — who is the director of the school — and the colonial theorist and scholar J. M. da Silva Cunha.

Equally important was to impress upon the secondary-school and university students an awareness of the overseas provinces, principally Africa; out of this awareness might come an increased immigration of educated young men and women to Angola and Moçambique. This campaign, not very successful, extended into the middle 1940's, when other factors, such as colonial prosperity and a higher standard of living, began to accomplish what repeated official urgings had not been able to do. The line of persuasion taken by the New State was one that sought to raise a challenge to the adventurous spirit of the Portuguese youth. He was told not only of the great opportunities offered by the colonies, but that he should be interested in serving his nation, not himself. In addition to working for the good of his country, he would have the personal satisfaction of being regarded as the "white chief, who knows all and can do all . . . He can stimulate culture . . . explore forests, open roads, irrigate fields . . . organize trading centers . . . build infirmaries . . . He will be a man of action, not a bureaucrat." [18] To give vitality to this educational campaign in the middle 1930's summer cruises to the West African possessions were organized for university students under the direction of Marcelo Caetano, who was then beginning to emerge as one of Salazar's young leaders. On the occasion of the first cruise, in 1935, an editorial in O mundo português summed up the reason for the voyage and the significance of Africa for Portugal. "We must always keeps alive in the Portuguese people the dream of beyond-the-seas and the consciousness and pride of Empire. Africa is more than a land to be exploited . . . Africa is for us a moral justification and a raison d'être as a power. Without it we would be a small nation; with it we are a great country." [19]

The ultimate gesture of solidarity between Portugal and the African colonies under the New State has been the presidential voyages. Here the regime may pride itself on making a unique contribution to overseas unity. Through inertia or by policy previous Portuguese governments had almost studiously refrained from sending any dignitary or official of importance to visit Africa. The short trip of the crown prince in 1907 and that of Colonial Minister Bebiano in the 1920's were the only precedents. In the 1930's this attitude changed. In 1932 Colonial Minister Armindo Monteiro visited the colonies — thus initiating a series of inspection tours by colonial ministers — and in 1938 President Carmona went to Angola and a year later to Moçambique. In 1954 President Craveiro Lopes visited Angola and in 1956 Moçambique.[20] On each voyage Presidents Carmona and Craveiro Lopes have been accompanied by ranking members of the Overseas Ministry. The visits have not been casual affairs, but well-arranged tours through the greater part of each province. In addition to emphasizing the oneness of the Portuguese world, they have served the colonies as useful deadlines for the completion of major projects. Each visit has been attended by the inauguration of a dam, a bridge, an airport, a colonization scheme, a radio transmitter; vilas are raised to the categories of cities, colonial fairs and exhibits abound, and African delegations from almost every part of the colony greet the President with declarations of fidelity and solidarity.[21] And each visit gives administration leaders the opportunity to review the meaning of Portuguese endeavor in Africa. With these words the Governor of Manica e Sofala greeted President Craveiro Lopes in Beira in August 1956:

Here we are after more than four and a half centuries, here we are engaged today more than ever on a great and successful work, with the help of God, raising high the banner of Portugal, taming the wilderness, building towns and making them prosper, teaching, educating, and leading to a better life the rude mass of natives, disciplining their rudimentary instincts . . . molding their soul in the superior forms of Christianity, administering them justice with affectionate understanding . . . A task, or I should say, a mission, vast, difficult, and exhausting, but noble and dignifying as few are. It is our historical vocation emerging once again . . . Everything indicates that we are on the verge of a new era, a decisive phase of History, of our History, that we have ahead of us a great, auspicious, and obtainable future . . . Everything is for the common good and aggrandizement of the mother country.[22]

The parallel between the imperial mystique created by the New State, absorbed by many of its colonial administrators, and imposed, at least, superficially, on a surprisingly large segment of the Portuguese population, and the nationalistic attitude of the Union of South African government is inescapable. The words of Dr. Malan have a familiar ring. "The history of the Afrikaner reveals a determination and definiteness of purpose which make one feel that Afrikanerdom is not the work of man but a creation of God. We have a divine right to be Afrikaners. Our history is the highest work of the art of the Architect of the Centuries." [23] In the national mythologies of Portugal and South Africa the caravel and the oxcart seem to offer the same symbolic inspiration to the present generation. The Portuguese and the Boer are pursuing, albeit from different directions, the same goal: self-preservation in Africa, the Portuguese theoretically through a closer *rapprochement* with the metropolis and the Boer through the isolation and intensification of what he holds to be the traditional Afrikaner culture and way of life. The increasingly warm regard in which the South African and Portuguese governments hold each other today is more than a matter of economics. Events in other parts of Africa are driving the two countries to find common cause in their efforts to meet the implied threat of African nationalism with a revival of the simulated values of an exaggerated heroic past.

The spirit of the Salazar government's neo-imperialism is found not only in speeches and programs to whip up interest in the colonies. It is present as well in all overseas legislation dating from the Colonial Act of 1930; in fact these laws have often been the source for much of the theorizing on Portugal's past and present role as a colonizing power ("The development of spiritual relations between the metropolis and the overseas provinces shall be promoted for their mutual knowledge and *rapprochement* in all aspects of intellectual life; thus all institutions diffusing Portuguese culture in the overseas provinces should be protected and subsidized").[24] At the same time the colonial laws have reflected the sternly authoritarian attitude of the government and are of an intellectual piece with the Portuguese Constitution of 1933, the new labor statutes, and similar metropolitan legislation. It is logical that an administration which has successfully exalted morality, the family, and the privilege of the Portuguese majority to be poor should seek to disseminate these same virtues in the colonies, and much of recent Portuguese colonial legislation has been characterized by the same doctrines that pervade the laws governing Portugal.

The Colonial Act of 1930 was the work of Salazar, who served briefly as Minister of Colonies in that year, and his successor, Armindo Monteiro. The Act set forth the general principles for the conduct of affairs overseas. It provided for the unification of administration in the hands of the state and the cessation of administrative authority in the hands of private companies; the normalization of colonial administration and the end of the high commissionerships; and the nationalization of the colonial economies; it prohibited the use of African labor by private companies or individuals and reiterated the obligation to pay the African for his labor. Finally, it stressed the duty of the colonial administrators to sustain the sovereignty of Portugal. As is evident, the principal aim of the Colonial Act was to reverse the trend toward financial and political autonomy and to enable Portugal to put forth to the world a united imperial front.

For the defenders of the New State at home and abroad the Colonial Act has been seen as an inspiring affirmation of imperial destiny, "the calling of the colonies to closer communion with continental Portugal and a sternly vigorous declaration of Portugal's intention to maintain and perpetuate the legacy of history." [25] The reaction in the colonies has sometimes been more reserved, especially among long-time white residents of Angola and Moçambique who take a more practical view of the Act and subsequent legislation. They argue that the natural development of the provinces has been replaced by artificial stimuli and restrictions and even that Portugal has returned to her traditional policies of milking the colonies for the profit of the metropolis. Simões Vaz, publisher of As notícias de Lourenço Marques and one of the most distinguished Portuguese residents of the province, writes, in discussing the lack of adequate agricultural services in Moçambique: "The colony does not have, unfortunately, sufficient autonomy itself for such an undertaking. It is dependent on the Ministry of Colonies, and as in this Ministry they have the habit, in our view a mistaken one, of legislating in matters of this sort simultaneously and uniformly for all of the colonies, as if in each of them there did not exist different necessities, and as they do not have the facilities for taking prompt and energetic action in dealing with all of the problems of all of the colonies, the proposals which are submitted by the colonial governors are lost on one desk or another or are pigeonholed to be forgotten by everyone, including the Minister himself. . ." [26]

The progress of the Colonial Act illustrates the continuing efforts of the government to achieve economic and political solidarity — and to confront anticolonial sentiments springing up in many parts of the world. Modified in some details in 1935 and 1945, the Act, with additional changes, was incorporated in 1951 into the Portuguese Constitution as an integral part of the law of continental and overseas Portugal. Portuguese possessions were once again after 1951 given the designation of "overseas provinces," a term "considered to conform more with the principle of unity and with the closer co-operation now existing among all the peoples who constitute the Nation and the various parcels of Portuguese territory." [27] Thus Article 134 of the Constitution reads: "The overseas territories of Portugal are given the generic name 'provinces' and have a politico-administrative organization suitable to their geographic situation and their conditions of social environment." Article 135 states that "the overseas provinces as an integral part of the Portuguese state are linked to each other and to the metropolis," while Article 136 specifies that "the solidarity between the overseas provinces and the metropolis includes especially the obligation of making an appropriate contribution to guarantee the integrity and defense of the Nation as a whole . . ."

In reverting to a term used by the scorned Liberal government in the 1830's — which had, modern Portuguese spokesmen emphasize, no practical significance and was nothing more than an ideological chimera [28] — the New State was laying the groundwork for entrance into the United Nations, where she would be more vulnerable to charges of colonialism, and for closer collaboration with the nations of the Western alliance. Evidence of the success of this maneuver may be seen in Secretary of State Dulles' prompted remark in 1955 that the Portuguese state of Goa was a Portuguese province. In all United Nations debates on questions relating to non-self-governing territories, Portugal has refused to participate on the grounds that Portugal is a single state and that all Portuguese, whether born in the provinces of the metropolis or those of the *Ultramar*, enjoy, without distinction of race or religious creed, the same rights.

The general provisions of the Colonial Act have been elaborated and more carefully defined by other colonial legislation, principally the Organic Charter of 1933, modified in 1935, 1937, and 1946 and replaced in 1955 by the Organic Law, which establishes special provisions for the particular character of each overseas province; and the Administrative Overseas Reform Act of 1933, which remains in effect except where it has been modified by changes in the Portuguese Constitution and the Organic Law. But nothing in this legislation, or in more specific laws, has altered the essentials of the Colonial Act. Minor changes in the Organic Charter in 1946 gave a measure of financial and administrative freedom to the governors general of the colonies, and the consultative authority of the Legislative Councils in the colonies has recently been increased, but both Angola and Moçambique remain snugly beneath Lisbon's control.

Angola and Moçambique have undergone administrative divisions and regroupings since 1930. The changes have been designed to extend Portuguese authority more effectively into the remoter areas of each province and to expedite the transmission of authority from Lisbon through the provincial capitals to the lesser administrative centers, although basically the patterns of districts and circumscriptions established in the early part of the century have remained constant. Until 1956, that is, roughly, during the years when Angola and Moçambique were called colonies, each possession was divided into several large provinces, which in turn were split into districts, or *intendências*, and these into *concelhos* or circumscriptions. As established in a decree of 1946, Moçambique was divided into four provinces: Manica e Sofala, comprising the districts of Beira and Tete; Sul do Save, divided into the districts of Lourenço Marques, Gaza, and Inhambane; Zambézia; and Niassa, split into the three districts of Nampula, Lago, and Cape Delgado. Angola contained five provinces: Luanda, with its districts of Luanda, Cabinda, Zaire, Congo, and Cuanza Norte; Malange, divided into Malange and Lunda; Benguela, split into Benguela, Cuanza Sul and Huambo; Bié comprising Bié, Moxico, and Cuando-Cubango; and Huíla, made up of Huíla, Moçâmedes, and Cunene. Further division produced in Angola, for example, sixty-six civil circumscriptions, of which thirty-three were *concelhos*, and two hundred eighty-nine posts. Moçambique had fourteen *concelhos* and sixty-five circumscriptions. The number and shape of these lesser divisions has changed but slightly in the last fifteen years.

A decree of October 1954 — taking effect in 1956 — divided Angola and Moçambique, now officially overseas provinces, into districts which more or less corresponded to the districts making up the former provinces in the two colonies. These districts (with their capitals indicated in parentheses) are:

Angola
Cabinda (Cabinda)
Congo (Uige)
Luanda (Luanda)
Cuanza Norte (Vila Salazar)
Cuanza Sul (Malange)

Moçambique
Lourenço Marques (Lourenço Marques)
Gaza (Vila João Belo)
Inhambane (Inhambane)
Manica e Sofala (Beira)

Lunda (Henrique de Carvalho)   Tete (Tete)
Benguela (Benguela)   Zambézia (Quelimane)
Huambo (Nova Lisboa)   Moçambique (Nampula)
Bié-Cuando-Cubango (Silva   Cabo Delgado (Porto Amélia)
    Porto)   Niassa (Vila Cabral)
Moxico (Vila Luso)
Moçâmedes (Moçâmedes)
Huíla (Sá da Bandeira)

Simultaneous with the redistricting of Moçambique and Angola, first steps were taken to create an administrative organization similar to the one prevailing in Portugal. It is intended that as the work of civilizing the African peoples goes forward, the unit of government in the districts will become the *concelho*, an instrument of limited local self-government. In the meantime, however, the districts are divided as before into *concelhos*, where a civilized majority predominates, and circumscriptions in largely African areas. Some *concelhos*, however, are split into urban *freguesias* (parishes) and non-urban administrative posts. The unit of division in the circumscription continues to be the administrative post. In certain districts of the provinces where African policy is of primary importance, an intermediate division, the *intendência*, a grouping of circumscriptions and areas of African population within contiguous *concelhos*, is used to expedite native policy and development schemes.

The source of all important colonial authority is Lisbon and resides in three bodies: the National Assembly, the Council of Ministers, and the Overseas Ministry. The National Assembly has but a modest role in colonial policy and administration, serving only to legislate the proposals it receives from the Overseas Ministry through the Council of Ministers and to review the yearly reports from the overseas provinces. Among its 120 members are three deputies elected from Angola and three from Moçambique, but since these men need not be residents of the colonies and are candidates chosen by the government to stand for election, their influence on colonial conduct is as negligible as that of the rest of the Assembly's members.

The Portuguese government (*i.e.*, the Council of Ministers) acts in a general executive capacity on overseas affairs. It may legislate by decree for the national territory or for the individual provinces. It alone may permit the negotiating of loans by the provinces, which occurs only under exceptional circumstances, and it approves all concessions to foreign companies. The appointment and dismissal of colonial governors is also the business of the Council. Through various governmental boards, such as those controlling the production of certain crops (cereals and cotton, for example), and export-import commissions the government effectively dominates the economic life of Angola and Moçambique. Through the national labor laws the government extends its influence over workers and employers overseas.

In more specific matters the central organ of overseas administration is the Overseas Ministry, whose authority embraces all questions of general colonial policy. On particular levels this includes responsibility for administrative personnel, native policy, missionary matters, censorship, some aspects of the juridical system and the military organization, and public works programs. Ultimately the Overseas Minister is responsible for the political and administrative life of the provinces and their over-all financial organization; he must decide on all disputes arising between the governor general and the provincial legislative councils. No colonial legislation becomes law until the Minister has released the text for publication in the *Boletim oficial* of the province or provinces concerned. As Professor Martins Afonso remarks, "These dispositions clearly show that the unity of power resides in the Central Government and, especially, in the Overseas Minister, since it is he who superintends, directs, orients, co-ordinates, and controls on the highest level all overseas administration." [29]

Acting as a consultative body to the Overseas Minister, when he chooses to consult it — and even then he is not bound to heed its advice on any except juridical matters — is the Overseas Council, a permanent organization. Temporary consultative bodies are the Overseas Governors' Conference and the Overseas Economic Conference, which meet to discuss general policy when they are convened — infrequently — by the Overseas Minister. To keep in constant contact with the problems of each province the Minister relies on a corps of inspectors, who, while they have no administrative authority, are in a position to influence decisions through their reports to the Ministry and the colonial governors.

The supreme authority in each overseas province is the governor general, charged with representing and maintaining political unity. Appointed by the Council of Ministers, usually on the recommendation of the Overseas Minister, the governor general has a four-year term of office, which may be renewed for additional terms. He is forbidden to have any business interests in the province where he serves or to have any association with firms doing business there. He enjoys the honors belonging to the ministers of the government and has precedence over all civil and military officers serving in the colony. He may not leave the colony without permission of the Overseas Minister and must advise the latter when he leaves the provincial capital.

The governor general possesses extensive powers and responsibilities to administer the province under the terms of colonial laws and in areas which do not fall under the exclusive competence of another governmental or provincial body. He must inform the Overseas Ministry of current administrative events and problems. He is charged with assuming the protection under law of nationals and foreigners; at the same time, he may order the expulsion of, or refuse entry to, those Portuguese and foreigners whose presence would seem detrimental to provincial interests. He may appoint, promote, or dismiss all government employees whose appointments are not made by the Overseas Ministry or other independent bodies. The governor general is responsible for the administration and operation of all colonial departments; supervision of public magistrates and attorneys and other judicial officials, however, are beyond his competence. He exercises the power of the general police. He is obliged to visit at intervals the various regions of the province to inspect local administrations and to receive claims or petitions which may be directed to him.

The governor general is the financial authority in the colony, exercising the function of a controller of expenditures, and draws up the annual budget for submission to the consultative councils and the Overseas Ministry. The constraints on the governor general in the matter of the budget and expenditures are severe, for the government, remembering the 1920's, has ordered that he shall be liable to trial when, by his own initiative or against the opinion of competent government officials, he incurs expenditures not foreseen in the budget or in excess of those approved by the Overseas Minister. Under existing regulations the governor general may grant concessions of land and mines, commercial monopolies, construction contracts, navigation and fishing rights, and other privileges for the exploitation of the province so long as they do not imply the surrender of the state's sovereign rights.

The governor general is responsible for bettering the moral and material living conditions of the African, for the improvement of his aptitudes and natural facilities, and, in a general sense, for his education, security, and progress. He may establish, change, or suppress native taxes and regulate tax collection and the census. He is the protector of the African's rights and is the government's instrument for the carrying out of native policy, particularly those laws enacted for the defense of the African's life, freedom, labor, and property.

To assist them in the executive administration of the province, the governors general of Angola and Moçambique rely chiefly on three associates, the secretary general, the immediate subordinate, and two provincial secretaries. These men are chosen by the governor general and carry the rank, in the overseas hierarchy, equal to that of inspector. Their powers are defined by local ordinance, although in every case they are responsible to the governor general. Usually they are delegated authority over certain aspects of the provincial administration. In Moçambique, for example, in 1956, the secretary general was responsible for the general supervision of the education and health programs in the province, as well as of civil administration, police, and justice. One provincial secretary supervised the public-works program, the transportation system, communications, and the meteorological services, while to the other fell the administration of such diverse matters as agriculture, industry and mines, provincial statistics, commerce, and veterinary services.[30]

In legislative matters the governor general is assisted and theoretically guided by the Legislative Council. Formerly nothing more than a rubber stamp for local administrative decisions, the Legislative Council was granted expanded consultative powers in the early 1950's, although its principal function even now is to discuss and suggest local policy that is to be implemented in local legislation and to express an opinion on whatever matters are presented to it by the governor general or the Overseas Minister. Should the governor general refuse to accept the advice of the Council on any matter which he is obliged to discuss with it, he must report his differences in writing to the Overseas Minister. The Legislative Council exists partly as a safety valve for local resentments and partly to give overseas residents a sense of participation, however limited, in the provincial government. The Council meets twice a year for thirty-day periods beginning April 1 and October 1. The Legislative Council in Angola presently has twenty-six members (eighteen elected and eight appointed) and in Moçambique it has twenty-four (sixteen elected and eight appointed). Six of the appointed members, at least three of whom must be high administrative officials, are chosen by the governor general, while the other two are chosen by the Government Council from a triple list submitted by the governor general. Of the elected members, eleven in Angola and nine in Moçambique are elected by direct suffrage of citizens registered on the electoral rolls, two are chosen by municipal bodies, two by organizations representing cultural and moral interests (one of these members must be a Catholic missionary), one by organizations representing the laboring class, one by organizations representing employers' associations, and one by taxpayers of Portuguese nationality who pay a minimum direct annual tax of $350. While it is possible that all the members of the Legislative Council have the African's interests at heart, it is nonetheless significant that not one member directly represents the interests of the nine million Africans in the two provinces.

To assist the governor general in his executive duties, meeting only when he summons it, is the Government Council, a sort of advisory cabinet. The Council is made up of the secretary general, the provincial secretaries, the military commander of the province, the attorney general, the director of the treasury department, and two elected members of the Legislative Council designated by the governor general. The most important function of the Government Council is to aid in the preparation of the yearly budget.

The lines of authority in Angola and Moçambique pass from the governor general down to the district governors to the administrators to the chiefs of post. The district governors, named by the Overseas Minister, are the direct representatives of the governor general. Their responsibilities include civil authority and administration in the districts, economic control and development, protection of the African, and collaboration with the general administration of the province.

The administrators of the *concelhos* correspond in their authority and responsibilities to municipal magistrates in Portugal. This official directs the administrative activities of the *concelho*, prepares its budgets and annual reports, has charge of municipal services, and consults with the municipal council.

The administrator of the *circunscrição* continues to be the most important figure in the colonial administration, excepting the governor general, because the circumscription remains the primary unit of government in the African provinces. In addition to carrying out the usual administrative, economic, and civil duties, the *administrador*, in New State language, "represents in the middle of the native population, the sovereignty of the Nation, the authority of the Republic, the order, the dignity, the justice of Portuguese civilization." In more practical terms, he is still the white chief envisioned by Enes and Costa, for he and the *chefe de posto* are the colonial officers in most immediate contact with the people making up more than 95 per cent of the population in both provinces. He is registry officer for the African population, judge in their disputes (relying, in purely tribal

questions, on information supplied by African informants), super-
intendent of tax collection, stimulator of the African economy and
agriculture, and, in many circumscriptions, native-labor co-ordinator
and supply officer.

In the from two to six divisions, or *postos*, which comprise each
circumscription the administrative officer is the *chefe de posto* whose
functions are roughly those of the administrator, but on a reduced
level. The chief of post is ultimately the European in closest contact
with the tribal population.[31]

Because of their many activities and the nature of their work with
a rural African population, the administrator and the chief of post
are specified by Portuguese colonial law to be men of action. The
New State frankly admits that on their zeal, competence, and honest
conduct the success of the country's African policy rests. To fill these
lesser administrative positions the New State has attempted to create,
chiefly through the Colonial School, an elite to serve overseas. Viewed
against the desultory, if not negligent performance of many colonial
officials in the nineteenth and early twentieth centuries, the government's program must be regarded a success. The pay remains small,
but the standard of living has improved noticeably. Spacious houses,
official automobiles, paid vacations in Portugal, and the presence of
the administrator's family have helped change the rather desperate
conditions existing fifty and twenty-five years ago and have contributed to the generally acknowledged efficiency of Portuguese administrators in the African interior.[32]

Integrated into the administrative hierarchy as auxiliaries of the
overseas civil administration are various African officials. Their positions include that of the sepoys — usually men who have served in the
army — who form an African police force. There are also interpreters, whose knowledge of native languages and customs is indispensable to Portuguese administrators, and *régulos*. Completely subservient to the administrator or chief of post is the *régulo*, or African
chief, a man who has attained his position through succession or tribal
election or who is a soldier or local official rewarded for having
served Portuguese interests faithfully. The *régulo* is obliged to maintain public order, to assist in the collection of taxes, to try to convince
his people to fulfill their labor obligations, either through contracting
their services or working on their own account, and to keep Portuguese authorities apprised of village happenings. For their services,
the chiefs receive token honors, a salary of perhaps ten to twelve
dollars a month, and certain gratuities. Within each village in the
régulo's jurisdiction, a head man carries out the chief's instructions,

which are principally concerned with tax collection and road maintenance.

Through this formidable administrative service [33] — larger in proportion to the size of the territory and number of its inhabitants than that of any other colonial power in Africa — the authority of the Portuguese government extends directly from the Overseas Ministry to the individual African in the hinterland village. In terms of native policy it means that the activities of the African population are under the closest control, if not actual surveillance, and it must be considered one of the several reasons why the Portuguese may boast that their overseas provinces are the most peaceful and secure areas in the African continent. In terms of colonial development, political and economic, this bureaucratic channeling of authority, with its series of checks on almost every form of local initiative, is considered by many to be a discouraging and restricting force. The executive and legislative machinery of Portugal's governments has usually moved at a ponderous pace on colonial matters, and the present government is no exception. The lack of specific authority all along the line has in recent years increased the traditional Portuguese inclination to rely more on elaborate legislation, lengthy reports, and seemingly endless discussions than on responsible administrative action in Angola and Moçambique.

XII

THE NEW STATE IN AFRICA:
NATIVE POLICY

U NTIL recent years native policy was only incidental to the administration and exploitation of Angola and Moçambique. The African population in its majority was ignored, enslaved, or conquered depending upon the necessities of the age, and Portuguese actions and atttitudes, which in retrospect have been called policy, were based on little more than expediency. The slave trade was, of course, given its extent in the two possessions, a sort of native policy, but in a larger sense it was another aspect of Portugal's economic exploitation. Economic considerations still dominate colonial schemes, but not so nakedly, and a major effort of the New State's overseas policy has theoretically been based on the social, as well as the financial, integration of Angola and Moçambique. From the traditions deriving from Portuguese conduct in Africa in centuries past and from the authoritarian purpose and mystique of the present the Salazar government has evolved a philosophy for the African provinces: cultural assimilation. Still more precept than practice, this policy is advertised as the answer to Africanism and the ultimate hope for European colonialism in Africa.

Realistically, the heralded traditions of the Portuguese occupation in Angola and Moçambique are, as has been seen, not much more than the pattern of behavior followed by a handful of Europeans who barely survived four hundred years of African vicissitudes. The survival of Portuguese colonies on both coasts of Africa was more the result of the white inhabitants' ability to maintain a modest and uncertain *modus vivendi* with the African peoples than of Lisbon's sporadic efforts to transplant European cultural values. The state of the provinces in mid-nineteenth century is sufficient evidence of Portugal's lack of success in expanding either her political or cultural authority over the Bantu tribes. Apart from Luanda and the town of Moçambique, administrative centers more or less constantly refreshed through contact with the metropolis or other Portuguese colonies, no center of Portuguese activity could boast in 1900 of a continuous history of importance. The soldier or trader in the interior lived a precarious existence, subduing the nearby African villagers in good years and trying to negotiate with them in bad, but almost always mingling his blood with theirs. While the Portuguese did not always accept the African as an equal, they were usually willing to accept him, to trade with him, to allow him to hold minor administrative or ecclesiastical offices, and, on occasions, to be absorbed by him. This is the essential reality of the native policy practiced by the Portuguese in Africa. It is the only fact of the past which properly lends itself to transcendental discussions. All other talk — the nonextermination of the African (as if the Portuguese were ever in a position to kill off the African if they had wanted to), the perpetuation of Christian ideals, or the inappropriate analogies with Portuguese India or Brazil — is fantasy.

Perhaps the casual African-Portuguese relationship of the early centuries is manifest in the various terms used by the Portuguese to describe the Bantu inhabitants of Angola and Moçambique. *Negros, naturais, cafres* are the terms with the widest acceptance, although *nativo* was not unknown, and collectively the Africans were frequently referred to as *o gentio*, or the heathen people, or *a gente da terra*, people of the land. The absence of a single or even predominant term for the African is possibly more than accidental; it may reveal the limited extent to which the African figured in Portuguese policy and preoccupations. All of these names have been largely replaced by the word *indígena*, which gained currency in the nineteenth century and has since become both the legal and popular term; its acceptance has roughly paralleled the increasing concern of Portugal for such matters as native policy. *Preto* (black) is an expression widely used, sometimes affectionately, sometimes scornfully, in Portuguese Africa, while *negro* seems to be less used than formerly. Only in the last several years have the inhabitants of Angola and Moçambique been occasionally referred to as *africanos*.

Only in Angola, Moçambique, and Portuguese Guinea does the word *indígena* have legal significance (other fragments of the empire — Portuguese India, Macao, the Cape Verdes — are considered cul-

African agricultural project, Caconda, Angola

Agricultural project for Portuguese settlers, Cela, Angola

Quissama village, Angola

Convalescent center for African workers, near Beira, Moçambique

turally as well as politically assimilated with the metropolis and their inhabitants called Portuguese), and only in these areas do special policy and legislation exist for the majority of the population. Defined by a statute of 1954, the *indígena* is a person of the Negro race who is governed by the customs of his own society and has not yet evolved to a cultural level — or state of civilization — which would permit him to be governed by the same laws as a Portuguese citizen. Thus the inhabitants of the African possessions fall into two judicial categories: *indígenas* and *não-indígenas* (whites and assimilated Africans or mulattoes). In practice a third category, that of the assimilated African, or *assimilado*, is commonly recognized, if not legally sanctioned, and every provincial census contains statistics on this third category.

In affirming the bases for its present native policy, whose goal is specifically the elimination of the *indígena* as a separate element of the population in the African colonies and the ultimate identity of these areas with Portugal, the government has of course emphasized "the traditional principles and methods of Portuguese colonization." Beyond the aspirations of the sixteenth-century Congo experiment, the mission work of the Jesuits and Dominicans, and the humanitarian suggestions contained in the reports of a few enlightened colonial governors, contemporary enthusiasts have been hard put to find factual evidence for a positive native policy in the centuries past and have had to rely for the most part on abstractions and allusions to the multi-racial societies of Brazil and India. But since many Portuguese are convinced that the history of their relations with the African has a special character and since this conviction has to a certain extent determined present philosophies, the concept of Portuguese traditions in Africa cannot be ignored. One of its clearest expressions is by Bahia dos Santos, contemporary historian of Portuguese colonialism.

The traditional concern for the improvement of native peoples as a factor in the progress of the human condition, apart from the undeniable economic advantage which it represents, has always constituted one of the fundamental characteristics of our overseas policy. Thus it is that, contrary to what happened with the majority of other colonizing nations, Portugal has always succeeded in reconciling overseas the material interest . . . with the realization of a task of universal significance for the elevation of the mentality of the most backward peoples.

Endowed by nature with exceptional qualities of sympathy and attraction for their fellow men, the Portuguese were fortified in these sentiments by the sublime doctrine of Christ, which was the maximum stimulation for these very qualities. In the establishment of factories and in the campaigns of penetration, the navigators, explorers, and merchants were followed by priests and missionaries who began the first friendly contacts which, based on absolute equality, were designed to inspire in the neophytes those same principles which, followed by all men, would guarantee peace and prosperity in the whole world.

The gradual integration, or assimilation, which today is said to have been the characteristic of Portuguese native policy in the earliest days of our overseas action was nothing more, therefore, than a way of following the dictates of our moral and religious sentiments. It is a question then of a native policy more spontaneous than deliberate. In reality, the attitude of the Portuguese toward the native peoples was not in those early times adopted for any specific political purpose. In the beginning of the Portuguese colonization, in the matter of relations with the natives the means were the end. Only much later, in the face of techniques adopted by other colonizing powers, techniques which could not serve us as an example without going fundamentally against our characteristics of social behavior, does this attitude arise as a body of doctrines which is today called Portuguese native policy.[1]

"Our whole policy," writes Morais Cabral, "has been and continues to be to improve the cultural, economic, and social level of the Negro, to give him opportunities, to drag him from his ignorance and backwardness, to try to make of him a rational and honorable individual, worthy of the Lusitanian community." [2] Protection of the African, a detached humanitarianism, or an anthropological interest in his customs is not sufficient justification for a native policy in the Portuguese view; they argue that such a policy leaves the African in the same inferior position he has always held. The creative quality of Portugal's work in Africa, they say, is that it draws the African into a modern Christian community, gradually replacing his tribal values with the more substantial ones (i.e., the importance of the family and the dignity of labor) of Portuguese society. Historically this has been an accidental process; now it is national policy whose larger goal is complete spiritual assimilation and political unity. The insignificant trickle of Africans assimilated in the past and the fact that the present populations of Angola and Moçambique are increasing at a much greater rate than they are being culturally integrated does not seem to shake Portugal's convictions of the eventual triumph of her scheme.

By assimilation, however, the New State did not originally mean, as government spokesmen pointed out at great length in the 1930's and 1940's, assimilação uniformizadora, that is, the Liberals' policy of proclaiming the African subject to the same laws and political institutions as citizens of metropolitan Portuguese. Such ideas were regarded as harebrained philanthropy and a foolish and unrealistic attempt to compensate the African for centuries of slavery. Much of the admiration for Enes and Mousinho in the last thirty years has been because they led the resistance to these Liberal colonial policies. In the present decade, however, there is some evidence that the Salazar government is taking another tack in its colonial policy, is abandoning its earlier philosophy of what might be called selective assimilation, and is now directing its attention to the assimilation of the entire African population. Significantly, the attacks on the Liberal ideals of the nineteenth century have diminished. The colonies have become provinces, and the language used in the latest legislation has more than a vague similarity with that of nineteenth-century decrees. But it would be rash to suggest that any real change of attitude is taking place in the Overseas Ministry; it is more likely that the Portuguese government is preparing a legalistic fortress against the anticolonial attacks it must surely face.

Much of the legislation regarding the African has been a continuation of the *Estatuto político civil e criminal dos indígenas das colónias de Angola e Moçambique* of 1926. Drawn up by Colonial Minister João Belo, an Enes admirer, it had a hard conservativism beneath its theoretical visions of spiritual integration. The new law, according to Silva Cunha, was oriented by two dominant ideas:

One of these is to guarantee the natural and unconditional rights of the native whose tutelage is confided to us . . . and to assure the gradual fulfillment of his moral and legal obligations to work, to be educated, and to improve himself . . . The other is to lead the natives, by the means appropriate to their rudimentary civilization — so that the transformation from their own customs and their own habits may be gentle and gradual — to the profitable development of their own activities and to their integration into the life of the colony, which is an extension of the mother country. The natives are not granted, because of the lack of practical application, the rights associated with our own constitutional institutions. We do not impose on their individual, domestic, and public life, if it may be called that, our political laws, our administrative, civil, commercal, and penal codes, our judicial system. We maintain for them a juridical system consistent with the state of their faculties, their primitive mentality, their feelings, their way of life, but at the same time we continue to encourage them constantly, by all appropriate means, to raise their level of existence.[3]

The Statute of 1926 was replaced by another statute, very similar, made law by a decree of 1929. This legislation, and the general principles outlined in the Colonial Act, the Imperial Organic Charter of

1933, and the Overseas Administrative Reform Act of the same year, determined Portugal's policy until the early 1950's. The principles established in the several documents are these: the goal of Portuguese policy is to bring about the integration of the native peoples into the Portuguese nation; this goal "must be pursued prudently, always keeping in mind that the natives have a culture, a social organization, and a law of their own which must be respected and maintained"; the obligation of the state is to protect the African in his primitive condition against the abuses and control of the colonists, to protect his property, and to supervise his labor contracts with *não-indígenas;* the African's assimilation is to be obtained through the Portuguese language, education, instruction, and Christianity; the African is guaranteed, once he has acquired a civilized way of life, the same juridical privileges as a born Portuguese.[4]

In stressing the traditional Portuguese sentiments of racial equality and at the same time devising a policy founded on theories of cultural inequality, the Portuguese government was walking a conceptual tightrope. In reality, it was temporizing. Although the administrative machinery of the New State made it possible to establish a close control over the African population, whose customs the government professed to respect but whose local authority had been irrevocably broken, the task of educating, or "civilizing," the African in Angola and Moçambique could only have been regarded as a near impossibility by the most optimistic New State colonialist. Quite apart from the grinding abuse of African labor, the inherent poverty of Portugal, the economic backwardness of the colonies, the lack of minimal educational or medical facilities, and the absence of a technical personnel made the goal of assimilation in the 1930's and 1940's, as in the previous centuries, a legislative dream. Hence the reiterated precautions that the government must proceed slowly, that evolution of the African to a civilized state is a process of centuries (the example of other areas of the world notwithstanding), that native programs must be studied and carefully considered before being implemented. Hence the emphasis on the spiritual, not material, values of Portuguese culture. Hence the safety valve of individual or selective assimilation, which had served Portuguese interests so well in the past. The purpose of this eloquent legislation, in spite of its humanitarian language and its proposals for social and economic services for the African, was really nothing more than an attempt to maintain the *status quo.*[5]

Although in the mid-1950's the process of selective assimilation is no longer given the emphasis and publicity it received earlier, the assimilation of the individual African, it must be stressed, has not

ceased to be an integral part of native policy in Angola and Moçambique. Today, as then, the qualified African may attain, if he chooses,
full Portuguese citizenship and enter the ranks of civilized nonindig-
enous population of the province. The standards he must meet are
difficult and are stringently applied. The applicant must be at least
eighteen years of age and prove his ability to speak Portuguese. He
must demonstrate that he earns sufficient income for himself and his
family. He must be of good character and possess those qualities necessary for the exercise of the public and private rights of the Portuguese
citizen. He must not have evaded military service or have been declared a deserter. The candidate submits his application to the local
administrative authorities who, after reviewing the case, decide
whether to issue the proper identification card. Should his petition be
refused, the African may appeal directly to the district governor. The
wife and children, legitimate or illegitimate, of the *assimilado* may
acquire citizenship if they speak Portuguese and demonstrate their
good character and the qualities necessary to exercise the right of
Portuguese citizenship. These formalities may be waived and the
bilhete de identidade issued to any African who proves that he has
exercised a public charge, that he is employed in the colonial administrative corps, that he has a secondary-school education, that he is a
licensed merchant, a partner in a business firm, or the proprietor of
an industrial establishment.[6] The 1950 census in Angola recorded
30,089 *assimilados* out of a population of 4,000,000 people, and Moçambique's population of 5,733,000 contained a mere 4,353 assimilated
Africans. (A more recent — and very questionable — figure puts the
total of Moçambique's *assimilados* at about 30,000.) Both provinces
had about 25,000 mulattoes listed in the civilized segment of the
population. In neither province has the number of *assimilados* shown
any great increase in recent years.

A system as selective as assimilation, which in a period of twenty-
five years has affected the legal status of less than one half of one per
cent of the African population, has little to recommend it as an instrument of native policy — unless the purpose of the policy is to
maintain the degraded status of the greater part of the population.
Still less is it an effective weapon against the increasing foreign criticism of Portuguese activity in Africa. The division of the colonial
population into the categories of *indígena* and *não-indígena* gives an
altogether too accurate appearance of cultural racism and inequality.
Also, Portuguese authorities seem to be reaching the conclusion, reluctantly perhaps, that assimilation, with its attendant obligations and
doubtful advantages, is not a sufficient stimulation for the African, a

number of whom, although qualified, do not apply for the *bilhete*.

Straws in the wind, certain small changes in official pronouncements and attitudes, reveal that Portugal's policy may be taking another direction. Although government officials still warn of a premature total assimilation of Angola and Moçambique with the metropolis and re-emphasize that the work of civilizing a backward people to bring them to spiritual and political maturity must be a slow and studied procedure, there are signs that the abhorred nineteenth-century ideal of uniform assimilation may become a contemporary reality and that within the foreseeable future the African provinces will achieve the same status as Goa, the Cape Verdes, and Macao in the Lusitanian community. Such a decision will not necessarily mean that the government's program of spiritual assimilation has been accomplished. It will mean only that the government is aware that it cannot wait centuries for the complete success of its present policies and has chosen to strengthen its argument that Angola and Moçambique are integral parts of Portugal by abolishing those legal distinctions which clearly argue the contrary.

The first and most obvious step in this transformation was the change in terminology from colonies to overseas provinces. Other indications include discussions on the possibility of transferring certain authorities from the Overseas Ministry to other ministries (in 1949 supervision of the armed forces in the colonies was transferred from the Colonial to the War Ministry) and the tightening of economic ties between the provinces and the metropolis. The Organic Law of 1955 provides for the possible establishment in circumscriptions with a large number of "civilized," not assimilated, Africans of a municipal council, similar to that of the *concelho*, to assist and consult with the administrator; this may be considered a preparation for a semblance of local government by Africans. The Native Statute of 1954 for Guinea, Angola, and Moçambique is less doctrinaire than previous legislation of its kind. The token powers of the village chief are slightly increased. The definition of the *indígena* is not so precise, perhaps thus anticipating a more comprehensive inclusion of the African into overseas Portuguese society. In dealing with African customs, the *administrador* is cautioned to harmonize these as expeditiously as possible with the principles of Portuguese law. Marcelo Caetano has suggested that the classifications of *indígena* and *não-indígena* are too rigid to conform with the social realities of Angola and Moçambique and that the time has come when a reclassification, with appropriate legislation, is needed. Between the extremes of the assimilated African and the primitive villagers, he sees two distinct groupings of the African population: those who have not yet abandoned their tribal customs but who have begun to come under the influence of European civilization, and those who have abandoned their tribal ways but who, although having acquired a veneer of civilization, are not yet sufficiently Portuguese to become legally assimilated.[7] Finally, in debates in the National Assembly on colonial legislation, some deputies have held that the provisions of the Portuguese Constitution on citizenship should apply to a larger portion of the overseas population and that the distinction between natives and nonnatives should be reduced so as to extend to the former the rights of Portuguese citizenship.[8] In the one-party parliament of Portugal such remarks are seldom made at random and usually represent some tentative aspect of official thinking. But the practical gain the African may anticipate from such changes is negligible.

There are two closely related aspects of Portuguese colonialism in Africa, mentioned before, that have created more favorable conditions for cultural assimilation than may be found in any other part of Africa, including the French territories. These are miscegenation and a relative lack of a color bar. Although successive generations of colonial authorities have lamented the lawless ways of some mulattoes in Angola and Moçambique, calling them a threat to Portuguese sovereignty, there is a stronger element of truth in the words of an Angola governor that "these *mestiços* have been our best auxiliaries in the penetration of the territory." [9] Mulattoes in both provinces have held, and hold today, responsible positions in the colonial administrative and business world. Their numbers are probably much greater than the 1950 census figure of 25,000 in each colony. By law children with one Portuguese parent — who is willing to recognize them — are Portuguese citizens. Although Eduardo de Azevedo has recently expressed concern over the disturbing social condition created in Luanda by the growing number of fatherless mulatto children ("In the midst of the Negroes I notice many mulatto youngsters — boys and girls — children of a Negro woman and a white father. A casual white father who abandons them to a life in the native hovels with the future consequence that they will consider themselves victims of society and rebel against it"),[10] there is equal evidence that the parental love of the Portuguese, which Livingstone found so attractive, is still a predominant characteristic of many mixed unions. The children are accepted, brought up, and educated in the Portuguese manner and take their place without discrimination in Portuguese society. At the same time, however, the New State exercises an informal control over the political ambitions, whatever they might be, of the *mestiço* and he frequently finds that the higher administrative offices are beyond his attainment.[11]

The greatest source of Portuguese pride in Africa is a generally acknowledged lack of color consciousness. When in all other points of comparison with neighboring colonies the Portuguese are found wanting, they assert their traditional acceptance of the Negro as a fellow human. "Contrary to what happens with other nations who possess territories overseas, we do not practice segregation, nor is the establishment of color barriers consistent with our natural way of being." [12] Manifestations of racial discrimination — toward foreign visitors — at hotels and restaurants in Lourenço Marques have drawn rebuke and even apologies from the Portuguese administration and press.[13] For many travelers, especially those who enter Angola or Moçambique after a visit to other parts of Africa, a striking feature of the provinces is the lack of racial tension.[14]

For centuries the same racial tolerance prevailing in Portugal [15] has prevailed equally in Africa, and the Portuguese may justifiably claim, in spite of their slaving practices, that in the past as well as in the present their social attitude toward the African has been marked by an easy-going tolerance and some sense of human equality. But in the last half-century another attitude, partly originating in the inegalitarian concepts of the generation of 1895, has become increasingly apparent in Portuguese Africa; it has become especially more pervasive in the last twenty years. Incidents in Beira and Lourenço Marques, which the Portuguese explain away as the influence of British residents and the great number of tourists from the Union and the Rhodesias, are no longer isolated cases. Nor may the use of white waiters and maids in Luanda's better hotels (leading hotels in Beira and Lourenço Marques employ African waiters), white taxicab drivers in all parts of Angola and Moçambique, and sharp discrimination in public transportation be attributed solely to economic factors.

What is happening in Portuguese Africa is that the careful distinction between racial equality and cultural inequality cannot be maintained once the relatively large number of white immigrants has begun to make its presence felt. It is a logical human step, even in Portuguese colonies, to proceed from laws which distinguish between natives and nonnatives, especially when the second category is made up mostly of Europeans, to racial distinctions between black and white. It is likewise logical in a colonial society in which the white population subjects the African to a growing economic repression for the European to justify his position by the color of his skin. Signs on the doors of Angolan restaurants reading "Right of Admission Reserved" are not accidental phenomena any more than are the creation of almost exclusively white towns and colonization projects in the interior. They signify more than a legal distinction between a civilized man and an uncivilized one; they reflect a racist tendency intruding into the society of Angola and Moçambique.

The provinces are still free from the extreme racial prejudices which dominate life and thought in parts of the Union of South Africa. In cities and towns national schools accept black and white students — if there is space available for the African pupil. Municipal hospitals, on the other hand, have Negro and white wards. In a few provincial towns, principally Luanda, the border between the Portuguese and African sections is sometimes blurred — although the scene beyond the border in the African section is one of filth and poverty. But the mounting color consciousness in both provinces has became a matter of concern for thoughtful Portuguese, who take fierce pride in their country's racial tolerance,[16] and some pessimistically foresee the day when Angola and Moçambique may no longer be recognized as the most racially tolerant areas of Africa.

Do miscegenation and a professed lack of color prejudice provide a sufficient basis for an African policy in the middle of the twentieth century? Can these two forces alone create the conditions for the assimilation of the African into the Portuguese world? Can they compensate for the lack of education, the inadequate economic opportunities for the African, forced labor, a police-state paternalism? In the past the Portuguese attitude toward the African has been unquestionably responsible in part for whatever success Portugal has enjoyed in Angola and Moçambique. Portuguese tolerance and the ignorance in which the African has been plunged for centuries probably account for the comparative absence of racial tension in both provinces and permit the Portuguese to boast that they have no native problems. But what of the future? Will the African be content simply to furnish labor to the European and to be suppressed by an increasing white population? Will the black and white worlds in Portuguese Africa continue to live and work in harmony, as many Portuguese rhapsodists claim?

From their public utterances and writings it would seem that Portuguese officials and others of their conviction resolutely refuse to admit any other possibility. Freyre writes that whenever the Cardinal of Moçambique visits those Africans who have been subject to Portuguese influence, he is received with the greatest naturalness by people who call themselves Portuguese and Roman Catholics, and Eduardo de Azevedo says that "the Negroes will fight to the last drop of blood for the liberty of being Portuguese, for the greatest pride of the Negro is to belong to a country of men who are brothers." [17] And there is the longer, half practical, half mystical, view of Nunes de Oliveira, a high inspector in the Portuguese colonial service, who sees the work in Africa as just beginning.

The object and not the agent of civilizing action, the Negro must not be regarded by the European as a dreaded or troublesome rival. Moreover, his rivalry is not to be feared but desired. Only when the Negro is able to dispute with the European for those positions which the latter now reserves for himself or shares with the Asian, will we be able to consider him sufficiently evolved . . . and only then will we have the right to proclaim that it was not in vain that we occupied a large part of the African continent. It would be contradictory and absurd to want to civilize the native and flee at the same time from the fatal consequences of this civilization.

When that day, which still can only vaguely be made out in the very distant future, arrives, the ideas of the Negro will be our own ideas, his beliefs, ours . . . and the knowledge of this union will certainly be stronger and deeper than the antagonisms and susceptibilities provoked by the superficial gradations in the color of the skin.[18]

To assimilate the African population of Angola and Moçambique and to raise its standard of living to a level where the process will succeed in terms of the largest number of the provinces' inhabitants, the Portuguese government has evolved a series of programs designed to affect every aspect of African life. To a large extent these programs are a continuation and intensification of previous efforts; they demonstrate again the difficulty Portugal has always had in obtaining positive material results from her specific policies in Africa.

The judicial system established for the African is one of the least well defined aspects of Portugal's native policy. Although various decrees determine the competence of colonial courts and the judicial powers of the magistrates and the administrators, the relation between Portuguese law, which is used throughout the provinces, and African customs is indeterminate. The absence of native legal codes and even of satisfactory compilations of customary law may be more than oversight or the government's inability to collect and codify, at least superficially, the tribal usages of the most important areas of the two provinces. Early in the 1930's the hope was expressed that such a compilation would be made in order to assist administrators and chiefs of post in their duties, but although isolated tentative studies like José

Gonçalves Cota's *Projecto definitivo do código penal dos indígenas da colónia de Moçambique acompanhado de um relatório e de um estudo sobre direito criminal indígena* (Lourenço Marques, 1946) have appeared, no really comprehensive work has been done. It is possible that in the meantime the Portuguese overseas administration has found the vacuum convenient both for the extension of Portuguese authority into African life and for the assimilation of the African, and has no real intention of pursuing the project.

The only law officially recognized in Angola and Moçambique is Portuguese common law, the civil and criminal codes of the metropolis. Nevertheless, the prevailing legal situation for the African is ambiguous, for successive statutes have defined the African as "an individual of the Negro race . . . who still is not sufficiently enlightened and does not possess the individual and social customs to permit the integral application of the public and private rights of the Portuguese citizen" and have stated that "except where the law disposes otherwise, the *indígenas* are ruled by the uses and customs of their respective societies." [19] The administration has sought to reconcile this apparent incongruity by an informal arrangement. Since there are no native courts, civil cases involving *indígenas* are generally heard by an administrator or chief of post acting as justice of the peace. In his mediations he is assisted by two African advisers, either chiefs or other men versed in the traditions of the region, who inform him of local customs, and on the basis of this information he attempts to make a judgment consistent with tribal law and Portuguese policy. No lawyers may represent the contestants. Although such a procedure is in keeping with Portugal's paternalistic philosophies in her conduct of African affairs, it raises serious problems besides the denial of legal counsel, since so much depends on the experience and understanding of the official and since there are many complex tribal issues for which such a system cannot provide any satisfactory form of adjudication.

In civil cases involving an *indígena* and a *não-indígena* Portuguese common law is applied, unless there exist special circumstances, and Portuguese law applies in all criminal cases. Explaining the latter point, Silva Cunha observes that "it is necessary to protect the colonists and the natives against mutual violence and depredations, and it is evident that this protection is not contained in native traditional law. Nor can one forget that from contact with colonizers results the transformation of the moral concepts of the native and that the Criminal Code, closely linked to morality, should accompany this evolution." [20]

Colonial courts fall into two categories: ordinary courts, which are presided over by the administrative official in most native cases, and special courts, presided over by judges, which consider more serious cases and act as courts of appeal. Final appeal must be made to the High Court in Lisbon.

There is no African penal code for Angola and Moçambique, and the Portuguese code, with local modifications, applies for Africans sentenced under the criminal code. In passing sentence the judge is instructed to take into consideration the influence that tribal customs may have had on the African. This modified Portuguese code provides for reparations to be made for damage done, a graduated system of punishment conforming with the seriousness of the crime, and the use of the African prisoner on provincial work projects. Minor crimes may be punished by correctional labor in the region and major crimes by assignment to public-work details in another part of the province. The indiscriminate application of the metropolitan criminal and penal codes in Africa has been criticized with surprising sharpness by Silva Cunha, who points out that nothing is more dangerous than to apply to a people of a different culture a legal system conceived for Europe; he urges that a profound revision of the system be made to serve the practical realities of African life.[21]

There is some evidence that the Colonial Ministry is aware of the problems and confusions growing out of the disparity between native traditions and Portuguese law, but there is little evidence that any serious changes are contemplated. In the preamble to a decree of 1954, relevant to the organization of municipal courts in Angola and Moçambique, the makeshift position of the government on an African juridical regime may be found.

The peculiar circumstances of the overseas provinces do not permit, or even recommend, that the administration of justice be handled exclusively by regular magistrates. On the one hand, it is necessary to give special heed to native questions, submitted for the most part to the traditional laws of the *indígenas*, the knowledge of which implies an intimacy, as profound as possible, with local life. Only the direct representative of the Administration, protector of the natives and constant agent of Portuguese culture, is the appropriate person to resolve, in principle, native questions, using the prestige of his authority, which thus appears indivisible, to obtain the peaceful fufillment of all decisions.

And even when problems arising from the conflict between Portuguese law and native law demand adherence to the former and justify in such a case the intervention of common tribunals [*i.e.*, a Portuguese court] the process must be kept uniform, as simple as possible, because the obligation to protect the native justifies the elimination of complex legal processes, since these would be incomprehensible to the *indígena* . . .

On the other hand, the judicial occupation of the whole territory cannot prescind the intervention of the administrators in the preparation and judgment of questions completely subject to common law. Since, however, the complexity and multiplicity of tasks assigned to the administrators do not permit them to handle involved judicial problems, which only specialists can solve, the system has been evolved of assigning to his competence only the most simple and urgent cases; otherwise, he acts as a delegate of the common court, receiving for each case the orientation necessary. It is believed that in this manner the judicial occupation of the territory and the respect for legality will be simultaneously assured.[22]

The loosely defined legal apparatus in the provinces does not imply a corresponding lack of Portuguese control over the African population. Through an administrative system which penetrates into almost every African village, a series of native labor laws, and the necessity for the male *indígena* to possess a *caderneta* (an identification card and pass-book), Portugal maintains a sufficiently close surveillance over the African population in Angola and Moçambique to have avoided in recent years disturbing incidents like those that crop up from time to time in other European colonies (the Portuguese claim that this tranquillity is the result of the more idealized aspects of their policy). But this control is not the police-state oppression existing in the Union of South Africa, and the total police force in Portuguese Africa is considerably less than in the metropolis.

The presence of African informants, sepoys (the sepoy, generally chosen from the ranks of African soldiers, is an indispensable element in policing the colonies), and reliable chiefs in the midst of the African population have helped contain dissatisfaction and nascent sentiments of Africanism. Censorship, border control, ruthless police action, and a supervised educational system have prevented the formation of an effective leadership capable of arousing resistance to the Portuguese administration. Literature and phonograph records — the latter used to circumvent the high illiteracy rate in the provinces — of suspicious nature are confiscated, and the amount of political literature circulating in Angola and Moçambique is small. It is not unknown for Africans educated in Portugal to be kept from returning home. Africans suspected of agitation, including those who have made unhealthy associations in the Congo or the Rhodesias, are quickly jailed, frequently beaten, and usually sent to a penal camp or exiled to a remote point in the colonies, in Angola to the desert-bound fishing town of Bahia dos Tigres. A mild disturbance in Lourenço Marques in 1948 was the last outward sign of serious trouble; about two hundred people were arrested, the majority, including one chief, apparently being sent off to the island of São Tomé.[23] A more recent manifestation of dissatisfaction among the Moslem communities of northern Moçambique — where Pan-Arab pamphlets and portraits of Nasser have circulated — has been summarily dealt with.

Lesser offenses of nonpolitical nature are punished more casually, either through correctional labor or corporal punishment or a strong mixture of both. In keeping with the paternalistic concept of the African, Portuguese administrators rely on corporal punishment. I have been seriously told by a high Angolan official that "we Portuguese regard the native as a child and like good parents we have to spank him from time to time." Other residents of the provinces speak less paternally of the *chicote*, a hide whip, and the *palmatória*, a wooden paddle with holes in the striking surface, used on the open palm of the offender, often a runaway worker or an African accused of insubordination to his white employer. Police beatings of women and children are not unknown in Angola and Moçambique. Such excesses have been common Portuguese practice in Africa for centuries; it remained only for the New State to bring a police-state efficiency to an informal apparatus of terror.

The most effective control over the African is established through the *caderneta*, a booklet which contains the tax record and labor record of the African male as well as the names of his wife, or wives, and children — who are responsible for paying the tax in the event of his disappearance — and photographs and fingerprint identification. The bearer must show his *caderneta* on demand to officials and must have it properly visaed before he moves from one part of the province to another. Since each African male is subject to an annual tax (there are exceptions such as chiefs, soldiers, traders, pupils, the aged, and administrative officials) of up to ten dollars a year, depending on the region where the taxpayer lives,[24] and since he must show evidence of having satisfied Portuguese labor requirements, through the *caderneta* the African is kept in close contact with the administration. Should he lose his papers or should they fail to be in order, the African may suffer unpleasant consequences, jail or correctional labor. The repressions associated with the *caderneta* have in the recent past been one of the causes of a considerable emigration of Africans from the border regions of Angola and Moçambique into neighboring territories.

Any organization of Africans is regarded with disfavor by the colonial administration, although there do exist in Angola and Moçambique government-sponsored African societies and co-operatives.

From time to time there spring up in different parts of the provinces religious sects which the Portuguese regard as inflammatory and quickly suppress, scattering their leaders. Even the officially approved Liga Africana [25] has recently had a difficult time in Angola for allegedly trying to make representations to the United Nations. The government has also given its support and guidance to the more tractable Associação dos Naturais, which includes both Portuguese and *mestiços* among its members. These organizations are primarily social clubs of limited membership. The one loud voice of the almost nonexistent Portuguese African press, *O brado africano* ("The African Cry"), a Lourenço Marques newspaper, has been softened to a respectable whisper. But before the Salazar government got around to extending its censorship to an insignificant Moçambique journal, *O brado africano* published in 1932 a ringing editorial, entitled "Enough," which ran contrary to all the traditional proclamations of the African's satisfaction with Portuguese rule.

We are fed to the teeth.

Fed up with supporting you, with suffering the terrible consequences of your follies, your demands, with the squandering misuse of your authority.

We can no longer stand the pernicious effects of your political and administrative decisions.

We are no longer willing to make greater and greater useless sacrifices . . .

Enough . . .

We want you to manifest, not by laws and decrees, but by deeds, your elementary obligations . . .

We want to be treated as you treat yourselves.

We do not want the comforts with which you have surrounded yourselves at the cost of our sweat . . .

We do not want your refined education . . . since we do not want a life dominated by the idea of robbing our fellow men . . .

We prefer our savage state, which fills your mouths and your pockets.

But we do want something . . .

We want bread, we want light.

We don't want to pay, but to receive . . .

We don't want to pay for services which are of no use to us . . . for institutions whose benefits we never feel . . .

We no longer want to suffer the bottomless pit of your excellent colonial administration!

We want of you a more humane policy . . .

We repeat that we don't want hunger, nor thirst, nor disease, nor discriminatory laws founded on the difference of color.

We have the scalpel ready.
We shall dissect your work . . .
We are daring, the result of ignorance.
We shall learn how to use the scalpel . . .
The gangrene you spread will infect us and later we will not have the strength to act. Now we do . . . It is the instinct for self-preservation. We are beasts of burden and like them we possess it . . .
Enough, gentlemen. Change your ways. There still is time.[26]

Scenes of potential unrest are the growing urban centers in Angola and Moçambique where a rapid influx of African villagers has already begun to create considerable problems for the colonial administration. The transition of these cities from provincial or district capitals and outposts of commerce to modern cosmopolitan centers of provincial government and international trade has been attended in the last several decades by the same social ills afflicting Johannesburg, Nairobi, and Lagos. An increasing African population, brought to the cities as labor or drawn by the color and the economic promise they seem to offer, has resulted in the creation of ugly swollen slums in Luanda and Lobito and, to a lesser extent, in Lourenço Marques and Beira. The populations of these cities have doubled in the last twenty years. In the *senzalas*, or African sections, thousands of rootless Africans exist in poverty and filth, suffering an absolute lack of sanitation and, in many areas, even of water. Juvenile delinquency, a growing crime rate, drunkenness,[27] are only a few of the by-products of the social ferment. Foreign criticism of these slums ("At Lobito the African quarter lies in simmering confusion. . . Most of its huts and hovels are made of straw and mud, and none of its inhabitants can be said to enjoy anything in the nature of 'security of tenure'. . . All these people [20,000] take their fresh water from five water-points with three taps each")[28] is more than matched by the concern of some Portuguese. Azevedo refers to the naked children of the Luanda senzala, "the faces and houses corroded by misery." Everything — food, transportation, water — is a struggle for the African. "It is impossible to be objective about the lives these people live, impossible to forget their human condition, impossible to consider this picture of desperate misery picturesque." [29]
To the present each provincial government has been more concerned with imposing its authority over these foci of unrest than it has with elementary facilities or housing. Infirmaries and schools are inadequate, and housing developments for the African have not been pushed with the same energy as have those for the white population. No African housing project can hope to keep pace with the popula-

tional growth, but the seeming reluctance of authorities in Portugal and in Africa to deal with the situation realistically has been a discouragement to both African and Portuguese residents of cities like Luanda and Lobito. They feel that these slum conditions will grow worse and inevitably result in bitter resentments against the European population.

The problems of rural Portuguese Africa have not been as pressing as those of the city, although their eventual importance to the development and stability of the two colonies may be greater. The government's land policies seem, on the whole, to be equitable. A series of decrees from 1900 have provided that large sections of Portuguese Africa will remain available to the African population. In 1901 all land not privately owned was declared the property of the state. Subsequent decrees have reserved large areas for the exclusive use of the African, and these may not be taken away. Outside of these reserved lands the African may occupy vacant land, from which he may be removed only if he is compensated and granted an equal tract of land elsewhere, usually in the reserves. If the African has chosen to be governed by Portuguese common law, he may acquire real rights in terms of inheritance and sale over the land he has occupied; otherwise he may have no individual rights to it. A general statement on the African land policy is Article 38 of the 1955 Native Statute for Angola and Moçambique. "Natives who live in tribal organizations are guaranteed, in conjunction, the use and development, in the traditional manner, of lands necessary for their villages, their crops, and for the pasture of their cattle." The actual rights of the African villagers remain vague, however, as do the location and extent of the native reserves. Points of dispute between Portuguese colonizers and Africans have up to now been comparatively few, although some traditionally African land has been absorbed by European coffee *fazendas* in northeast Angola, and some Africans have been resettled in Moçambique to make room for sugar plantations. Nevertheless, government policy, flexible though it seems to be, has drawn criticism from Portuguese colonists in Africa. "One can neither understand nor justify the principle by which the best and even the largest areas of land in Moçambique have been reserved for the natives and closed to occupation and exploitation by European capital. . . The native, with an ingratitude that is only matched by his condemnable ignorance, does not have the slightest interest in the soil, this sacred soil which prodigally offers him everything he needs in order to live. . . He exploits it as long as it produces, and when it doesn't produce . . . he moves off with his family to another area." [30]

The long view of New State ideology sees the ultimate creation of a modern peasant society — held to be an expression of social concepts developed in Latin communities under Catholic influences — in Angola and Moçambique. Salazar believes that to attempt to go in a single step from a tribal way of life to a modern industrial society (even should conditions permit in Portuguese Africa a transition which has not yet taken place in continental Portugal) is sociological madness. Thus an agrarian society is to be achieved through the settlement of Portuguese peasants in government colonization projects, in some of which the African is to participate, and through the establishment of African agricultural colonies, under the direction of Portuguese administrative and technical authorities, which will create the conditions favorable for the economic and spiritual assimilation of the African. What this policy, still in its formative stage, really envisions is the creation of a semiliterate population of Africans and Portuguese holding rural Portuguese values, hard working, dedicated to the land, and politically conservative. Presumably such a society would absorb or divert the energies of the emergent African and at the same time would not be a threat to the large European-owned estates, which are the main economic support of both provinces.

One of the earliest projects of the Salazar government was the formation of new villages to draw the African out of his isolation into a peripheral contact with the Portuguese world. These village settlements, with their schools, infirmaries, and co-operative farm services, were also intended to make the African more available for labor, and the few steps taken toward their establishment in the 1930's were failures, partly because the African preferred his isolated village to the disadvantages of being forced to work.[31] But the government did not forget its native colonization schemes. Its concern was given urgency by the continuing migration of Portuguese Africans to the Belgian Congo and the Rhodesias, which offered them a higher standard of living. In 1940 the Colonial Ministry drew up a draft for the organization of the indigenous populations. African villages of at least twenty families were planned, each with common ground and farm buildings. Places in these villages were to be allotted to healthy males, twenty-five to forty years of age, preferably those who had military service or had worked on large agricultural concerns. The colonial administration and the Catholic missions were to work together for the effective management of the villages' social, spiritual, and educational needs. Medical and technical assistance was planned;

taxes were to be waived the first year of occupancy; and the self-supporting African would be exempt from the labor draft.[32] Colonial governors were instructed to consider the most appropriate ways of administering and nationalizing these villages.

After twenty years of such attempts and studies, the New State began to take action in the early 1950's — at about the same time the white colonization projects took definite shape — on the African *colonatos*. At Inhamissa, in Moçambique's Gaza district, an elaborate drainage project is under development to render the fertile lands in the Limpopo delta useful for native agriculture, principally the production of rice. Still in its early stage, the Inhamissa scheme foresees the re-settlement of thousands of African families in the area.[33] Further up the Limpopo, at Guíja, a combination European-African *colonato* is under construction in connection with a dam across the Limpopo and an extensive irrigation system. One of the most publicized of the New State's African enterprises, the Limpopo colony is still mainly a European settlement project. The neat little village in 1956 was inhabited by Portuguese immigrants, the Africans living, reportedly because they preferred to, in thatched huts on the margin of the farming land. Ultimately the colony will contain three thousand Portuguese colonists and two thousand Africans. Each Portuguese family receives four hectares of tillable land and twenty-five for grazing; each African, two and twelve hectares.

In Angola a similar project in the southern part of the province, near the Cunene River, is being pushed to provide for the settlement of six thousand Portuguese families and three thousand African families. At Caconda the nuclei of eight African settlements — containing some forty small villages — have been established. By the end of 1957, about four thousand Africans, that is, 750 families, lived, according to official figures, on the Caconda *colonato*. The government prepared the land (over 600,000 acres have reportedly been set aside), built an irrigation system, and supplied the necessary seeds. Strictly administered by an agricultural engineer and a director, Caconda is a model paternalistic society in which man, woman, and child are equally engaged in work. Each village has its own farm buildings and implements. Production goals are assigned each family, and those who do not achieve them because of indolence are removed from the colony.[34] Whether this latter-day re-creation of the Jesuit work farms will prove successful in the over-all program of African integration cannot yet be known, but first official Portuguese accounts of the work at Caconda are enthusiastic. Northeast of Luanda at Damba, Bembe, and Loge three African co-operative colonies are emerging and now contain about one thousand families engaged in the growing of rice, beans, and coffee.

The number of Africans who live or who will live in these new villages and *colonatos* in Angola and Moçambique is a very small part of the total population. Experimental projects like those at Inhamissa and Caconda are expensive. Even should they prove successful beyond the wildest Portuguese dreams, similar settlements cannot be indiscriminately set up throughout the interior. The Colonial Ministry is aware of these difficulties, but speaks hopefully of using to good advantage the experience gained at the model projects to establish other more modest African villages and colonies.

Hand in hand with the government's efforts to improve the material life of the African is the Portuguese missionary program to improve his spiritual and intellectual life. Reaffirming the traditional role of the Catholic Church in Angola and Moçambique in bringing civilization to the African, Article 140 of the Portuguese Constitution states that "Portuguese Catholic missions overseas and those establishments preparing personnel for that service . . . shall be protected and aided by the State as institutions of instruction and assistance and instruments of civilization." This is a restatement of the government's position as elaborated in the Colonial Act. Thus once again, after the Liberal interlude in the nineteenth century and the brief period from 1911 to 1919, when the Republic withdrew subsidies and suppressed Portuguese Catholic missions, the function of the Church "to Christianize and educate, to nationalize and civilize" is officially recognized. The present Catholic missionary program in Angola and Moçambique is governed by appropriate provisions of the Constitution, the Missionary Accord of 1940 (which develops the principles contained in the Concordat of May 7, 1940, between the Vatican and the Portuguese government), and the Missionary Statute of 1941. As a result of the agreement of 1940, property confiscated from the Church by the Republic was returned wherever possible.

The various provisions of this legislation define the organization and purpose of the Catholic missions. The overseas provinces are divided into dioceses and missionary circumscriptions corresponding as closely as possible to the administrative divisions. At the present time Angola has five dioceses (the archdiocese of Luanda, and the dioceses of Malange, Nova Lisboa, Silva Porto, and Sá da Bandeira) and Moçambique four (the archdiocese of Lourenço Marques, and the dioceses of Beira, Quelimane, and Nampula). Mission work in the field is subsidized by the governments of the respective provinces, while missionary institutes in Portugal are subsidized by the metropolitan government. In principle missionary personnel must be of Portuguese nationality, but in cases of necessity — and the necessity exists in both provinces, for the lack of missionary inclination continues in Portugal — foreign missionaries may be called into service under three conditions: the express agreement of the Holy See and the Portuguese government; the foreign missionary's renunciation of the laws of his own country and submission to Portuguese law; and proof of the missionary's ability to speak and write the Portuguese language correctly. All Catholic missionaries, while not public functionaries, are held to be personnel "in the special service of national and civilizing utility."

Among the activities specified by the Missionary Statute of 1941 as pertaining to the Church's work are "the founding and directing of schools for European and African students, elementary, secondary, and professional schools, seminaries, catechism schools, as well as infirmaries and hospitals." The Catholic missions have been entrusted by the government with much of the educational program designed primarily for African students in Moçambique and Angola; this service is largely underwritten by the Portuguese government. Preparation of African teaching personnel is carried out in missionary normal schools designated by the provincial prelate.

Both Angola and Moçambique today have over one hundred mission and parish churches served by secular priests and fathers of various religious orders, including the Franciscans, Dominicans, Benedictines, Lazarists, and those of the Holy Ghost Congregation. They are assisted in their labors by sisters from different orders. In 1957 the number of priests in Angola was 387 and in Moçambique, 310. The Catholic population of the two colonies, according to the 1950 census, did not show the same equal proportion: 1,500,000 in Angola (possibly an exaggerated figure) and 210,000 in Moçambique.[35]

A strong antiforeign sentiment still exists against the Protestant missions. While it would be incorrect to say that the various Protestant missions are permitted by the New State to remain in Portuguese Africa by sufferance, one can hardly say that they are warmly welcomed. Visa control, expulsion, and continuing petty annoyances characterize the official reaction to their presence. Much depends on local conditions, and in recent years the Protestants in Angola have fared better than their co-religionists in Moçambique, who in the 1950's are having a difficult time. But the Protestants are not without Portuguese defenders. "In the Protestant missions . . . a meritorious

hospital work goes on, directed by doctors of great competence. . .
The Protestant missions have been, and are still today, accused of
practising denationalization among the natives over whom they exert
religious influence. If this danger existed . . . there are no present
reasons to suspect that it has continued." [36]

During the years of the present Portuguese government the Protestant missionary program in the two provinces has been mainly one
of consolidation in Angola and of survival in Moçambique. Of the
forty-eight mission stations in Angola, for example, only eight were
established between 1930 and 1937 and none between 1937 and 1950.
In Angola, however, the Methodist Board's work in the vicinity of
Malange and the joint American-Canadian Board's work at Dondi
have made striking contributions in the medical and educational
fields. Over 300 Protestant missionaries serve in Angola and about
200 in Moçambique. The 1950 census showed 540,000 Protestants, including about 2,000 Europeans, 800 mestiços, and 6,000 assimilados,
in Angola, and about 60,000 Protestants in Moçambique.

Education in the African provinces, in which the Catholic and
Protestant missions have an important role, seems to be distinguished,
insofar as the African is concerned, by three aspects: the official position of the government that education is an indispensable instrument
for promoting African assimilation; the perhaps unconscious sentiment that education for the mass of the African population represents
an implicit threat to Portuguese interests; and the inability of both
church and state to create an educational system that will serve more
than a small percentage of the inhabitants of Angola and Moçambique.

Portuguese educational policy is founded in the New State's
mystique of Lusitanian identity. The duplication in Angola and
Moçambique of the metropolitan primary and secondary school system is one manfestation of this concept. Like their fellow students
in Portugal, European and African pupils in primary schools are
introduced at an early age to the glories of the maritime discoveries,
the miracles of Our Lady of Fatima, and the Salazarian philosophy
of faith, toil, and family. Students in the rudimentary schools, which
are almost exclusively for the African youth, usually learn the elements of the Portuguese language and history as well as a few funda-
mentals of agriculture and hygiene.[37] In this introduction to European
learning, colonial policy sees one of the formative elements in the
African's preparation for assimilation. Through further education

and contact with civilization these rough beginnings are to be shaped
and developed into traditional Portuguese values. There is no place
in this policy for African traditions and institutions — a field of study
apparently reserved for Portuguese anthropologists. To the contrary,
through the use of the Portuguese language and the emphasis on
Portuguese ways, every attempt is made to bring the African to break
with his tribal world.

Within the overseas educational system there are various levels
and types of instruction. In addition to the rudimentary, primary,
and secondary courses, both the state and the missions offer technical
or professional instruction on the primary and secondary levels. In
urban areas and in those parts of the provinces where there is a
substantial civilized population, a four-year course of instruction,
ensino primário elementar e complementar, is offered by government,
private, and a few mission schools — although the mission schools
are not primarily for the "civilized" population. In predominantly
indigenous areas, the Catholic missions, or where this is not possible,
Protestant missions or the government, offer *ensino primário rudimentar* (called *ensino de adaptação* since 1956) to African children;
this provides a very elementary program of instruction of from three
to five years. On the same primary school level, the government and
the Catholic Church have established arts and crafts schools, *ensino
primário professional*.

Secondary education, open on the basis of state examinations to
those students who have completed the *ensino primário elementar*,
is offered by the few *liceus* in the provinces. An African graduate of
the more elementary *ensino primário rudimentar* may qualify by com-
pleting his primary instruction in the primary-elementary school and
then passing the entrance examination. There are five *liceus*, or seven-
year high schools, in Angola, two at Luanda, and one each at Sá da
Bandeira, Benguela, and Nova Lisboa; and two in Moçambique, at
Lourenço Marques and Beira. The course of studies in the *liceus* may
lead to entrance into Portuguese or foreign universities. There are
also private secondary schools in both provinces as well as government and private technical schools on a secondary-school level. There
are several normal schools whose purpose is to prepare African students to be teachers in the rudimentary schools in the interior.

The accompanying table shows the state of education in Portuguese Africa in 1954.

The difficulties which the African student must surmount in the
overseas educational system are many and account in part for the
illiteracy rate of 99 per cent among the African population in 1950

NUMBER OF SCHOOLS, TEACHERS, AND STUDENTS
IN MOÇAMBIQUE AND ANGOLA, 1954

	Moçambique			Angola		
	Schools	Teachers	Students	Schools	Teachers	Students
Primary						
Government	71	208	7,634	139	293	10,979
Catholic	55	147	5,920	24 ⎫		
Protestant	2	2	802	42 ⎬	280[b]	6,454[b]
Private	27	31	1,161	132 ⎭		
Rudimentary						
Government	35	35	3,835	—	—	—
Catholic	1,356	1,543	172,313	784	800	24,618[c]
Protestant	26	40	6,654	135	341	10,743[c]
Private	2	2	290	—	—	—
Elementary professional						
Government	12	54	428	7	24	614
Catholic	51	106	2,764	—	—	—
Private	2	10	649	—	—	—
Commercial and technical						
Government	2	74	2,094	5	61	950
Private [a]	—	—	—	6	51	513
Ecclesiastical						
Catholic	8	15	125	—	—	—
High schools						
Government	1	56 ⎫		2	55	1,283
Private [a]	5	44 ⎭	956[b]	20	160	1,547
Normal schools						
Government	—	—	—	1	8	13
Catholic	4	18	341	1	11	153

Source: Based on *Anuário de ensino da província de Moçambique, 1954* (Lourenço Marques, 1955), pp. 397–433, and *Anuário estatístico da província de Angola, 1954* (Luanda, 1956), pp. 158–185.

[a] The majority of these private secondary schools are sponsored by religious organizations.

[b] The source gives no breakdown for these figures.

[c] This is the number attending at the end of the year.

(the Portuguese rate was only 23 per cent, well below continental Portugal's 40 per cent). In addition to being obliged to master a foreign tongue, he encounters age limitations, restrictive regulations, and lack of space in rural elementary schools. The maximum age limit for entrance into the *liceus* is thirteen, by which age most African students are unable to complete their elementary education. In Moçambique, government elementary schools are open only to assimilated Africans, with the result that of the 7,634 students in elementary schools there in 1954, only 322 were Africans. In most Angolan elementary schools Portuguese students are given first consideration for the limited space available. The African student finishing rudimentary schools who wishes to continue must pass an official state examination before he is allowed to enter the third year of the elmentary school, if there is an elementary school available to him.

In 1954, some 183,092 Africans were enrolled in Moçambique's rudimentary schools, but in the same year only 3,898 were admitted to the final examinations, and only 2,774 passed the examinations. In Angola, 35,361 were enrolled, but only 1,712 were admitted to the examination, of whom 959 passed. Education is a selective process for the African in Angola and Moçambique. The number of Africans in high schools is negligible, although more attend the technical schools; the elementary arts and crafts schools are primarily for African students. In 1954, of the fifty students enrolled in the Vieira Machado Agricultural School at Tchivinguiro in Angola not one was an African. Although color may play no part in the suppression of the African's educational opportunities, cultural and economic distinctions have the same prejudicial effect.

While the number of students and schools in Portuguese Africa has doubled, and in some cases tripled, in the last few years (on December 31, 1956, there were a total of 85,000 students in Angolan schools and some 284,000 in Moçambique schools, an increase of about 30 per cent over the 1954 figures), the number of Africans going beyond the first year of *ensino rudimentar* has remained small. Much of the government's expansion of educational services in the cities and towns has been able to absorb only the swelling number of white students, and education for the African remains on a catch-as-catch-can basis. The number of African teachers being trained at the Catholic mission normal schools can scarcely keep pace with a rising African birth rate. The quality and content of African instruction is, as it is designated, rudimentary, and often does not provide the basis for more advanced studies, even when the African is in a position to continue.

Not only is there no provision for popular African education in Portugal's colonial schemes, but there is no attempt to create an educated elite. In 1948 a governmental decree provided for the establishment of four training schools, two each in Angola and Moçambique, for tribal leaders. The eldest sons and daughters of chiefs were to receive five years of instruction in Portuguese, local government, administrative practices, agriculture, hygiene, treatment of tropical diseases, and road construction, after which they would return to their villages to assist in the program of assimilation. By 1956, however, these schools were not yet in operation.

Portugal's insistence that all instruction be given in Portuguese, save for the permitted use of the vernacular in religious instruction and in elementary instruction in teaching the Portuguese language to the African, has unquestionably hampered the African youth in his progress. While the Portuguese may argue that "they prefer to raise the African to their own level, rather than lower themselves to his," [38] in practice they often succeed in confusing and discouraging the African student. The necessity of using Portuguese as a language of higher instruction may not be questioned so readily, but the wisdom of basing elementary instruction on the acquisition of a foreign tongue may be seriously debated.[39]

As with the educational system, both the government and the missions collaborate on the medical and social services that are available to the African. The African's need for such assistance is as desperate as it is for education, and less adequately provided for. In the cities and larger towns, state and private hospitals serve the urban population, although they may be said to take care largely of the European residents, and great companies like Diamang, the Benguela Railway, and Sena Sugar Estates have hospitals for their employees. With few exceptions these government and company hospitals offer the most obvious examples in the African provinces of racial discrimination. Separate wards and operating rooms in the Luanda Hospital, for example, exist for European and African patients. In the interior the government has established a number of rural infirmaries, but they can only take care of minor illnesses and injuries, and have been called by some residents of the colonies as another case of "para inglês ver," "for the English to see." Small maternity hospitals are located in some circumscriptions, but they are insufficient to care for more than a very small part of the population.

Compared with past performances, the present government has made modest advances in colonial health services, although, viewed absolutely, these gains have only kept up with the rising birth rate which these services have helped bring about. A large modern leprosarium has recently been built in Angola — in a most unlikely location, near the Rhodesian frontier. Under the technical direction of the Institute of Tropical Medicine in Lisbon research in tropical diseases, notably sleeping sickness, and preventive inoculations have benefited the African. In 1954 Angola had fifty-three state-operated hospitals and fifty-five private hospitals, many of these quite small and antiquated, and sixty infirmaries. Moçambique had fifty government hospitals, thirty private ones, and eighty-two infirmaries. For Angola the *Anuário estatístico* also listed 156 government doctors (about one hundred private and missionary doctors also practice), 293 nurses for the infirmaries, 16 midwives, and an undefined 681 medical assistants. The Moçambique figures were about the same. For a population in both provinces of almost ten million people, the combined government-mission effort would seem inadequate.

The cornerstone of Portuguese native policy continues to be the African's obligation to labor. If the goal of Portuguese policy is assimilation, its achievement lies in the necessity for the African to put his services to profitable use — for the state, for private employers, for himself. For centuries labor has been the essential point of contact between the colonial administration and the African; today this relationship is complicated by economic pressures for the development of the provinces and the need for defending Portuguese policy in Africa before the world, but these complexities have not substantially altered Portugal's position, so bluntly stated sixty years ago by António Enes, that the African should be forced, by every means available, to work. In a sense, all other attempts to raise the African's cultural and economic level, to assimilate him into a single Portuguese community, whether by education, administrative tutelage, missionary work, health programs, or colonization schemes, are peripheral to this overriding obligation.

A large part of the New State's colonial legislation and philosophizing has been directed to the problem. While the brutal implications of slavery and of the forced-labor regimes of half a century ago have been softened, the attitude that produced them has changed little. Unmoved by the comments of both Portuguese citizens and foreigners, the Salazar government has followed in the path of tradition, answering all criticism with the remark that Portugal must be permitted to do things in her own way, which will eventually be acknowledged as the only way. Smarting under the memory of past humanitarian attacks and determined to keep the colonies inviolate from the attentions of world organizations, Portugal has refused to sign the Forced Labor Conventions of 1930 and 1946 or the Indigenous Workers Convention of 1936, although she did sign the Slaving Convention of 1926.[40]

The belief that the African must be obliged to work is a part of Portugal's vision of herself as a civilizing force in a primitive world inhabited by lazy children. "The blacks in Angola have to be directed and indoctrinated by Europeans . . . The Africans have not learned how to develop alone the territories they have inhabited for thousands of years, they have produced not one useful invention, made no valuable technical discovery, no conquest that has counted in the evolution of Humanity, and have done nothing that can compare to the accomplishments in the lands of Culture and Technics by the European or even by the Asian." [41] Having by implication placed Portugal in the mainstream of European culture, which historically she has been dedicated to implanting in Africa, New State colonialists further imply that this human progress has been the result of discipline and hard work and argue that the success of their country's policy in Africa rests squarely on inculcating the indigenous population with these virtues. Former Colonial Minister Vieira Machado wrote:

It is necessary to inspire in the black the idea of work and of abandoning his laziness and his depravity if we want to exercise a colonizing action to protect him.

If vagrancy and crime in whites are punished, we cannot condone it in blacks . . . If we scorn the white who lives on the work of a woman, we cannot permit the African to do the same.

If we want to civilize the native we must make him adopt as an elementary moral precept the notion that he has no right to live without working.

A productive society is based on painful hard work, obligatory even for vagrants, and we cannot permit any exception because of race.

The policy of assimilation which I conceive of must be complete. Therefore it is necessary to establish a rule of conduct for the black which exists for the white, making him acquire a sense of responsibility. It is to be an unenlightened Negrophile not to infuse the African with the absolute necessity for work.[42]

The problem facing the Colonial Ministry in 1926 — the year in which the restrictive *Regulamento de 1899* was substantially altered for the first time — and for the overseas planners in the subsequent Salazar government has been, on the one hand, how to achieve the two goals of the economic development of Angola and Moçambique and the assimilation of the African and, on the other, how to avoid the abuses associated with labor practices in the past. To a considerable extent, the issue has been academic, for the very existence of native labor codes implies a restriction of the African's freedom, and as long as colonial legislation contains provisions that the African must engage in productive work, repressive exploitation of him will ensue.

Nevertheless, the Portuguese government has attempted to curtail the most obvious injustices growing out of the use of African labor. A decree of 1926 declared that forced labor could only be used in the public interest — which included many private projects — and had to be remunerated. The Indigenous Labor Code of 1928 defined the whole area of overseas labor relations and through a series of specific articles sought to give added protection to the African. The Colonial Act of 1930 stated that "the system of native contract labor rests on individual liberty and on the native's right to a just wage and assistance, public authority intervening only for purposes of inspection," a clause reaffirmed in the Imperial Organic Charter three years later and in the Organic Overseas Law of 1953. Articles 32, 33, and 34 of the 1954 *Estatuto dos indígenas das províncias da Guiné, Angola e Moçambique* declared: "The State will try to make the native recognize that work constitutes an indispensable element for progress, but the authorities can only impose work upon him in the cases specifically covered by the law" (Article 32); "The natives may freely choose the work they want to carry out, either on their own account or for another . . ." (Article 33); "The use of native labor by *não-indígenas* rests on [the African's] freedom of contract and on his right to a just wage and assistance, and must be inspected by the State through its appropriate organs."

The Native Labor Code of 1928, with some unimportant alterations introduced by later legislation, is the law governing the African worker in Angola and Moçambique.[43] It is a lengthy document, vague in some parts, precise in others. It specifies the responsibilities of the colonial administrator, the employer, and the worker, describes the various types of contracts, and provides for the recruitment of labor. Philosophically it is of a piece with previous African labor legislation, for although it attempts to correct those sections of earlier labor laws which led to the unchecked use of the African as *mão de obra*, the *Código de 1928* permits almost equal abuse, particularly in the matter of labor recruitment.[44]

In a general sense, given the Portuguese policy that the African must be taught or obliged to put his services to practical use, all labor in Angola and Moçambique is obligatory; but since 1926, when the vagrancy clause was eliminated as an integral part of labor legislation, the term "obligatory labor" has had a special significance, and is one of the three categories into which African labor may be divided, the other two being voluntary and contract labor. Article 20 of the Colonial Act states that *indígenas* may be compelled to work only "on public works of general and collective interest, the results of which will benefit them, to fulfill judicial sentences of a penal character, and to fulfill fiscal obligations." The use of obligatory labor is forbidden — except in urgent and special cases. The public needs for which forced labor may be requisitioned are public works, when voluntary workers are not sufficient; assistance in case of disaster or disease; for the cleaning and sanitation of African sections; for protection from dangerous animals; for local road details; for cultivation of certain lands of the African reserves in the proximity of the village.[45] Such labor must be compensated except when directly benefiting the African — such as building and repairing roads. Correctional labor sentences may be imposed upon the African for crimes punished under the Criminal Code or for infractions of the Labor Code. With regard to financial matters, the African may be obliged to work to supply the payment of taxes to which he is subject. In Angola, the delinquent is put to work on public projects. In Moçambique, failure to pay the head tax may result in correctional labor.

The distinction between the other two categories of African workers, the *contratados* and *voluntários*, is a practical one not contained in Portuguese legislation. The *voluntário* is the African who contracts directly with an employer; the *contratado* is the African who is recruited, under the supervisory inspection of the provincial administration, for work on private, and sometimes public, projects. The Labor Code recognizes both as free labor, and although there may be real differences in the length of contract, wages, and terms of board and keep, the law establishes certain conditions for the employer and the worker, whether the African is a voluntary or contracted employee. The *voluntário* usually contracts his services in the area in which he lives, although he may seek work in another circumscription; his contract, not subject to the administrator's intervention, may be for varying periods of time. The *contratado* is usually recruited for work outside his region. Until 1951 Africans thus recruited could be engaged for two years within the province and for three years outside of it (*i.e.*, on São Tomé and Príncipe, although not in the Union or the Rhodesias), but the maximum time limit on contracts for work within the province is now one year, and a six-months' contract is not uncommon. A special dispensation has been made to the Diamond Company of Angola to permit the extension of contracts made by them up to fifteen months, and the Angolan fisheries may contract a worker for eighteen months. Any African whose *caderneta* shows that he has worked six months (although quite frequently his work is not entered in the *caderneta*) during the last year or that he is presently employed is theoretically exempt from immediate liability to contract his services. Children under fourteen and Africans who are sick or advanced in age may not contract their services; women may sign for employment outside their villages only when accompanied by a male relative. These regulations are not stringently observed in either colony.

The obligations of the employer, as fixed by the 1928 Code, are (1) to fulfill conscientiously the terms of the contract; (2) not to demand tasks beyond the worker's ability or impose on women and children tasks reserved for men; (3) to give the worker nutritious food and hygienic lodgings when the contract calls for these; (4) to provide social, medical, and educational assistance to the worker and his family; (5) to refrain from obliging him to buy goods from company stores or his agents; (6) not to withhold any part of his wages which are supposed to be paid locally; (7) not to take financial advantage of him; (8) to keep the worker for the time stipulated by the contract and not to dismiss him without due cause; (9) to allow the worker to live with his family if he chooses; (10) to prohibit the sale, distribution, or manufacture of any distilled alcoholic beverages; (11) to refrain from subcontracting the worker's services without his consent and that of the administration; (12) to return the worker to his village, paying for his transportation and food and lodging en route, at the end of his contract.

The obligations of the worker are: (1) to obey all the orders of his employers which are in accord with the Labor Code; (2) to do his work industriously, consistent with his strength and abilities; (3) to repay his employer for loss and damage which he has deliberately caused; (4) not to leave his job without authorization from his employer.

The recruitment of those Africans in Angola and Moçambique who cannot prove that they are able to pay their taxes or feed, clothe, and house themselves and their families (that is, those who are not *voluntários*, farmers marketing a surplus, or men exempt for administrative reasons) is handled by agents or companies licensed by the government. European-owned farms and factories, unless fairly large, usually rely upon the services of independent licensed recruiters. The provincial government receives applications for the number of workers needed and grants a yearly quota to the companies or their agents. Since the African population in both provinces is usually not sufficiently concentrated in the area of greatest industrial and argicultural need, there is seldom enough voluntary labor available, with the result that plantations and companies must seek contract labor where they can get it. In the past, two types of labor-recruiting licenses have been granted, those permitting the recruiter to contract without

the help of the local authorities and those which have provided for
administrative assistance. This help is limited by law. The administrator
of the circumscription is instructed to give the recruiter only the
names and addresses of Africans seeking work. Recently the overseas
government has sought to reduce this kind of recruitment, holding
that if working conditions and pay scales are made sufficiently attractive, private companies will be able to attract workers without
the administration's acting as an employment bureau. In effect, however, the administrative system of the circumscription and the post
and the great authority held by the Portuguese officials over the
African there make the distinction between the two types of licenses
somewhat illusory.

All contracts made with the African worker are subject to the
approval of the colonial government, either locally, when local assistance is given in recruiting, or in the provincial capital, when it
is not. Through a series of instructions the Labor Code establishes
official protection for the African laborer. Living conditions are to
be inspected and the other various clauses of the Code relating to the
treatment of the worker guaranteed. The administration must hear
the worker's complaints and cancel those contracts whose terms have
not been observed. Administrative personnel must legally represent
the worker in all matters regarding the contract. Both employers and
officials guilty of malfeasance are to be punished.[46]

Practice and precept are not yet one in Angola and Moçambique.
Although African labor laws may hardly be called models of an
enlightened colonial policy, they still bear little resemblance to reality.
Labor practices mentioned in Chapter VI continue to characterize,
though less intensively, the recruitment and use of the African
worker. Periodic scandals involving colonial officials accused of accepting bribes for furnishing workers, the helpless often cynical attitude of employers who say they are forced to purchase contract
labor, and a Luanda newspaper advertisement offering to supply
native workers, all give evidence that the minimal requirements of
the law are not being met. That government policies have not been
fully effected is implicit in Governor General Sá Viana Rebelo's
reminder to a Nova Lisboa audience in 1956 that "the natives are
human beings, endowed with an intelligence and a capacity for work
and, therefore, it is necessary that they be used properly without
being exploited." [47] The complaints are many: inadequate wages, illegal extensions of contracts, the use of women in advanced pregnancy and children on local road projects, the unlawful sale of
alcoholic beverages to contract laborers, the illegal recruiting of

School children, Moçâmedes, Angola

Liceu Salvador Correia, Luanda, Angola

Delegation to greet Portuguese President Craveiro Lopes, Angola, 1954

Chieftains of the Mambone region, Moçambique

voluntários and African farmers, the extensive use of child labor on the tea plantations of Niassa and on Angolan coffee plantations, corporal punishment of *contratados* by administrative officers.

The governments of Angola and Moçambique are no less open to criticism in these matters than private enterprise. Occupying a privileged position in Portuguese labor laws, they make extensive use of contract and obligatory labor on harbor and transportation projects, and the official treatment of the African worker offers small example to the nongovernmental employer. The African continues to be regarded as *mão de obra* — in spite of all New State contentions. The indiscriminate use of his labor can hardly strengthen his convictions on the value of Portuguese culture. Even the staunch defender of Portuguese policy in Africa, Colonel F. C. C. Egerton, mildly questions the ultimate result of the contract labor system: "The avowed object of the Portuguese is to make the primitive natives realise, first, that progress is a good thing, and, second, that it can be obtained only by accepting the duty to work. Taking a man, contrary to his inclination, from his family and from the lands he regards as his own to work, let us say, for twelve months in the diamond mines or on a coffee plantation, may, at least temporarily, be a necessary measure, but its cultural effect is more likely to be harmful than otherwise." [48]

Probably the most persistent irregularities in the administration of the labor code occur, as in the past, in the actual recruitment of the worker. In many cases recruiting practices are more flexible and informal than the law foresees. One common procedure seems to be for an employer to request a certain number of workers from a *chefe de posto*, who fills the quota with tax delinquents or men whom he persuades the local chief to supply. The official is usually rewarded for his intervention. The problems of large companies, whose needs are greater, are more complex since their requisitions involve more officials, but in many parts of the provinces the same procedure prevails. The manager of one company has remarked that without bribes and intrigue he could not obtain sufficient labor for his plantation. Recent dismissals and public trials of officials have not yet succeeded in eliminating these practices.

Now more than ever before the concept of the African as a source of cheap labor is being shaped by economic factors. This is especially true in Angola where the pace of development is quicker and the number of workers scarcer. In Moçambique, more leisurely, more deliberate, the European attitude toward African labor is perhaps less aggressive and demanding. The need for labor in the comparatively rapidly expanding economies of both provinces, but particularly in Angola, and the natural reluctance — to use Portuguese phraseology — of the African to do manual labor have intensified a problem which has been growing since the beginning of the century. It is apparent that the legislation introduced by the New State has not solved the problem. Nor has the technological progress of the two colonies been rapid enough to reduce or equalize the demand for workers. In the continuous discussion on how to resolve this classic colonial dilemma two lines of argumentation may be seen. One, less frequently expounded but nonetheless popular, maintains that present labor laws are not firm enough to get the maximum labor from the available supply ("As long as the natives enjoy six months of holidays every year and can emigrate to the neighboring colonies . . . the problem cannot be solved").[49] A second view maintains, with many references to other European territories, that the African is offered no incentives, only compulsion, to take up regular employment ("Nothing has been done by the European to give him a new mentality. On the contrary, the low prices paid him for his goods [and services], the high prices charged him for what he needs, drive him to further abstinence and keep him from acquiring new habits which would lead to new and higher production").[50] This reasoning is in part valid, for the wage scale for African labor in the Portuguese provinces is among the lowest on the continent.

For the Portuguese government, committed both to stimulating the material growth of Angola and Moçambique and, on paper, at least, to the cultural elevation of the African and the development of native agriculture, the existing labor laws are at best a compromise. But can a satisfactory solution to this economic and human problem be found as long as the government and provincial employers continue to think of the African as nothing more than labor to serve European interests and as long as a newspaper editorial, from which the following quotation is taken, can be said to reveal a fundamental Portuguese attitude?

But for all the effective resources of the overseas soil and subsoil to be exploited and developed, for their intensive and extensive exploitation, much work, much perseverence, much human effort is absolutely necessary. Translated into everyday speech, this means that an abundant, permanent, and very reliable *mão-de-obra* becomes fundamentally indispensable. Now, this laboring force can only be supplied by the native . . .

It has been more than once demonstrated that the white man in Africa cannot carry out heavy tasks, which demand a fatiguing and exhausting human effort. The climate . . . does not permit it. He may only be given the task of directing and of guiding, administratively and technically. Other tasks are naturally reserved for the Negroes, since they are the only ones capable of carrying them out, because of their physiological function and their ancestral adaption to an environment which, though harmful to the European, is familiar to them. And one should not be amazed that this is what happens.[51]

The Portuguese African labor supply has been constantly diminished by temporary or permanent emigration from the colonies to surrounding territories. A large part of this emigration is regulated by various accords between the Portuguese government and the Union of South Africa and the Rhodesias or by provisions of the Labor Code, when workers in Angola or Moçambique contract to work in the islands of São Tomé and Príncipe. The number of workers annually recruited by the Witwatersrand Native Labour Association in Moçambique for the Transvaal mines now runs from about eighty to one hundred thousand, and the yearly total working in the Rhodesias is over one hundred thousand. From fifteen to twenty thousand Angolan laborers annually contract for work in Northern Rhodesia and South-West Africa, while perhaps six thousand, mostly now from Moçambique, go to the Portuguese islands. All the contracts are for one year, with provision for a six-month extension, and repatriation is insisted upon. The arrangement is not an entirely satisfactory one for the colonial governments, since the number of Africans contracting for work in other territories is a serious drain on the local labor supply, and there is also the danger, in recent years, that a part of the workers may become politically contaminated during their stay outside Portuguese frontiers. But these inconveniences are outweighed, especially in Moçambique, by economic advantages and the realization that it is more profitable and safer to regulate the emigration as much as possible.

There is a comparable clandestine immigration into the Congo, Nyasaland, the Rhodesias, and the Union. The number of Portuguese Africans fleeing the labor policies of the two provinces or seeking higher wages and a relatively higher standard of living elsewhere can only be estimated, for frequently the African returns to Portuguese territory after a short period abroad. Marcelo Caetano calculates the number of Portuguese Africans living outside Angola and Moçambique at about five hundred thousand for each province.[52] Other estimates run as high as one million for Angola alone. These high figures present some embarrassment to Portuguese colonial officials, revealing as they do some inadequacy in Portugal's policies in Africa.

Government spokesmen attribute much of the emigration to the African's "childish desire for useless gewgaws." They also point with pride to the delegations of Portuguese Africans living in the Congo or the Rhodesias who gather to welcome Portugal's president on his visits to the overseas provinces; these spontaneous gatherings are said to reveal the purity of the African's Portuguese sentiments. At the same time employers in the overseas provinces are urged to raise wages as one means of counteracting this flow.

The international controversies over native labor policies in which Portugal has been embroiled for one hundred and fifty years temporarily abated in the early years of the Salazar regime. Humanitarian attentions, drawn to other parts of the world, were directed only occasionally to Portuguese Africa, and from 1930 to 1945, Angola and Moçambique were undisturbed by any except passing criticism. Also, new colonial legislation and official pronouncements gave the impression that the government was making serious efforts to correct past abuses.[53] Intermittent reports and correspondence from the International Labor Office and a small controversy in the middle 1930's were the sum of the criticism. Since the Second World War, however, Angola and Moçambique have begun to receive their share — small, but growing — of the revived interest in the African continent. Not only that section of the English press (such as the *Manchester Guardian*, *The Anti-Slavery Reporter*, and the *New Statesman*) which have long questioned Portuguese African policy, but other newspapers, periodicals, and studies have touched on labor conditions in the two provinces. A. T. Steele, writing in the *New York Herald-Tribune* in 1948, summed up in familiar language the situation in Angola: "When an Angola plantation owner requires labor, he notifies the government of his needs. The demand is passed down to the village chiefs, who are ordered to supply fixed quotas of laborers for their communities. If the required number is not forthcoming, police are sent to round them up. These contract laborers are paid a wage sufficient for their sustenance, but no more." [54] Brian Parks, writing in the *Johannesburg Star* (March 7, 1958) tells the story of economic bars, forced labor, and the bad treatment of Africans in Angola. Quoting a Portuguese official, he writes: "The state can conscript them for six months' labour for work on the roads, the railways, the plantations — for anything. We feed them and clothe them. Of course, we pay them. We pick them up, we use them, then we return them to where they came from . . . We can transfer trouble-makers from one of our provinces to another and we do so." The journalist's conclusions are: "There is no doubt their treatment is shocking. Floggings and beatings are the rule rather than the exception." In the American periodical, *Africa Today*, Elizabeth Landis scoffs at Portugal's contention that Angola and Moçambique are parts of Portugal and do not come under Article 73 (E) of the United Nations Charter. Maintaining that the colonies are non-self-governing territories, Miss Landis quotes liberally sections from letters reportedly sent from Angola to the Secretary General. Labor gangs, exile, terror, poverty, malnutrition, abuse of pregnant women, children, and the aged are the substance of this correspondence.[55]

The sentencing in 1958 by the Portuguese government of Captain Henrique Galvão to sixteen years imprisonment for alleged political crimes brought a storm of criticism from various segments of the English press and a formal protest from the English Liberal Party to the Salazar government. The *Manchester Guardian* reviewed the history of Galvão's trouble with the regime — previously told by Basil Davidson in *The African Awakening* — which dated back to his 1947 report on forced labor conditions in Angola. Galvão, a high inspector in the colonial service and deputy for Angola as well as an eminent historian, submitted to the Colonial Ministry a report on neoslavery in Angola. The report was subsequently published by the opposition, and in 1951 Galvão was jailed during an election campaign. His fate has become identified with repressive Portuguese policy in Africa, and the *Manchester Guardian* saw in the extended sentence an attempt by the Salazar government to gag any future criticism of this policy.[56]

But the *bête noire* for the present government has been the Englishman Basil Davidson who, in articles appearing in *Harper's Magazine* and the *New Statesman* and in his book on the Belgian Congo and Angola, *The African Awakening* (1955), angrily established himself in the tradition of Nevinson, Cadbury, and Ross. Commissioned by *Harper's* to write an article to commemorate the fiftieth anniversary of Nevinson's visit, Davidson went to Angola in 1954. He saw little change from the days of *A Modern Slavery*. *Serviçais* had become *contratados*, but the system of labor exploitation continued unabated ("Forced labour is the economic flywheel in Angola"). In Davidson's eyes, brutality, appalling living conditions, unreasonable taxes, and racial discrimination characterize Portuguese treatment of the African in Angola. He concludes that the Portuguese administration has shown itself unable to alter its course and is surely driving toward ruin.[57]

Portugal's response to Davidson's philippic was prompt, if not convincing. In 1955, the General Agency for the Overseas Territories published a thirty-page pamphlet, *Angola without Prejudice*, defined by its author, F. C. C. Egerton, as "Some comments on the misrepresentations of a remarkably hasty investigator." Egerton's technique in answering Davidson's charges is in a familiar mold: he argues that Davidson was in Angola only ten days, hardly a sufficient time to get a comprehensive picture; he points out that Davidson does not name many of his informants (Egerton does not mention administrative harassments suffered by those who have given derogatory information in the past); he attempts to trace Davidson's steps and get contradictions from the people with whom Davidson admits having spoken; he quotes government spokesmen and statistics to prove that Davidson was either wrong or inaccurate (he says that where Davidson spoke of 379,000 *contratados*, official government figures showed only 142,674 in 1953 and 99,771 in 1954). The gist of *Angola without Prejudice* is that in Angola Portuguese labor policy is one of humane tolerance and enlightenment. The right of the Portuguese government to force the African to work Egerton seems to accept without question. Nor does he discuss the point raised by Davidson that racial discrimination is becoming a reality of Angolan life under the influx of white immigration. In many ways Egerton's pamphlet does not answer Davidson's essential condemnations.

More important than the issue of contract labor is Portugal's native policy in its totality: its mystique, its attitudes, its legislation, and the reality. So long as this policy is founded on the assumption that Angola and Moçambique are to be white men's colonies, it will fail to serve the legitimate interests of some ten million Africans. The New State has brought to the provinces the ideological trappings of a pseudo-benevolent paternalism and a superficial prosperity, enjoyed mostly by several thousand Europeans, but it has not broken with the unrewarding traditions of the past. It has instead accepted them, used them when possible to practical advantage, and sought to create from them an intensely nationalistic colonial policy. It may well be true, as the Portuguese themselves sometimes confess, that they have the vice of history, for, as I have remarked elsewhere, they seem strangely intent, as far as the African is concerned, on perpetuating the past into the future.

XIII

THE NEW STATE IN AFRICA:
PROJECTS AND PROBLEMS

THE attentions of the Salazar government have been directed
to other aspects of Portuguese Africa besides native policy and colonial
administration. To a large extent these questions — economic policies,
colonial development, immigration, and international relations —
have been approached in typical New State fashion, rhetorical
abandon and practical caution. Since Portugal's policy in dealing with
these problems is of recent improvisation and since they are so closely
tied to changing events in both Portugal and the rest of the world,
it is almost impossible to do more than suggest general patterns that
have emerged in recent years. But since past performance in Portuguese Africa has usually pointed the way into the present, it may be
that the present is a fairly secure indication of future progress in the
colonies.

Where the results of the New State's native policies, for example, have been largely sterile, in material development the provinces have shown genuine moderate progress, especially since the
middle 1940's. This has been a period of general prosperity in Africa
in which the Portuguese colonies have naturally shared, and it may
be, as some have claimed, that Angola and Moçambique would have
shown an even greater expansion had metropolitan controls over
the provincial economies been less and the government's policies
more imaginative. But it was Salazar's rigorous bookkeeping which
pulled Angola from backruptcy after the chaotic 1920's and set a
conservative economic pattern which carried both colonies through

the financial crises of the 1930's, thus permitting them to take advantage of the favorable conditions of the 1940's and 1950's.

Identity with the metropolis is the government's goal in the economic organization of the colonies, although the goal is still unrealized because of special circumstances prevailing in Portuguese Africa. What is envisioned is the gradual integration of all colonial economies into the general economic complex of the Portuguese nation; specifically, this seems to mean the free passage of citizens, capital, and products within the national territory. The economic character of each province, it is realized, will create local differences in their financial policies, but the interests of all the overseas provinces will be considered together and economic programs established in accordance with the general orientation of the metropolis. Both Angola and Moçambique now enjoy some financial autonomy and submit their own budgets, which are evolved within the patterns established by Lisbon. The provinces, however, are restricted from contracting foreign loans, and all charter concessions of importance are arranged by the Lisbon government.

The economic problems of the provinces were one of the first tasks undertaken by the new government in the early 1930's. Even in 1929, Salazar remarked that "it would be in vain to restore the finances and economy of the metropolis if a similar effort were not realized in the colonies, principally Africa, and particularly Angola . . . Our colonial possessions must have balanced budgets which contain normal provisions for the operations necessary for programs of development and economic expansion." [1] As a part of a general plan to activate the business life of the colonies and to create a sound economic structure in each, Colonial Minister Armindo Monteiro made an inspection of Portuguese Africa in 1932. In the following year was held the first Conference of the Colonial Governors, whose purpose was to study the reorganization of the colonial economies and to forge a new solidarity between Portugal and the overseas territories. Although not all the suggestions made by the Conference were implemented, the meeting did establish a general economic program which has been followed in the last twenty-five years.

Among the steps considered by the Conference were to increase and adjust colonial production within the realities of the world market; to replace, wherever possible, foreign products with colonial products in the home market; to abolish colonial reliance on trade barriers and artificial forms of protection; to encourage a selective immigration of Portuguese colonists; to attract capital to Portuguese Africa; to introduce new agricultural techniques into the colonies.

The Conference also concentrated on plans to revise the overseas financial structures and to rest them on bases similar to those established in Portugal by Salazar. The Conference further proposed an overseas tariff commission to study a general reform of tariff policies. Finally, the Conference stressed the necessity for publicizing the Portuguese overseas possessions through a series of exhibits, publications, and similar programs.[2]

The budgets of Angola and Moçambique have been balanced since 1931, and in most years have shown a respectable credit balance. From 1946 to 1953, for example, the budget of Moçambique showed an annual surplus of about seven million dollars. In the 1930's and 1940's this was accomplished by a ruthless curtailment of imports and by a somewhat more efficient financial administration overseas. In the last fifteen years, the economic expansion of Angola and Moçambique has further increased this credit balance (the value of Angola's exports in 1954, for example, was twelve times that of the average for the years 1926–1930). The budget for each province in 1956 was approximately seventy million dollars, as contrasted with typical budgets of the early 1930's, which averaged from six to ten million dollars a year. The major portion of each budget is still allotted to administrative expenses, although the amounts going into provincial development projects increase each year. Nevertheless the funds available for medical and educational services are totally inadequate, and the provisions in the budgets for direct assistance to the African are negligible. Among the proposed 1957 expenditures in Angola were two items for $140,000 each, one for public monuments and the other for African housing.

Only since 1948 has the overseas tariff policy undergone serious changes. Traditional Portuguese practice through the first half of the century — and even earlier — had been to collect import duties on all goods entering the African provinces, whether from Portugal, other Lusitanian colonies, or foreign countries; Portuguese goods, and to a lesser extent nationalized goods, enjoyed a strongly preferential position. Duties on foreign goods were generally two to five times higher than on those of Portuguese origin. Most of the duties were collected on an *ad valorem* basis, although certain articles, notably those intended for the African trade, such as cotton goods, shoes, hoes, and wines were subject to specific duties. The changes introduced in the tariff regimes of Angola and Moçambique in the last ten years have not drastically altered Portugal's mercantilist policies. But the barriers on trade between the imperial colonies, though not with the metropolis, have been lowered and may soon be eliminated. Other changes have been introduced; to accelerate colonial development, import duties on machinery, tools, vehicles, and selected raw materials were reduced. Portuguese industry, however, continues to benefit from a preferential tariff, especially on such items as manufactured cotton, alcoholic beverages, cork, glass, matches, and when either the high cost of these Portuguese articles or the superiority of the same articles manufactured elsewhere nullifies the advantage of this preference, limitations or even prohibitions are placed on foreign goods by an import control board. In addition to normal import duties, colonial imports are frequently subject to sur-charges, municipal tariffs, and a development fund tax. In neither colony have the new schedules reduced the colonies' essential budg-etary reliance on import duties. Business men in both provinces com-plain that in reality tariffs have increased, not decreased, on most goods coming into Portuguese Africa and that the customs charges are so high that its economic growth is being held back.

One of the most significant triumphs of Salazar's economic policies is that the colonial governments may now count each year on a rea-sonable income from the direct taxation of companies and individuals. Until very recently the mainstays of provincial budgets were import and export duties, the African head tax, and the contributions of concessionary companies, and these still form the largest part of an-nual income. But with the customs reforms of the late 1940's and early 1950's, revisions in the overseas tax structure were introduced: in-dustrial taxes, professional income taxes (which run from 1 per cent to a maximum of about 7 per cent), a building tax, taxes on com-panies exploiting the resources of the land and sea, and a surtax on large personal or business incomes were put into effect. These taxes are scarcely high enough to discourage personal or business initiative (the head tax takes, comparatively, from the African a much higher percentage of earned income), but in the last few years they have brought in substantial revenue to the provinces and indicate the changing economic patterns of Angola and Moçambique.[3]

But the economic picture is not entirely favorable. Portuguese Africa's reliance on goods of foreign manufacture, its high tariff policies, and the Portuguese merchant's disposition to put excessive mark-ups on imported commodities have created a high cost of living in the colonies. Although no accurate price index exists, it is reliably estimated that the cost of living has more than doubled in the last twenty years with no corresponding increase in income for either the African or the majority of the European population. The African's purchasing power in the provincial economy is low; high taxes, low wages (in 1956 the minimum wage for the agricultural worker in Moçambique was from two to eight dollars a month, depending upon the region, for the industrial worker from about three to ten dollars a month, and for the African craftsman about a dollar and a half a day), and the fixed ceilings on the prices he receives for his crops have kept the African worker and farmer in a chronically depressed state. For the Portuguese worker who comes to Africa to escape the poverty of the metropolis, life is difficult. Only the higher administrative officials, the merchants, and the successful *fazendeiros* prosper in Angola and Moçambique. One Portuguese visitor to Angola estimated that 80 per cent of the white population lived on the edge of poverty. "The cost of living is the greatest absurdity I encountered on my Angolan trip . . . being, without exaggeration, 100 per cent higher than in the metropolis." [4]

The major development projects in Angola and Moçambique up to 1930 were primarily subsidized by foreign capital.[5] The ports of Lourenço Marques and Beira, the Benguela Railway, and Diamang owed little to Portuguese capital or initiative. Since 1930, however, the development projects carried out in the African provinces have been financed almost exclusively by the provincial or national governments; in 1951 a credit of 455 million dollars was granted by the Economic Co-operation Administration to Portugal for overseas development. Until recently the government has been determined that no extensive foreign concessions would be made again, but the tight Portuguese budget in the last several years and a growing foreign trade deficit are modifying Salazar's fears about foreign investment and outside capital is being circumspectly sought for use in the colonies.

National funds available for large-scale development schemes in Portuguese Africa are limited and apportioned only after long careful study. Consequently the advances in both provinces have been slow in comparison with those in neighboring territories. But expansion and improvement programs have gone ahead uninterruptedly for the last ten years and show signs of continuing unabated. In general, these funds have been spent conservatively on programs essential for the colonies' growth; in a few cases, as in continental Portugal, money has been used on splashy structures or projects designed "to honor Portugal." [6]

At the end of the 1930's the government began a series of minor development plans which, though partly interrupted by the war, have been successfully carried out. Each new plan since then has been more ambitious; gradually these programs are transforming the life of Angola and Moçambique — for a small part of the population at least. The earlier improvement programs, utilizing the annual surplus in the colonial budgets and loans by the National Treasury, were mostly concerned with expanding port facilities and transportation systems. In Moçambique the national government made a loan of about thirty million dollars to improve transit communications, particularly the rail system. In 1950 the two provinces each undertook a co-ordinated campaign to expand public utilities and communications and to provide for increased white colonization. These five-year plans were incorporated in 1953 into the Portuguese National Development Plan, a six-year program extending through 1958. Under this plan Angola was allocated one hundred million dollars and Moçambique, about eighty-five million dollars. A second six-year plan was to be initiated in 1959: 237 million dollars will be spent in Angola, 125 million dollars in Moçambique. Over half the total for each province will be used for colonization schemes and for expanding roads and railroads.

In Moçambique the most important project in this period has unquestionably been the Limpopo Valley Immigration Project, which was some twenty-five years in a planning stage. A dam across the Limpopo at Caniçado provides irrigation for almost one hundred thousand acres — and provides as well a bridge across the river for the extension of the Lourenço Marques rail system into Southern Rhodesia. Here the government is establishing its largest agricultural colony in the province. Limited work on a similar irrigation and colonization scheme in Niassa near Vila Cabral has also begun, presumably to coincide with the final extension of the railroad from the coast. The tea and tobacco country around Gurué and Malema also figure in the development plans. To provide hydro-electric power for Lourenço Marques, the construction of a dam on the Movene River at a point twenty miles from the capital will be undertaken. A lesser dam on the Revué River east of Vila Pery has already been completed to furnish power for local industry and the port of Beira. Port facilities at Beira and Nacala are being expanded, bridges built, and roads improved to permit an expansion of Moçambique's commerce and industry.

In Angola the ports of Luanda and Lobito were enlarged and modernized in the late 1940's and early 1950's, and the European colonization project at Cela — model for similar projects in both colonies — has had a successful start. The most important project under the National Development Plan is being carried out in the south of Angola in the middle Cunene valley. Over thirty million dollars will be spent in preparing the Matala-Capelungo and Quiteve-Humbe regions for the largest of Portuguese African colonization schemes. As a part of southern Angola's development, the port of Moçâmedes is building a deep-water quay and the Moçâmedes Railroad is being extended toward the Rhodesian frontier. The Matala irrigation and hydro-electric project is under construction, reportedly to be completed in 1960. It will provide power for Sá da Bandeira and the vicinity, water to be carried in a twenty-five-mile-long canal for the Cunene colonization settlements, and will provide a bridge for the rail extension. Two other power plants at Biópio and Mabubas, the latter now in limited operation, will supply electric power for the Benguela-Lobito and Luanda areas respectively. In the Cuanza valley another scheme calls for the construction of a hydro-electric plant and irrigation system near the Duque de Bragança Falls. The Luanda Railroad will be extended and roads and airports built.[7]

Although the development of Portuguese Africa has scarcely matched that of the Belgian Congo or the Rhodesias, against the memory of the unfulfilled programs of the early twentieth century the achievements of the Salazar government are little short of extraordinary, especially in view of the limited capital available for such enterprises. Portugal has not until recently encouraged foreign investment in the colonies, except on its own rigid terms. Portuguese fortunes are seldom employed in Angola and Moçambique except under near-monopolistic guarantees. Local capital is also scarce. "Only fools or careless people, or those who have a passionate love for this colony — those whom we call 'good colonists' because they bury here everything they make, frequently losing it — dare to use their wealth here in new undertakings. Everyone else takes from the province all that he makes and invests it where he may have the certainty of greater and surer gain without work or worry."[8] There are some indications that the colonies' present economic stability is at last beginning to attract serious Portuguese investments.

While the Government of the National Revolution has not solved the problem of how to attract Portuguese capital to Africa, it seems for the present to have solved, by design or by accident, the equally ancient problem of Portuguese immigration into Angola and Moçambique. Although the white population of Angola remained constant, or perhaps even declined, in the uncertain decade from 1930 to 1940,[9] in the following ten years the number of white residents rose from 44,000 to 78,000 and to 110,000 by 1955. Moçambique has also shown an increase in European population that has been more consistent though less spectacular: 18,000 residents in 1932; 27,500 in 1940; 31,200 in 1945; 48,000 in 1950; and probably 60,000 by 1960.[10] In the 1950's Angola has been the promised land, next to Brazil, for the Portuguese emigrant; its booming economy, its relative proximity to Portugal, and a more receptive administration (the Moçambique government has adopted a policy of keeping to a minimum untrained "poor white" immigrants) give Angola advantages over Moçambique. But the growth of both provinces has been startling and shows no signs of dropping off. Poverty at home and exaggerated stories of the prosperity in Africa have succeeded where other persuasions have failed. The combination of this free immigration and the controlled colonization on the government's agricultural settlements is an important factor in the changing complexion of Portuguese Africa.

How much of the populational gain has been the result of Portugal's educational and colonization policies is uncertain, apart from the specific number of farmers Lisbon has recruited for the agricultural colonies at Cela and in southern Angola and at Guíja in Moçambique. But if the general trend of migration is from an area with a low standard of living (the average annual income in continental Portugal of about two hundred dollars a person is the lowest in Western Europe) to one which offers or promises a higher standard, then the upsurge in white population has been mostly a consequence of the colonies' new prosperity in the last twenty years, a period in which life in Portugal has become more and more difficult for a majority of the people.

In the 1930's the government followed a wavering policy on settling Angola and Moçambique with a large white element. In 1933 Armindo Monteiro spoke of the "tragic situation which would be created by a government's transferring any considerable number of its citizens to colonial areas with the idea of solving the unemployment and poverty questions at home. After the expenditure of fabulous sums, it would merely have created a vast white proletariat in regions where it would be difficult to succour them." [11] In short, the government was not prepared and not able to sponsor the white settlement of Portuguese Africa. At the same time, however, through an erratic campaign in Portuguese schools and publications the Colonial Ministry attempted to convince a youthful elite to dedicate their lives to service in Africa. Appeals were made to Portuguese women to accompany their husbands. These campaigns seem to have been principally a way of marking time, an attempt to create a colonial mentality which could be exploited at a later date, and by 1940 it had had little practical result. As late as 1945 the colonialist Eça d'Almeida was urging a massive effort to colonize Angola and Moçambique; some of his proposals were forced contributions from provincial firms, regulations obliging teachers and soldiers to serve a term in Africa, laws to force large colonial companies to establish white settlements, and direct government assistance to Portuguese colonists.[12]

The most effective action the government has taken has been the establishment of the agricultural colonies already mentioned. The importance of these projects in Portugal's long-term plans must not be minimized. Cela and Guíja are more than showplaces for the foreign journalist. They are part of Lisbon's vision for colonial development. In 1943 Salazar remarked that "the rich extensive colonial lands, undeveloped and sparsely populated, are the natural complement for metropolitan agriculture, especially for ordinary crops and for the raw materials for industry. In addition they will take care of that part of the metropolis' excessive population which Brazil does not wish to accept." [13] The agricultural colonies grew out of several experiments in planned immigration made in both provinces in the 1940's, but principally in the Huíla plateau of Angola. Partly because of the hasty selection of the colonists, the lack of adequate programs to prepare them for their new life, and the totally different environment into which they were plunged, these early experiments were not notably successful, in spite of assistance by colonial administrations which gave the colonist land, a house, and livestock.[14]

Profiting from these mistakes, the Colonial Ministry began in the 1950's to carry out a more co-ordinated program designed to establish Portuguese villages, not isolated farms, in selected areas of Angola and Moçambique. By 1954, 260 families had been installed at the Cela colonato on Angola's Amboim plateau,[15] where eventually two thousand families are expected to be located. The colonists are grouped in small farming villages of about twenty-five homes each; each village has a combination school-church and a community farm building. The family receives a house, livestock, seeds, and over one hundred acres of farming and grazing land. Wherever possible an effort has been made to re-create the life of Portugal; preferably all the inhabitants of one village are from the same section of Portugal. The cost of establishing one family at Cela is estimated at five thousand dollars, which the immigrant is expected to repay to the government over a twenty-five year period. The initial reaction of the colonists was not entirely enthusiastic, and some families returned to Portugal, but the application list has steadily grown, and the success of Cela — and of the Limpopo project at Guíja — seems assured.[16]

The expansion of the *colonato* system seems certain, particularly in the south of Angola and in the north of Moçambique, since Portugal is committed to establishing its own social and economic patterns in Africa. Since the colonists are forbidden to use African labor and since there is a relative abundance of land in the two colonies, which precludes for the time being the creation of a white highlands as in Kenya, the points of friction between the African and European should be kept to a minimum. But the continued increase of Portuguese population in Angola and Moçambique does create other problems. The available funds and the attentions of the Portuguese government are now largely spent on development projects which primarily benefit the European. Angola and Moçambique are taking on the appearance of European colonies in which the African is at best a second-class citizen. This policy has already begun to reduce the economic opportunities of the African in Angola as the poor Portuguese immigrant is now taking manual and semiskilled jobs formerly held by African laborers. With this increased Portuguese immigration has come a hardening color consciousness, and if present tendencies continue, it seems likely that Angola and Moçambique will bear more resemblance to other European territories in Africa than to Brazil, as the Portuguese now predict.

The growth of urban areas in the two provinces has been even more pronounced than that of the rural regions of the interior. The clearest indication of Portugal's fortunes in Africa has traditionally been found in the state of its cities and towns. In a general sense the history of Luanda and Tete, for example, would tell the history of Angola and Moçambique, their successes and their failures. From the cautious thirties into the formative forties and prosperous fifties Portuguese settlements have mirrored the recent transition of Angola and Moçambique. The steady sedate development of Lourenço Marques and the explosive growth of Luanda in the last ten years reflect the changing personalities of the two colonies. Only the island of Moçambique seems to have remained impervious, but even here a modern municipal swimming pool marks the advance of a new order.

Ancient towns like Benguela and Quelimane have acquired new life; towns like Nova Lisboa and Nampula, only place-names on a map in the 1920's, have became rising centers of Portuguese life and commerce: new towns like Vila Luso and Vila Cabral record the expansion of colonization into the far interior. New and old, large and small, these towns bear the uncompromising stamp of continental Portugal, for now, more than at any other time in her history, Portugal is re-creating her cultural image in Africa.

Lavish cinema theaters, attractive shops, metropolitan bus services, tourist hotels and restaurants, and imposing administrative and commercial buildings, place Luanda, Beira, Lobito, Nova Lisboa, and Lourenço Marques among the most modern small cities in Africa,[17] setting a standard which other Portuguese African towns strive to imitate, and help insulate their European residents against the primitive realities of the countryside. Many cities have their own newspapers and small broadcasting stations, and various sports clubs sponsor athletic and social events. Luanda, Benguela, Lourenço Marques, and Nampula have excellent small museums. In these towns and cities of Portuguese Africa one may see at least one success of the New State's policy of forging a single identity between the provinces and Portugal, but in the process it has contributed to the formation of two distinct societies, one African and the other European, in the colonies.

No longer are the Portuguese African provinces regarded with suspicion by their white neighbors; no longer are they a source of continuous, often ill-informed attacks on Portuguese policy and behavior. Angola and Moçambique live in harmony with the other territories below the equator. The bonds of friendship in Africa are more than economic, although the essential relationship of Portuguese Africa to the Rhodesias and the Union of South Africa is based on financial self-interest. The Portuguese desire to remain in Africa is shared equally by the white Rhodesian and South African. Portugal's respect for the economic success of her neighbors in Africa and their discovery that Portuguese policy is not greatly different from their own have drawn the various areas into closer rapport. A remark made by the Governor General of South Africa, Dr. Ernest Jansen, on a state visit to Lisbon ("By a happy accident we are neighbors. I believe that we should be grateful to history for this accident") [18] is more than diplomatic courtesy. It is an expression of awareness that the governments of the African lands below the equator have for the moment a common cause — their survival.

Although the friendship between Portuguese Africa and the

white governments of neighboring lands is a source of great pride to the small nation, accustomed in the past to being regarded with possessive hostility, the proximity of these areas to Angola and Moçambique may be the source of future dangers. The two Portuguese colonies can no longer be considered isolated segments of the African continent, and the turn of events in neighboring lands will surely have repercussions in Angola and Moçambique, where the examples in the rest of Africa have not passed completely unnoticed. Both the policies of the new African Republic of the Congo and the dead-end policies of the Union hold a distinct threat for Portuguese Africa, and there is reason to assume that an emancipation of the Congo or erupting tensions in South Africa (and perhaps in the Central African Federation) will have their effect in the Portuguese provinces.

In spite of Portugal's good relations with colonial governments since 1930, particularly since the end of the Second World War, a small segment of European humanitarian opinion, predominantly English, was openly critical in the 1930's of Portuguese policy in Angola and Moçambique. The issues were the Portuguese use of African labor and discussions in the League of Nations on the possibility of setting up international regulations on the sale and distribution of vital raw materials; at times these issues took on overtones of larger political controversy, growing out of the Salazar government's open admiration for the Fascist regimes in Germany and Italy and the support of the Franco rebellion in Spain.

Throughout the 1930's — and the 1940's — Portugal refused to sign the Forced Labor Convention drawn up by the International Labor Conference, arguing that she was not in agreement with clauses restricting the use of conscripted African labor to public works and that local conditions demanded that each colonial power should be permitted to deal with the problem of labor in its own way and not be subject to conventions that could not be satisfactorily applied.[19] Portugal's reluctance to sign caused occasional sharp commentary abroad in the middle 1930's. At the same time Portugal turned down a loan from the League of Nations for colonial development, believing that it would place her colonies under foreign economic control. The New State was equally distrustful of suggestions raised by the International Economic Conference in 1933 for a study to be made of the possible free circulation of raw materials to equalize existing irregularities. A speech made by Anthony Eden in the House of Commons in 1936 supporting this general proposal and a blunt editorial in the *London Daily Express* (July 23, 1937), stating that Portugal had learned nothing in four centuries of African rule and that it would be a blessing for the native population of these lands if they were taken from Portugal and given to some one else, seemed to confirm Portugal's suspicions that her colonial integrity was again in danger.

Portugal's position was made clear by Salazar in a speech of 1937 on the colonial situation. He concluded with these words: "Contrary to what everyone may believe, we will not sell, we will not cede, we will not rent, we will not partition our colonies . . . Our constitutional laws do not permit it, and in the absence of these, our national conscience would not permit it." [20] Other government spokesmen were more pointed in their denunciations, classifying all of Portugal's real and supposed critics as meddlers, Bolsheviks, and members of international Jewry. Only Hitler and Salazar, "in whose voice vibrated, strong and sincere, the soul of the Portuguese people," knew how to stand up against their aggressive intentions.[21]

These intermittent controversies were exaggerated by Portuguese sensitivities and by the government's desire to take a strongly nationalistic position in the public view. More serious has been the recent mounting opposition from many Arab and Asian nations to what they consider oppressive Portuguese colonialism in Africa and Asia. While most of Portugal's disputes in the nineteenth century with other European powers over her African possessions were, stripped of their moralistic cloak, economic or territorial in essence, the present attacks are primarily ideological. The developing debate is pointed up by the Indian-Portuguese argument over the enclave of Goa, a bit of territory economically worthless, but significant to Portugal as a remnant of her past and to India as a final barrier to national hegemony.

In both the 1956 and 1957 sessions of the United Nations the status of Portugal's overseas provinces has been discussed. A group of Arab-Asian nations, vigorously supported by Russia, has suggested that the provinces are in effect non-self-governing territories and that, under Chapter XI of the United Nations Charter, Portugal should be obliged to furnish the United Nations with periodic technical reports on these areas.[22] In both sessions a motion was introduced to censure Portugal for having failed to submit such information, and only the skillful tactics of some Western bloc representatives kept it from being adopted. In withstanding these motions, Portugal plainly replied that she had no responsibility to the Council, since her overseas provinces were political extensions of Portugal, governed by the same constitution and enjoying the same privileges as the metropolitan provinces. It is not likely that the issue will disappear, however; it seems more likely that it will intensify and possibly force Portugal to make major revisions in her colonial policies.

For four hundred and fifty years in Africa, the Portuguese have survived disease, native wars, neglect, and foreign attacks, surely the most remarkable endurance record in colonial history. Today, according to former Foreign Minister Paulo Cunha (speaking at a New York press conference in 1955), Angola and Moçambique are the last outposts of Western civilization in Africa. Although Dr. Cunha's hyperbole may not be entirely flattering to Portugal's neighbors in Africa, inherent in his remark is the affirmation of what Portugal has come to consider her traditional colonizing role in Africa — to implant there the alleged national and Christian values of Portuguese society. That this "fundamental faith of Portuguese colonization" which the New State has sought to reassert has had at best a shadowy reality and that the history of Portuguese Africa has long been marked by the disparity between principle and practice is of little consequence, for it is on this philosophic ground that Portugal seems determined to confront the challenge of the future with its materialistic and "separatist" ideologies.

There are forces leavening in modern Africa which will test the ancient capacities of the Portuguese. Speaking on the rise of Africanism, Lord Hailey observes that "no country can expect to isolate itself indefinitely. There is a wind blowing through Africa, and it will be felt in the Congo and Moçambique as surely as it is being felt (though not, I hope, with such bitterness) in French North Africa today." [23] To such prophecies the New State, following the affirmations of Salazar, replies that Pan-Portuguese nationalism ("Empire without imperialism") will prevail against these sentiments for African self-determination. The answer to racial tensions is the universal spirit of brotherhood in the African colonies which transcends color, race, and civilization. The answer to economic unrest is the Portuguese respect for the individual dignity of the worker. The answer to materialistic doctrines is Christianity. Thus Portugal is confident she can avoid the turbulence of other colonial areas, contain the sentiments of African nationalism, and in the end culturally absorb the entire population of Angola and Moçambique into a Christian Portuguese community.

Portugal is determined to prevail. She is presently determined to remain in Africa and to convince the African — and perhaps the rest of the world — that it is right for her to be there. But how much longer the disembodied colonial mystique evolved by the New State or a traditional racial tolerance will serve Portugal's cause in Africa is uncertain. The present tranquillity of Angola and Moçambique is no sure indication of future harmony. As I have attempted to show in earlier chapters, it is as much the result of ignorance and isolation as it is of successful Portuguese policy. For the future Portugal will need to temper her doctrines and experience with more wisdom and understanding of human aspirations than she has shown in the past.

NOTES

1. The Companhia de Diamantes de Angola, the formidable Diamang, mines about twelve million dollars' worth of gem diamonds each year. Capitalized mostly by British and Belgian interests making up the Union Minière Company, an extension of the international diamond monopoly, Diamang has been since its foundation in 1920 the most important single force in Angola's economic life. Diamonds were the main financial support in the colony's lean years from 1920 to 1940; in recent years their importance in the total economy of the province has been overshadowed by the tremendous expansion of coffee exports. A new contract negotiated in 1955 extended indefinitely the company's exclusive prospecting rights, gave the Portuguese government 11 per cent of the capital stock (it had previously held only 6 per cent), and established a redistribution of annual profits which gave the government an additional $450,000 a year.

Diamang is a small monopolistic empire in Angola. It is exempt from taxes, pays no import duties on mine machinery and no export duties on diamonds, and has at its exclusive disposal the African work force of the Lunda area. Its privileged isolated position has drawn through the years a clamor of odd-assorted protests from nationalists, who believe that Portugal was hoodwinked by clever foreign capitalists; from liberals, who have scored the wide scope of authority granted the company; from colonists in Angola, who resented the special favors received by Diamang; and from traditional defenders of Portuguese policy in Africa, who think that the company's clinical efficiency, its *hauteur*, and its isolated position represent the antithesis of Portugal's colonizing spirit. In reality, Diamang, which is the largest private employer of African labor in Angola, has a record no better and no worse than that of any other concessionary company in the Portuguese colonies.

Whether the oil strike near Luanda will rival the importance of diamonds in the Angola economy cannot yet be known, but the discovery of oil in 1955 was heralded as one of the great events in twentieth-century Portuguese Africa, and it was then estimated that upwards of a million tons yearly would be processed. The pilot refinery completed in 1958, however, has a capacity for only 100,000 tons a year, not sufficient for the province's own use.

The Portuguese government, tempering its reluctance to allow foreign capital in the overseas provinces, has been obliged to permit a Belgian company, the Compagnie Financière Belge des Pétroles (Petrofina) to develop its nascent oil industry. The terms of the contract provide for, among other things, 55 per cent of the stock in the exploiting company to be in Portuguese hands and for 5 per cent of the annual liquid profits to go into the Angolan Reserve Fund.

The two colonies export small quantities of other minerals, uranium and manganese from Angola (mineral surveys have located scattered deposits of copper), and insignificant amounts of beryl, bauxite, and davidite from Moçambique. A trickle of gold occasionally comes out of the mines of Manica — which since 1510 have been Portugal's greatest disappointment in Moçambique — and about 175,000 tons of coal are mined near Tete each year.

2. Sugar refineries and cottonseed and vegetable oil extracting plants produce the other main export items of local industry. Colonial textile production takes care of a small part of each province's needs, while beer, cigarettes, cement and asbestos products, bricks and tile are manufactured in sufficient quantities for local demands.

3. One of the major problems Portugal has attempted to solve in the colonies is how to stimulate African agriculture. The present Portuguese government has set up various programs, controls, and pilot schemes to assist the African toward better cultivation of his land to check soil erosion. Cereals and cottons have been designated almost exclusively African crops, and open compulsion has been used to increase their production. Frequently, however, the prices of these crops have been fixed at levels generally considered inadequate to stimulate production. The government's efforts have had the effect at times of forcing the African to sacrifice the cultivation of other food crops he has traditionally grown. It has also been difficult for the government to reconcile the development of African agriculture with the increasing demands for African labor made by European farms and industry and by the colonies' own public-works programs.

4. In Angola, coffee, now principally grown on European *fazendas* northeast of Luanda, accounts for about 50 per cent of the colony's annual exports, while sugar, sisal, and palm oil make up another 10 to 12 per cent. In Moçambique, African-cultivated cotton is the leading export, but sisal, sugar, and copra from the vast concessionary coastal plantations — many of them internationally financed — and tea from the highland estates of Gurué and Milange make up the larger portion of the province's agricultural production. Cashew nuts, citrus fruits, and bananas are gaining in importance as export crops from Moçambique.

In 1955 the leading exports from Angola were, in order, coffee, diamonds, fish products, sisal, cotton, corn, and sugar. Those of Moçambique were cotton, sugar, tea, copra, cashew nuts, and sisal.

5. Unfortunately, from the Portuguese point of view, much of the wealth that passes through these ports comes from other countries in Africa: through Lobito goes the mineral ore from the Belgian Congo's Katanga province; through Beira, much of the Rhodesias' ore and tobacco; and through Lourenço Marques, about 50 per cent of South Africa's Rand traffic. By a series of international conventions (see Chapter VI for a discussion of the Moçambique–Union of South Africa Convention) the Portuguese ports are guaranteed a percentage of the traffic to and from the Congo, the Rhodesias, and the Union. Constant expansion of port facilities has barely kept pace with the increasing traffic, and both Lourenço Marques and Beira are frequently congested with cargo and shipping. Lourenço Marques now handles about five million tons of cargo a year and Beira another three million tons.

6. Although Portugal is still the main supplier of colonial imports (chiefly wine, cotton textiles, and simple agricultural tools), imports from the me-

tropolis are now only 30 to 40 per cent of the yearly total, with goods of English, German, or American manufacture making up another 40 per cent. Portugal now takes only from 25 to 30 per cent of the provinces' exports, and in recent years the United States, purchasing large quantities of Angolan coffee, has frequently replaced the metropolis as the main market for Angolan exports. Preserved fish from Angola is used in the Congo and French Africa; Moçambique's sugar and fruit go to the Union of South Africa and her cashew nuts are shipped to India.

The fluctuations of trade in Portuguese Africa and the transitory nature of such information are such that I have only sought to give the most general indications. Continuing publications such as the United Kingdom's "Overseas Economic Surveys" and the United States Department of Commerce's economic reports on world trade give a comprehensive picture of trade and economic patterns in Portuguese Africa. The most recent publications in these series are: Cyril W. Andrews, *Portuguese East Africa*, "Overseas Economic Surveys" (London, 1949); G. Edgar Vaughan, *Portuguese East Africa*, "Overseas Economic Surveys" (London, 1952); Bryce J. M. Nairn, *Portuguese East Africa*, "Overseas Economic Surveys" (London, 1955); T. C. Shannon, *Portuguese West Africa*, "Overseas Economic Surveys" (London, 1954); "Basic Data on the Economy of Angola," *World Trade Information Service Economic Reports*, Part 1, No. 57–51; "Economic Developments in Mozambique, 1954," *World Trade Information Service Economic Reports*, Part 1, No. 55–47; "Economic Developments in Mozambique, 1955," *World Trade Information Service Economic Reports*, Part 1, No. 56–47; "Economic Developments in Mozambique, 1956," *World Trade Information Service Economic Reports*, Part 1, No. 57–48.

Much of the information in these publications comes from the *Anuários estatísticos* published by each province. These statistical annuals and their supplements are indispensable for any close examination of the colonial trade and economy. C. F. Spence's *The Portuguese Colony of Moçambique* (Cape Town, 1951) is very useful for a general economic guide to Portuguese East Africa.

7. The Benguela Railway traverses central Angola from Lobito to the Belgian Congo frontier at Dilolo. The Lourenço Marques–Transvaal system finished in 1955 a branch line northwestward to the Southern Rhodesian frontier at Pafuri, thus connecting Lourenço Marques directly with the industrial and mining areas of the Rhodesias. The Beira-Umtali road has recently been improved to carry larger quantities of freight to and from the Rhodesias. Both rail lines are government owned. The Beira-Umtali line is in turn connected with the British-capitalized Trans-Zambezia which runs north into Nyasaland; a Portuguese spur line connects the latter road with Tete.

The queen of these railroads is undoubtedly the Benguela Railway, one of the great pioneering roads of the continent. Probably no other feature of Angolan life in this century has attracted so much attention as the Benguela Railway as it progressed its thousand-mile way up from Lobito to the Bié plateau and across Hungry Country to the Belgian Congo frontier. The Benguela Railway was big, it was imaginative, it was expensive. The concession to build the road was obtained by a group headed by Robert Williams, one of Rhodes's men, who had discovered copper deposits in the Katanga and conceived the notion of building a railroad from the Congo to Benguela-

Lobito. Williams' Tanganyika Concessions provided most of the original capital for the road. Begun in 1903, the line did not reach the Congo frontier until 1929. The cost of construction exceeded forty million dollars, of which over 80 per cent came from British sources. As a colonizing and commercial force the Benguela Railway has made an invaluable contribution to the development of Angola.

8. The two most important local lines are those which are under construction from Moçambique's port of Nacala to Lake Nyasa (four hundred miles of track have now been laid) and from the Angolan port of Moçâmedes toward the Northern Rhodesian frontier (by the end of 1958 the four hundred miles of track had reached Vila Serpa Pinto). With the completion of these two lines all of the most productive areas of both colonies will be connected with the coast. In addition, the government-owned Luanda-Malange line in Angola is being extended eastward to the Lui River and a 165-mile road is under contruction into the Portuguese Congo. In Moçambique, several small systems, none more than one hundred miles in length, run along the coast and penetrate the near interior from the ports of Lourenço Marques, Chai-Chai, Inhambane, and Quelimane.

CHAPTER I. THE CONGO EXPERIMENT

1. Basil Davidson, *The African Awakening* (London, 1955), p. 49.

2. A court poet of the first third of the sixteenth century gives what must have been a fairly common conception in Lisbon of the Congo scene. The following is a free translation of a passage from Garcia de Resende's *Miscelânea*, edited by Mendes dos Remédios (Coimbra, 1917), pp. 22, 24. "I shall begin in Guinea and the Congo where it is well known that they have the custom of eating each other up. They eat men like cattle, selected, well cared for. The slave-wives kill them and cook them in pots; they eat them also broiled . . . They have fearful elephants, snakes of great size, terrifying alligators, fragrant civet cats, stately trees, rice, bananas, palm trees, cats of many different kinds, and different sorts of birds, powerful hippopotamuses which walk along the shore."

3. The best sources for information on the Congo and its people in this early period are: J. Cuvelier and L. Jadin, *L'Ancien Congo d'après les archives romaines* (Brussels, 1954); J. Cuvelier, *L'Ancien royaume de Congo* (Bruges, 1946); Théodor Simar, *Le Congo* (Brussels, 1919).

4. Quoted in Alfredo de Albuquerque Felner, *Angola* (Coimbra, 1933), pp. 22–23.

5. R. E. G. Armattoe, *The Golden Age of West Africa* (n.p., 1946), pp. 29–30.

6. Quoted in Ralph Delgado, *História de Angola* (3 vols.; vols. I and II, Benguela, 1948; vol. III, Lobito, 1953), I, 84.

7. Of the original five missionaries who went to the Congo in 1490, at least two remained until 1506. There may have been, in addition to individual priests arriving from São Tomé, a party sent out by Manuel in 1504, but details are lacking.

8. Probably the most accessible version of the *regimento* is in Felner's *Angola*, pp. 383–390. Felner's work is in many respects a treasure.

9. "Letter from Afonso, King of the Congo, to King Manuel, October 5,

1514," in Visconde de Paiva Manso, *História do Congo* (Lisbon, 1855), pp. 13–31. This plea was followed by another in May 1515, when Afonso asked for teachers, priests, and technicians. Manuel responded by enjoining the apostolic vicar of São Tomé to investigate the situation in the Congo. Father Rui de Aguiar visited the kingdom in 1516. He wrote admiringly of Afonso's intense faith and scholarship and recommended that Lisbon send more missionaries. During his sojourn the São Tomé father established a school which, according to one enthusiastic report, had more than a thousand students.

10. The subsidies given the missionaries were generally cowrie shells or slaves. If the former, the vicar took them and any other money given the priests by parishioners and had slaves bought. The slaves were sold by the procurator of the diocese who in turn recompensed his brothers in the Congo with needed supplies. It is at once apparent that the recommendation by João III that this traffic be carried out with discretion and honesty was not always kept.

11. In still another letter of the same year, Afonso expressed a desire to have doctors and pharmacists in residence to treat the Portuguese, who were dying in substantial numbers. He also placed his usual request for teachers, masons, and carpenters.

12. The devastating climate and fevers surely contributed to Portuguese bad temper. Farinha quotes a contemporary letter (c. 1515): "The climate is so unhealthy for the foreigner that of all those who go there few fail to sicken, and of those who sicken few fail to die, and those who survive are obliged to withstand the intense heat of the torrid zone, suffering hunger, thirst, and many other miseries, for which there is no relief save patience, of which much is needed, not only to tolerate the discomforts of such a wretched place, but what is more, to fight the barbarity, ignorance, idolatry, and vices, which seem scarcely human, but rather those of irrational animals." António Lourenço Farinha, *D. Afonso, Rei do Congo* (Lisbon, 1941), p. 19.

13. In the 1530's and 1540's probably 4,000–5,000 slaves a year were shipped from the Congo.

14. Paiva Manso, *História do Congo*, pp. 93–96.

15. The migrations and devastations of the Jaga warriors are described in Gladwyn Murray Childs, *Umbundu Kinship and Character* (London, 1949), pp. 181–190.

16. Duarte Lopes was a Portuguese merchant and explorer, long resident in the Congo. He sailed from Pinda in 1583 with letters for Philip II. After a number of accidents and detours he arrived in Spain to deliver his messages and set out for Rome to get approval for two projects he had in mind, a house for the missionaries in the Congo and a hospital there for Christians. While in Rome, Duarte Lopes told his Congo adventures to Filippe Pigafetta who published the account in Italian in 1591 under the title *Relatione del reame di Congo*. Editions in Latin, Dutch, and English appeared before 1600, but not until Rosa Capeans' edition did the work appear in Portuguese. See Duarte Lopes and Filippe Pigafetta, *Relação do Congo e das terras circunvizinhas*, trans. by Rosa Capeans (2 vols.; Lisbon, 1949–1951).

The account gives interesting anthropological and geographical details of the Congo, although the comments on Portuguese-African relations in the sixteenth century are disappointingly sketchy. Duarte Lopes subsequently became an important figure in the great controversy which has raged (on the Portuguese side anyway) for almost one hundred years on the priority of exploration in central Africa. The Portuguese attitude is best summed up by Leon Cahun in his preface to a French translation of the relation (Brussels, 1883). I quote from the Portuguese translation of Cahun in Capeans' edition, I, 23–26:

"Comparing a map of Africa, made in 1850, before the voyages of Barth, Livingstone, and Speke, with a map of the end of the sixteenth century, after the great Portuguese explorations of Diogo Cão, Francisco Gouveia, and Duarte Lopes, one may see that the interior of this continent was less well known thirty years ago than it was three hundred years ago . . . In a lecture given after his return he [Speke] cleared up the great African mystery thus: 'If the ancients had known that Equatorial Africa is the region of the great rains, they would not have racked their brains seeking the origin of the Nile.' And we say: 'If Speke had read the description of Africa published in 1598 by the Bry brothers, he would not have boasted of having uncovered the secret of the origin of the Nile, which Duarte Lopes discovered and the Bry brothers divulged 280 years before his voyage.'"

Cahun goes on to ridicule Stanley's claims of discovery in the Congo and also the voyages of Serval, Griffon de Bellay, and de Brazza, suggesting that they could have saved themselves much trouble by reading Duarte Lopes first. He finishes up with the much quoted remark: "Unhappily, scholars who read ancient books almost never travel, and travelers who explore the land personally never read."

17. Father Barroso, quoted in Farinha, *D. Afonso* I, p. 84.

CHAPTER II. MOÇAMBIQUE AND THE TRADITION

1. Two important aspects of Moçambique history I shall omit in the present chapter, principally for reasons of organization. The *prazo* system is treated in Chapter IV on Portuguese colonization in Africa; the story of the missions in Moçambique is included in Chapter V on the missionary effort in Angola and Moçambique.

2. Whether João received the report is not known. If the Portuguese court did not receive the letter, it at least did receive much information of Covilhã's travels and the sights he witnessed.

3. Originally the supreme command was offered to Vasco's father. On his death, it was rejected by the eldest son Paulo, the third choice being Vasco.

4. The reasons for the mutual disenchantment are complicated and in part the result of initial confusions over religious identities. The sheik was not altogether blameless. At the same time, da Gama's men, before and after the cannonading, played the role of kidnappers and brigands.

5. This is one of the incredibly heroic stories of the Portuguese in the East, giving substance to their boasts of valor and the faith they inspired in the local population.

6. See Eric Axelson, *South-east Africa, 1488–1530* (London, 1940), pp. 108–127.

7. The captaincy at Sofala and Moçambique included jurisdiction for the whole coast. Sofala at first was the home of the captain, but after a period of six-month alternations the permanent residence was established on the island.

8. Throughout this work, unless I make specific reference to the modern

administrative district of Zambézia, I use the term Zambézia in its original sense, that is, the area of Portuguese penetration on both sides of the river into the interior.

9. A second important source of itinerant knowledge on African customs and Portuguese vicissitudes in southeast Africa is found in a number of accounts of shipwrecks taking place off the coast of Natal in the century 1550–1650. George McCall Theal, *Records of South-East Africa* (9 vols.; Cape Town, 1898–1903) has translated the greater part of these into English. The accounts are further discussed in James Duffy, *Shipwreck and Empire* (Cambridge, Massachusetts, 1955).

10. Far more important than the Dutch attacks on São Sebastião was the establishment in 1652 of a Dutch settlement at Table Bay on the continent's end. That the Portuguese did not occupy at least a small portion of this coast may have been a grave mistake.

11. Madeira was fearful that the jealous captain at Moçambique would somehow obstruct his messengers or else turn the discovery to his own advantage. He therefore entrusted the samples to two friends, a Dominican priest and Gaspar Bocarro. The priest, above suspicion in his clerical garb, got the glad tidings to Lisbon after boarding a homeward-bound carrack at Moçambique. Bocarro, to avoid sailing from the island, journeyed overland from Tete, by the southern edge of Lake Nyasa, to the mouth of the Rovuma, penetrating an area of the province not thoroughly explored by another European until the travels of Livingstone.

CHAPTER III. ANGOLA TO 1858

1. The island of Luanda and the coastal strip opposite were apparently not subservient to the Ngola. Through the century this land was under the control of the Manicongo.

2. For a fuller description of the Ovimbundu, their origins and relationships, see Childs, *Umbundu Kinship and Character*, especially pp. 167 ff.

3. Felner, *Angola*, pp. 166–169.

4. The suggestion had a double purpose: to make use of these celebrated fighers in the difficult campaigns and to rid Brazil of some of its unwanted subjects.

5. Baltasar Rebelo de Aragão, "Terras e minas africanas," in Luciano Cordeiro, *Memórias do ultramar* (Lisbon, 1881).

6. Ravenstein's edition of the Battell account is one of the classic studies in the African field. E. G. Ravenstein, ed., *The Strange Adventures of Andrew Battell of Leigh* (Hakulyt Society; London, 1901).

7. Charles R. Boxer, *Salvador de Sá and the Struggle for Brasil and Angola* (London, 1952), p. 270.

8. The hero has now attained the highest official recognition. In 1955 the two national secondary schools in Angola were Liceu Salvador Correia de Sá in Luanda and Liceu Diogo Cão in Sá da Bandeira (the high school in Lourenço Marques is the Liceu Salazar).

9. Henrique Galvão and Carlos Selvagem, *Império ultramarino português* (4 vols.; Lisbon, 1950–1953), III, 81.

10. J. J. Lopes de Lima, *Ensaios sobre a estatística das possessões portuguesas* (4 vols.; Lisbon, 1844–1846), III, 34.

11. One of the most serious ills from which Angola now suffered was populational. A census of the period gives the following figures for the area of Portuguese occupation: 1,832 whites (150 women), 5,770 mulattoes, 292,270 free Africans, 86,708 slaves. Luanda had a white population of a little over 1,500 souls, 135 of them women. In the late 1840's over three hundred emigrants from Brazil were transported to Moçâmedes, some of them making their way to the highlands of Huíla. It was a small beginning, but from it was to proceed an uneven growth in the colony's inhabitants.

CHAPTER IV. COLONIZATION AND SETTLEMENT

1. The matter of colonization in the twentieth century will be taken up in Chapters X and XIII.

2. As a general rule Portuguese colonizing activities in Angola and Moçambique fall into three phases. First came the merchant who traded with the Africans along the coast and gradually penetrated the interior, following, in Moçambique, routes established by Arab and native traders. A trader was seldom able to continue or expand his activities without armed support to protect the centers of commerce and the routes leading to the coast, and thus small stockades and even substantial fortresses were constructed and became isolated outposts of Portuguese civilization. In the footsteps of the merchant and the soldier, sometimes preceding them, was the missionary, who in some instances sincerely sought to implant in a primitive consciousness the moral ideals and cultural attainments of Europe. The second phase was the military occupation of the colonies, a move which was motivated by the necessity to protect Portuguese Africa against foreign intrusions and to assure its peaceful occupation by white settlers. The perennial wars in Angola against the great chiefs and lesser *sobas* were almost exclusively for the purpose of protecting or fomenting the slave trade, and it was not until the end of the nineteenth and the beginning of the twentieth centuries that the second phase was completed in Angola and Moçambique. The third phase is basically a contemporary phenomenon: the creation of a stable white population in towns and on farms and the emergence of a noticeable European female population. See Gastão Sousa Dias, *Ocupação de Angola* (Lisbon, 1944), p. 7.

3. See Armindo Monteiro, "Inimigos da colonização," *O mundo português*, I (1934), 194.

4. José A. Gomes dos Santos, *As nossas colónias* (Lisbon, 1903), pp. 5–6.

5. Mabel V. Jackson, *European Powers and South-East Africa* (London, 1942), pp. 23–24.

6. Henry Salt, *A Voyage to Abyssinia . . . and an Account of the Portuguese Settlements on the East Coast of Africa* (Philadelphia, 1816), p. 45.

7. Joaquim Mousinho de Albuquerque, *Moçambique* (2 vols.; Lisbon, 1934), II, 190–191. Although the first volume of this edition is entitled *Livro das campanhas*, both volumes are usually referred to by the title *Moçambique*.

8. F. Torres Texugo, *A Letter on the Slave Trade* (London, 1839), pp. 38–39.

9. António Norberto de Barbosa de Villas Boas Truão, *Estatística da capitania dos Rios de Sena no anno de 1806* (Lisbon, 1889).

10. Manuel Joaquim Mendes Vasconcelos e Cirne, *Memória sobre a província de Moçambique* (Lisbon, 1890), pp. 26–27.

11. Ernesto de Vilhena, *O regime dos prazos da Zambézia* (Lisbon, 1916), p. 7. For much of my information on the *prazo* I have relied on this classic little study and Marquês do Lavradio, *Portugal em Africa depois de 1851* (Lisbon, 1936).

12. Frederick D. Lugard, *The Rise of Our East African Empire* (2 vols.; Edinburgh, 1893), I, 29–30.

13. Mousinho de Albuquerque, *Moçambique*, II, 172–176.

14. *Relatório da comissão encarregada de estudar as reformas a introduzir no sistema dos prazos de Moçambique* (Lisbon, 1889). The Committee based its report on documentary material and a visit to the province.

15. *O regime dos prazos*, pp. 9–11.

16. For the story of the Cruz family fortunes I used mostly two indispensable works: J. J. Teixeira Botelho, *História militar e política dos portugueses em Moçambique de 1833 aos nossos dias* (2nd ed.; Lisbon, 1936) and Filipe Gastão de Almeida de Eça, *História das guerras no Zambeze* (2 vols.; Lisbon, 1953–1954). Almeida de Eça's work is a remarkable contribution to Moçambique bibliography and offers a quite different interpretation of the Zambezi wars.

17. The best source for factual information on the land companies in Moçambique is in *A Manual of Portuguese East Africa* (London, 1920), a work compiled by the Geographical Section of the Naval Intelligence Division of the British Admiralty.

18. An interesting sidelight on the comparative native policies of the Moçambique and Zambézia Companies is found in a contemporary tract whose author claims that the African population in the Moçambique Company lands increased 84 per cent from 1900 to 1904 because of the Africans seeking refuge there from the territories of the Zambézia Company. His explanation is that the Moçambique Company accepted payment of the head tax in goods or money while the Zambézia management demanded payment by labor. Lopo Vaz de Sampaio e Melo, *Política indígena* (Oporto, 1910), p. 250.

19. Francisco José de Lacerda e Almeida, *Diário da viagem de Moçambique para os Rios de Sena* (Lisbon, 1889), pp. 6–7.

20. Lyons McLeod, *Travels in Eastern Africa; with the Narrative of a Residence in Mozambique* (2 vols.; London, 1860), I, 154–155.

21. Parker Gillmore, *Through Gasa Land and the Scene of the Portuguese Aggression* (London, 1890), p. 4.

22. Montague George Jessett, *The Key to South Africa: Delagoa Bay* (London, 1899), pp. 22–23; Amadeu Cunha, *Mousinho* (5 vols.; Lisbon, 1935–1936), IV, 70.

23. William Miller Macmillan, *Africa Emergent* (rev. ed.; London, 1949), p. 21.

24. Mary H. Kingsley, *West African Studies* (London, 1899), p. 284.

25. William F. W. Owen, *Narrative of Voyages to Explore the Coasts of Africa, Arabia, and Madagascar* (2 vols.; London, 1833), II, 384–386; W. Winwood Reade, *Savage Africa* (2nd ed.; London, 1864), pp. 301–302.

26. Gastão Sousa Dias, *José de Anchieta* (Lisbon, 1939), pp. 46–47.

27. Daniel Crawford, *Thinking Back* (London, 1914), pp. 4–5.

28. Quoted in Jofre Amaral Nogueira, *A colonização do Huambo* (Nova Lisboa, 1953), p. 5.

29. Quoted in Sousa Dias, *José de Anchieta*, p. 18.

30. Amaral Nogueira, *A colonização do Huambo*, pp. 26–27.

31. Sousa Dias, *Ocupação de Angola*, pp. 52–53.

32. For the story of the trek gathered in part from conversations with Boers who participated in it, see: Willem Jaspert, *Through Unknown Africa*, tr. by Agnes Platt (London, n.d.), pp. 97–98; Lawrence G. Green, *Lords of the Last Frontier* (London, 1953), pp. 113–125.

33. Alberto de Almeida Teixeira, *Artur de Paiva* (Lisbon, 1937). See also Paiva's correspondence edited by Gastão Sousa Dias in *Artur de Paiva* (2 vols.; Lisbon, 1938).

34. Henry W. Nevinson, *A Modern Slavery* (New York, 1906), pp. 67–68.

35. H. H. Johnston, "The Portuguese in West Africa," *Journal of the African Society*, XII (1913), 115–116.

The Brazilian sociologist Gilberto Freyre has used Huíla as a sociological object-lesson to indicate the superiority of Latin colonizing abilities in tropical lands over those of Nordic races — a view which ignores three centuries of Portuguese failures to colonize Africa and which mistakenly regards Huíla as a tropical area, when it has climatically more in common with large sections of the Union of South Africa, colonized in part by Nordic races, than it does with the Congo or the Luanda areas. In fact the Moçâmedes-Huíla region of Angola is the scene of the only triumph of Portuguese white colonization in her two African provinces until the twentieth century, and there are those who consider this success the workings of fortune. See Gilberto Freyre, *Aventura e rotina* (Rio de Janeiro, 1953), p. 399.

36. Macmillan, *Africa Emergent*, p. 94.

CHAPTER V. THE MISSIONARY EFFORT

1. These disputes, generally of a personal nature involving local problems, are evident in a great debate in the Chamber of Deputies in 1879. Bishop Pires de Lima, in response to Andrade Corvo's charge that the history of Portuguese missions was filled with examples of abuse, replied: "You may be right, sir . . . Missionaries in the past practiced abuses, missionaries in the present probably do the same, and so will those in the future. The fact that they are missionaries does not make them lose their human nature . . . But who has committed greater folly overseas than the governors and employees who have been appointed there? And because part of the personnel chosen has been bad, very bad and even detestable, does anyone suggest that the colonies be left without authorities? To avoid the abuses of appointees, does anyone seriously propose the abandonment of our overseas administration?" Quoted in Eduardo d'Almeida Saldanha, *Colónias, missões, e Acto Colonial* (Vila Nova de Familacão, 1930), p. 97.

2. Mousinho de Albuquerque, *Moçambique*, II, 231.

3. Manuel Alves da Cunha quoted in Gastão Sousa Dias, *Um grande missionário, Padre Ernesto Lecomte* (Lisbon, 1946), p. 3.

4. J. P. Oliveira Martins, *Portugal em Africa* (Lisbon, 1953), p. xxiv.

5. Quoted in J. Alves Correia, *A dilatação da fé no império português* (2 vols.; Lisbon, 1936), II, 40–41.

6. "In the whole history of African missionary activity, excepting possibly the early days of the Congo, the action of Portuguese missionaries never

equaled either in quality or extension, the work of the Italian Capuchins."
Paiva Manso, *História do Congo*, p. 213.

7. Owen, *Narrative of Voyages to Explore the Coasts of Africa, Arabia, and Madagascar*, II, 65-66. The charges are echoed by Mabel Jackson (*European Powers and South-East Africa*, pp. 39-40), basing her remarks on Portuguese letters of the period.

8. Bartle Frere, *Eastern Africa as a Field for Missionary Labor* (London, 1874), p. 66.

9. Manuel de Brito Camacho, *Pretos e brancos* (Lisbon, 1926), pp. 147-148.

10. Quoted in António Lourenço Farinha, *A expansão da fé na África e no Brasil* (Lisbon, 1942), pp. 191-192.

11. Luís Silveira, *Um missionário português no Congo nos fins do século XVIII* (Lisbon, 1943), p. 5.

12. For a survey of the many activities of the Protestant missions in Angola and Moçambique up to about 1930, two works are invaluable. They are John T. Tucker, *Angola, Land of the Blacksmith Prince* (London, 1933), and Eduardo Moreira, *Portuguese East Africa* (London, 1936).

13. James Johnston, *Reality Versus Romance in South Central Africa* (London, 1893), pp. 55-58.

14. I was told by a Portuguese citizen in Angola that in his opinion the Protestants had done more for Angola in fifty years than his church had done in three hundred. Any comparison of this nature is essentially unfair, since it is partly based on social service contributions which in previous centuries were secondary in Catholic missionary concepts.

15. The dispute arose from a smuggling raid on the island by Portuguese authorities. The crew of a mission boat were taken captive, and in the ensuing scuffle the Portuguese corporal fatally shot an English missionary.

16. Mousinho de Albuquerque, *Moçambique*, II, 235.

17. *Umbundu Kinship and Character*, pp. 222-223.

CHAPTER VI. THE SLAVE TRADE, SLAVERY, AND CONTRACT LABOR

1. In recent years these attacks have been met with impatient scorn by Portuguese officials, who point out that their country has been in Africa longer than any other European people, during which time they have learned how to live and work with the African population, a statement — from their point of view — undoubtedly true. In a Lourenço Marques interview with a representative of France Presse in August 1956, Portugal's Craveiro Lopes said that Portugal made only one request, that she be allowed to get on with her work in Africa without the interference of people who know nothing about Africa. Quoted in *O século de Lisboa*, August 8, 1956, p. 1.

2. In the early 1900's the British consul at Beira wrote enthusiastically.

Whilst in our own colonies we have educated the native, and petted him, and done everything we could think of to impair his value as a worker by endeavoring to fit him for positions for which he is not by nature intended, the Portuguese, on the other hand, throughout the centuries of their occupation of East Africa, have never viewed him in any but a proper and practical light; for them he is first and last the "mão d'obra" (laboring hand), and any proposition tending to lessen his value in the capacity would never, and will never, be entertained by them for a single moment. I have always observed, over a considerable number of years, that in whatever direction the Portuguese have achieved but qualified success, they have always known how to deal with the negro, and want of respect on the part of the latter is scarcely ever seen. I do not mean that this respect is extorted by cruelty; I do not believe the Portuguese master is in any sense a cruel person — indeed, I must confess to having seen much more ill-treatment of natives among the foreigners of the Mozambique province — but wherever one may come in contact with him, whether it be Mozambique in the north, the Zambezi in the center, or Beira in the south, one will never see the insolent demeanour of the black man toward the white which is such a constant and lamentable spectacle of everyday occurrence in our Colonies and Protectorates in almost all parts of Africa. R. C. F. Maugham, *Portuguese East Africa* (London, 1906), pp. 302–303.

3. The native policies of the present Portuguese government will be discussed more fully in Chapter XII.

4. See Carter G. Woodson, *The African Background Outlined* (Washington, 1936), pp. 221–222, and W. E. Burghardt DuBois, *The World and Africa* (New York, 1947), p. 47.

5. Humorously exaggerated lines like these from a contemporary poem (1516) are not to be taken at face value.

> We see so many captives
> Come into the realm,
> And so many Portuguese leave
> That it soon may be that they,
> In my opinion, will outnumber us.

Garcia de Resende, *Miscelânea*, p. 37.

6. António Brásio, *Os pretos em Portugal* (Lisbon, 1944).

7. Gilberto Freyre, "Slavery, Monarchy, and Modern Brazil," *Foreign Affairs*, XXXIII (1955), 624–633.

8. Charles R. Boxer, *Salvador de Sá*, p. 255.

9. The most concise appraisal of West African history in this period is found in John William Blake's introductory essay to *Europeans in West Africa, 1450–1560* (Hakluyt Society; 2 vols.; London, 1941–1942), I, 3–63. Edmundo Correia Lopes, *A escravatura* (Lisbon, 1944), is very useful in spite of a haphazard arrangement of material. Most of my slaving statistics come from these two sources. See also Donald Pierson, *Negroes in Brazil* (Chicago, 1942), pp. 32–34. Neither the statistics nor the authorities cited by Pierson are completely convincing.

10. Correia Lopes, *A escravatura*, p. 87.

11. *Ibid*, p. 175.

12. Boxer, *Salvador de Sá*, pp. 236–239.

13. Maria Teresa Amado Neves, "D. Francisco Inocêncio de Sousa Coutinho," *Os portugueses em África* (3 vols.; Lisbon, 1938), I, 126–133.

14. William Law Mathieson, *Great Britain and the Slave Trade* (London, 1929), pp. 20–21.

15. Thomas Fowell Buxton, *The African Slave Trade* (2nd ed.; London, 1839), p. vi.

16. Lawrence F. Hill, "The Abolition of the African Slave Trade to Brazil," *Hispanic-American Historical Review*, XI (1931), 169–197.

17. Lugard, *The Rise of Our East African Empire*, I, 15–16.

18. Lacerda, *Diário da viagem*, pp. 23–24.

19. Torres Texugo, *A Letter on the Slave Trade*, pp. 14–15.

20. See Owen, *Narrative of Voyages*, I, 287. "The introduction of the slave trade stopped the pursuits of industry, and changed those places where peace and agriculture had formerly reigned into the seat of war and bloodshed. Contending tribes are now constantly striving to obtain by mutual conflict prisoners and slaves for sale to the Portuguese, who excite these wars and fatten on the blood and wretchedness they produce. The slave trade has been a blight on its prosperity."

21. MacLeod, *Travels in Eastern Africa*, II, 32.

22. Henry Rowley, *The Story of the Universities' Mission to Central Africa* (London, 1866), pp. 64–65.

23. Frederick Courtney Selous, *Travel and Adventure in South-East Africa* (London, 1893), pp. 57–58; Daniel J. Rankin, *The Zambesi Basin and Nyassaland* (Edinburgh, 1893), pp. 106–107.

24. Verney Lovett Cameron, *Across Africa* (2 vols.; New York, 1877). "Coimbra [a mulatto slave trader and son of the captain-major of Bié] arrived with a gang of fifty-two women tied together in lots of seventeen or eighteen. Some had children in their arms, others were far advanced in pregnancy, and all were laden with huge bundles of grass-cloth and other plunder. These poor, weary, and footsore creatures were covered with weals and scars, showing how unmercifully cruel had been the treatment received at the hands of the savage who called himself their owner. To obtain these fifty-two women at least ten villages had been destroyed, each having a population of from one to two hundred, or about 1,500 in all. Some may, perchance, have escaped to neighboring villages, but the greater portion were undoubtedly burnt when their villages were surprised, and shot whilst attempting to save their wives and families, or doomed to die of starvation in the jungle . . ." (II, 136). So troubling were the charges made by Cameron that they were debated in the Lisbon parliament.

On the other hand, both Lord Mayo (D. R. W. Bourke) and Sir Harry Johnston, who visited Angola extensively in 1882, made only passing references to slavery. Of the Portuguese occupation of Angola, Johnston wrote for *The Graphic*: "But . . . we must not forget to give the Portuguese their due. Of all the European powers that rule in tropical Africa none have pushed their influence so far into the interior as Portugal. And the Portuguese rule more by influence over the natives than by actual force. The garrisons at Dondo, Malange and other places in the interior range perhaps from fifty to two hundred men, and these are nearly entirely native soldiers. The country is so thickly populated that the inhabitants could in a moment sweep away the Portuguese if they disliked their rule." Quoted in Roland Oliver, *Sir Harry Johnston and the Scramble for Africa* (London, 1957), p. 30.

25. "If the goal was the dignification of the black man, the abolition of slavery created around him conditions of non-protection which harmed him more than slavery had previously." Francisco Bahia dos Santos, *Política ultramarina de Portugal* (Lisbon, 1955), p. 128.

26. Quoted by Jaime Batalha Reis, "Portugal e a colonização da Africa na sessão do VI Congresso Internacional de Geografia em Londres," *Estudos geográficos e históricos* (Lisbon, 1941), p. 208.

27. The number of slaves officially registered with the colonial authorities

in 1854 was ridiculously low, and probably represented a Luanda-Benguela figure. The slave owner was doing himself no favor by complying with the required registration law of 1854, and most residents certainly submitted negligible and inaccurate figures.

28. António Francisco da Silva Porto, *Viagens e apontamentos de um portuense em Africa*, ed. by José de Miranda and António Brochado (Lisbon, 1942). Silva Porto was writing in 1869; in 1890 he committed suicide under extraordinary circumstances predicted in the quotation given. See Chapter VII.

29. Reade, *Savage Africa*, p. 317.

30. António Júlio Belo de Almeida, *Operações militares na região da Sanga, no concelho de Novo Redondo* (Lisbon, 1942), pp. 7–9.

31. From a section of the "Relatório da Comissão" published in *Antologia colonial portuguesa* (Lisbon, 1946), p. 25 et seq.

32. For the substance of the native labor legislation I have relied on J. M. da Silva Cunha, *O trabalho indígena* (2nd ed.; Lisbon, 1955). See also G. St. John Browne, *The African Laborer* (London, 1933), 194–198.

33. The Portuguese themselves have not been reticent in pointing up abuses in Angola. "The black knows that the whites, those who are not Portuguese, at least, faithfully fulfill their contracts, pay them generously for their services. The Portuguese colonist considers the native as a beast of burden, an agricultural machine with no rights or privileges; he deceives him in his contracts, defrauds him in the products of his work, prompts him with exaggerated punishments condemned by law. Anyone who visits the highlands of Angola knows that it is not uncommon to find on the roads discarded slave collars or the hippo whip with which the back of the Negro is still beaten." Gomes dos Santos, *As nossas colónias*, p. 147.

The most authoritative spokesman is Norton de Matos, governor general and later high commissioner in the second and third decades of the century. Defending his own policies in Angola, he says that before his arrival native labor, with rare exceptions, could not be called free, but that by the end of his term in 1915 the remains of ancient slavery and the new disguised forms had disappeared. When he returned in 1919, Norton de Matos found that corruption had broken out again and that only through his decrees of 1921 did Angola again pass from a regime of forced labor to free contracted labor. Norton de Matos believed that the surest way to win the African was to pay him well, clothe and feed him, and introduce him to a way of life superior to his own. As high commissioner he set about immediately, he says, to correct the exploitation of the native's contract and forbid absolutely the use of forced laborers by private concerns. José Mendes Ribeiro Norton de Matos, *A província de Angola* (Oporto, 1926), pp. 126 ff.

That Norton de Matos was more enthusiastic than accurate about the effect of his decrees and the permanent influence they had on Angolan Portuguese may be seen in a speech given by Vasco Dias de Oliveira at a meeting of the Angola Agricultural Association, wherein the speaker referred to the Africans as a backward race who should be forced to work and not have the same liberties as civilized people. The speaker also pumped for government conscription of labor for private farms. Vasco Dias de Oliveira, *Mão-de-obra indígena* (Luanda, 1924).

34. "Correspondence with British Commissioners," *Accounts and Papers* *1865*, XXVII, 91–92; *1868–1869*, XXIII, 22–24; *1870*, XXI, 92–93.

35. I have been unable to obtain Biker's article, " A ilha de São Tomé," which was published in the *Revista portuguesa colonial e marítima* in 1903. I rely on a summary and quotations from Gomes dos Santos, *As nossas colónias*, pp. 110–117. The quotations I use are Biker's.

36. Henry W. Nevinson, *More Changes, More Chances* (London, 1925), pp. 38–39.

37. Nevinson, *A Modern Slavery*, pp. 27, 118–119.

38. Nevinson, *More Changes, More Chances*, pp. 74–75.

39. *Ibid.*, pp 77–79.

40. *Correspondence Exchanged between Mr. William A. Cadbury and a Committee of Planters of the Islands of São Tomé and Príncipe in December, 1907, and January, 1908* (Lisbon, 1908), p. 9.

41. *Ibid.*, pp. 13–20.

42. William Cadbury, *Labour in Portuguese West Africa* (2nd ed.; London, 1910), pp. 76–77.

43. John H. Harris, *Portuguese Slavery: Britain's Dilemma* (London, 1913), p. 9.

44. *British Documents* 993 (LIX), 938 (LX), 941 (XLV), and 947 (XXIII).

45. Lord Cromer, "Portuguese Contract Labor," *The Spectator*, September 18, 1915, pp. 359–360; *Journal of the African Society*, XVI (1917), 343.

46. Quoted in E. D. Morel, *The Black Man's Burden* (New York, 1920), pp. 156–157. Colonel Statham, en route to Angola in 1920, records a talk with the British vice-consul who "convinced me that, in the economic as well as humanitarian aspects of cocoa planting, the Portuguese have little or nothing to learn from any other colonial power. . . The native laborers are well fed, housed, and hospitalized and appear well treated and content." Statham goes on to say that the whole scandal may not have been justified and that the English press may have supported a campaign started by England's enemies! J. C. B. Statham, *Through Angola, a Coming Colony* (Edinburgh, 1922), pp. 25–28.

47. Mary H. Kingsley, *Travels in West Africa* (London, 1897), p. 49.

48. Notable Portuguese answers to English charges are: August Ribeiro, *O cacau de São Tomé — Resposta ao relatório da missão Cadbury* (Lisbon, 1910); António A. Corrêa de Aguiar, *O trabalho indígena nas ilhas de São Tomé e Príncipe* (São Tomé, 1919); Francisco Monteiro, *A mão-de-obra em São Tomé e Príncipe* (Lisbon, 1910); Lopo Vaz de Sampaio e Melo, *Política indígena* (Oporto, 1910), pp. 303–335.

49. That part of Portuguese native policy not immediately associated with the labor problem will be taken up in Chapter X.

50. Edward Alsworth Ross, *Report on Employment of Native Labor in Portuguese Africa* (New York, 1925), p. 12.

51. *Report on Employment*, pp. 58–59.

52. F. M. de Oliveira Santos, *Resposta às acusações que o americano Professor Edward Alsworth Ross fez à administração dos portugueses num relatório . . .* (Luanda, 1927), pp. 125–127. Four years after Ross's visit, T. A. Barns remarked that "labor conditions in Portuguese West Africa are not quite as bad as they have been made out." T. A. Barns, "Through Portuguese West Africa," *Journal of the African Society*, XXVIII (1929), 227.

53. Thomaz de Almeida Garrett, *Um govêrno em Africa* (Lisbon, 1907), pp. 218–219.

54. Defending his patriotism, the high commissioner responded that he had not furnished the workers, but had only given permission for recruitment. He stated he thought 16,000–18,000 workers a year was a small contribution for the development of the lower Zambezi. Brito Camacho, *Pretos e brancos*, pp. 48–49.

55. Sheila T. Van der Horst, *Native Labour in South Africa* (London, 1942), p. 135.

56. The best available sources for the subject are: Van der Horst, *Native Labour, passim; The Colonial Problem* (London, 1937), pp. 395–396; *The Official Yearbook of the Union of South Africa*; C. F. Spence, *The Portuguese Colony of Moçambique, an Economic Survey* (Cape Town, 1951), pp. 85–87; *Manual of Portuguese East Africa* (London, 1920), pp. 171–182.

57. W. C. A. Shepherd, "Recruiting in Portuguese East Africa of Natives for the Mines," *Journal of the African Society*, XXXIII (1934), 253–360.

58. António Augusto Mendes Correia, *Raças do império* (Oporto, 1943), pp. 546–548. There is some truth in Mendes Correia's assertions of denationalization in parts of Moçambique as a result of recruiting there. Carol Birkby says that Gazaland might as well be called "Wineland" (after WNLA) from the number of recruits going and coming from the mines in this district. *Limpopo Journey* (London, 1939), p. 261.

CHAPTER VII. LIVINGSTONE AND THE PORTUGUESE

1. *Boletim oficial do governo-geral da província de Angola*, June 28, 1854, pp. 2–3.

2. *Missionary Travels and Researches in South Africa* (London, 1857), p. 227.

3. *Ibid.*, p. 217. His cryptic account here is fuller in the original journal. See Frank Debenham, *The Way to Ilala* (London, 1955), p. 86. Silva Porto's version appears in *Viagens e apontamentos*, pp. 124–129.

4. *Missionary Travels*, p. 362.

5. *Ibid.*, p. 435.

6. Quoted in Reginald Coupland, *Kirk on the Zambezi* (Oxford, 1928), pp. 68–69. George Seaver in his recent biography of Livingstone cites many instances of Livingstone's gratitude to the Portuguese, but he also quotes a curious paragraph from one of the explorer's letters. "In a postscript of a letter to Tidman, marked *private*, he says shrewdly: 'I may remark that the Portuguese in Africa have a good character for polite hospitality, but I came amongst them in a peculiar manner. I came out from behind them. It would, I suspect, be a different story if a missionary had come to Loanda and wished to go in from thence.' " George Seaver, *David Livingstone: His Life and Letters* (New York, 1957), p. 224.

7. *Missionary Travels*, pp. 369–370.

8. *Ibid.*, pp. 371–372.

9. *Ibid.*, pp. 395–396.

10. *Ibid.*, pp. 394–395. He gives the city's population as 12,000 (830 whites, of whom 160 are female), and estimates that the whole colony can boast of only about 1,000 Europeans.

11. *Ibid.*, p. 405.

12. *Ibid.*, p. 437.

13. *Ibid.*, p. 653. Elsewhere: "The Portuguese here are as kind as they were in Angola, and that is saying a good deal. Somehow or the other, I had imbibed a sort of prejudice against them. But actual intercourse has fully convinced me that we are liable to form a very wrong opinion of the majority from the contumacious acts of a few." David Chamberlain, ed., *Some Letters from Livingstone, 1840–1872* (London, 1940), p. 256.

For their part, the Portuguese have acknowledged Livingstone's prowess as an explorer. Serpa Pinto, who crossed the continent some years later, wrote that, "Livingstone is the only man who has known how to explore the *sertões* of Africa and his peaceful disposition is well known." Quoted in Alves de Azevedo, "Serpa Pinto, explorador invencível," in *Os portugueses em Africa*, I, 385.

14. *Missionary Travels*, pp. 642, 660. Dr. Gladwyn Childs informs me that he has seen in the 1857 *Boletim* of the Government General of Angola a letter written by Livingstone from Tete to the governor general of Angola. Livingstone offered his services to the Portuguese government to assist in the establishing of a chain of governmental and commercial posts across Africa from Angola to Moçambique. Their purpose would be to drive out the slave trade and establish legitimate trade in the interior. I have been unable to obtain a copy of this communication.

15. Livingstone's ideas about the aims of the expedition went beyond those of simple exploration. In a letter written a few days before his departure from England, he stated that his objects "have something more in them than meets the eye. They are not merely exploratory, for I go with the intention of benefiting both the African and my own countrymen. . . All this machinery has for its ostensible object the developing of African trade and the promotion of civilisation, but what I tell to none but such as you, in whom I have confidence, is this. I hope it may result in an English colony in the healthy high lands of Central Africa." Debenham, *The Way to Ilala*, p. 130.

16. Coupland, *Kirk on the Zambezi*, p. 89.

17. Debenham, *The Way to Ilala*, p. 134.

18. Charles and David Livingstone, *Narrative of an Expedition to the Zambezi and its Tributaries* (New York, 1866), pp. 163–164.

19. *Ibid.*, p. vii.

20. *Ibid.*, p. x.

21. *Ibid.*, pp. 427–428.

22. *Ibid.*, p. 259.

23. *Ibid.*, pp. 485–486.

24. *Ibid.*, pp. 636–637.

25. For typical communications from Lisbon to the Moçambique governors, see Jackson, *European Powers and South-East Africa*, pp. 251–267.

26. Francisco José de Lacerda, *Exame das viagens do Doutor Livingstone* (Lisbon, 1867), p. 25.

27. I have failed to do justice to Lacerda's close and caustic arguments. See *Exame das viagens*, pp. 288–293.

28. The notion of a prior Portuguese *travessia* still has as many defenders as does Atlantis or the Baconian authorship of Shakespearian dramas.

29. See Charles R. Boxer, "Sisnado Dias Bayão: Conquistador da 'Mãe de

ouro,'" in *Os portugueses em Africa*, I, 99–115. See also Visconde de Soveral, "Apontamentos sobre o domínio de Portugal no continente africano," *Boletim da Sociedade de Geografia e História de Lisboa*, X (1891), 145–156.

30. F. V. Bruce Miller, "A Few Historical Notes on Feira and Zumbo," *Journal of the African Society*, IX (1910), 416–423; E. H. L. Pool, "An Early Portuguese Settlement in Northern Rhodesia," *Journal of the African Society*, XXX (1931), 164–168.

31. Richard F. Burton, *The Lands of Cazembe* (London, 1873); see also Francisco José de Lacerda e Almeida, *Diário da Viagem*, and Sidney R. Welch, *Portuguese and Dutch in South Africa, 1640–1806* (Cape Town, 1951), pp. 620–633.

32. The date of their departure is not clear. Quirino da Fonseca gives 1801, Gastão de Sousa Dias, 1804. See Quirino da Fonseca, "João Baptista, pioneiro da dupla travessia de Africa em princípios do século XIX," *Boletim da Sociedade de Geografia e História de Lisboa*, LIII (1935), pp. 141–157, and Gastão de Sousa Dias, "O reino de Angola e as suas conquistas . . . ," *História da expansão portuguesa no mundo*, edited by António Baião and others (3 vols., Lisbon, 1937–1940), III, 212.

33. The information on the strange meeting of these two men who represented in so many ways prevailing national attitudes in England and Portuguese Africa is slight. The material on Silva Porto is completely inadequate for a man of his importance. The only substantial works are several edited collections of his writings and a biography by Gastão de Sousa Dias, published in Lisbon in 1948.

34. Quoted in Ruy Miguel da Cruz, "Silva Porto," *Esmeraldo*, no. 10, 1956, pp. 49–54.

35. See Joaquim Rodrigues Graça, "Expedição ao Muatayanvua," *Boletim da Sociedade de Geografia e História de Lisboa*, IX (1890), 365–468.

36. João de Andrade Corvo, *Estudos sobre as províncias ultramarinas* (2 vols.; Lisbon, 1883), I, 211–212.

37. Quoted in José de Almada, *A política colonial de João de Andrade Corvo* (Lisbon, 1944), p. 31.

38. Perhaps the outstanding work published by the society was Cordeiro's collection of sixteenth- and early seventeenth-century accounts of commerce and conquest in Angola, *Memórias do ultramar* (Lisbon, 1881). In the *Boletim* published by the society appeared many valuable articles of contemporary and past events in Africa.

39. Stanley spent more than a month with Capelo, Ivens, and Serpa Pinto in Luanda waiting for a ship to take him from Africa. Several amusing anecdotes of this association appear in Alexandre Alberto da Rocha de Serpa Pinto, *Como eu atravessei África* (2 vols.; London, 1881), I, 23–27.

CHAPTER VIII. INTERNATIONAL DISPUTES

1. Quoted in Mabel Jackson, *European Powers and South-East Africa*, p. 53. A survey of French interest in Moçambique is contained on pp. 42–63.

2. *Ibid.*, pp. 137–138. For detailed analysis of the turbulent decade, see pp. 122–153. A study of the Delagoa Bay negotiations, 1823–1875, is in Raymond W. Bixler, "Anglo-Portuguese Rivalry for Delagoa Bay," *The Journal of Modern History*, VI (1934), 425–440.

3. Almada, *A política colonial de João de Andrade Corvo*, p. 22.

4. For much of my information here and on the Conference of Berlin I have used S. E. Crowe, *The Berlin West African Conference* (London, 1942).

5. J. Holland Rose, *The Development of the European Nations* (5th ed.; London, 1915), pp. 546–547.

6. J. Scott Keltie, *The Partition of Africa* (2nd ed.; London, 1895), pp. 147–148.

7. *Ibid.*, pp. 241–242. See also Charles Lucas, *The Partition and Colonization of Africa* (Oxford, 1922), pp. 92–93; Luis Vieira de Castro, "A Conferência de Berlim e seus efeitos imediatos," in *História da expansão portuguesa no mundo*, III, 339; Charles E. Nowell, "Portugal and the Partition of Africa," *The Journal of Modern History*, XIX (1947), 13.

8. Pursuing her new-found policy of positive diplomacy, Portugal demanded in 1886–87 that the Sultan of Zanzibar remove his customhouse and posts from the whole of Tungue (Tungi) Bay, which lay some twenty miles south of the Rovuma's mouth and had long been, by mutual understanding, the frontier between the dominions of Zanzibar and Moçambique. The Sultan, who had recently been bullied by more important European countries, refused to cede his half of the bay to the pretensions of Portugal. Portuguese gunboats thereupon began to patrol the coast and Consul Serpa Pinto lowered the flag on the Portuguese consulate, preparatory to departure. The Portuguese government issued an ultimatum and occupied Tungue and the shores of the bay. England and Germany remonstrated, but the Portuguese refused arbitration and no solution was reached. For the English, who could read of the action in a series of articles in the *Times* by no less a journalist than Henry Stanley, the incident was but another indication of Portuguese irresponsibility in Africa.

9. A remark much quoted in Africa and Europe summed up a popular attitude: "Let the Portuguese have only the territory where the whites can't live." The *Natal Mercury* pumped for German occupation of Moçambique. "It is better to have one small German settlement near us than any number of miserable and wretched Portuguese colonies which never have and never can benefit either settlers or aborigines, but which are simply a curse wherever they have taken root on African soil. . . To speak of Portuguese colonies in East Africa is to speak of a mere fiction. . . The very fact that for three hundred years the flag of Portugal has waved along the East Coast involves the condemnation of Portuguese rule." Quoted in Joaquim Carlos Paiva de Andrade, *Relatório de uma viagem às terras dos landins* (Lisbon, 1885), pp. 29–30.

10. Leonard Woolf, *Empire and Commerce in Africa* (London, 1920), p. 174.

11. Eduardo Moreira, "Portuguese Colonial Policy," *Africa*, XVII (1947), 186–188.

12. The meeting between the Englishman and the Portuguese was in the best Kipling tradition. Johnston received champagne and delicacies and a letter of safe conduct through Portuguese territory. Serpa Pinto's Lt. Coutinho told Johnston that "we are both doing our best for our respective countries, and however much our political views may differ, that is no reason why one white man should quarrel with another in Central Africa." Johnston notes that "this was indeed the keynote of Portuguese demeanour towards me, then and thence-

forth, and I feel it only just to place these facts on record, for I have been often vexed at the unjust aspersions which have been cast upon the Portuguese in the British Press." H. H. Johnston, *British Central Africa* (New York, 1897), pp. 80–89. See also Oliver, *Sir Harry Johnston and the Scramble for Africa*, pp. 158–159. Johnston was one of the few Englishmen of his day who liked and, in some cases, admired the Portuguese in Africa, and in later life he seems to have had some misgivings about the validity of England's pretensions in 1889–1890.

13. J. P. Oliveira Martins, *Portugal em Africa*, pp. xiv–xv.

14. F. A. Oliveira Martins, ed., *O "Ultimatum" visto por António Enes* (Lisbon, 1946).

15. In all of her troubles with other nations Portugal has had no more loyal defender than Mary Kingsley. "It must be noted, for one thing, that Portugal was the first European nation to tackle Africa in what is now by many people considered the legitimate way, namely by direct governmental control. Other nations left West Africa in the hands of companies of merchant adventurers and private individuals for centuries. Nevertheless, Portugal is nowadays unpopular among the other nations engaged in exploiting Africa. I shrink from embroiling myself in controversy, but I am bound to say I think she has become unpopular on account of prejudice, coupled with that strange moral phenomenon that makes men desirous of persuading themselves that a person they have treated badly deserves that treatment.

"The more powerful European nations have dealt scandalously, from a moral standpoint, with Portugal in Africa. . ." Mary Kingsley, *West African Studies* (London, 1899), p. 282.

16. The best presentation of the shifting frontiers and demands is found in *A Manual of Portuguese East Africa*, pp. 492–503.

17. The clash did take place, at Macequece, in May, too late to influence the final negotiations. The Portuguese volunteers were dispersed with considerable losses. João de Azevedo Coutinho, *O combate de Macequece* (Lisbon, 1935).

18. A dispassionate analysis of the foregoing conflict is hard to find. The bibliography is extensive, but generally intemperate. Valuable material, however, may be found in Amadeu Cunha, "O 'Ultimatum,' suas repercussões até ao tratado de 1891," in *História da expansão portuguesa no mundo*, III, 345–358; Luis Vieira de Castro, *D. Carlos I* (3rd ed.; Lisbon, 1943); José Justino Teixeira Botelho, *História militar e política dos portugueses em Moçambique*, II, 319–399; *Manual of Portuguese East Africa*, pp. 479–503. An excellent survey, containing much new information, is found in Oliver's *Sir Harry Johnston and the Scramble for Africa*, pp. 124–196.

19. Jessett, *The Key to South Africa: Delagoa Bay*, p. 86. This is a monumentally fatuous, uninformed, and imperialistic work, but quite representative of an attitude prevailing in South African and English opinion.

As usual, Mary Kingsley had kind words for the Portuguese. "The thing she is taxed with nowadays is that she does not develop her possessions. Developing African possessions is the fashion, so naturally Portugal, who persists in going about in crinoline and poke bonnet style, gets jeered at. This is right in a way, so long as we don't call it the high moral view and add to it libel." *West African Studies*, p. 283.

20. The area was returned to Portugal after the First World War.

21. See "Conflict over Delagoa Bay and the Future of the Portuguese Empire in the Nineties," Appendix II of *The Colonial Problem*, pp. 383–385; Arthur Ribeiro Lopes, *A convenção secreta entre a Alemanha e a Inglaterra sobre a partilha das colónias portuguesas* (Lisbon, 1933); Louis A. C. Raphael, *The Cape-to-Cairo Dream* (New York, 1936), pp. 156–160, 207–214.

22. Prince Lichnowsky, *My Mission to London, 1912–1914* (London, 1918), p. 16.

23. Arthur Berriedale Keith, *The Belgian Congo and the Berlin Act* (Oxford, 1919), p. 300. Keith goes on: "A system such as that in force in Angola, under which land could not be acquired by other than Portuguese subjects, and exports which paid 3 per cent shipped in Portuguese bottoms were mulcted in 15 per cent if carried in foreign vessels . . . is not seriously to be defended . . . especially when the result of the policy is stagnation pure and simple. Portugal must also reform in essential aspects her treatment of the natives who go to labour in San Thomé. . ."

CHAPTER IX. A NEW ERA

1. João Alexandre Lopes Galvão, "A ocupação económica das colónias portuguesas," in *Os portugueses em Africa*, III, 128.

2. Oliveira Martins, *Portugal em Africa*, p. 32.

3. Eduardo Lupi, ed., *Aires de Ornelas* (3 vols.; Lisbon, 1936), I, 72.

4. Quoted in Amadeu Cunha, *Mousinho*, I, 29.

5. Quoted in Lupi, *Aires de Ornelas*, I, 72.

6. Brito Camacho, *Pretos e brancos*, p. 12.

7. Quoted in Lourenço Cayolla, *Sá da Bandeira* (Lisbon, 1935), p. 27.

8. António Enes, *Moçambique* (3rd ed.; Lisbon, 1946), p. 58.

9. *Ibid.*, p. 63.

10. *Ibid.*, p. 251.

11. *Ibid.*, p. 96.

12. *Ibid.*, pp. 401–420.

13. *Ibid.*, pp. 229–236.

14. *Ibid.*, p. 75.

15. António Enes and others, "O trabalho dos indígenas e o crédito agrícola," *Antologia colonial portuguesa*, pp. 28–29. Enes' strong attitude on forced labor was influential in revisions of the Native Labor Code of 1899.

16. Cunha, *Mousinho*, I, 13.

17. Mousinho believed that only a military *coup d'état* could save Portugal from third-rate governments. This military regime would have a nonpolitical leader. He was unable to convince Carlos, however, that a government could exist without political parties.

18. Mousinho de Albuquerque, *Moçambique*, II, 17–18. Although he holds the Liberals responsible for the final collapse of Moçambique, Mousinho admits that it was the end of a process which began in the middle of the seventeenth century, caused by the incapacity and indiscipline of public officials, lack of military strength, and the rise of the mulattoes and Canarins.

19. Cunha, *Mousinho*, III, 17–18.

20. *Ibid.*, III, 28.

21. *Ibid.*, III, 12–13; II, 50.

22. The circumscription was the major unit of administrative division in

each district. There remained in unpacified areas a military command and in the centers of white or civilized population, *concelhos*, or municipalities, administered by local councils.

23. Eduardo Costa, "Princípios de administração colonial," in *Antologia colonial portuguesa*, p. 93.

24. After the establishment of the Republic in 1910, both Paiva Couceiro and Aires were prominent in monarchist resistance, especially Paiva Couceiro who assumed command of the monarchist forces in exile. Both men played leading roles in the abortive revolt of 1919.

CHAPTER X. PROMISE AND DISAPPOINTMENT, 1895–1930

1. Not even the accomplishments of the African explorers and the generation of 1895 were above reproach. Teixeira de Sousa, Minister of Marine and Overseas from 1900 to 1903, vented his impatience on these men too. "From romantic Africa we have got nothing but anecdotes. What did Sr. Serpa Pinto bring us? Anecdotes. Sr. Capelo and Sr. Ivens? Anecdotes. What did Sr. Mariano de Carvalho give us? What did Sr. António Enes bring us? Anecdotes. Stories to entertain children and administrative folly to make cynical bureaucrats laugh." Arménio Monteiro, *Conselheiro Dr. António Teixeira de Sousa* (Lisbon, 1937), p. 34.

2. Enrollment was irregular in the first years (14 in 1906, 87 in 1913, 24 in 1915, 9 in 1918), but increased steadily after 1926. António de Almeida and João F. Rodrigues, "O ensino colonial na metrópole e a sua influência sobre a nossa administração ultramarina," *Estudos gerais* (3 vols.; Lisbon, 1938), III, 301–405, is a useful study of the Colonial School.

3. Gomes dos Santos, *As nossas colónias*, pp. 11–13.

4. João Lopes Carneiro de Moura, *A administração colonial portuguesa* (Lisbon, 1910), pp. 259–260.

5. J. Pereira do Nascimento and A. Alexandre de Mattos, *A colonisação de Angola* (Lisbon, 1912), pp. 7–8.

6. The war was a disaster for Portugal. Although it meant a great deal to the small country's national pride, participation in the conflict created serious economic problems with political repercussions that went on beyond 1918. Both Angola and Moçambique, on the other hand, enjoyed a short-lived upsurge in prosperity, and Portuguese East Africa regained the sliver of Quionga territory which she had lost to Germany in the 1890's. The African campaigns have furnished much grist for the mills of Portuguese publicists in spite of the military reverses suffered by Portugal. The incident at Naulila on Angola's southern frontier in 1914 was a massacre, an act of wanton arrogance by German troops, of seventy Portuguese and native soldiers. The East African campaigns were equally undistinguished; General von Lettow moved almost at will through Moçambique north of the Zambezi and northeast Rhodesia. Early in 1916, Portuguese forces crossed the Rovuma into German East Africa, but the triumph was brief and for the rest of the war, Portuguese action was mainly defensive. The rout of her forces in a small clash near Quelimane was particularly humiliating to Portugal because of unkind British comments.

The popular defense of the Quelimane incident is that Portuguese forces broke ranks and fled through no lack of courage but because they were uninstructed. "Nor could we count on the natives because wherever the Germans went native revolts against Portuguese authority followed." Those English who take pleasure in humiliating the Portuguese are reminded that with more men and better equipment they also failed against von Lettow. See A. Duarte de Almeida, *História colonial de Portugal* (Lisbon, n.d.), pp. 227–228.

7. Armindo Monteiro, "As grandes directrizes da governação ultramarina no período que decorreu entre as duas guerras mundiais," in *História da expansão portuguesa no mundo*, III, 432.

8. The leading newspaper of Angola, *A província de Angola* (October 17, 1955, p. 1) printed a long article on the beginning of a subscription campaign in the city of Nova Lisboa to build a monument to the memory of Norton de Matos, about whom the Salazar government has mixed emotions. May one read significance in this gesture by the Portuguese in Angola who constantly chafe under the restrictions of Lisbon?

9. Quoted in d'Almeida Saldanha, *Colónias, missões e Acto Colonial*, p. 27.

10. Brito Camacho, *Pretos e brancos*, pp. 6, 219, 268.

11. In Malcolm Burr, *A Fossicker in Angola* (London, 1933), T. Alexander Barns, *Angolan Sketches* (London, 1928), and Consul Maugham's two studies on Portuguese East Africa one may find numerous references to the tidy house and garden of the Portuguese administrator in the bush. The traveler was sometimes more impressed with the garden than with the work done by the administrator.

12. Norton de Matos, *A província de Angola*, pp. 219–223.

13. D'Almeida Saldanha, *Colónias*, pp. 97–99.

14. *A província de Angola*, p. 201.

15. Júlio Ferreira Pinto, *Angola* (Lisbon, 1926), pp. 114–115.

16. *A província de Angola*, pp. 248–250.

17. Van der Horst, *The Colonial Problem*, pp. 110–111.

18. Quoted in Sampaio e Melo, *Política indígena*, p. 110. More succinctly Artur de Paiva suggested in 1892 that the Portuguese stop calling the African a child and treat him like a man. Alberto de Almeida Teixera, *Artur de Paiva*, p. 41.

19. I realize that these generalities are unfair to many Portuguese colonists, but I believe they are in essence true. In the strange complex of Portuguese attitudes toward the African one will find a willingness to intermarry, a readiness to accept the civilized African as an equal, a sometimes benign tolerance toward the *indígena*, but one seldom finds, save in some administrative and missionary circles, any practical concern for the African's welfare.

20. See C. P. Groves, *The Planting of Christianity in Africa* (3 vols.; London, 1948–1955), II, 272–277.

21. *Moçambique*, II, 185–188. Mousinho also suggested that his country might be able to persuade the Transvaal government to permit the sale of Portuguese wines in the Rand mines.

22. Almeida Garrett, *Um governo em Africa*, p. 141. A long section of his report is concerned with the devastations created by alcoholism.

23. Cadbury, *Labour in Portuguese West Africa*, p. 70.

24. *A província de Angola*, p. 141.

25. Barns, *Angolan Sketches*, p. 104.

26. These transitory schools were always in Luanda or Moçambique and were mainly for the education of officials' children. In 1808, for example, the

wife of Angola's Governor Saldanha da Gama gave classes in French and music to the daughters of Luanda's illustrious families.

27. Avila de Azevedo, *O problema escolar de Angola* (Luanda, 1945), p. 12. A royal decree of 1852 called for a training center in Moçambique for African girls, and a year later a seminary was created in Luanda; an occasional political exile offered courses out of altruism or boredom, but these were scarcely important contributions.

28. Mousinho de Albuquerque, *Moçambique*, II, 138–139.

29. Sampaio e Melo, *Política indígena*, pp. 119–120.

30. *Ibid.*

31. Thomas Jesse Jones, *Education in Africa* (New York, 1922), pp. 224–247 (Angola); Thomas Jesse Jones, *Education in East Africa* (New York, 1926), pp. 296–315 (Moçambique). The reports were attacked by Portuguese spokesmen as distorted, but, apart from several doubtful generalities, the conclusions of the commission coincided with statistics and complaints made by Portuguese officials in the same years.

32. D'Almeida Saldanha, *Colónias*, p. lxxiv.

33. Camacho, *Pretos e brancos*, pp. 198, 234, 245, 266–267, 295. The high commissioner's observations refer to the entire province. Of a visit to a mission school outside of Lourenço Marques, Brito Camacho tells (p. 267) the following anecdote. "The priest who says Mass is the same one who teaches school, and it seems to me that God fated him for neither of these jobs. I attended a class to see how it was taught. The first thing the teacher asked one of the little black students was 'What are *palavras esdrúxulas* [words accented on the antepenultimate syllable]?' When the little boy did not answer, he asked him another question, 'What are polysyllabic words?'

"I told the teacher that if this was the way he taught the black boys, they would easily come to know as much as the professor, but they would never know enough to start down the road of life."

34. Quoted in Vaz de Sampaio e Melo, *Política indígena*, pp. 87–89.

35. Some Portuguese maintain that proof of their success is contained in two clichés which gained currency in the early twentieth century. One is that to the native, an Englishman is always an Englishman, a German is a German, and a Frenchman, a Frenchman, but the Portuguese is always a white man (the pride the Portuguese take in relating this anecdote — which reveals an attitude quite contrary to their professed lack of color consciousness — shows how much Portugal sought to adopt the colonial manners and prejudices of the major powers after the Conference of Berlin). The second remark stressed the point, which is very true, that so few Portuguese could live among so many natives without fear and could go safely from one end of Portuguese Africa to the other.

36. Vaz de Sampaio e Melo, *Política indígena*, p. 70. Although foreigners have been generally charmed by the seemingly domestic serenity of the Afro-Portuguese household and its happy mulatto offspring (Livingstone had said that Portuguese policy did credit to their hearts), a number of governors were less impressed. Norton de Matos saw the degeneration, or "cafrealization," of the white man, while Brito Camacho complained that the abandonment of mulatto children by their parents was a serious problem for the province, since the boys usually grew up wastrels and the girls, prostitutes.

37. Kingsley, *West African Studies*, p. 290. Consul Nightingale held no hope

for the future, however, without sharp revisions in the economic restrictions strangling Angola.

38. Carneiro de Moura, *A administração colonial*, p. 262.

39. Elemér Böhm, *La mise en valeur des colonies portugaises* (Lille, 1933), pp. 212–216.

40. *Ibid.*, p. 183; Vicente Ferreira, *Estudos ultramarinos* (4 vols.; Lisbon, 1943–1945), IV, 168. Vol. IV is chiefly a collection of Ferreira's essays on the problems of colonization and reveal the preoccupations and sentiments of his day.

41. *Angola*, p. 156.

42. Lourenço Marques' new status was not achieved without incident. When Brito Camacho asked the local golf club to print its rules in Portuguese as well as English, he was attacked by his countrymen for his "shocking bad taste" — and he replied accusing them of "a lamentable lack of national pride." *Pretos e brancos*, pp. 265–266.

CHAPTER XI. THE NEW STATE IN AFRICA: MYSTIQUE AND ADMINISTRATION

1. Even the much quoted remark, "We Portuguese will be the last Europeans to leave Africa," seems to have much less currency than it did a few years ago.

2. Armindo Monteiro, "Portugal in Africa," *Journal of the African Society*, XXXVIII (1939), 259.

3. António de Oliveira Salazar, "A nação na política colonial," in *Antologia colonial portuguesa*, p. 328. In a speech made over the national radio on November 1, 1957, Salazar still emphasized the historical character of Portugal's policy, which is dedicated to the spread of Portuguese culture and faith among the peoples of other colors and races in lands discovered by the Portuguese.

4. João Ameal, "Mostruário do Império," *O mundo português*, I (1934), 97–101.

5. Marcelo Caetano and others, "Discursos pronunciados. . . ," *O mundo português*, III (1936), 378, 381.

6. Conde de Campo Belo, "A mentalidade imperial através da expansão portuguesa no mundo," in *Estudos gerais*, I, 408.

7. António Leite de Magalhães, "Na estrada do Império," *O mundo português*, V (1938), 154. The translation does not do justice to the original.

8. António Leite de Magalhães, "Raízes de Portugal," *O mundo português*, IV (1937), 363.

9. Sidney R. Welch, *South Africa under King John III* (Cape Town, 1948), p. 139.

10. Quoted in João Ameal, "Os três chefes do Império," *O mundo português*, I (1934), 164–165. The transition from empire and colonies to nation and overseas provinces, an interesting study in semantics, will be discussed later.

11. Among the Agency's publications have figured prominently the writings of the generation of 1895 and studies on its various members.

12. Fernanda Reis, "O jornalismo colonial na metrópole," *Conferências na Escola Superior Colonial* (Lisbon, 1943), pp. 327–346.

13. No comprehensive study of the influence of the overseas expansion on Portuguese thought exists.

14. Rodrigues Junior complains that there is no lack of writers, but a lack

of books. He says that a writer in the colonies, with their inadequate print-ing facilities, cannot afford to pay for the publication of his work, especially since the amount of the prize is less than the cost of publication. Rodrigues Junior, *Literatura colonial* (Lourenço Marques, 1953), pp. 29-32.

15. "The future of native Angolan literature in Ki-mbundu . . . is now practically assured. J. Cordeiro da Matta, the negro poet of the Quanza River, has abandoned the Portuguese muse in order to consecrate his talents to the nascent national literature. The autodidactic and practical Ambaquistas of the interior have begun to perceive the superiority, for purposes of private cor-respondence, of their own tongue . . ." Heli Chatelain, *Folk Tales of Angola* (Boston, 1894), p. viii.

16. In addition to the need for a colonial literature, more enthusiastic writers have voiced the need for a colonial architecture to reflect both the dynamic and traditional in Portuguese overseas culture. See José Osório de Oliveira, "Necessidade de uma arquitectura portuguesa nas colónias," *O mundo português*, V (1938), 173-175.

Gilberto Freyre expressed mixed emotions on Angolan architecture. He was dismayed at Lobito, finding there no vigorous expression of the modern, but of Luanda he wrote: "Happily I find here people who have respect for the past as something to be defended, not with the exaggerations of an anti-quarian, but with a pleasure for those eternal Portuguese values which cut through conventional notions of time to form a kind of 'alwaysism' . . . *Aventura e rotina*, pp. 475-476.

17. Most old-time residents of the colonies speak well of the Colonial School graduates, commenting particularly on their diligence and honesty.

18. Marcelo Caetano, "Carta a um jovem português sobre o serviço do Império," *O mundo português*, I (1934), 264. During the 1936 cruise, Caetano spoke in Angola of the Portuguese university's role: "The university must be — if it desires to fulfill its high mission — a school of permanent devotion to science, of constant national exaltation, of extensive and intensive moral vibrance . . . The Portuguese university cannot remain apart from the pre-occupations, difficulties, and hopes which in every moment and for every generation arise in our country . . . And in the first level of the Portuguese university's preoccupations there stands today the colonial problem." "Dis-cursos pronunciados . . ." *O mundo português*, III (1936), 377.

19. *O mundo português*, II (1935), 218. A cruise in the other direction took place in 1940 on the occasion of the Exposition of the Portuguese World. A group of old colonists and soldiers was shipped by the government to Portugal to participate in the ceremonies.

20. Salazar has so far not made a trip to Portuguese Africa, although he is said to have remarked that such a visit would satisfy one of his greatest desires. Nevertheless, more outward manifestations of a Salazar cult are present in Africa than in Portugal. Streets, towns, schools, ships, all bear his name.

21. I was in Moçambique about six months before the arrival of Craveiro Lopes. On a trip through the interior of the province, our car was greeted by African children standing along the road with cries of "Viva Carmona!" The driver wryly observed that they would have to be re-educated before the arrival of Craveiro Lopes.

22. Quoted in *O século de Lisboa*, August 13, 1956, p. 5.

23. Eric Robbins, *This Man Malan* (Cape Town, 1953), p. 7. Sheila Pat-

terson's brilliant study, *The Last Trek* (London, 1957), brings out many concepts of Afrikanerdom which are suggestive of attitudes taken by the Portuguese in the last twenty-five years.

24. Article 80, chapter viii, of "Proposta de lei no. 231," in *Nova legislação ultramarina* (2 vols.; Lisbon, 1953-1955), I, 132.

25. João Ameal, "Mostruário do Império," *O mundo português*, I (1934), 99-100.

26. Manuel Simões Vaz, *Problemas de Moçambique* (Lourenço Marques, 1951), p. 42. With Portuguese colonial legislation in general, Simões Vaz is impatient: "The legislation in effect in Moçambique, both that emanating from the Colonial Ministry as well as that published locally is a 'skull-breaker' for anyone who trys to consult it. The laws and the decrees undergo constant changes and clarifications, and it is necessary to be a specialist to understand how they ought to be applied. Even specialists get confused and make mistakes which the tax payers inevitably have to pay for." *Problemas de Moçambique*, p. 29.

27. Bahia dos Santos, *Política ultramarina*, pp. 152-153.

28. Insofar as anyone has clarified the terms used in referring to the Portuguese possessions, Marcelo Caetano's summary is as good as any other: "Before the nineteenth century one does not find the official designation 'provinces' used in referring to the territories we today call 'colonies.' Against the term 'colony' there exists an unjust prejudice, created especially after the advent of the republican regime by the political sectarianism of the enemies of the new government.

"Looking through the documents of the period prior to the nineteenth century, we see that the territories conquered, colonized, or occupied by the Portuguese were generally called 'overseas dominions' and at times '*conquistas*' . . .

"The designation 'colony' is found in the seventeenth century and becomes current in the eighteenth century. 'Overseas provinces' are only introduced into official language in the nineteenth century under the influence of ideas of political and administrative assimilation which denied to the colonial territories the need for a juridical administration different from that of Portugal — which was patently absurd." Marcelo Caetano, *Do Conselho Ultramarino ao Conselho do Império* (Lisbon, 1943), pp. 29-30.

29. A. Martins Afonso, *Princípios fundamentais de organização política e administrativa da nação* (5th ed.; Lisbon, 1956), p. 156.

30. Although working in collaboration with the governor general's office and subject to its general supervision, certain administrative services, such as the military corps, as well as the judicial and treasury offices, are a part of national services.

31. In addition to the Provincial Statutes of Angola and Moçambique, authorized in 1955 by the Organic Overseas Law, for information on the administrative organization, I have relied on: A. Martins Afonso, *Princípios fundamentais*, pp. 156-160; Lord Hailey, *An African Survey* (rev. ed.; London, 1957), pp. 228-231, 353-357; F. Clement C. Egerton, *Angola in Perspective* (London, 1957), pp. 114-117; and various legislation contained in *Nova legislação ultramarina*.

32. At the same time, however, there is evidence that some officials have not yet attained the dedication demanded by the government. Silva Cunha

writes: "Unfortunately there has been noted recently a certain dissatisfaction . . . which has been translated into neglect of duty, discouragement, and lack of faith. It is necessary to eliminate the causes of the discontent of these functionaries and try to restore them to healthy optimism, to love and pride of the profession. Only thus will our Native Policy carry out successfully its mission." J. M. da Silva Cunha, *O sistema português de política indígena* (Coimbra, 1953), p. 233.

It is not clear whether Silva Cunha had in mind administrative abuses associated with the recruiting of African labor; in this regard the procedures of some officials, especially chiefs of post, have been open to much criticism.

33. The selection of colonial officials is of some interest. The office of governor general is customarily occupied by a high official from the Portuguese armed services. To a lesser extent, the governor general's immediate associates and the district governors also come from outside the colonial administrative hierarchy, either from the armed services or the professions. Directors of colonial services are usually professional men, many of whom have had long careers overseas. The ranks of the lower administration, as we have seen, are filled by men directly trained for the position. With the recent redistricting of Angola and Moçambique, it may be expected that a larger number of *administradores* will be promoted to district governors.

Admission to the colonial service is theoretically open to all qualified applicants, regardless of color, but European Portuguese predominate. Claims of discrimination against local recruits are not unheard of, and very few *assimilados* from Angola or Moçambique have progressed up the administrative ladder. Oden Meeker remarks that the colonial service is highly stratified, but that the head of an important department might be very black. He cites the case of an African *administrador* in Moçambique who had been trained in Lisbon. Oden Meeker, *Report on Africa* (New York, 1954), p. 224.

CHAPTER XII. THE NEW STATE IN AFRICA: NATIVE POLICY

1. Bahia dos Santos, *Política ultramarina*, pp. 81–82.
2. Morais Cabral, "A vitória do nosso espírito colonizador," *O mundo português*, VI (1939), 216.
3. Silva Cunha, *O sistema português*, pp. 140–141.
4. *Ibid.*, pp. 143–144.
5. Nevertheless, the philanthropic wording of legislation like the Colonial Act was disturbing to Portuguese colonists in Africa, usually more conservative in their views on native problems than the government. Of the Colonial Act, Eduardo d'Almeida Saldanha wrote: "Dr. Oliveira Salazar, in complete ignorance of the constitutional and physical differences between the white man and the black man and only influenced by the doctrine of equality of the idealists of the French Revolution . . . has concerned himself only with creating a constitutional dogma largely favorable to the Negro." *Colónias, missões, e Acto Colonial*, pp. xviii–xx.
6. Articles 56–64, chapter iii of Decreto-lei no. 39,666, "Estatuto dos indígenas portugueses das províncias da Guiné, Angola, e Moçambique," in *Nova legislação ultramarina*, II, 202–204.
7. Marcelo Caetano, *Os nativos na economia africana* (Coimbra, 1954), pp. 17–20.

8. Silva Cunha, *O sistema português*, p. 145; see also p. 115.

9. Quoted in Remy, *Goa, Roma do Oriente*, trans. by M.G. (Lisbon, 1955), p. 17.

10. Eduardo de Azevedo, *Terra de esperança* (Lisbon, 1954), p. 150.

11. The government's attitude is approximately summed by the anthropologist Mendes Correia:

Miscegenation in certain special cases (scarcity of Portuguese colonists from the metropolis, difficulty of acclimatization for the European) is a recourse for consolidation and development in the exploitation of territories, according to modern processes and in a spirit of collaboration between the Portuguese immigrants and the natives.

As human beings, tied to our race by the sacred bonds of origin, the mulattoes have a right to our sympathy and help. But the reasons which we have propounded do not permit the political role of the *mestiços* to go beyond the limits of local life. However brilliant and effective may be their professional, economic, agricultural, or industrial action, they, as naturalized foreigners, must never hold high posts in the general politics of the country, except perhaps in cases of proved and complete identification with us in temperament, in will, in feeling, in ideas, cases which are both exceptional and improbable.

A. A. Mendes Correia, *O mestiçamento nas colónias portuguesas* (Lisbon, 1940), pp. 22–23.

12. Bahia dos Santos, *Política ultramarina*, p. 165. Another Portuguese colonialist writes: "So sincere is our esteem for those who belong to the primitive races of Africa that . . . we accept them in our very midst without feeling for them the least repugnance, thus departing radically from the restrictions and prejudices which are manifest principally in the Anglo-Saxon and Germanic races." Jorge Pedro de Figueiredo Marinho da Silva, *O sentido do imperialismo português* (2 vols.; Lisbon, 1942), I, 50.

13. Commenting on these incidents — which still occur — the Brazilian Gilberto Freyre takes his Portuguese cousins sharply to task. "A Portugal that is pretentious and imperially European, ethnocentric, 'Aryan,' is a Portugal which has as little future in Africa as Holland has in Asia . . . The Portugal capable of eternalizing herself in Africa is the Portugal who remembers that she is Arabic or Moorish, and not only Nordic, in her origins and in her culture, character, and actions." *Aventura e rotina*, p. 483.

14. "It [Luanda] was Portugal but fused into Africa. Natives and half-castes sat at the wine shops, and children of every grade from black to white played in the streets. It was often difficult to distinguish which of the population were European and which African . . .

"Europe at its lowest standard of living is not far removed from Africa. The Portuguese peasant does not live so differently from the African peasant. The African makes an implicit caste distinction between the big white and the small white; he refers to the Portuguese as the black man of Europe and reacts to him as an equal.

"Nor to the Portuguese is he essentially inferior. Thus the two races have absorbed one another quite comfortably. I have seen them in school, in hospital, in prison together. They have the same rights, the same judicial system, and . . . the same language." Patrick Balfour, *Lands of the Equator: An African Journey* (London, 1937), p. 79.

15. See C. G. Woodson, "Attitudes of the Iberian Peninsula," *Journal of Negro History*, XX (1935), 190–243.

16. Manuel Récio records a conversation he overheard at the Lumbo airport in Moçambique. "Alongside of me are two ladies talking about the natives. One of the ladies is a teacher and condemns all Negroes without exception . . .

" 'Animals . . . savages . . . Don't trust them, don't speak to them!'

" 'Pardon me . . . I don't think so,' protests the other lady, who is not a professor, who has no official responsibilities. 'They are human beings, worthy of our respect and our aid . . .'

" 'Fancy words. I am the one who knows them well . . . Animals! And after all, there's the question of race, the white skin.' And the *professora* slaps her bare, pink, fleshy arm.

"The other lady repeats softly in either sorrow or indignation, 'Race . . . color . . . But what do race and color have to do with humanitarian sentiments?' " Manuel Récio, *Homens no mato* (Lisbon, 1952), p. 117.

17. Freyre, *Aventura e rotina*, p. 490; Azevedo, *Terra de esperança*, pp. 114–115.

18. Júlio Nunes de Oliveira, "Moçambique: Alguns aspectos e problemas da sua vida política, económica e social," in *Conferências na Escola Superior Colonial* (Lisbon, 1943), pp. 59–60.

Mendes Correia takes a similar view. "Angola can support a white population greater than that of the metropolis . . . But it will be necessary to treat equally the natives and the populational groups resulting from the mixing, whatever the policy may be . . . All Angolans will recognize our firm desire that Angola be forever Portuguese and very Portuguese." *Raças do império*, p. 482.

19. Articles 2 and 3, chapter iii, of Dicreto-lei no. 39,666.

20. Silva Cunha, *O sistema português*, p. 205.

21. *Ibid.*, p. 207.

22. Preamble to Dicreto no. 39,817. In *Nova legislação ultramarina*, II, 223–224.

23. Details on matters of this sort are hard to come by. See A. T. Steele, "On the Edge of Africa's Racial Troubles," *New York Herald-Tribune*, November 26, 1952, p. 16.

24. These taxes, formerly one of the financial supports of the provinces, now provide only about 7 to 8 per cent of the yearly total revenue.

25. The Liga Africana was perhaps more representative of African aspirations in the 1920's, although it has never effectively counted for much in influencing Portuguese policy. W. E. B. DuBois speaks of the Third Pan-African Conference he attended in Lisbon in 1923, at which the Liga Africana was host. He quotes a Portuguese deputy on the function of the Liga: "The great association of Portuguese Negroes, with headquarters at Lisbon, called the *Liga Africana* is an actual federation of all the indigenous associations scattered throughout the five provinces of Portuguese Africa and represents several million individuals . . . The *Liga Africana* . . . has a commission for all the other native organizations and knows how to express to the government in no ambiguous terms, but in a dignified manner, all that should be said to avoid injustice or to bring about the repeal of harsh laws. That is why the *Liga Africana* of Lisbon is the director of the Portuguese African movement, but only in the good sense of the word, without making any appeal to violence and without leaving constitutional limits." W. E. B. DuBois, *The World and Africa* (New York, 1947), p. 241.

26. *O brado africano*, February 27, 1932, p. 1. These selections do not reveal the full protest of this very long editorial.

27. The colonial administration continues to find it difficult to curb excesses in the distribution and sale of wine, which remains one of the most important import commodities, and drunkenness, even alcoholism, is a serious problem in parts of both colonies.

28. Davidson, *The African Awakening*, p. 223.

29. Azevedo, *Terra de esperança*, pp. 148–150. "To solve the problem," Azevedo goes on, "the government must make a real effort. Good intentions and words are not enough."

30. Simões Vaz, *Problemas de Moçambique*, p. 53.

31. See Teófilo Duarte, "Aldeamento indígena," in *Estudos coloniais* (Lisbon, 1942), pp. 113–128.

32. "Social and Economic Organization in the Portuguese Colonies," *Colonial Review*, II (1941), 121–122.

33. See José Firmo de Sousa Monteiro, *Relatório sobre o resgate dos "machongos" do Sul do Save* (Lourenço Marques, 1955).

34. Egerton, *Angola in Perspective*, p. 220.

35. Moçambique had about one hundred thousand Mohammedans. For giving me figures on the number of missionaries presently in the two colonies, I am indebted to Mr. Kenyon E. Moyer of the Missionary Research Library in New York and to the Reverend Frederick A. McGuire, C.M., of the Mission Secretariat in Washington. For other statistics I have relied on the *Anuários estatísticos* of Angola and Moçambique.

36. Afonso Costa Valdez Thomas dos Santos, *Angola, coração do império* (Lisbon, 1945), pp. 92–93. He continues: "The native is not easily denationalized . . . However exclusive has been his education in a Protestant religious mission, no Negro will stop wanting to imitate Portuguese customs on leaving his academic life."

37. The Organic Overseas Law defines the *ensino rudimentar* and relates to Portugal's colonial policy: "Instruction especially intended for natives in the provinces where the native regime still prevails will, in those regions where Portuguese Catholic missions are established, be entirely entrusted to missionary personnel and their assistants. In localities where these missions cannot carry out the function, instruction will continue to be the charge of the State.

"The instruction of natives in private schools must be subordinated to the same general orientation to which it is submitted when administered by the State.

"In the instruction of natives there is envisioned their perfect nationalization and moralization and their acquisition of habits and aptitudes of work in keeping with their sex, condition, and local economic conditions.

"Native languages may be used as an instrument in the teaching of Portuguese." Quoted in Bahia dos Santos, *Política ultramarina*, p. 164.

38. Hugo Rocha, "No império português ensina-se a falar a língua de Portugal," *O mundo português*, I (1934), 184.

39. See Childs, *Umbundu Kinship and Character*, pp. 142–143.

40. Having converted the colonies to provinces in 1951, several years before her admission to the United Nations, Portugal declares that she has no obligation for submitting reports on non-self-governing territories to the

United Nations. This argument, as shall be seen later, has not been universally accepted.

41. Marcelo Caetano, *Os nativos na economia africana*, p. 16.

42. Quoted in "A estadia do Sr. Ministro das Colónias nas terras africanas do Império," *O mundo português*, X (1943), 554. Such a statement is altogether consistent with the government's stated view that the Portuguese laborer should find joy through work — no matter whether poorly recompensed. The Portuguese economic system is not much less exploitative at home than it is overseas.

43. For the last several years, the government has spoken of preparing a new native labor code, but at the moment of writing (December 1957), I am not aware that one has appeared.

44. Even so, the 1928 code and the native labor principles stated in the Colonial Act were regarded by conservative Portuguese colonists as nonsense, conceived with no sense of the provincial need for a constant labor supply. See d'Almeida Saldanha, *Colónias, missões, e Acto Colonial*, pp. xxxiii-xlix.

45. Exempt from the draft are children under fourteen and people over sixty, the sick and invalid, sepoys (who usually are in charge of the labor brigades), Africans employed in public service, Africans working for themselves or others, recognized chiefs, women — except in special cases — and workers during the first six months after their return to their village. These exceptions are not always closely observed.

46. For this synthesis of labor laws I have relied principally on Silva Cunha, *O trabalho indígena*, pp. 201-270. See also Egerton, *Angola in Perspective*, pp. 258-262; Bahia dos Santos, *Política ultramarina*, pp. 159-160; Hailey, *An African Survey*, pp. 1371-1375; Lucy P. Mair, *Native Policies in Africa* (London, 1936), pp. 250-260.

47. Quoted in *A Huíla*, May 19, 1956, p. 1.

48. *Angola in Perspective*, p. 264.

49. Manuel Récio, *Homens no mato*, p. 51. The Diamond Company of Angola has stated that the twelve-month limitation on contracts has "prejudicial and pernicious effects" on the company's operations. *Relatório relativo ao exercício de 1955* (Lisbon, 1956), pp. 49-50.

50. Valdez Thomas dos Santos, *Angola, coração do Império*, p. 91.

51. "A protecção dos menores do ultramar," *O século de Lisboa*, August 4, 1956, p. 1.

52. *Os nativos na economia africana*, pp. 34-35.

53. Such efforts, according to d'Almeida Saldanha, were pointless. Speaking of the Colonial Act, he wrote: "It is useless to intrude these precepts [freedom of labor] into the constitution of the country, or even to publish them again, because foreigners are convinced that although our laws are excellent (and they are not always that) the better they are, the less we carry them out." *Colónias*, p. 83.

54. A. T. Steele, "Forced Labor is Common for Angola's Natives," *New York Herald-Tribune*, February 15, 1948, p. 13; see also Steele's report on Moçambique in the *Herald-Tribune*, November 26, 1952, p. 16.

55. Elizabeth Landis, "UN Stepchildren," *Africa Today*, January–February, 1958, p. 15.

56. *The Manchester Guardian*, February 27, 1958, p. 9, and March 9, p. 1.

57. Basil Davidson, "Africa's Modern Slavery," *Harper's*, July 1954, pp. 56–64; *The African Awakening* (London, 1955), pp. 190–232; *New Statesman*, May 8, 1954, p. 585, and May 15, 1954, p. 621.

CHAPTER XIII. THE NEW STATE IN AFRICA: PROJECTS AND PROBLEMS

1. Américo Chaves de Almeida, *O problema da Africa oriental portuguesa* (2 vols.; Lisbon, 1932), I, 249.

2. Carmelo Viñas y Mey, *La nueva política colonial portuguesa* (Santiago de Campostela, 1934), *passim*.

3. In 1952, for example, the following direct taxes were collected in Angola (figures given in *contos*, a *conto* being worth thirty-five dollars): industrial taxes, 58,000; professional income taxes, 13,800; property taxes, 6,400; taxes on agriculture, forestry, and fishing, 48,000; surtax on income, 112,000; African head tax, 93,593. Figures from *The African World*, November 1953, p. 56.

4. Azevedo, *Terra de esperança*, p. 218.

5. Writing of the Portuguese occupation of Africa prior to the New State's regime, Professor Macmillan observed that "the Portuguese record established in advance the truth of at least one fundamental principle . . . that there is little to be got out of Africa except by those able and willing to put a great deal in." W. M. Macmillan, *Africa Emergent*, pp. 94–95. He goes on to say: "Slight as it was, the Portuguese achievement compares favorably with that of any European rivals in the tropical parts of Africa."

6. Simões Vaz is most critical of the way the government has spent money in Moçambique, too much going, he argues, for show and not enough for well planned projects. He mentions a two-lane bridge over the Matala where a one-lane bridge would have been sufficient, since the road is straight on either side and the traffic is light. But, he adds, "It is a work which honors us!" A second example is the Liceu Salazar in Lourenço Marques with its marble halls and elevators but with smaller laboratories than in the school it replaced. The government could have built two large simple schools, he concludes, for the price of this one. *Problemas de Moçambique*, pp. 35–40.

7. The National Development Plan makes practically no provision for the expansion of medical or educational services; these programs continue to depend on the colonies' yearly budget appropriation.

8. Simões Vaz, *Problemas de Moçambique*, pp. 25–26.

9. The census figures for some of these years are inaccurate and misleading. The number of white persons was estimated in 1927 to be 42,843, in 1931 to be 59,493, and in 1940 to be 44,000. The 1931 figure, however, includes a portion of the mulatto population while the 1940 total does not. Many Portuguese did leave Angola in the 1930's, but a small immigration and the local birth rate almost counterbalanced the difference.

10. Moçambique's Indian and Chinese population, about 10,000 and 1,500 respectively, has remained fairly constant. The British Indian remains a vexing problem for the Moçambique administration, since he prefers to send his profit out of the country — in spite of currency restrictions — instead of investing it in the province. In recent years the local government has moved to restrict their migration and trade in the interior.

11. Quoted in *The Colonial Problem*, p. 345. See also Armindo Monteiro, *The Portuguese in Modern Colonization* (Lisbon, n.d.).

12. Genipro de Eça d'Almeida, *Colonização, um problema nacional* (Lisbon, 1945), pp. 59–63.

13. António de Oliveira Salazar, "Após 15 anos de governo," *O mundo português*, X (1943), 693.

14. Similar projects sponsored by the Benguela Railway have not worked out well.

15. This figure is given by Luis C. Lupi, "The Portuguese President's Historic African Tour," *African World Annual*, 1954, p. 25. Egerton gives only 150 families for the same year in *Angola in Perspective*, p. 241.

16. The *colonatos* had not yet made much contribution to the money economy of their province.

17. Luanda may hardly be called a small city any longer, having a population of over 200,000, of whom about 40,000 are European. Lourenço Marques has about 100,000 inhabitants and Beira, perhaps 50,000. Nova Lisboa with 38,000 people, and Lobito and Benguela with 32,000 and 16,000 each are the next largest cities in Angola. These figures include Africans and Europeans.

18. Quoted in *Notícias de Portugal*, August 10, 1957, p. 2. Even Rhodesian complaints against the congestion at Beira and the reluctance of the Portuguese to make foreign concessions in Moçambique have drawn rebuke. "It is unfair to lay the blame for the existing state of affairs on the Portuguese. Any close student of the history of the relations between the Portuguese colonies of Moçambique and Angola and their hinterland neighbors during the past half century well knows that they have had some unfortunate experiences and these have enhanced the nationalist sentiment of dislike for concessions which, in their view, impaired their sovereignty over the territory." *African World*, February 1949, p. 10.

19. See Silva Cunha, *O trabalho indígena*, pp. 273–288, for a summary of the Portuguese position. Portugal does participate in the Inter-African Labor Conference, whose views she finds more congenial, and was host to the fourth session of the Conference at Beira in 1955.

20. Quoted in *O mundo português*, IV (1937), 53.

21. See António Leite de Magalhães, "O problema das matérias primas," *O mundo português*, IV (1937), 55–59, and Conde de Penha Garcia, "O Império colonial e os internacionalismos," *O mundo português*, IV (1937), 5–7.

The natural tendency of Portugal's authoritarian regime to sympathize with the governments of Italy and Germany in the 1930's is well known. During the early years of the war Lourenço Marques was a miniature Lisbon as a center of espionage and intrigue. Persistent reports refer to a short-wave radio station outside of the city which from 1939 transmitted shipping news and other intelligence to Germany and directed German submarine attacks in the Indian Ocean. See Selwyn James, *South of the Congo*, pp. 233–262, and Roderick Peattie, *Struggle on the Veld* (New York, 1947), p. 93.

22. Hailey, *An African Survey*, pp. 233–262, has a detailed presentation of the general problem of international trusteeships and the United Nations.

23. Quoted in Alan Grey, "Lord Hailey and the African Survey," *African World*, December 1957, p. 9.

INDEX